CANADIAN CRIMIN...
Strategies and Perspectives

Third Edition

CANADIAN CRIMINOLOGY
Strategies and Perspectives

Third Edition

James C. Hackler
University of Victoria

Prentice Hall

Toronto

To Bunny, for her patience

National Library of Canada Cataloguing in Publication Data

Hackler, James C., 1930-
      Canadian criminology : strategies and perspectives

3rd ed.
First ed. published under title: Crime and Canadian public policy.
Includes bibliographical references and index.
ISBN 0-13-042794-2

1. Criminology—Canada. 2. Crime—Sociological aspects. I. Hackler, James C., 1930- . Crime and Canadian public policy. II. Title.

HV6807.H33 2003   364'.0971   C2002-901010-1

ISBN 0-13-042794-2

Vice-President, Editorial Director: Michael Young
Acquisitions Editor: Jessica Mosher
Marketing Manager: Judith Allen
Associate Editor: Patti Altridge
Production Editor: Tara Tovell
Copy Editor: Jim Leahy
Proofreader: Wayne Jones
Production Manager: Wendy Moran
Page Layout: Susan Thomas
Interior Design: Julia Hall
Cover Design: Jennifer Federico
Cover Image: Getty Images

  4 5   06 05 04

Printed and bound in Canada.

Contents

Preface

If the reader were to turn to the last two chapters of *Canadian Criminology: Strategies and Perspectives* and reflect on the recommendations offered there, he or she might think that I am somewhat radical in my thinking. Similarly, much of this book suggests that I am to the left of the political centre. On the other hand, the chapters on scientific theory and on statistics support the use of empirical data to understand crime and guide policies. Both impressions are correct. For me, social science begins with empirical evidence rather than with ideology. However, the way I would like to use science is definitely influenced by my social concerns.

Of course, a book on crime—and on how knowledge about crime can be used to influence public policy—should present a range of perspectives born of diverse historical contexts, which this book does. Knowing the past is necessary to understand developments in the present.

The explosion of research and information in criminology requires a rethinking of general texts. It is not possible to summarize everything, so one must select limited areas. It is also more difficult to choose the best references. In order to reduce the bibliography and make it more useful, I have used more review-type articles. These sources will allow the reader to find the basic research that informs the topic.

In one sense, authors trying to summarize ideas become much more selective simply because of the volume of material available. Readers should therefore be cautious about the claims and conclusions made in this book. The references will help the reader pursue a topic in greater depth and possibly reach different conclusions.

Part I, "The Criminological Enterprise," concentrates on how crime has been studied, on the questions that should be asked, and on some of the debates over how research should be done. Part II, "Explanations of Crime," begins with explanations of individual behaviour, gradually adding more social-psychological elements and then exploring aspects of the larger society. Toward the end of this section questions are raised about these traditional views through the introduction of the conflict perspective. Part III, "The Shape and Form of Modern Crime Patterns," attempts to bridge traditional and conflict thinking. The chapters on violent crime and property crime draw on historical as well as contemporary themes, while the chapters on women's issues, drug crime, the criminalization of sex, and corporate crime suggest that traditional theories might not be appropriate. Different perspectives are needed. Part IV, "Responding to Crime," focuses on the criminal justice system and criminogenic conditions in Canadian society. For those interested in reform, this last section may be of greatest interest.

The seemingly radical conclusions of this book should not be surprising. Despite differing views among criminologists, the majority would agree that structural changes are needed in order to reduce crime. Some of the recommendations made in the final chapters fit more than one particular perspective because they draw on evidence produced by a variety of orientations. Furthermore, the majority of criminologists probably share my view that government policies for the past two decades have emphasized punishment rather than crime reduction.

Acknowledgments

A book is often an accumulation of ideas and information from sources that the author has sometimes forgotten. Thus, let me simply list names of those who have helped in a variety of ways while apologizing to those I have overlooked: Herbert Costner, Clarence Schrag, Bob Ratner, Fran Shaver, John Lowman, Erin Van Brunschot, Francis Cullen, Louise Biron, Elizabeth Stanko, Holly Johnson, Angela Browne, Steve Messner, John Laub, Robert Sampson, Paul and Pat Brantingham, Karen Rodgers, Doug Wahlsten, Don Kuiken, Patricia Erickson, Neal Shover, Joan Nesbitt, Scott Menard, Richard Tremblay, Ezzat Fattah, Meda Chesny-Lind, Nikos Passas, Ray Paternoster, Sibylle Artz, Robert Crutchfield, Leroy Gould, Rick Linden, Bob Silverman, John Hagan, Staff Sergeant P. J. Duggan, Gwynne Nettler, Dan Koenig, Bill McCarthy, Louise Bohachyk, Jana Grekul, Laura Hargrave, Edem Frank Avakame, Elizabeth Comack, Det. Insp. Kim Rossmo, Jim Creechan, Andrew Donohue, Tim Hartnagel, Les Kennedy, Sergeant Colin Milton, Marianne Nielsen, and Sabrina Park. Ron Hinch's input, as reviewer, is particularly appreciated.

Thanks also to Pearson Canada's Patti Altridge and Tara Tovell, and to Jim Leahy for his keen editorial eye.

Statistics Canada information is used with the permission of the Minister of Industry, as Minister responsible for Statistics Canada. Information on the availability of the wide range of data from Statistics Canada can be obtained from Statistics Canada's Regional Offices, its World Wide Web site at http://www.statcan.ca, and its toll-free access number 1-800-263-1136.

The most useful source of Canadian crime statistics is probably the Juristat series produced by Statistics Canada. The series is available on-line at http://dsp-psd.pwgsc.gc.ca/Collection-R/Statcan/85-002-XIE/85-002-XIE.html.

I must also acknowledge the important impact of the writings of John Kenneth Galbraith on my overall worldview. Scholars such as Galbraith reinforce my view that crime, like so many human activities, is deeply enmeshed in the economic and social structure of a society. This book argues that effective social policies relating to crime cannot be studied intelligently in isolation from this larger social picture.

James C. Hackler
University of Victoria

THE CRIMINOLOGICAL ENTERPRISE

Chapter 1 discusses what and whom we should be studying under the label of criminology. Our reasons for labelling certain behaviour and certain individuals are not always logical. Chapter 2 argues that we make certain assumptions about human beings that influence our attempts to explain crime. Scholars also operate from certain perspectives that mould their conclusions. Assumptions shared by the dominant society often dictate and guide these perspectives. The scientific perspective is one of these. Although oversold at times, the scientific approach has certain merits. Chapter 3 focuses on the use of crime statistics. Although these data can be misused, they can provide insights when analyzed appropriately.

WHAT IS CRIME?
WHAT IS DEVIANCE?

This chapter will:

- Distinguish between crime and deviant behaviour.
- Note the importance of norms and settings to definitions of crime.
- Discuss why certain wrongs are considered more criminal than others.
- Debate the issue of who should be considered a criminal.
- Note areas of agreement and disagreement among criminologists.

THE DISTINCTION BETWEEN CRIME AND DEVIANCE

Imagine that you have a glass of water in your hand. See how clear it is. It is fresh water from Banff National Park. Sip it. It is cool and refreshing. Now spit into the glass. Spit again. Notice that the saliva has made the water a bit cloudy. Clear your throat. Now spit that phlegm into the glass. The water has losts it clarity; it is no longer very attractive. And now, put the glass to your lips and drink the contents.

When I go through the above exercise in my criminology classes, the expressions of disgust are obvious. But why? Before you spit into the water, the saliva was previously in your mouth. So, why do you object to putting it back into your mouth? The reaction of disgust is not "rational," and yet there is almost universal agreement in the way Canadian students respond to the above situation. Although we find certain things objectionable, it is sometimes difficult to explain just why we feel the way we do. Similarly, our responses to crime and deviance are not always rational, or at least based on seemingly objective criteria. On the other hand, much of human behaviour doesn't make a great deal of sense when viewed from a distance.

Crime and deviance overlap, thus making the boundary between the two difficult to draw. As a result, crime and deviance are often falsely treated as one and the same, but, despite their commonalities, they are two distinct terms. For example, are all deviant acts criminal? The hippie and punk movements are good examples of deviant behaviour—that is, behaviour that deviates from the norm—but they are not classified as criminal. Are all criminal acts deviant? In some parts of the Canadian wilderness people hunt and fish out of season. This is a crime, but to many of those who live in wilderness areas, it may not be seen as a deviant act.

These are precisely some of the problematic issues that this chapter wishes to address. In order to distinguish between crime and deviance, we will discuss three factors that influence the way society responds to different types of behaviour: the role of norms, settings, and sanctions.

The Role of Norms

All societies develop normative systems. These norms can be viewed as having two parts: *prescriptions* and *expectations*. **Prescriptions** are the formal rules laid down by society. Although these prescriptions might not necessarily be written down, they do spell out what members of that particular society *should* do. By contrast, **expectations** are what we anticipate people *will* do. Norms, then, include both the formal and informal rules and expectations of society.

For example, there are norms regulating a professor and a class. The *prescriptions* indicate that professors as well as students are to arrive on time. When students arrive late, most of them are aware that they are violating the norm and that their late entrances are somewhat disruptive. Thus, most late students slip into their seats quietly. Now imagine that a professor *always* arrives five minutes late. Does she establish new expectations? Does the class adjust, even though she violates the prescriptions? The class might also fall into a predictable pattern of arriving a few minutes late, corresponding to a newly established expectation but contrary to the prescription. What would happen if this same professor arrived on time one day and immediately distributed a very brief quiz, telling everyone that they had just five minutes to complete it? In one sense, this action is within the prescriptions, but even so, the expectations had developed so that students would anticipate that the class would actually begin five minutes late.

We can see this violation of expectations, as distinct from prescriptions, in many types of behaviour. The corporation that dumps toxic waste into a stream may not be committing a crime according to the laws, the formal prescriptions. However, most people would agree that this behaviour violates societal expectations. Laws may not prohibit eating human flesh, but it is clearly against social norms.

One aspect of "being a crime" usually includes the fact that many people feel that "something should be done." The violation of the prescriptions might not trigger such a reaction, but the violation of some expectations, including expectations that differed from the prescriptions, could lead to a genuine sense of outrage on the part of those affected.

Crimes, in a formal and legal sense, can only be the violation of prescriptions, not expectations. We can only prosecute people for violating the *law*, those prescriptions that have been formalized in a certain way. Theoretically, the professor who gave the unexpected quiz may not have violated formal rules, and thus it might be difficult to sanction her. But, as criminologists, should we limit our studies to the violation of prescriptions, or is the violation of expectations also within our range? Should we dabble on the fringes?

The Role of Settings

Nudity offers an interesting illustration of the way in which we respond to deviance and crime. In this case, the setting is all-important and the difficulty in defining the borders is apparent. The lack of clarity as to where the borderlines lie makes nudity a useful behaviour pattern to study. There are limits, but those limits differ depending on a variety of circumstances.

One summer, my wife and I were walking along English Bay in Vancouver. We were wearing shorts, and I had bathing trunks in my knapsack. As we walked west around the end of the peninsula, we approached Wreck Beach, which is located below the cliffs near the campus of the University of British Columbia. The number of nude bathers gradually increased until we reached Wreck Beach itself, where thousands of naked bodies were sunbathing or leaping about. Clothing was rare, with perhaps only an occasional shirt, but bottoms were virtually non-existent. Clearly, my wife and I were the deviants, and it amused us.

Should these nude bathers be considered criminals? Which is more important, the laws or local tradition? Occasionally, a few citizens object to the nudity on Wreck Beach by trying to get the police to make arrests and by holding protest marches (by wearing clothes) on the beach. However, those who strive to uphold the law or the prescriptions have been, to date, unsuccessful. It is the *expectations* of nudity that express the true norms on Wreck Beach. Despite this reality, there seems relatively little chance that the law will be changed in the near future in order to conform with the actual behaviour.

Another side of this issue concerns the limits of the expectations. Violating the prescriptions—that is, the laws—is one thing, but how far can one stretch the unwritten expectations? How far along the beach is it acceptable to be nude? Where are the boundaries and where do the police start enforcing the law? A display of nudity in downtown Vancouver is clearly unacceptable, and people who defy this condition are subject to social as well as legal sanctions. Thus, students of crime and deviant behaviour must be alert to different shades of grey, as well as to the borders of acceptability. It is also of interest just how norms are established and how people determine when the line between acceptable and unacceptable behaviour is crossed.

But what has this got to do with crime? Clearly, behaviour by itself is not enough. It must take place within a social context. This social context is a product of a specific culture which has, over the years, developed norms that regulate the behaviour of all its members.

In his novel, *A Single Pebble*, John Hersey described an American who took passage on a Chinese junk going up the Yangtze River some years ago. After depositing two blasts of nasal phlegm into a square of cloth, he hid these excreta in a pocket. This was revolting to the cook, who requested that the American be put ashore. Whose behaviour is "superior"? When the British established control over Hong Kong, they were horrified at the Chinese custom of spitting. Instead, Englishmen cherish the custom described above, blowing hard into a handkerchief, driving the germs into the sinus cavities where they will prolong a head cold, then depositing the contaminated cloth in a pocket, usually next to a warm thigh where the bacteria can breed nicely. Hands are rarely washed after such an operation. Handshakes and other practices guarantee the efficient spread of the infection. The Chinese prefer spitting, but medical facts are irrelevant. Those in power choose the customs, and the Chinese in Hong Kong have adjusted to a degree. Now that the Chinese have taken over Hong Kong, it will be interesting to see if they reject the barbarous English customs regarding nose-blowing.

Are Multicultural Settings More Likely to Have Crime?

While spitting or nose-blowing may seem like trivial examples, the modern world is organized into societies where there is diversity in cultural practices. Those practices often come into conflict. One could argue that simple societies have very little crime. Everyone knows the rules, and informal social control keeps people in line. However, the readers of this book are clearly more interested in complex, heterogeneous societies. Canada is typical of modern countries that have a diverse cultural heritage. While such diversity does not necessarily result in crime, it increases the likelihood that some of the cultural conflict will be criminalized. When a dominant culture invades another, the behaviour of the indigenous culture is judged by the rules established by the dominant culture. When there is culture conflict, the behaviour of those conquered may be criminalized.

In Canada, there is much soul-searching and debate regarding multiculturalism. Many would argue for greater tolerance towards other cultures. While this diversity can enrich a nation, there are some areas in which conflict is inevitable. What is seen as acceptable in one culture may be sanctioned in another. For example, when Europeans came into contact with Australian Aborigines, they had much difficulty understanding, much less appreciating, the latter's value system. For the Aborigines, work was not seen as meritorious in itself. If you had food or material goods, it was expected that you would share with others. As work was seen as a means to an end and not the end in itself, you did minimal work to achieve what you wanted. Since women were the property of men, trading young girls to white men was an easy way to make money. The goods obtained were then shared with others, making it unnecessary for Aborigines to work for Europeans. Thus they lived in ease and idleness. Whites had to make the Aborigines dependent before they would work (Reynolds, 1981).

Such attitudes and values were, and still are, incompatible with mainstream European thinking. The solution has been to resocialize these peoples, get them to adopt our values, and of course to destroy their old value system. In the early part of the twentieth century the Canadian government and the churches established a system of residential schools for Native children. The people in power felt that by destroying the Native way of life, they could resocialize the children to accept the norms of the white society. Such practices occur when cultural conflict is prevalent and the culture with the power wishes to weed out the other culture. During the last half of the twentieth century Canadians began to appreciate Native cultures and see merit in the preservation of that identity.

When there is culture conflict, the behaviour of those conquered may be criminalized. In general, it is not hard to find illustrations of practices that criminalize Native peoples. For example, the Plains Indians took pride in stealing horses. Young males who excelled in this activity were held in high regard. But how did this go over with the invading Europeans?

In Canada and the U.S. today, Native peoples have higher-than-average crime rates. To explain this as just the criminalization of a weaker group by a more powerful one does not take into account many other factors, but the generalization is often valid. More vivid examples arise as Third World people immigrate to countries with European cultures. In parts of Africa, conscientious fathers, concerned about the morality of their daughters, would use a piece of glass or razor blade to cut out their clitoris. This was to ensure that they would not enjoy sex, and would therefore grow up to be better wives. After immigrating to Canada the conscientious father might feel that when his daughter becomes a teenager it is time to perform the traditional operation on the kitchen table. The teenager, however, may have become part of the North American culture, and may resist the father's attempt to do what he feels is appropriate. Whose culture should be respected? Should this behaviour be treated as criminal?

In the above case, most of us would not face a serious dilemma. We would insist that the father respect the rules of his new country. But let's change the situation somewhat. Imagine that the father was part of a powerful invading army which had conquered your country and insisted that Canadian fathers follow the more civilized practices of their superiors. (Those who win the battles are obviously superior.) According to the new morality, Canadian fathers should get out their razor blades and do their duty to protect the virtue of their daughters. Since most of the readers of this book are part of the conquering cultures, it is difficult even to contemplate such a situation; but if you were an Aboriginal in Canada or an Aborigine in Australia, you might understand the point more easily.

The Role of Sanctions

Social groups have sanction systems, which they use to punish people who violate their norms. That is, the group exerts social control over its members. However, sanctions are not used every time a rule is violated, as was illustrated by the anecdote about nude bathing on Wreck Beach in Vancouver. When are sanctions used? Who has the authority (or power) to use them? Do societies sanction everyone?

Some individuals are not sanctioned, even though they violate clear prescriptions. Children, for example, "don't know any better." However, we try to teach them to follow the rules, using mild sanctions such as a frown or a sharp word. In general, we give people a chance to learn, but our tolerance varies considerably.

A friend of mine travelling in rural India was trying to be alert to the customs of the country. He carefully watched what others were doing and tried to imitate their behaviour. When invited to share a meal, he noticed that everyone reached into the common plate with fingers and used pieces of bread to scoop up the other food. After watching carefully, he reached into the plate and immediately noticed a shocked reaction on the faces of his hosts. His action caused the others to stop eating. He had done something wrong, but what was it? After a while he discovered his social error. Being left-handed, he naturally reached into the plate with his left hand. However, this was the "unclean" hand. (One used the left hand after going to the toilet; only the right hand was used for eating.) When he used his right hand, things went much better.

When the child, ignorant foreigner, or colleague behaves badly or expresses ideas that are highly divergent, our first efforts are to educate the individual. If that does not produce the desired effect, more stringent sanctions are imposed. Those who learn quickly are forgiven for their previous mistakes, especially if they are repentant.

Acts of a criminal nature, on the other hand, are sanctioned by a codified set of formal laws. The criminal law differs from other sanctioning systems in that it is *specific*. It spells out who can be sanctioned for what behaviour. The official sanctioning of criminal behaviour is usually delegated to certain people who follow specific rules. While those rules are often written into criminal codes, they may also evolve as part of a common law based on decisions that have been made in the past. In some societies, the rules may never be recorded in written form, but certain individuals are given the responsibility for knowing the rules and enforcing them.

Many centuries ago, under English common law, specific categories of people, such as children, the insane, and women, could not be considered guilty of certain crimes because they lacked the capacity for crime. As all men knew during these past periods, women were not capable of making many types of decisions and simply lacked the intelligence and initiative to commit most crimes. Despite the fact that rules are violated, the status of the offender will influence the likelihood of sanctions being applied. Some individuals are not sanctioned even though they violate clear prescriptions. The actions of Madonna and similar celebrities are prime examples of deviant behaviour, but instead of facing social sanctions from society, they have risen to star status.

WHY STUDY CRIME?

Judging Crime According to the Economic Costs

It is understandable to ask why we should study crime. Crime seems to be undesirable, and, therefore, we may wish to reduce it. One reason most people would give for studying crime is "cost." The argument has been made that crime should be studied so that the most "expensive" crimes could be reduced. Should cost be measured in terms of dollars or in terms of the "harm" done to people? Let us begin with the economic costs of crime.

How much does crime really cost? Think of the way goods are distributed. Does crime redistribute some goods? If my computer were stolen, I would be annoyed. However, the insurance company might replace it. The insurance company hires people, collects premiums, and in general contributes to the welfare of the community. The company that makes computers is not hurt by the theft. If the thief sells the computer to a fence who ends up selling it to an unsuspecting college student, it is possible that the student would use the computer more productively than I did. Did the society lose in economic terms? The transfer of goods by theft may represent damage to an individual, but not necessarily to the society.

A safe-cracker once told me that he kept safe companies in business. He specialized in supermarkets, and considered his profession comparable to manufacturers who produced deceptive packaging. He didn't hurt people, the insurance company covered the costs and sold more policies, and the safe companies were constantly well funded so they could upgrade their technology. It is difficult to assess the economic impact of the redistribution of wealth through crime.

It may be difficult to envision robbery and burglary as beneficial to the economy, but let us look at a less dramatic example, such as prostitution. We pay entertainers to make us happy. Their salaries and related activities contribute to the gross national product (GNP). How about prostitutes? Should their earnings be added to the GNP? Many economists feel that this would make good sense. Entertainers buy food and clothing, pay rent, and redistribute the money they earn, thereby stimulating the economy. So do prostitutes. How does one compare the economic worth of prostitution with that of other activities?

What about all the services and institutions that are directly linked to crimes? Why are prisons considered burdens? It is not rare for prisons to be located in some area because a local politician saw it as a way of bringing jobs to the community. Building a road to a tar-sands plant in northern Alberta is seen as an "investment," but building a road to a prison is seen as a cost. The prison "industry," however, keeps many people employed. What about the cost of maintaining a police force? Would the economy be better off if these people were working elsewhere? Do the police provide other services in addition to fighting crime? The old saying, "crime does not pay," no longer applies. Crime pays—for all the people working in jobs related to the criminal justice system.

In economic (not moral) terms, crime is similar to other social activities. We can find parallel economic consequences between most legal and illegal activities. It is not reasonable to talk about the economic burden of crime when we fail to calculate the economic cost of other activities in the same manner. Perhaps we should talk about costs in terms of the *damage* done to the individual or society.

Judging Crime According to the Non-Economic Damage

If damage to the individual or society were the main criterion for assessing crime, we would probably be studying different things in criminology. For example, the use of alcohol and tobacco would be central topics. Our response to damage-producing situations, however, does not always make sense. Imagine a mother and father sitting in front of a TV. Both are smoking and Daddy has a small child on his lap. Mother is pregnant, and each parent is holding a drink. They are watching a TV program on marijuana, and one asks the other: "What is it that makes kids do such silly things?"

One hopes that the reader will see the irony in the above situation, but many do not. Over twenty years ago I was at a program on the prevention of drug use, and one of the speakers was a government official from Ottawa. While delivering his talk on the evils of drug use, he puffed on a cigarette and said, "We adults have learned to handle our alcohol and tobacco, but kids don't know how to handle marijuana." Even at that time most people were aware that adults handle alcohol and tobacco very badly, but comments almost as asinine as the one made by this official are common.

When making comparisons between conventional crimes and the tobacco industry, we have trouble estimating non-economic gains and losses. Health and Welfare Canada tells us that alcohol, nicotine, caffeine, and prescription medicines are most responsible for public health problems (Beauchesne, 1997). Clearly, illegal drugs do not do as much damage as alcohol or tobacco. How does one assess the use of good agricultural land in Ontario being used to grow tobacco? Smokers work less than non-smokers, cost employers thousands of dollars each year, are absent from work more, and are responsible for more property damage. Should this expensive behaviour be criminalized? The point is: *damage to society or the individual plays a fairly modest role in terms of selecting behaviour patterns that we wish to define as criminal.*

How, then, do we decide what we should study as crime and whom we should study as the criminal? In the next section I review some conventional guidelines that direct our choices, but we have little trouble justifying our concern with crime. It has broad implications for society. If there were less stealing, less violence, less corporate crime, less illegal industrial pollution, and so on, we would clearly have a better-quality society. Crime, even if we have trouble knowing the borders, tears at the fabric of society. We may not agree on which crimes tear the fabric the most, nor will we all agree which behaviour should be criminalized, but it is reasonable to assume that citizens should be concerned about that fabric.

Different Types of Wrongs: Which Ones Should Be Crimes?

There are many types of "wrongs" in society, but not all of them can be considered crimes. If someone drives an automobile in a negligent fashion and causes you damage, you could try to obtain compensation in the courts. In the case of torts, it is up to the individual to initiate action. The state will not come to your aid automatically. Your quarrel is, in one sense, a personal one. The goal is primarily compensation rather than punishment.

In the past, many wrongs were treated as torts. In some simpler societies, murder was treated as a **tort** (a civil wrong requiring compensation for damages). Individuals or their families responded to the murder themselves. The society as a whole did not intervene. If one of your relatives were murdered, you might respond. The nature of that response would be dictated by other social rules, but the initiative would have to come from your family. The community might support you in your actions, but the conflict was primarily between the family of the victim and the family of the murderer. As societies became more complex, there was an evolution towards having the state take on the responsibility for initiating action against individuals who had committed wrongs. In fact, individuals were no longer allowed to take punitive actions against offenders.

During the early Middle Ages, kings and others in power were not particularly concerned if a traveller was robbed while passing from one kingdom to the next. However, the king sometimes sent his messenger to the next kingdom, and it was annoying when the messenger was knocked on the head and robbed. Robbers did not always distinguish between ordinary victims and a messenger for the king. Thus, kings proclaimed that anyone committing robbery on the King's Highway would have to answer to the king. Making certain actions offences against the state was probably pragmatic rather than idealistic. While kings may have been primarily interested in their own mail service, it was more practical to make all forms of theft offences against the state.

Even during modern times, some serious crimes have led to responses by the family and friends of the victim, so that feuds and revenge murders have taken place. One can see, however, that such activity would create chaos in a modern society. Just as the king found it more practical to deal with all robbers, rather than just those who attacked his messengers, so other authorities found it more reasonable to define a broader range of wrongful behaviour as requiring state control. Thus, individuals' responses have been repressed by modern states; state agencies have a monopoly on the use of certain types of force (i.e., police, army, courts). To a large extent, then, we can define modern crimes as *offences against the state, and we expect the state, not individuals, to take the appropriate action.*

In recent years, criminologists have also studied crimes *by* the state. Since September 11, 2001, certain governments have been identified as sponsoring terrorism. In addition to pointing to the crimes of dictatorships, such as Nazi Germany, illustrations of systematic criminal behaviour among the secret service agencies of Western democracies are coming to light. Thus, traditional definitions of crime are rather restrictive.

The O. J. Simpson case raises another challenge to the conventional view that crimes are just offences against the state. The state found Simpson not guilty of murdering his wife, but a civil court, where the burden of proof is different, found him guilty and ordered him to pay over $50 000 000 in damages. Is O. J. Simpson a criminal?

Shifting from One Category of Wrong to Another

While criminologists concentrate their efforts on offences against the state, the borderlines between various types of wrongs can certainly overlap. We saw how torts became crimes as the king expanded his role to protect others. Other powerful groups can have certain behaviour "criminalized" to serve their interests.

The *Carrier* case provides an illustration (Chambliss, 1964). During the medieval period, the wool merchants in England hired others to carry their bales of wool. If a carrier decided to run off with a merchant's wool, it was not the problem of the state. The merchant had to deal with the culprit. But, in the famous *Carrier* case, the court ruled that the state would now intervene on behalf of the merchant. Obviously, this decision was of major importance to those in commerce.

Later, we will ask why these criminal laws came into being. Is it because a powerful group, such as the wool merchants, wanted the laws for their own good, or is the overall good of the society the important factor? Clearly, the *Carrier* case and other legislation extended the reach of the criminal law to what had earlier been viewed as a tort. Similarly, wife-beating was formerly treated as a family affair; now administrative decisions have led to the enforcement of laws that already existed. Similarly, child abuse is no longer seen as outside the jurisdiction of social control agencies operated by the state.

Just as torts can become crimes, so can sins. In the earlier part of the twentieth century, a number of people, including the members of the Women's Christian Temperance Union, considered the use of alcohol a sin. These people were able to convince governments that this behaviour should be criminalized. In a later period, others convinced the government to reverse the ruling prohibiting the use of alcohol. Clearly, there has been a shift in both directions between crimes and sins.

Abortion, the use of drugs, and homosexuality are just some of the areas in which moral issues, sin, and crime get intertwined. One might argue that criminologists should not deal with behaviour in this area. It isn't "real" crime. But I would argue that, while there is a difference between deviant lifestyles and crime, it isn't the behaviour alone that helps us to define our area of crime. It is not criminal to be gay. It is a crime, though, to carry on sexual activities in a public restroom at a shopping centre, and people are being arrested, charged, convicted, and jailed for such activities in Canada today (Desroches, 1991). If a behaviour can result in such sanctions, it clearly falls within the realm of criminology. However, the modern criminologist might be much more interested in the question, "What are the consequences of different types of police responses to certain types of activities?" In the past, many criminologists were only asking, "Why do they do it?"

Despite grey areas, we can use some traditional guidelines for determining what we mean by *crime*. Crime means:

1. *Law enforcement machinery may be used.* We must emphasize the *may*, because for most crimes the law machinery does not come into play. While part of this is due to the fact that much crime is undetected, there are deliberate decisions made at various stages in the process to remove the case from the system. John Braithwaite (1989) and others would argue that there are considerable advantages to *not* using the formal system.

2. *Crimes and criminal court procedures are (supposedly) very explicit.* Some sanctions can be applied somewhat haphazardly, but, in principle, crimes are to be handled very explicitly. The crime itself must be clearly defined. During the Middle Ages in England it seems that common law permitted cows to be executed if they damaged property or did some other terrible thing. The story goes that a cow was on trial for something that could lead to death. The jury was not keen on executing the cow, and someone pointed out that this particular cow had never given birth. Thus she was really a heifer and not a cow. The common law applied to cows, not heifers, and thus the heifer was spared.

3. *Intent is usually necessary.* Accidents are usually not crimes, even if they are caused by negligence. There must be *mens rea*, or a guilty mind. However, there can be *transferred intent*. If George has decided to kill William and shoots at him, but misses and kills Robert instead, George cannot plead lack of intent. Similarly, if George shot at Robert thinking he was William, George would still be guilty of murder.

4. *Criminal laws are general in their applicability.* In principle, criminal law applies to everyone regardless of social status, race, sex, and so on. Neither rich people nor poor people are allowed to sleep under bridges at night, as the old saying goes. In practice, this principle is violated frequently. Those who have lower status in our society are often more subject to criminal laws than those with higher status. This particular bias is one of the factors we must take into account in explanations of crime, and also when we consider any policies that may be relevant to the reduction of crime.

Crime, then, is not just any sort of nasty behaviour. You and I may disagree as to what things should be considered crimes. I think everyone who mows a lawn should compost their lawn clippings instead of putting them in plastic bags to be hauled to a landfill, that power boats should not be allowed on many lakes, and that city and provincial governments should provide their employees with public transit passes instead of parking spaces; but no matter how strongly I feel about certain behaviours or how harmful they are to society, they are not crimes unless they meet the criteria listed above. On the other hand, if I could get support from enough people to pass certain laws, I might get some of those behaviours, which I feel are "bad," classified as crimes.

Crime and deviance are not the same. Deviance is much more inclusive. Crime depends on a political process that permits the use of institutions such as the police and courts. Having worked out a rough definition of crime, one might assume that it would be fairly easy to identify those who are criminals. As we attempt to identify criminals, other factors must also be considered.

BOX 1.1   Who Is the Criminal?

Two surgeons defrauded the Ontario health system of $700 000 and were disciplined by the College of Physicians and Surgeons. There was no indication that they had to repay the $700 000 or that they could never again receive payment from the public health system.

A single pregnant woman in Sudbury received an unauthorized overpayment from welfare. The Ontario government, besides going after the overpayment, attempted to have her banned from receiving future benefits.

Welfare fraud in Canada may be approximately $46 million per year; medical fraud around $600 million per year.

Who is the criminal?

PERSPECTIVES ON WHO IS THE CRIMINAL

Thorsten Sellin: The Conflict of Conduct Norms

In 1938, Thorsten Sellin wrote an influential book which argued that criminal law should be regarded as part of a larger body of rules that (1) prohibit specific forms of conduct and (2) indicate punishment for violations (Sellin, 1938). The character of these rules, the kind or type of conduct they prohibit, and the nature of the sanctions will depend on the character and interests of those groups in the population that influence legislation. The general argument made by Sellin fits into a framework often referred to as **conflict theory**. Using this perspective, we will attempt to identify individuals who are likely to become criminals.

Sellin argues that the social values that receive the protection of the criminal law are ultimately those values cherished by *dominant* interest groups, those who have the power. Notice that this does not refer to the interests of the *majority* of society, but rather of those who are dominant. It is possible that the interests of the dominant and those of the majority are similar, but it is not a certainty. Sellin was one of the earlier sociologists to suggest that the values and interests of dominant groups differed from those of the majority. Thus, those with little influence in the society, who might not share the values of the dominant groups, would be more likely to run afoul of the laws passed by the powerful.

In addition, laws tend to change over time. Sellin argued that everything the criminal law of any state prohibits today might not be prohibited at a given time in the future, unless complete social stagnation sets in. While this may be somewhat extreme, it points to changes in societal values as well as changes that can take place in the dominant groups. Sellin feels that criminologists should study *normal* versus *abnormal conduct*, i.e., conduct that is in accord with or deviates from a conduct norm. Since behaviour is classified as right or wrong depending on the social values of a particular group, conduct norms are found wherever social groups are found. They are not the creation of *one* normative group and they are *not necessarily embodied in law,* as different social groups will have different norms.

While Sellin feels that social scientists cannot really understand crime unless they study the broader concept of conduct norms, and develop theories that explain abnormal conduct, he recognizes that crimes are unique. They are the product of laws, whose creation requires explaining as well.

Paul Tappan: The Emphasis on the Justice System

While many social scientists share Sellin's general view that the study of crime should embrace concepts broader than those found in criminal law, Paul Tappan (1947) disagrees and would restrict the study of crime and the criminal to a narrow legal conceptualization. Criminals are those who are arrested, charged, and convicted. Those people found not guilty are not criminals. Although he is not opposed to the study of conduct norms, Tappan believes specific study of the law violator is needed for social control purposes.

Thus, Tappan has little interest in the study of "white-collar" or upper-world crime. Unless these people are duly convicted, they are not criminal in any meaningful sense. Unconvicted white-collar criminals, violators of conduct norms, and antisocial personalities may be undesirable individuals, but they are not criminals. When it comes to studying, explaining, understanding, and controlling criminals, Tappan believes that *adjudicated* offenders represent the closest possible approximation to those who have in fact violated the law. They have been carefully selected by the sieving process of the law. No other area of social control attempts to ascertain the breach of norms with such rigour and precision.

The Debate over Who Is the Criminal

These two perspectives set the stage for a continuing debate over who should be considered criminal, who should be studied, and who needs to be controlled. Examining the career of the past president of the International Olympic Committee, Juan Antonio Samaranch, we see a fascist who abused power and who was at the centre of a network of corruption. Similarly, some heads of corporations sit on the boards of other corporations and vote each other outrageously high salaries. Neither their shareholders nor consumers of their products approve. When others take your money without your permission we call it robbery. When heads of corporations do it by abusing their power, it is called "responding to market forces." Should criminologists study people who abuse others?

And then there are those who assist criminals to profit from their crimes. Vast amounts of money from the drug trade are laundered through major financial institutions. They know this is "dirty money." Should these money handlers be considered criminal? Stockbrokers are supposed to know their clients. When the client repeatedly calls collect from prison to invest money, should the stockbroker realize that his client is laundering illegal funds? The stockbroker may be barred from trading stock, but would he be charged with a crime? Many "bad" people, or people who do bad things, do not get convicted or even charged. Should they be studied in criminology classes? I think they should, because we need to understand, not only the individual behaviour, but the structure of a society that allows or encourages such behaviour.

The case of Larry Causey raises another issue. Diagnosed with colon cancer, and living in the U.S. with little money and no medical insurance, he found it almost impossible to get treatment. He went into a Louisiana bank, slipped the teller a robbery note, and waited for the police to arrive. He was able to get treatment in jail. At first glance, one might argue that Causey should not be considered a criminal—that some people have so few options that they see criminal acts as their only alternative.

Other factors, such as social stigma, can also influence the labelling of someone as criminal. Low-status people get labelled criminal more easily than high-status people. Ronald Reagan could not conceive of Richard Nixon as being a criminal even though he broke many laws as part of the Watergate scandal. He did not have a "bad character." However, Reagan would probably consider someone who defrauds the welfare system to be a criminal.

Other unusual situations make the definition of the criminal even harder to determine. Consider the example of the fire chief who was once an arsonist. Even after becoming a firefighter, he continued to set fires. The question is: should the fire chief be considered a criminal, since he committed 2000 crimes, even though he has been reformed for many years? Do we look at current status or past activity?

The assignment of stigma is quite complex. A professor could be labelled a communist for advocating universal medical care; a First Nations man might not be labelled criminal for committing spousal assault. Frequently, lifestyle influences the attribution of a deviant character. John Lofland (1969) notes that school teachers possess normal character, while males who wear dramatic eye makeup take on a deviant character. Those seen to have deviant characters are more likely to be seen as criminal.

Can one shed stigma? In Canada an ex-offender sometimes receives an official pardon, but as John Anderson (forthcoming) notes, "stigma, like sap from a pine tree, has an adhesive quality that resists removal."

When terrorists flew passenger planes into the World Trade Center buildings in New York City, criminologists were asked to explain this type of crime. However, when atrocities involve martyrs and a variety of political and religious issues, conventional definitions of who is a criminal become difficult. Thus, our perspective is somewhat limited to those who live within a particular culture.

Other situations are easier to resolve. During the Second World War, Canadians of Japanese ancestry were interned and given criminal records. One might assume that those records would not become a problem at a later time, but some Japanese Canadians have found that their "criminal records" came back to haunt them. However, as criminologists, it is unlikely that we would find these particular people suitable objects of study as criminals. On the other hand, should the actions of the government that interned them be considered criminal? When lands were taken from Native peoples during the Second World War for military purposes and kept illegally, was this a criminal act?

Increasingly, criminologists are looking at the criminal behaviour of people in power. For a long time police have provided drugs to addicts who act as informants. Committing minor illegal acts as a way of getting convictions for major crimes has long been tolerated in the police forces of almost all countries. Arguments have been made that such activity is for the greater good of society. However, when the CIA laundered money from drug sales by using a bank in Sydney, Australia, it was less clear what "greater good" was being achieved.

Some of the criminal acts by powerful individuals do not require new conceptual thinking. If executives from Enron lie before the U.S. Congress, if the CEOs of tobacco companies testify that they did not know tobacco is addictive, or if a president perjures himself about his sexual activities, we have little problem labelling these activities as illegal, even though we realize the powerful may never be punished. It is less clear when the leaders of a nation *collectively* decide to engage in illegal behaviour. Even if the illegal behaviour is obvious, the collective decision-making process renders the identification of a single person as criminal very difficult.

After World War II, several German leaders were singled out and tried as criminals. Identifying such individuals as criminal is more likely to occur if a nation is beaten in war. Thus, Slobodan Milosevic has been charged with 66 counts of crimes against humanity in Croatia and Kosovo and for genocide in the 1992–95 Bosnian war. The International Court of Justice in The Hague has already convicted Radovan Karadzic, the psychologist responsible for many deaths in Kosovo. One could argue that these people are criminals. However, powerful people from nations that *win* wars are rarely labelled as criminals.

John MacArthur points out in an article in *The Globe and Mail* (August 4, 2001) that a retired French general who confessed to personally torturing and killing 24 Algerian prisoners has not been charged. French President Jacques Chirac proposed no sanction more serious than suspending him from the Légion d'honneur. We could also raise questions about former FBI director J. Edgar Hoover, whose blackmailing activities directed at various influential people are well documented.

Crimes by states and by the leaders of states are getting more attention. This book will not cover this area in depth, but criminologists are legitimately interested in explaining why states and powerful individuals commit crimes, and also why and how some avoid the appropriate convictions and labels.

A focus on conventional criminals alone yields a limited perspective. Therefore, we must look at borderline groups, not because we wish to see them prosecuted or formally defined as criminals, but because understanding how they behave and how society responds to their behaviour is important in order to understand the larger picture. Just as most of us have, in fact, engaged in crime in one form or another without being considered criminals, bank robbers also spend the bulk of their time in non-criminal activities. Understanding crime requires that we take a reasonably broad look at the people around us, the institutions that influence our lives, and the society in which we live.

Must We Have a Clear Definition of Crime or of the Criminal?

Rather than thinking in terms of criminals versus non-criminals, we can think of some people as being *more* criminal than others. The bulk of the population has committed infractions of the law. The law and the agencies of social control have developed imperfect, and sometimes illogical, strategies for defining crime and the criminal. Some harmful acts, such as smoking, drinking alcohol, and pollution are legal, while behaviours that are less harmful, such as nudity, are illegal. In this book, we will find it useful to include activities on the fringes.

We can also function with contradictions. Law and practice do not always correspond. Some crimes are "popular." For example, during Prohibition, when alcohol sales were forbidden, drinking was an "acceptable" crime. Laws that do not reflect the will of many people should probably be changed, since having laws on the books that the people do not support leads to corruption. Others argue that the laws reflect principles that should be stated, even if not always upheld in practice. Still others believe that laws represent the will of the powerful and that it is naive to think that they will reflect the will of the majority.

Discussions about crime make some people pessimistic. The world seems to be getting worse, but there may be grounds for optimism. Let us look back to England in 1712. A club of young men of the higher classes was accustomed to sallying forth each night into the streets to victimize other citizens (Geis, 1965). One of their favourite amusements was to squeeze the nose of their victim flat upon his face and to bore out his eyes with their fingers. Or they would form a circle around their prisoner and prick him with their swords until he fell exhausted. Another game was to set women on their heads and commit a variety of indecencies. Maidservants, as they opened their masters' doors, were waylaid, beaten, and their faces cut. Matrons were enclosed in barrels and rolled down steep and stony slopes. Watchmen were beaten unmercifully and their noses slit.

In the past, upper-class people could commit some crimes with relative impunity. Today we may actually be safer. We may have been able to control at least some of the more obvious violence of the upper classes. The current violence that appears to be so rampant according to the media is not a recent phenomenon. It has characterized most of history. Even the interest in criminology classes can have mixed interpretations. Is it a morbid fascination with the seamy and vicious side of life? Or is it a genuine concern with deficiencies of our society, with the hope for improvement?

Areas of Agreement in Identifying Causes of Crime

Some would argue that the level of agreement in most areas of criminology is not great enough to allow for clear policy-making. Perhaps this is true for some areas, but there is considerable agreement that poor quality of family life, inequality of opportunity, and racism are all factors which directly or indirectly affect the level of crime. Many of our theories of crime involve the family. The arguments differ, but there is considerable overlap, and frequently they are compatible in terms of intervention strategies. Everyone agrees with strengthening families, including politicians. But when governments decrease support for kindergartens and day care, it hurts families, decreasing their crime-inhibiting potential.

In addition to the importance of the family, there is growing evidence that inequality is related to crime (Hagan and Peterson, 1995). This argument will be explored in a later chapter, and admittedly the implications are far from clear. However, there is enough evidence that the increased disparity between rich and poor, along with an ideology which professes equality, has been criminogenic. It is not simply the distribution of wealth which is important but our attitudes toward material wealth and how opportunities are distributed. Inequality within a society can be modified by governmental strategies, and by doing so we can reduce criminogenic conditions.

Another area in which policies can influence crime is in the area of racism. Canadians like to point to the U.S. as having problems that are different from ours. Admittedly, there has been significant progress in North America, but progress has slowed and considerable inequalities still remain.

Most of these ideas are traditional themes in criminology. In recent decades, however, many criminologists have focused on different questions.

The Conflict (Radical, Critical) Approach in Criminology

Traditionally, criminologists have tried to explain how criminals, troubled youth, and other deviants differ from "normal" people. This approach to crime ignores the role of institutional authority, and ignores the probability that social institutions and agencies of social control are the more crucial players in determining who is the criminal and what is crime. Colin Sumner (1994) would have us pay more attention to those agencies which engage in "moral censure," those having the power to make fundamental judgments as to who should be treated as deviant.

Some criminologists view society as different groups in conflict, struggling to gain advantages over others. Powerful groups win these struggles. Many of the ideas originally offered by conflict theorists are now accepted as part of mainstream criminology, although one might not get that impression from reading some of the debates. Criminologists with different perspectives often identify similar weaknesses in the way society is organized.

In this book, ideas from the conflict perspective have been grouped into macro-, micro-, feminist, and left realist perspectives. The *macro-level* arguments focus on the larger structure of society. The Marxist conflict theorists would fit here, and will be summarized in a later chapter. Much of the *feminist* literature could be viewed as using the conflict perspective to comment on the structural aspects of society. (See Chapter 13, on violence, and Chapter 11, on women's issues.) *Micro-level* arguments often focus on the criminal justice system, agencies which define, process, and punish criminals, or attempt to rehabilitate them. This research critically examines various agents of social control.

The *left realist* perspective criticizes some radical views for romanticizing crime and for assuming that the only serious crimes are those committed by the powerful. The left realist notes that poor people are frequently victimized by other poor people, that women are frequently abused and harassed by poor and marginal men, and that the abuse of children is influenced by a complex web of circumstances. When dealing with a number of criminological issues, it may be difficult, as well as unprofitable, to try to distinguish between a conflict perspective and a liberal-reform orientation.

I wish to argue against a tendency to see conflict (radical, critical) criminology as a domain that is distinct from current mainstream criminology. Nor is it necessarily helpful for scholars to remain "pure" in their ideological orientations. Depending on the questions and issues, a criminologist might find it useful to pay more or less attention to different ideological perspectives. John Hagan's work, for example, ranges widely: some of his research reflects a conflict orientation while other work does not. Similarly, Ezzat Fattah (1997) takes a very critical view of the powerful in his recent writings, but he has also pointed out that it is not the elite who push for repressive strategies in criminal justice, as many conflict theorists argue, but rather the lower classes. In sum, ideological consistency may not be particularly advantageous for understanding crime.

The Response to Crime by Agents of Social Control

Traditionally, criminologists have focused on factors that are relevant to criminal behaviour, but they have spent less time on the way society responds to behaviour that is perceived to be criminal. Because of space limitations, this book will touch only briefly on the role of agencies of social control, and ask to what extent the response of these agencies can amplify deviance, if not actually create it. For years, many people assumed that the police and other agencies merely respond to crime. Criminals do bad things, and the police and courts are simply reacting to these criminal acts in a rational manner. We now know that agencies of social control can do more than just react. As a result, these agencies of social control can affect the level of crime by the actions that they do or do not take.

Social scientists in the U.S. have done more research on the agents of social control than elsewhere in the world. Such work is not as common in Canada, but the principles seem to operate here as well. It is clearly an oversimplification to label all agencies of social control as nasty bureaucracies, or to label the individuals who work in these agencies as selfish bureaucrats. Instead, we find great similarities between individuals who work in agencies of social control and members of other organizations. The fact remains, however, that these agencies can contribute to the crime problem instead of reducing it. On the one hand, these influences may not be as important as the structural features of society mentioned above. On the other hand, changes in these agencies' functioning and, hence, changes in their impact on crime, may be more amenable to rational policy decisions and modification than the major changes needed in the larger society.

Even though making changes at the agency level may seem like tinkering rather than basic change, there is no reason to forgo gains in this modest manner if they can be accomplished more easily than fundamental changes. Tinkering can proceed while changes are being considered which are more basic to society. The final chapter has some specific suggestions for tinkering.

CRIME IN THE FUTURE

This book argues that crime is the product of broad societal forces that cannot be influenced significantly by police, courts, and prisons. We have made progress in some areas, such as violence against women and children. These measures may have reduced crime. At the same time, we may be marginalizing a minority of people who have less control over their lives in a time of rapid change. With the current emphasis on globalization, we may be neglecting the basic fabric of society. These failures may haunt us with more crime in the future.

SUMMARY

1. Although crime and deviance overlap, several factors influence the way society responds. Various norms and settings in which acts take place influence the definition of crime.

2. Some wrongs are considered more criminal than others, but economic and non-economic costs do not always provide good guidelines. Some wrongs become crimes because they are of concern for the larger society.

3. Crime means that: law enforcement machinery may be used, crimes are explicit, intent is usually necessary, and criminal laws are general in their applicability. Crime depends on a political process that permits the use of institutions such as the police and courts.

4. Deciding on who is actually criminal can be contentious, but those with higher status and with greater power are better able to resist a criminal label.

5. Despite differences among criminologists, there are many areas of agreement on the causes of crime. A growing interest in conflict approaches has expanded the focus of criminology from explaining the behaviour of individuals to understanding the workings of the larger society.

KEY TERMS

conflict theory	12	prescriptions	3
expectations	3	tort	9

WEBLINKS

www.library.utoronto.ca/libraries_crim/centre/centre.htm
The University of Toronto Centre of Criminology offers graduate programs in criminology. In the library section research can be found on a broad range of issues.

www.sfu.ca/criminology
Simon Fraser University, School of Criminology, offers graduate programs in criminology.

www.grad.uottawa.ca/programs/masters/criminology/index.html
The University of Ottawa offers graduate programs in criminology.

www.fas.umontreal.ca/CRIM
Université de Montréal offers graduate programs in criminology.

EXPLAINING CRIME:
CONTRASTING APPROACHES

This chapter will:

- Review assumptions about instinct, learning, and socialization that are made when we study crime.
- Note the distinction between explanations assuming free will and those assuming determinism.
- Discuss different strategies for "explaining" crime.
- Explain the difference between perspectives and knowledge.
- Describe a scientific theory and show how it is tested.
- Show that variables consist of concepts and operational definitions.
- Note the problems and usefulness of scientific theories.
- Use ideas from Durkheim to illustrate the application of a general theory of crime.
- Offer some illustrations of pseudo-science.
- Recognize the growth and contribution of interpretive criminology and the use of qualitative data.

THE ASSUMPTIONS WE MIGHT MAKE

None of us approaches a topic without preconceived ideas. These assumptions influence the perspectives we select in trying to understand the world. We assume that other animals do not commit crimes, at least in the sense of committing transgressions against a moral code. What is it about *Homo sapiens* that presents the potential for crime? *The following opinions on human characteristics will be oversimplified and will not necessarily be shared by all social scientists, but these assumptions can mould the way we regard crime.*

It appears that early humans were able to adapt to a wide range of environmental conditions, even with minimal tools. Crucial to this learning process was intelligence and a variety of conceptual skills. For example, the Bushmen in the southern part of Africa were aware of a variety of techniques for conserving water, a commodity that was very scarce at times. They gathered the bi plant, which had a watery, fibrous root, scraped it into pieces, squeezed it, and drank the juice. The scrapings were then placed in a shallow trench. They urinated on those scrapings and, during the heat of the day, would lie on the scrapings to conserve this scarce moisture. In other words, early humans, in a variety of environments and extreme climatic conditions, displayed an extensive knowledge of their resources and developed skills for utilizing these resources, which required intelligence and the understanding of cause and effect. Modern humans share these characteristics: the ability to learn and the flexibility to adapt. This leads to a traditional debate: which is more important, instinct or learning?

Instincts, Learning, and Socialization

Some have argued that humans, especially males, are instinctively criminal. Others claim that *some* people are born criminal; i.e., it is in their genes. I argue that learning is the major factor in determining criminal, or any other, behaviour. This is not to say that genetic characteristics do not provide limitations and opportunities; the very nature of *Homo sapiens* and the characteristics that have led to the many and varied societies that have developed would not have been possible without an animal that was first and foremost a learner. Since the very survival of human beings depends on their ability to innovate, a fixed pattern of behaviour to which nothing could be added or modified would be dysfunctional. In other words, innate behaviour—i.e., instincts—would be counterproductive to a creature who must adapt to a variety of situations.

Early humans depended on this ability to learn and to adapt their behaviour to their environmental conditions. This ability allowed early humans to survive while stronger and better-equipped predators did not. One example of this survival involved *Dinofelis*, a cat less agile than a leopard or cheetah but more solidly built. It had a straight, dagger-like killing tooth and was a combination of a sabre-tooth tiger and a modern one. The bones of this heavily built, extinct tiger were found in the Transvaal, where early humans existed.

The Early Search for Instincts and Why It Failed

A number of classic experiments, conducted by psychologists trying to explain instinctual behaviour, actually led most current social scientists to reject the notion of instincts in humans. One experiment placed a baby monkey in a cage with a python that had been fed a pig. Clearly, the python was not interested in eating. It had been assumed that monkeys were instinctively afraid of snakes, but the baby monkey was simply curious. He inspected the python, twisted its tail, and poked at the head. The well-fed python could not be bothered with another potential meal. Then, the mother monkey was placed in the cage. She shrieked at the sight of the python, grabbed the baby monkey, and huddled, terrified, in the opposite corner. The mother was removed and, when the baby monkey was returned to the cage, *it* now shrieked and huddled in the corner. Socialization and learning provide a better explanation of these events than instincts.

Another experiment involved raising kittens with three different types of mice. The assumption: cats instinctively kill mice. However, kittens who were raised with different types of mice tended not to kill that particular species as they grew older. By contrast, kittens who were raised with mothers who killed mice in their presence did kill mice. Again, the type of mouse made a difference. When mothers killed a certain type of mouse, the kittens chose that type of mouse rather than other types. As in the case of the monkey, instincts do not explain the behaviour adequately; the kittens learned from their mothers. With a number of such experiments, psychologists changed their views about instincts as they realized that learning played a more important role than had previously been thought. To simplify, lower animals rely more on instinct, but the higher up the ladder of animal species one goes, the greater the reliance on learning.

How much can we transfer to humans from the study of animal behaviour? We learn that monkeys who are denied mother-love become poor mothers themselves. Among humans, we also find a correlation between children who received little love from parents and their ability to provide affection to their children a generation later. In other words, the study of social behaviour among monkeys and other primates has helped us to understand how humans learn to become normal, non-criminal adults. One concludes that learning rather than instinct provides a better explanation for almost all complex behaviour.

How do we transfer this simplified argument to crime? Basically, we reject the notion of criminal instincts in favour of learned behaviour. This acknowledges, of course, that people can also *fail* to learn prosocial behaviour, and that antisocial behaviour may have been learned haphazardly; but most sociologically oriented criminologists today would not find instincts, or some innate compulsion to commit nasty deeds, adequate to explain criminal behaviour.

The Interaction of Social Learning Processes

When one claims that behaviour is a product of needs, experience, and culture, it does not make it easy to predict specific behavioural outcomes. For example, the cultural setting does not determine behaviour, but it can provide the context in which behaviour is defined as acceptable or not. This can be illustrated by a telephone conversation one of my colleagues had with his baby daughter. "You went to the bathroom by yourself today, Shawnee? My, that's being a big girl. Mommy didn't have to help you? Daddy's proud of you. Where did you go? On the sidewalk?!"

Socialization takes time, and children learn imperfectly and at an uneven pace as their experiences unfold. Shawnee was part of a camping and hiking family. Squatting behind trees or by the side of a trail was one of many options that she had learned. However, she had not yet worked out all of the refinements. A few years later, we had another illustration of the complexities of the socialization process.

We were on a camping trip on a beach with several families. As we were setting up the tents, Shawnee, now about five, was fascinated with Thelma, my wife's former roommate, who was now visiting us. For Shawnee, the amazing thing about Thelma was her dark skin colour. "Why are the palms of your hands a lighter colour than the rest of your skin?" Thelma responded, "Because I'm a Negro." (This was back in the days before "black" became the more acceptable term.) Shawnee, with the innocence and energy typical of five-year-olds, relentlessly pursued the topic, with detailed questions that no adult would dare to ask. Fortunately, Thelma, a school teacher, was both more skilled and more at ease coping with the situation than the rest of us. Obviously, Shawnee had lived in a rather segregated and sheltered world, despite our assumptions that we sociologists and our families were relatively sophisticated on racial issues.

The adults in our group were torn between amusement and discomfort, not knowing whether it was best for a child to explore the questions of race at the top of her lungs in a crowded campground, or if she should be diverted to some other topic of inquiry. Finally, the tents were erected and sleeping spots were assigned when Shawnee came bounding down the beach yelling at the top of her voice, "I want to sleep with the Negro! I want to sleep with the Negro!", again making her the focus of attention for the campground.

Why use such illustrations in a criminology text? Learning to behave in a complex social world is difficult, time consuming, and occurs at differing rates. Most children become more skilled with time and, like Shawnee, become normal, gracious adults, while others do not have the opportunity to learn appropriate social behaviour. In addition, there are those who appear to be surrounded by law-abiding adults in normal settings but who still become criminals. Other children are raised in criminogenic settings, but manage to grow up to become non-deviant adults. It is clear that socialization is important, but there is considerable debate over which factors are the most important.

FREE WILL VERSUS DETERMINISM

The assumptions we make about humans influence the direction of our thinking and, to some extent, limit the explanations we hold regarding crime. Another perspective that moulds our basic thinking is the free will versus determinism debate. During the decades following World War II, this discussion engaged the interest of many academics. Although the issue is less prominent today, it is still implicit in much of our thinking about crime. The goal of this book is not to resolve the debate, or even to suggest that it *is* resolvable, but to simply note that where one stands on the free will versus determinism issue can influence how one does criminological research or interprets information.

Most social scientists follow a deterministic model, which presupposes that all human behaviour is determined by antecedent conditions. All events, including all human actions, are the result of preceding causes. Human behaviour is seen as determined by the events of the past, which includes biological heredity as well as the social and cultural environment. **Determinism** rejects the notion of free will or free choice, which assumes that people decide on a course of action of their own accord.

In the literature, one will often see the terms *positivism* and *empiricism* associated with determinism. **Positivism** is the use of the scientific method to explain crime, and borrows from methods used by the physical and life sciences. Knowledge can be gained only through sensory experience. Positivism emphasizes measurement in contrast to intuition, metaphysical speculation, and pure logic. Early criminologically oriented positivists measured parts of the body, and so forth, and produced studies that had many weaknesses. Because of these errors, some scholars have assumed that all studies measuring biological characteristics are suspect. However, this approach is not dependent on the type of variable. Biological, psychological, and sociological variables are all potentially useful. In fact, we are even able to use relatively "soft" data, that is, information that is difficult to count or classify precisely. The key factor is that one creates *testable* hypotheses. Ideas are stated in such a way that information can be gathered that could reject those ideas. **Empiricism** holds that generalizations can be held to be valid only when tested by objective techniques and verified by the senses. Although it may be an oversimplification for some specialists, this book will treat positivism and empiricism as equivalents. Both views are compatible with a deterministic view of the world.

A significant minority of criminologists do not share this view. These critics would argue that these "facts," which scientifically oriented criminologists use, are not facts at all, but rather are value-loaded concepts which are very subjective. Therefore, even when manipulated in a scientific manner, these facts produce conclusions that are not truly scientific. This perspective seems to have more followers among criminologists in England than in the United States, with Canadian criminologists being influenced by both streams of thought.

Radicalism and Anti-Positivistic Views

Some people equate many of the radicals with those who oppose positivism. While in certain cases this may be true, there is no inherent reason to automatically link those who favour dramatic social change, or those who are highly critical of the economic structure of capitalism—for example, the Marxists—with one methodology or another. In fact, one of the better-known radical criminologists, David Greenberg, publishes work in mathematical criminology (1979), and applies a scientific logic to his radical criticisms of the social order. Another illustration of a well-known radical criminologist who uses scientific tools is Barry Krisberg, president of the National Council on Crime and Delinquency. Krisberg's position requires that he work with a relatively conservative board of directors on policy issues relevant to the United States. To develop credibility with those who would influence policy, Krisberg and his fellow researchers support their arguments with statistical data and the types of analysis used by positivists.

On the Canadian scene, Marie-Andrée Bertrand has taken radical positions on many issues, arguing, for example, for the legalization of marijuana, but she works within a framework of empirically based knowledge. There are also economists with Marxist orientations who are sophisticated users of empirical data. On the other hand, some radical criminologists reject the use of empirical data.

The Different Types of Determinism

Many years ago, before I studied sociology, I heard a geographer give an impressive lecture, pointing out how power sources determined the ascendancy of nation-states. England had cheap coal, which led to the Industrial Revolution and England's dominant role on the world scene during the nineteenth century. The speaker was convinced that solar power would be the next major factor in determining national influence. Thus, Africa, which has more sunshine than the other continents, would lead the world by the end of the century. Today, I realize that this well-known professor was simply wrong. The nature of social structure and cultural elements enables countries such as Singapore and Japan, with modest natural resources and power sources, to overcome these limitations. Of course, I am convinced of this perspective. I was trained as a sociologist. Is it possible that I tend to be a "social determinist," while geographers tend to be "geographical determinists"?

If we extend this logic somewhat, is it surprising that some geneticists believe that "it is all in the genes"? Is it surprising that psychologists have greater faith in various sorts of counselling than do sociologists? In other words, a general acceptance of a deterministic model of behaviour does not necessarily lead to agreement on the *factors* that are most influential, or what sort of social programs might bring about desirable changes.

In this chapter, I do not set out to convince the reader that any one specific perspective is correct, but rather that we must be aware that *the way scholars are socialized into various disciplines and perspectives is also a social phenomenon that must be seen as part of the explanatory process.* The way we think and the beliefs we hold are socially constructed.

EXPLAINING CRIME: THE SCIENTIFIC METHOD

There are many routes to gaining knowledge. Philosophers, artists, and scholars of literature go at the knowledge business differently than social scientists. Historians construct reality using techniques that are quite different from physicists. In criminology, some postmodernist thinkers even raise doubts about the possibility of knowing what is "the truth." During the last two decades qualitative research within the social sciences has broadened the way criminologists search for knowledge (Kvale, 1996; Prus, 1996). Should criminologists be philosophers or social scientists? I certainly will not resolve such debates here. However, basic to what many criminologists do are the questions: How do we know what we know? Which version of reality is the best? There is much to be gained by understanding conventional scientific thinking. The scientific procedure has certain advantages. It provides clearer guidelines to let you know when you are wrong. It does not necessarily tell you when you are right; but criminology has so much useless baggage that anything that will reduce the load is helpful.

The Distinctions among Perspectives, Information, and Knowledge

Imagine that you have entered a huge diving bell, in order to view life in the ocean. In addition, imagine that some of the windows of this diving bell magnify and others distort in different ways. Furthermore, the glass is also of different colours. People looking out the different windows would see things differently. No one would actually see the truth. However, the view seen through each window has a certain amount of validity. Each person could stand at her window and argue vigorously that sea life is truly represented by her window and that others must be wrong. Many criminologists today recognize that we use different windows, but they somehow assume that everyone must stay at her original window. I prefer a diving bell in which people wander from window to window, gaining different perspectives. Soon, discussion arises about the *nature of the windows themselves*, and then we begin to ask just how each window distorts the outside world and how one might get a better picture of reality, despite the fact that *all* the windows distort reality. Most criminologists prefer certain types of windows, while others utilize more than one. A "perspective" is not the same as knowledge, nor is knowledge the same as information. The way information is assembled and interpreted will determine whether or not genuine knowledge has been created.

Social scientists have used the scientific method with a certain amount of success. It is certainly not the only way of understanding crime; however, it has particular advantages over other perspectives. The student of human behaviour should be aware of different viewpoints and should peer at the world through a variety of distorted windows, but it would be a mistake to ignore the scientific window; its distortions are better understood.

Creating and Testing a Scientific Theory

Many esoteric books have been written on the topic scientific theory, but the basic ideas of science are not as complicated as many assume. Imagine sitting in a large classroom. Just beneath the ceiling, balloons and sheep's bladders filled with helium are floating. They are connected to one another by a variety of ropes and sticks. However, we cannot see this network of balloons and bladders because of a thick smog, which lies just below the ceiling. In fact, we will never be able to see this framework because the smog is permanent;

but we are sure something is up there and that it will remain fairly constant. We will call that network of balloons and sheep's bladders "reality." Since we cannot see it directly, we must look for techniques to help us describe it indirectly. One ingenious student suggests that we tie a string to a ball of tar. By wandering about the room with these balls of tar and by throwing these balls up through the smog, we will occasionally strike a balloon. If we throw the ball and hear a dull thud, we assume that we missed a balloon and hit the ceiling instead. However, if we hear a *boing*, we will assume that we struck a balloon. If we hear a long, deep *boo-wang*, we will assume that we struck a sheep's bladder.

We then tie a small bell to the end of each string that we suspect is attached to a balloon, and a large bell to those suspected of being connected to a sheep's bladder. By examining the location of those strings with bells attached to them, we attempt to draw a "map" of the invisible network. Scientists are continually drawing maps, or models, or theories, which attempt to describe reality.

Next, we would like to know just how these hidden balloons and sheep's bladders are related to one another. We notice three strings with bells attached hanging in a straight line. Therefore, we might hypothesize that the three balloons are attached to one another by means of a piece of rope. If this were true, and we were to pull on the first string, the bell on the second string would jingle fairly vigorously, and the bell attached to the third string would jingle less vigorously. We perform such an experiment and find that the bells jingle as predicted. We have support for our hypothesis.

Since our hypothesis predicts that our three bells are connected in such a way, we can perform another test. If we hold the second string firmly, so that it cannot move, jerking on the first string will not make the third string and its bell jingle, or at least not very much. We have intervened by controlling the movement of the intervening string and bell. In a similar manner, a researcher can statistically "control" for a variable that intervenes between two others.

But another student has drawn another map. Using the same information, he argues that our three bells are connected to each other by a large sheep's bladder located in the centre of the room. If someone were to hold the string attached to the hypothesized sheep's bladder and keep it from moving, then the second and third bells would not ring if the first bell were jingled. As the reader can see, a variety of tests can be made to test the accuracy of our map of "reality." Even after many tests, our map could be quite incorrect. We will never know if we have found all of the balloons. Furthermore, some of our basic assumptions may be wrong. But as we proceed, our ever-improving map helps us to predict what will happen as we jingle one bell after another.

The above analogy of balloons and sheep's bladders may not satisfy the sophisticated reader. Following Hempel (1952), a scientific theory is a network of concepts and hypotheses. The concepts can be represented by knots, and the hypotheses, which link the concepts together, represented by threads connecting those knots. The network floats above the plane of observation and is anchored to it by rules of interpretation, like strings that link points (concepts) in the network to the plane of observation. The network can then function as a scientific theory; by observations, we ascend, via an interpretive string, to the theoretical network and then proceed, via hypotheses, to other points, and descend, by another interpretive string, to the plane of observation. Stated more simply, theories are created when we link concepts together in some systematic way by means of hypotheses, but they must be tested with observable measures.

At one time physical scientists believed that theories were reasonably accurate and resembled "reality." Few hold that view today. Rather, many theories are good approximations. When the modern physicist jingles her bells, she can chart the jingling of others accurately. Her models may not be absolutely correct, but they are surprisingly good for predictive purposes.

The Components of a Theory: Variables, Concepts, and Operational Definitions

Scientific theories require **variables**—that is, something that varies. Sex is a variable. We can classify people as either male or female. There is nothing sacred about a variable. It may be oversimplified. The simplification of sex into male or female is not 100 percent accurate. However, sex is handled conveniently in two categories. Crime is sometimes treated as if it were a two-part variable; that is, criminals and non-criminals. For some explanations, this simple dichotomy may have some utility. However, we find that most of the people who are criminals resemble those who are not criminals. Thus, this simple dichotomy is often inadequate. One response to some of these difficulties is to create a number of categories of criminals. Still another approach has been to treat delinquency in the way physicists measure heat. Something can be hotter or colder. By being able to measure the variable "heat" precisely, the physicist has been able to improve on his predictions. Attempts have been made to measure criminality on a continuum. The problem with classifying criminals or crime, and the variables related to them, is of considerable magnitude; but the logic of the problem is the same as that used by physical sciences.

The variables scientists use do not exist in their own right. They are only abstractions, which we assume are reflections of reality. In the study of crime we have a series of pet variables: the deteriorating family, bad genes, the opportunity structure, and so on. Crime might be approached using different variables. People could be classified as those exploited and those who do the exploiting. We could ignore the behaviour of potential criminals and focus instead on the behaviour of social control agencies. Or, we may wish to focus on the conflict that arises as a result of the interaction between those social control agencies with authority and those who are subjected to that authority. "Conflict," "power," "types of agencies," and so forth, can all be seen as variables in a scientific theory. They reflect the particular interests of specific criminologists. In order to work with variables, however, we need to break them down into two components: concepts and operational definitions.

A **concept** could be seen as an attempt to communicate what we mean by a certain variable. For example, when someone says she is going to describe "crime," it is not always clear what she has in mind. The concept *crime* may take on different meanings to different persons. Therefore, a researcher may spend quite a bit of time making it clear what she means when she uses the word *crime*. Simply defining the concept does not designate anything new; it is neither right nor wrong, and it makes no claims. A concept is a word or short phrase that takes the place of a paragraph of discussion and tries to get us to understand what the concept is all about.

An **operational definition** specifies the procedures of observation that are necessary to identify the concept or measure the variable. We might define crime operationally by using "crimes known to the police." If we go back to our model of the balloons, tar balls, and strings, we can see that the balloons are the concepts and the bells are the operational definitions. We have linked the two together. However, we can *only* work at the operational level; that is, we can only use the bells. Reality remains invisible. We have described our concept as a balloon filled with helium. It may be quite different, but the smog will never let us see it (see Figure 2.1).

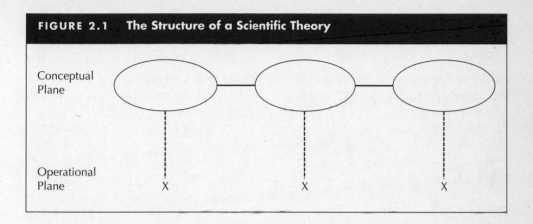

FIGURE 2.1 **The Structure of a Scientific Theory**

Conceptual Plane

Operational Plane   X   X   X

Scientists must *work* at the level of the operational plane, but they *think* at the level of the conceptual plane. In Figure 2.1, we must work with the operational definitions (jingle the bells, compute our statistics, etc.), but we are concerned with the linkage among the concepts (balloons that we can only imagine). This logic might be understood more easily if we use a model from physics, Boyle's law (see Figure 2.2).

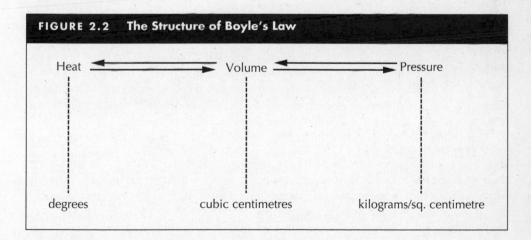

FIGURE 2.2 **The Structure of Boyle's Law**

Heat ⟷ Volume ⟷ Pressure

degrees   cubic centimetres   kilograms/sq. centimetre

The model or theory suggests that there is a direct relationship between heat, volume, and pressure. If volume is constant and the heat increased, the pressure will increase. The operational definition of "heat" may be the height of a narrow column of mercury in a glass tube. Today, we have many types of thermometers, but they are all operational measures of the concept "heat."

Sometimes concepts are understood only partially. For example, heat can be described as the rapid movement of molecules; but if we had a simpler notion of heat, could we still test the theory? Even if I know nothing about the movement of molecules, I know that a fire makes heat. Boyle's law can be tested with a test tube, a cork, and a fire. When the air in a test tube is heated, the pressure builds, and the cork blows off. The test is crude, but we often test theories with crude instruments. In criminology, the instruments are primitive, but other sciences did remarkably well with unsophisticated measuring devices at an earlier time.

Finding Appropriate Operational Definitions and Concepts

We can make considerable progress using and testing theories without refined concepts or precise operational definitions. Let us assume that we measure the concept *crime* as "crimes known to the police." We probably would like to include criminal acts unknown to the police as well, but where can we get such data? Immediately, we can see a dilemma: finding a measuring device, or operational definition that exactly fits our concept will be difficult. Our operational definition may be a poor measure of the concept it attempts to measure.

Criminology is not alone in lacking clear concepts and accurate operational definitions. For example, the gross domestic product (GDP) has been considered a useful concept in economics for some time. People seem to know what it means. When one looks at it more carefully, however, the concept is really not that clear. There is a temptation to define the concept by simply giving its operational definition. However, describing how a concept is measured is not the same as communicating the essence and meaning of that concept.

Even the operational definition could be questioned. The gross domestic product includes the value of automobiles with defective brakes, a worthless product like Coca-Cola which destroy teeth, and fees paid for questionable and even dangerous services. Should it also include the fees paid to prostitutes? If we include the fees of other entertainment, why not prostitutes as well? If a dishonest clerk charges a customer 10 dollars but records a sale of 5 dollars, which figure should be a part of the GDP? If an accountant does a farmer's income tax and accepts a side of beef in payment, does it become part of the GDP? Should it? The point is that the GDP can be somewhat unclear as a concept and imprecise in the way it is measured, but it is still useful. When we begin to treat concepts and operational definitions as sacred, we can be led astray. Unclear concepts and crude measuring techniques can still be useful. Therefore, we should not let such problems paralyze our efforts to understand crime.

Our ability to conceptualize is limited by our experience. Western medicine has developed certain conceptual frameworks for understanding illness. Those who use acupuncture use a different set of concepts, and communication across these two mental sets is not easy. Concepts, then, are not necessarily "true." They are judged by their clarity. Theories may be useful. They are like road maps. They are not necessarily precise, but are designed for utility. If you drive from Vancouver to Montreal, I can provide you with aerial photographs along the Trans-Canada Highway. They will be more precise than the road maps, but the design of the road map makes it more useful than the aerial photograph. Theories, like maps, are creations. Some are more useful than others.

The Utility of Theories

In Boyle's law, as presented above, we have a parsimonious theory with only three variables: heat, volume, and pressure. However, there are times when our untested theories contain many variables, and we are unable to measure some of them. By systematically linking together those variables that we can measure, we can develop a reasonable explanation even when we have only partial knowledge. Theories can extend the knowledge that is available to us.

Maximizing Partial Knowledge: The Case of the Lobster

Every concept does not have to be measured before progress can be made. I have a theory about lobsters and their gravity organs. I hypothesize that lobsters have a gravity organ in the side of their head, which is something like a small hole lined with a membrane sensitive to pressure. Inside that gravity organ is a piece of sand. The weight of that piece of sand resting against the membrane tells the lobster whether he is right side up or whether he is moving forward or backward. When the lobster sheds his exoskeleton and leaves his old shell behind, the piece of sand in his gravity organ drops out. While the lobster is growing his new shell, he must find a new grain of sand to stick in his gravity organ. After the new exoskeleton has hardened, the lobster has a new grain of sand in his gravity organ and is able to function as before.

My students don't take me seriously when I describe this theory of the lobster and his gravity organ. However, a clever biologist once placed lobsters in salt water where iron filings replaced the sand. The biologist reasoned that when the lobster shed his exoskeleton he would lose the grain of sand in his gravity organ and would grope around for another one. It is unlikely that the lobster would be able to find the same grain of sand; thus, he would probably pick up one of the small pieces of iron and stick it in his gravity organ. After waiting an appropriate length of time, the biologist held a magnet above the lobsters. What do you think happened? Soon, there were several confused crustaceans flipping over on their backs. The biologist had made a test of the theory of the lobster and his gravity organ.

Let us look at the logic of the argument more closely. Although the biologist made only one test, he linked many facts and assumptions together. Should the biologist open up the lobster's head to see if a piece of iron was contained inside? This, of course, would be a further test of the theory. It might also be difficult for observers to see whether or not the lobster actually picked up a piece of iron filing in his claws. In other words, the "theory" links together concepts and ideas. In the final test with the magnet, use was made of other knowledge: iron is attracted by magnets. Furthermore, a logical argument is offered that if the iron filing is drawn upwards to the top of the gravity organ, the lobster would confuse the pull of the magnet with normal gravity and would respond accordingly. The credibility of the entire test lies in the fact that the researcher *made his predictions in advance*.

In the study of crime, and in many other disciplines, scholars frequently provide ***ex post facto*** explanations, that is, explanations after the fact. Admittedly, calling one's shots in advance is difficult; but it lends credibility to one's ideas. If one is attempting to design a crime prevention program, a clearly articulated explanatory argument, a "theory," should be spelled out *in advance*. In the social sciences, we are not always careful about making such predictions. After the evidence fails to support our predictions, which is common, then we should turn to *ex post facto* interpretations, which are useful in considering new theories for testing. However, we should not fall into the trap of giving these interpretations the credibility of predictions made in advance. In the case of the lobster study described above, a single dramatic test provided credence to the entire linkage of ideas because an integrated theory was developed in advance.

Durkheim's Theory of Deviance

How can stating concepts and linking them together systematically with hypotheses help in the study of crime? A classic work by Émile Durkheim (1858–1917) provides a useful illustration. At the end of the nineteenth century, Durkheim studied suicide in Europe. Our simplified version of the theory contains three concepts: individualism, social cohesion, and deviance. The argument goes as follows: when people live in communities that have a common culture, they share common values and are in agreement on the important issues in life. This similarity in thinking leads to social cohesion. Social cohesion makes people sensitive to the social demands of society and hence leads to the reduction of deviant behaviour.

Durkheim's research showed that Protestant communities, which may be more individualistic, had higher suicide rates than Catholic communities, which may be more oriented toward collective thinking. One can generalize the argument from the specific act of suicide to deviance and crime in general, as illustrated in Figure 2.3.

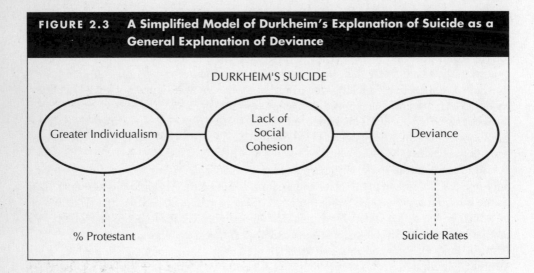

FIGURE 2.3   A Simplified Model of Durkheim's Explanation of Suicide as a General Explanation of Deviance

DURKHEIM'S SUICIDE

Greater Individualism — Lack of Social Cohesion — Deviance

% Protestant   Suicide Rates

Durkheim did not use a measure for social cohesion. Today, social scientists have measures for social cohesion, but it is important to demonstrate that a scientific theory can be tested even though some of its concepts cannot be measured. If the theory is correct, we would expect individualism to have an impact on social cohesion, and social cohesion would then have an impact on deviance. That is, individualism would have an impact on deviance via social cohesion.

Deviance was measured by suicide rates. At the operational level, then, we can test the theory by asking about religion and assuming that Catholics are more collective in their thinking and Protestants more individualistic. The theory utilizes assumptions and logical connections, but the data tend to support the overall pattern. These ideas are useful, even though there are major weaknesses. Individualism was measured crudely. Obviously "individualism" could reflect many things besides religion. In a similar manner, suicide may not be a particularly good measure of deviant behaviour. Other measures of deviance might also be deficient but still have enough validity to provide a crude test.

Different and imperfect operational definitions have been used in Durkheim's work and similar research that followed, but these initial ideas, despite the use of crude measures and concepts, have been very influential.

Choosing Theories to Suit Our Purposes

While Durkheim's ideas may be compatible with the way some people feel the world *is*, these simplifications could make others uncomfortable in terms of the way we feel the world *ought* to be. Durkheim suggests that individualistic communities have more crime. Does this mean we should all live in ghettos? There are people in Canada who think that we should live with people of "our own kind," whatever that means. Theories do not necessarily provide us with clear policy directions. Personally, I believe that Canada has been enriched by its many ethnic groups and that modern nations must accept the reality of considerable variety in their populations. At the same time, I am also aware that individualism and heterogeneity cause strain. Thus, I select theories with certain purposes in mind, and my choices are influenced by personal values. My preference is for theories that tell me how crime can be reduced in individualistic and *heterogeneous* societies, which I feel are both inevitable and desirable in the modern world.

Applying Theory to Modern Criminology

With many different attempts to explain crime, can we use scientific theory to support one argument or another? Simple debate, without referring to some criteria for truth, may lead nowhere. Those who utilize science state hypotheses that can be tested. This permits agreement on some points and enables scholars to move to more adequate theories.

Figure 2.4 suggests that social class is related to crime. In general, those from the middle and upper classes do not get convicted of crimes as often as those in the lower classes. At least two explanations are possible. The first might emphasize the power of the upper classes to manipulate society. The powerful influence legislation so that their values and sense of what is right are written into the laws. In addition, their social clout may make it less likely that they would be arrested, charged, and convicted.

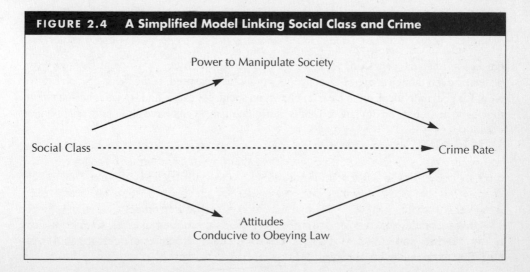

FIGURE 2.4   A Simplified Model Linking Social Class and Crime

Power to Manipulate Society

Social Class

Crime Rate

Attitudes
Conducive to Obeying Law

The second explanation might argue that upper- and middle-class people are simply more law-abiding, because they have attitudes that are conducive to obeying the law. Lower-class people, this view contends, are not as well socialized, have more delinquent attitudes, and, therefore, commit more crimes. Both explanations suggest that in Figure 2.4 the arrow connecting social class and crime is spurious. That is, there is no real direct link between social class and crime; thus, the link is indicated by a thin, broken line. Instead, the relationship exists due to intervening variables, which translate the meaning of social class into something that leads to crime. The first argument chooses the "power to manipulate society" as that intervening variable, while the second argument chooses "attitudes" as the appropriate intervening variable.

If a researcher were to gather the appropriate data, she could test both ideas at the same time, in order to see which model fits the data best. Unfortunately, many researchers selectively choose data that fit their argument. By utilizing a proposed theory we can clarify the argument and increase the likelihood that our findings can be interpreted in a manner that will actually move knowledge forward.

The Increased Use of Interpretive Research in Criminology

After the Second World War, some social scientists believed that science was an all-inclusive tool for understanding human behaviour. The scientific approach was oversold. In the 1970s the pendulum appeared to swing the other way with a reaction against empirically based work and quantitative data. Tolerance was often lacking on both sides.

Space does not permit an adequate discussion of the more recent and extensive use of *interpretive* criminology. Some criminologists argue that science misses a vital part of the social world: *meaning*. Interpretive criminologists see reality constructed by individuals as part of daily interaction. Instead of **quantitative data**, they favour **qualitative data**, such as the perceptions of how people understand their surroundings. For example, the work by Philippe Bourgois on street addicts discussed in the chapter on drugs illustrates an attempt to understand the world as seen by the addicts themselves. Thus, one should not assume that the scientific approach is necessarily the best or only way of studying crime.

Progress in the explanation of crime depends on contrasting views. Unfortunately, criminologists are like a baby with a new toy. Give the baby a new hammer and she will pound everything with it. Similarly, some social scientists use only one tool. Sometimes they try to convince others that theirs is the *only* tool. While this chapter emphasizes traditional science, qualitative methods are better suited for studying natural settings. Subjective thoughts and feelings, which might be seen as bias by traditional science, become central to interpretive criminology.

SUMMARY

1. Before we can explain crime, we must acknowledge the assumptions we make about human beings. Some people believe crime is instinctual, but most social scientists assume that humans are primarily moulded by learning and socialization.

2. Most social scientists believe that behaviour, including crime, is *determined* by the surrounding world rather than by *free will*. However, individuals interact with that environment. They are not passive.

3. Criminologists use a variety of strategies for explaining crime. Depending on the questions asked, different strategies might be more useful. Perspectives provide windows through which we view the world. The information may be faulty or partial. Sometimes we can put that information together and create knowledge.

4. Scientific theories utilize *variables*, which are composed of *concepts*, the way we describe things, and of *operational definitions*, the way we measure those concepts. Although scientific theories may not be as useful for understanding the meaning of social interaction as interpretive strategies, they have other advantages. For example, they are more testable.

5. Durkheim's theory of suicide provides an illustration of a general theory about the linkage of individualism, social cohesion, and deviance that has influenced explanations of crime.

6. Recently, interpretive criminology and the use of qualitative data have broadened our understanding of the meaning of social interaction and have extended our grasp of different forms of crime.

KEY TERMS

concept   26

determinism   22

empiricism   22

ex post facto explanations   29

operational definition   26

positivism   22

qualitative data   32

quantitative data   32

variables   26

WEBLINKS

www.ccsd.ca/
The Canadian Council on Social Development: a national, non-profit organization focusing on research in the areas of employment, government social policies, poverty, and child welfare.

www.cprn.com/cprn.html
The Canadian Policy Research Networks: information on social and economic issues.

www.ciaj-icaj.ca/index.html
The Canadian Institute for the Administration of Justice: a national, non-profit organization looking at the administration of justice in Canada.

THE MEANING
OF CRIME STATISTICS

This chapter will:

- Review factors that influence crime statistics.

- Discuss the meaning of statistics at different stages in the criminal justice system.

- Note trends in crime and its distribution in Canada.

- Explain how some measures are better for making comparisons.

- Identify some misperceptions about crime, particularly youth crime, created by the media.

- Note the use of victimization and self-reported rates.

COMMON ERRORS IN DATA GATHERING

Crime rates can be influenced by a number of things: changes in the way police respond to crime, a growth in police force strength (Koenig, 1996), and changes in the law. An example of the latter occurred when Section 266 of the Criminal Code was amended in 1983 under Bill C127, making it easier for police to arrest on a reasonable suspicion of assault. This led to a dramatic increase in assault arrests (Kingsley, 1996). The increase in *reported* assaults does not mean that there was an increase in *actual* assaults. This is only one type of error which plagues users of statistics, but there are often ways of dealing with various problems.

Errors exist in all data, but some cause more problems than others. *Random* errors can be handled differently than *systematic* ones. Let us assume that the police in Montreal, Toronto, and Vancouver record thefts in the same manner, but they occasionally make mistakes. Assuming that the police in all three cities make mistakes with similar frequency and in a random fashion, and that they make their mistakes about as often in one direction as in another, we can still use the data and compare the three cities. In other words, we can usually handle **random errors** by assuming that they balance each other out. In a similar manner, some small detachments of police scattered about a province might over-report certain crimes; other detachments might under-report the same crimes. If we assume that those detachments are similarly distributed in Ontario and in British Columbia, then these errors are randomized, and we can still compare Ontario and British Columbia when these statistics are averaged.

Systematic errors present a different problem. When census takers approach a home, they sometimes meet the man of the house at the door. When asked how many children he has, the man might respond "three." Is the wife home? No, she is in the hospital, having a baby. Has the baby been born? Yes, it arrived yesterday. Is that your third child? The husband hesitates. "Oh that's right. I have *four* kids now!" Husbands *systematically* forget their newborn children in counting offspring. This systematic error is not a problem for the census experts in Canada. Sophisticated demographers know how to adjust the number of children reported to get a more accurate count.

A similar systematic error occurs for women aged 39. Every census produces a surplus of women who are 39 and a shortage of woman aged 40 and 41. Our population experts are not fooled, however, and they correct this error with little trouble. While systematic errors that are understood can be handled, there are times when something that appears to be systematic may not be. For example, we might wish to compare crime rates for men and women. If the errors made in recording crime for men and women are random, we have few problems. If the errors are systematic but similar—for example, if we neglect both old women and old men—we might still compare men and women. But if the errors are systematic one way among women but systematic in a different way among men, we would have trouble comparing the sexes. However, we still might be able to make comparisons *within* the sexes.

In Canada the Centre for Justice Statistics is aware of the problems mentioned above as well as others. For the last two decades they have produced the Juristat series, which present statistics and discussion on certain crimes. These useful and readable documents also include cautions about the interpretation of crime statistics. Most of the statistics presented in this chapter come from Juristat publications.

DIFFERENT WAYS OF USING CRIME STATISTICS

While it is difficult to do a national study that would sort out factors influencing crime rates, concentrating on a single police department increases the odds of identifying problem areas while utilizing statistics effectively. Two studies will be summarized to illustrate how criminologists use crime statistics in a skillful manner. The first focuses on crime rates in Edmonton from 1984 to 1994 (Kennedy and Veitch, 1997). Crime rates in Edmonton climbed until 1991 and then decreased steadily. The pattern was similar for both violent and property offences. But what did the statistics actually mean? A sophisticated analysis of the official data, along with other data, suggested that actual crime did not decrease. However, police resources were used more effectively. They targeted problem areas and focused on root causes. Rather than simply responding to calls, they tried to solve problems and used more discretion in reporting incidents. Most criminologists agree that police activity cannot have a great impact on crime directly, but when police deal with root causes, they probably have an impact in the future. Thus, the changes in Edmonton in the 1990s appear to reflect an intelligent shift in the use of police resources, rather than actual decreases in criminal behaviour. Statistics helped us to understand the situation and document what may be a trend in many police forces in Canada.

In the second study, Tim Hartnagel (1997) makes quite different assumptions. Western Canadian provinces persistently exhibit higher crime rates than the rest of Canada, while the Atlantic provinces tend to have lower rates. Hartnagel is aware that police reporting can differ from actual criminal behaviour; but as one averages statistics from many different police departments across the country, he assumed that any differences in data-gathering procedures "balance out." Similarly, the relationship between police statistics and actual crime should not vary systematically across the provinces. In addition, more reliable rates, such as murder rates, show the same pattern. Thus, it is reasonable to assume that persistent higher crime rates in the west are real.

Hartnagel suggests that geographic mobility, which leads to weakened social controls in communities, would be accompanied by higher crime rates. Using data over a twenty-year period (1962–1982), Hartnagel finds that geographic mobility *is* associated with both violent and property crime rates. It would be reasonable to extend this logic to a variety of deviant behaviours which might be inhibited by stable and cohesive communities.

We have all heard the cliché about how easy it is to lie with statistics. Like many clichés, this one misses the central issue. The real issue concerns the meaning and interpretation of statistical data. Hartnagel assumed that the official data were appropriate for comparing regions. Kennedy and Veitch assumed that the official data measured police dynamics. Both studies illustrate how statistics can be a useful tool.

In the pages that follow I explore the utility and limitations of crime statistics. Some criminologists mistakenly claim that crime statistics are invalid and useless. Crime data can be useful, but they can also be misused. Crime statistics do not necessarily measure criminal behaviour; they measure the *response* of various agencies to their *perception* of crime. These data may permit estimates of criminal behaviour. Usually, however, they measure what social control agencies do.

Interpreting Incidents, Cases, and Charges

The most frequently cited crime statistics are incidents based on the Uniform Crime Reporting Survey (UCR), i.e., those reported to the police. If the police were able to record all incidents, these statistics would be an accurate measure of crime. However, not all crimes are reported. There are also regional differences which influence police reporting. Another way to measure incidents is the victim survey, which will be discussed later. These have problems of their own, but have advantages when we attempt to compare different regions. Unfortunately, victimization categories do not always correspond to police recorded categories.

When potential offenders are charged, we move into court statistics. Data are sometimes available on *charges* and sometimes on *cases*. Researchers who are primarily interested in juveniles favour data on cases, since they are usually interested in the numbers of juveniles involved in crime, rather than the number of offences. However, some data provide crimes known to the police or the number of criminal charges. If the police have picked up a juvenile who has committed a series of break and enters and also stolen a few cars, they could charge her with many offences. On the other hand, once having recorded a few offences, is there much point in adding many more to the list of charges? Thus, a police department that lays many charges, compared with one that lays few, may be dealing with a similar number of juveniles.

If we are interested in individual offenders, we may use one set of data, but if we are interested in the amount of crime, we may look at other data. Both strategies require different assumptions and estimates. When attempting to study the Canadian juvenile justice system, Diane Cossins (1991) was really interested in the number of cases, but she only had data on charges. However, the police laid about two charges per case, with the exception of Quebec, which laid about three charges per case. In other words, a fairly *systematic* ratio was similar for most of Canada. This enabled her to make comparisons among provinces.

In addition, Cossins knew that the Montreal police screened many juveniles involved in shoplifting, a practice common in some other cities in Quebec as well. When these minor offences were handled informally, fewer cases were sent on to the court. These police practices, which make sense, of course lowered the recorded crime rate. It also meant that court cases tended to be more serious and thus could easily involve more charges than cases in other Canadian youth courts. Knowledge about ratios between charges and cases, and an awareness of some local police practices, enabled Cossins to interpret crime statistics more accurately and to make cautious comparisons among the provinces.

Measuring Crime Data at Different Stages in the System

The activities of recording agencies at the early stages will influence recording activities later in the process. If the police screen many minor offences initially, the remaining cases, which are probably more serious, should result in more charges being laid per case (this appears to be the situation in Quebec). The cases sent to court would be more serious and more likely to receive punitive sanctions in court. By contrast, Youth Courts that receive more trivial offences should give more lenient sanctions. For example, 40 percent of the sentences in Youth Courts in Ontario 1999/2000 were to secure or open custody (Sudworth and deSouza, 2001). In Saskatchewan the comparable figure was 34 percent. However, the rate of cases appearing in Youth Court was 428 per 10 000 youths in Ontario and 941 in Saskatchewan. Did the larger number of court cases in Saskatchewan include less serious cases? Probably. Thus, 40 percent given custody in Ontario might be more lenient than the 34 percent given custody in Saskatchewan if the Ontario court cases represented more serious offences. The point is: *one cannot compare court statistics from place to place without taking into account the nature of the steps that lead to cases going to court.*

If some of these operations produce *systematic* differences, and we can assess that systematic bias, we can still make intelligent comparisons. It appears, however, that even though the provinces take in different numbers of juveniles at various stages, the proportion of those found guilty who go into custody is relatively similar across provinces (Doob and Sprott, 1996). The same pattern appears in adult criminal justice. Provinces and communities vary more in the way they process putative offenders at the front end of the system than in incarcerations.

Making Sense out of Problem Statistics

P. J. Giffen (1965) provided some helpful illustrations of problem statistics by using data on fraud from Canada's three largest cities, Montreal, Toronto, and Vancouver, in 1960. He found that Toronto had 2536 cases of fraud compared with 18 in Montreal and 60 in Vancouver. Should we assume that Torontonians cheat more than those living in Montreal or Vancouver? Or did the police classify fraud differently in the three cities?

A decade later, Giffen (1976) continued this discussion. According to 1962 data, the rates (per 100 000 persons) for fraud for the three largest Canadian cities were: Toronto, 364; Montreal, 81; and Vancouver, 340. The 1960 pattern persisted somewhat into 1962. But how long do patterns continue? In 1971, the rates for fraud were: Toronto, 557; Montreal, 171; and Vancouver, 601. Have the con artists moved to Vancouver? In 1996, the rate for Ontario was 321, Quebec was the lowest with 250, and BC was higher than average with 387 (Janhevich, 1998). The pattern still persists somewhat.

Today's data are clearly superior to those of the 1960s, but there is still the possibility of defining or reporting fraud differently across the country, with Quebec screening out more and British Columbia pulling more into its net. Instead of trying to interpret statistics without background information, it is wiser to supplement our knowledge about a specific system. My discussions with police in Montreal in the 1980s suggest that juvenile thefts are more likely to be handled informally than in other Canadian cities. Usually the police record about twice as many thefts as break and enters (B&Es). This fits with common sense: people shoplift more frequently than they break into houses. However, Montreal has produced official statistics for juveniles indicating more B&Es than petty theft. This could be the result of the police handling some of the shoplifting informally. Traditionally, petty theft (as well as common assault) has appeared to be lower in Quebec than Ontario. Victimization studies do not show such great discrepancies among the provinces.

The historical approach provides insights. My guess is that the screening patterns in Quebec, which appear to be an intelligent use of police resources, lower the minor property crime rates, thereby making all property crimes appear lower. Instead of saying that the statistics are "wrong," it makes more sense to say that they tell us something about the way police respond to certain types of events. The purpose of this section has been to make the reader cautious. Crime data can be useful even though they have certain limitations. In the next section we will see that some comparisons are easier to make than others.

CHARACTERISTICS THAT COMPLICATE COMPARISIONS

At this point, the reader may feel that making sense out of crime data is hopeless. The more we learn about these statistics, the warier we become, but we also gain insights about the settings in which crime statistics are produced. With these insights we make some comparisons but are hesitant to make others. Sometimes we would like to compare provinces. At other times we would like to compare cities. If all of the cities in Quebec and Ontario do things the same way, then comparison between the two provinces is possible. However, if cities themselves do things differently or have different characteristics, comparisons among provinces or within provinces can be misleading. Therefore, it is important to look at some features of cities and the impact they might have on crime statistics. Let us first consider the "central city phenomenon."

The Central City Phenomenon

As every experienced police officer knows, crime is more likely in areas where there are goods to be stolen or victims to be robbed. Cities surrounded by populated areas, such as suburbs, are more likely to act as "magnets" for people living nearby. Some cities, such as Calgary or Saskatoon, have small suburbs. There are no large surrounding populations that might use Calgary or Saskatoon for criminal exploitation. Central cities are not only attractive for work and culture, they also provide many well-known targets for crime (Boggs, 1965).

The Centre for Justice Statistics deals with this problem by using **census metropolitan areas (CMAs)**, which include adjacent urban and rural areas that have a high degree of economic and social integration. Victoria, BC, is now a CMA with adjacent communities such as Saanich and Esquimalt. But in the 1980s, Victoria offered one of the best illustrations of the **central city phenomenon** in Canada (Hackler and Don, 1989).

According to official data, Victoria displayed surprisingly high crime rates when compared with other cities, but did not get much attention in the media because it was not one of the larger metropolitan areas. In a city where you can purchase flowers in front of houses by putting money in an unattended box, the residents have difficulty thinking of their town as the crime capital of Canada. However, Victoria is a central hub for a half-dozen communities on the Victoria peninsula, each with its own police department. The CMA is approximately 300 000 people with Victoria as the central city. If you are a drug dealer living in one of the suburbs and are looking for action, you will probably head for Victoria. Similarly, if you are a young person living in the suburbs and decide to earn money by selling sex, you could try propositioning your neighbour while he is walking his dog, but you would probably do better in downtown Victoria. The central city phenomenon suggests that opportunities for crime in city centres attract the criminally inclined from the surrounding residential areas.

On the other hand, smaller residential areas could generate high crime rates for different reasons. For burglaries (B&Es in Canada), the police usually have little information. Without a suspect, it is difficult to make an arrest and lay a charge. If Mabel lives on a small island and notices that her TV set is missing, she may know the local police, and they may even know her TV set. They may check suspicious autos waiting at the ferry and check for Mabel's TV in the back seat. In other words, police in small communities may be more familiar with potential offenders and better able to lay charges, thereby increasing the "cleared by charge" category. B&E is probably less common on one of the Gulf Islands in BC than in Vancouver, but the *likelihood* of burglars being discovered and charged may be greater. Thus, some statistics may be augmented in small communities; others, such as public drunkenness, may be diminished. In small communities, the police may know the offenders and let them dry out in a cell or take them home. In larger urban centres such offenders may become part of the official statistics.

The central city phenomenon may differ by crime and by community. It can also differ when there is one large police department or many smaller ones. Going downtown to steal in Montreal keeps the statistic in the same police district, but going from Burnaby to Vancouver is a move from one police jurisdiction to another. Reporting crime using the larger CMA in Vancouver reduces the impact of the central city phenomenon but makes it more difficult to understand patterns within the area.

In Nova Scotia, does the bridge across the Narrows between Halifax and Dartmouth mean that it is easy to travel from Dartmouth into Halifax for certain illicit activities? Or is the distance a barrier? The central city phenomenon plays a different role in different parts of Canada and illustrates one of many factors that complicate the interpretation of crime rates.

Comparing Cities: Edmonton and Calgary as Illustrations

Each year, when crime statistics are released, journalists call local criminologists for explanations. The cautions about interpreting these figures usually have little impact on the media and are forgotten by the time statistics appear the following year. Edmonton is compared annually with Calgary, since Edmonton almost always displays much higher crime rates. The two cities are very similar in size and demographic characteristics. Edmonton typically joins Vancouver in the top three cities in the nation on a variety of offences, but Calgary invariably reports a lower crime rate. When the Canadian Centre for Justice Statistics (1990) studied crime reporting procedures, part of the differences in reported crime rates was attributed to the operation of the information systems in the two police departments (Silverman, Teevan, and Sacco, 1991: 57). The Calgary system screened more. It is inappropriate to assume that one system is "correct" or that one system was deliberately trying to mislead. Rather, it calls our attention to the variability which probably exists across different systems.

Fortunately, the two cities are aware of these differences, and Edmonton has not tried to make its statistics look "better." The shared information between these two police forces provides insights into the dynamics of the crime recording process, information that helps us understand crime data elsewhere in Canada. By 1999 the two cities were reporting more similar rates. Does the remaining difference suggest there is slightly more crime in Edmonton than in Calgary? We really don't know. The central city phenomenon might play a role. Calgary has smaller suburbs than Edmonton.

In general, inter-city and inter-regional comparisons are risky. If we wish to use crime statistics to compare cities, we should be aware that these indicators measure *the response of local justice systems to what they perceive to be crime*. This is a useful comparison, but it is misleading to think of such statistics as measuring the behaviour of criminals. On the other hand, if there is constancy in the way systems operate, statistics may be a reasonable indicator of *trends* for a country, province, or even a city. There are pitfalls, however, even when one attempts to examine trends. Let us turn now to some of these trends.

RECENT TRENDS IN CRIME

The Distribution of Homicide in Canada

Canada's police-reported crime rate decreased in 2000, the ninth consecutive annual drop (Logan, 2001). The main decrease was in property crime. Although violent crime went up by 3 percent in 2000, it had been declining for seven years. Youth crime decreased for eight years and then had a 1 percent increase in 2000.

Some violent crime rates are influenced by police practices. For example, schoolyard fights were rarely recorded a generation ago. Today they might be recorded as assaults. Similarly, drug offences are influenced by police strategies. Homicide, however, is more accurately measured and thus is used when looking at trends or comparing different areas.

Figure 3.1 shows the homicide rate in Canada from 1961 to 1999 (Fedorowycz, 2000). The peaking of homicide rates in the middle of the 1970s and the decrease since then seems to fit the pattern for most crimes in general. When we try to compare provinces or cities, the small number of homicides make comparisons difficult, but when we use a ten-year average, it is easier to see if there are systematic regional differences.

Nunavut, with statistics beginning in 1999, showed a rate of 7.40 with two murders. The rate for the Northwest Territories for the previous nine years is shown as 9.57 in Figure 3.2. This represents six homicides for the period. Although few, these homicides fit a long-time pattern of high homicide rates in the north. Similarly, PEI's ten-year rate of .75 is the

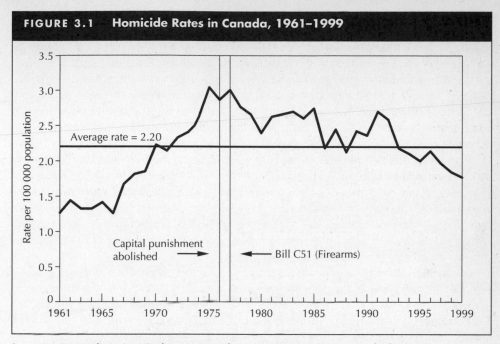

FIGURE 3.1   Homicide Rates in Canada, 1961–1999

Source: Statistics Canada, "Juristat" Catalogue 85-002. Vol. 20, No. 9, Page 2, Figure 1. Reprinted with permission.

result of a single homicide. But it fits a longer trend: homicide rates are significantly lower in the Maritime provinces and higher in the west and in the north.

Generally speaking, larger cities in Canada have slightly higher rates of homicide (2.35) (Fedorowycz, 2000); cities with 250–499 999 population have lower rates (1.72), and cities with 100 000–249 999 population have rates in between (1.97). Overall, rural and urban areas in Canada have very similar homicide rates.

Figure 3.3 supports the general theme. Most of the western cities have higher rates than eastern cities, with the exception of Montreal. This pattern exists in the U.S. as well. The New England states have lower homicide rates than the western and southern parts of the country. Many criminologists have tried to explain these differences. Tim Hartnagel's ideas about greater geographic mobility leading to weakened social controls makes sense. Other possible explanations, such as "subcultures of violence," are discussed in the chapter on violent crime (Chapter 13).

Exceptions to the Trends

While crime appears to be decreasing, other trends are more troubling. Homicide rates among First Nations people are approximately ten times greater than in the rest of the population. Later in this book, I will suggest that marginal groups in North America have suffered more than the dominant populations over the past couple of decades. The majority of First Nations homicide is intraracial (i.e., they kill each other). Similarly, the majority of African-American homicide is intraracial. Those who are well off have not endured the ravages of crime as much as those at the bottom of the social hierarchy.

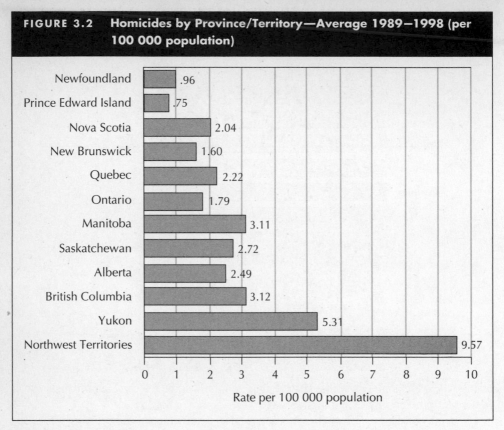

FIGURE 3.2   Homicides by Province/Territory—Average 1989–1998 (per 100 000 population)

Province/Territory	Rate per 100 000 population
Newfoundland	.96
Prince Edward Island	.75
Nova Scotia	2.04
New Brunswick	1.60
Quebec	2.22
Ontario	1.79
Manitoba	3.11
Saskatchewan	2.72
Alberta	2.49
British Columbia	3.12
Yukon	5.31
Northwest Territories	9.57

Source: Adapted from Statistics Canada, "Juristat" Catalogue 85-002. Vol. 20, No. 9, Page 4, Table 2.

Who Kills: Family, Friends, or Strangers?

Recent data on family violence are presented in the chapter on violent crime, but the pattern is clear. Family and acquaintances are more dangerous than strangers. Victims are more likely to be killed by a spouse, family member, or acquaintance than by a stranger. Male victims are more likely to be killed by strangers than female victims. A similar pattern exists for other violent crimes. Men are at greater risk because they are more likely to be in bars and other high-risk places, but women are more at risk at home. Wives and female partners are particularly at risk within the first two months after separation. There is some indication, however, that these rates are going down.

Many people assume that murders are measured accurately. But how many hunting accidents are actually murders? How many suicides are actually murders? At some point, we must work with what we have. While not perfect, murder and car theft appear to be reasonable indicators that permit comparisons within Canada; but can we make international comparisons?

Comparing Homicide Internationally

Obviously, we need to compare countries if we are to test some of our theories about crime. Murder rates appear to be the best indicator available. Even here one must be cautious because

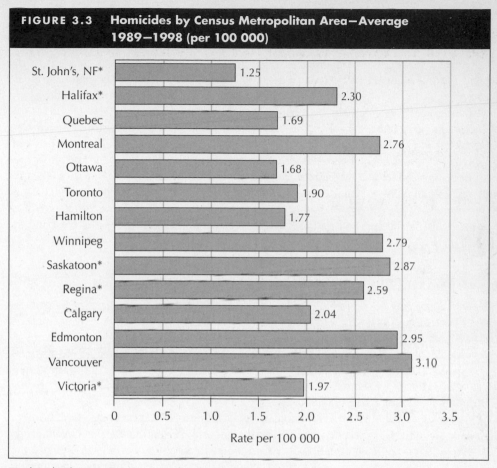

FIGURE 3.3   Homicides by Census Metropolitan Area—Average 1989—1998 (per 100 000)

St. John's, NF* — 1.25
Halifax* — 2.30
Quebec — 1.69
Montreal — 2.76
Ottawa — 1.68
Toronto — 1.90
Hamilton — 1.77
Winnipeg — 2.79
Saskatoon* — 2.87
Regina* — 2.59
Calgary — 2.04
Edmonton — 2.95
Vancouver — 3.10
Victoria* — 1.97

Rate per 100 000

*Population less than 500 000

Source: Adapted from Statistics Canada, "Juristat" Catalogue 85-002. Vol. 20, No. 9, Page 5, Table 3.

countries define homicide differently. Some include manslaughter, attempted murder, treason, and infanticide. Others do not. Thus comparisons are not as obvious as one would think. However, the Canadian homicide rate, which includes manslaughter and infanticide, is greater than Japan's. Since Japan includes attempted murder, we can safely argue that homicide is less common in Japan than in Canada. However, comparisons are not as straightforward as one would think.

In 2000, police in the United States reported a homicide rate of 5.5, down from 7.5 in 1996. The number of homicides has declined in both countries during the 1990s (Gannon, 2001). Two decades ago, the U.S. homicide rate was about four times that of Canada. Now it is about 2.5 times that of Canada. The two countries use comparable definitions. Comparing states, provinces, or states with provinces must be done cautiously, but it can be done. Vancouver, a city of about 600 000, may have 25 murders a year (the Vancouver census metropolitan area of 2 million may have 50 a year). The Bronx, a borough of New York City, with a population of about 700 000, may have about 400. Murder is clearly more common in the Bronx even if recording practices differ somewhat. Similarly, Chicago tends to generate as many murders as all of Canada.

In 2001 the downward trend in homicide was reversed in many U.S. cities. Fox Butterfield, in the *New York Times* (December 21, 2001), noted that murder in Boston increased 67 percent over 2000. However, Boston's homicide rate was comparable to that in Canadian cities in 2000 (Gannon, 2001). Even with the increase, Boston has one of the lowest murder rates of U.S. cities. In general, if a city has an extremely high or low rate one year, it is more likely to show a great change the following year. Thus, the tendency to dramatize yearly changes may be misleading.

In general, while we can use homicide rates to look at trends and make comparisons across Canada, we should be careful about international comparisons. Am I being overly cautious about the use of police-reported crime statistics? Possibly. Minor crimes influence crime statistics more than serious crimes and police departments differ somewhat in their reporting of minor crimes, but it is reasonable to assume that many of these biases will balance out when we look at provinces. Figure 3.4 depicts the total 1999 crime rate for the provinces across Canada. The general pattern is consistent with other evidence. The west and the north have higher crime rates.

The Perception of Violent Crime among Youth

Violent crime may be decreasing, but the perception and fear of crime do not necessarily respond accordingly. Clearly, the media are *reporting* more youth crime. For example, in Hawaii, between 1987 and 1996, juvenile arrests were quite stable, and arrests for serious offences decreased (Perrone and Chesney-Lind, 1997). Between 1992 and 1996, however, newspaper articles about delinquency increased fourfold. This could be an illustration of the "moral panics" that Bernard Schissel (1997) describes in Canada, in which public reaction is not based on underlying reality.

Although a majority of criminologists see a downward trend among youth crime in Canada (Doob, Marinos, and Varma, 1995), a minority see an increase in violent crime, particularly among female youths. Ray Corrado and Alan Markwart (1996) suggest that British Columbia differs from the rest of Canada in that violence among youth is going up. Focusing on young females, Sibylle Artz (1997a) points out that female youths in BC charged with non-sexual assault went from 209 in 1987 to 684 in 1996. Similarly, the number of females charged with robbery went up from 15 to 126. As a percentage of total persons charged, female youths contributed 2 percent in 1987 and 4 percent in 1996. For robbery, female youths contributed 2 percent in 1987 and 6 percent in 1996. If police response were a good measure of juvenile delinquency, the argument might be convincing. Despite public concern about the apparent increase in violence among young females and the occasional horrific crime, neither the numbers nor the rates of *serious* crimes by young females have increased in the past two decades according to official statistics and self-report surveys (Reitsma-Street, 1999). Over one-quarter of all charges against young females are now for administrative offences, such as "failure to comply with a court order." More female youths are in custody for breaches than for violent crimes.

Recently North America has been swept by concern over violence in school. But is such concern justified? The media ignore the fact that school violence, including homicide, is at an all-time low. Schools are much safer than homes. However, we are now spending millions of dollars on security guards, metal detection devices, security cameras, identity cards on neck cords, and bans on book bags not made of clear plastic. Although schools lack the

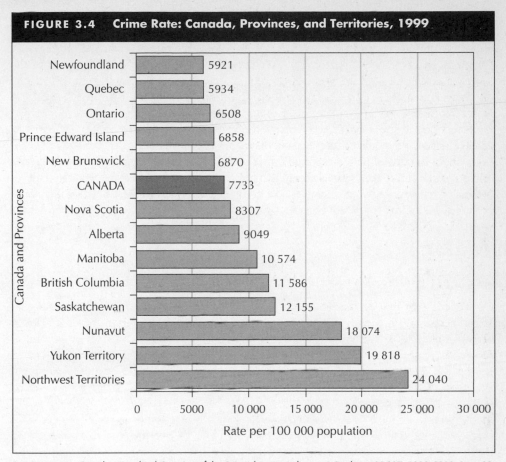

FIGURE 3.4   Crime Rate: Canada, Provinces, and Territories, 1999

Source: Statistics Canada, "Graphical Overview of the Criminal Justice Indicators," Catalogue 85-227, 1999–2000, Page 11. Reprinted with permission.

money to hire enough teachers or purchase library books, they find money to hire security guards and purchase metal detection devices.

Moral panics are damaging if they divert resources and attention from activities that matter. Later in this book I hope to show that malnourished, uneducated, unloved children with poor job prospects are more likely to commit crime. Investing in feeding and educating children and creating opportunities for meaningful employment provide a better return than investing in the security business. Public reaction and official responses have not been a reliable measure of underlying behaviour, as I will point out in Chapter 12.

Peter Carrington (1999) has looked at the rates of juveniles charged from 1977 to 1996. Because of unique experiences in any one year, he has used three-year moving averages. When the Young Offenders Act (YOA) replaced the Juvenile Delinquents Act in 1984, things were a bit confusing, so Carrington leaves that period blank. Prior to the YOA, Saskatchewan had a relatively low charge rate (Figure 3.5). After the YOA, that rate more than tripled. In general, Saskatchewan has displayed the most dramatic changes in juvenile justice statistics with the introduction of the YOA, going from a low rate to a high rate on many measures. Ontario also shows an increase in charges, while Quebec drops back to the rates of the 1970s. By the 1990s, Quebec, Ontario, and British Columbia were experiencing decreased charging.

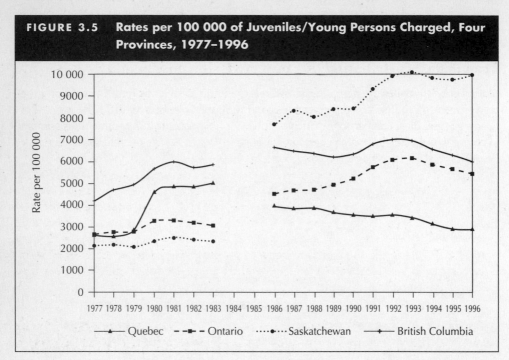

FIGURE 3.5   Rates per 100 000 of Juveniles/Young Persons Charged, Four Provinces, 1977–1996

Source: Based on Carrington, P. (1999). "Trends in Youth Crime in Canada, 1977–1996." *Canadian Journal of Criminology* 41:1–32.

Carrington suggested that prior to the YOA the police used more discretion and charged less. After 1984 they charged more. By the end of the 1990s, police may have been using more discretion again. Our juvenile justice systems may be resisting the unsubstantiated fears generated by the moral panics. From 1992 to 2000 there was a decline of 17 percent in the rate of youth court cases (Sudworth and deSouza, 2001). This decline may have been influenced by greater screening of minor cases by the police. Overall, violent youth crime was unchanged while property crime cases decreased by 38 percent. On the other hand, the number of cases involving failure to comply with a previous disposition increased by one-third. Data on juvenile crimes and court appearances are harder to interpret because of disparities in the way communities respond to youth. However, these data often help us to understand the way police and courts operate, which is also very useful information.

Self-Reported Delinquency Rates

Another strategy for getting at crimes not reported to the police has been to use self-reported data on delinquency. Despite some earlier opinions to the contrary, youths seem willing to acknowledge delinquent behaviour to researchers. A study of 12–13-year-old youths indicated that property crimes and aggressive behaviour were relatively high in the Prairies (Sprott,

Doob, and Jenkins, 2001). Quebec's 12–13-year-olds report the lowest level of aggressive behaviour. Youths from the Atlantic provinces and Quebec reported less involvement in property crimes. It is surprising, however, that 12–13-year-olds in BC reported less property crime than others. In addition, Ontario did only slightly better than the Prairies. Admittedly, the differences are not great, but it makes no sense to have low crime rates among youth in BC but high rates among adults. Or do children get worse over time in BC?

Trends and Distribution of Property Crime in Canada

Statistics on juveniles are particularly difficult to interpret, so let us return to data on property crimes for adults. The police can respond to property crimes in different ways. This makes geographical comparisons difficult. However, if we assume that communities continue to record data as they have in the past, the measure of *trends* may be reliable. Break and enter (burglary in the U.S.) is a serious but common crime.

Figure 3.6 shows that B&Es increased during the 1960s and 1970s, declined slightly in the 1980s, and then increased during the early 1990s (Kowalski, 2000). Since 1991 the rate has dropped 33 percent. In 1999 it reached its lowest rate in 25 years. Unfortunately, the term "home invasion" may have confused things. A "home invasion" involves a premeditated confrontation with a victim with the intent to rob. Thus, it may actually be closer to robbery than B&E. However, these crimes are infrequent compared with ordinary B&Es. In addition, if we assume that the biases are similar across the country, we could still make some geographical comparisons.

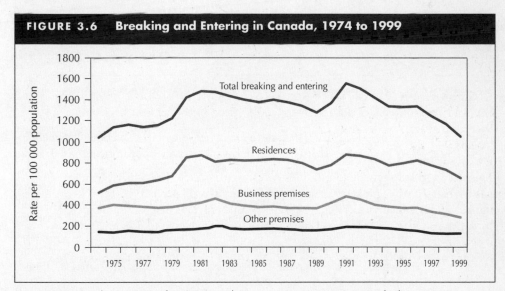

FIGURE 3.6   Breaking and Entering in Canada, 1974 to 1999

Source: Statistics Canada, "Juristat" Catalogue 85-002. Vol. 20, No. 13, Page 3, Figure 3. Reprinted with permission.

In general the east-west differences noted for homicide persist with property crimes (see Figures 3.7 and 3.8). Among smaller metropolitan areas, Regina had a rate of 2361 B&Es in 1999, and Saskatoon a rate of 1799, significantly higher than the larger Canadian cities. Before

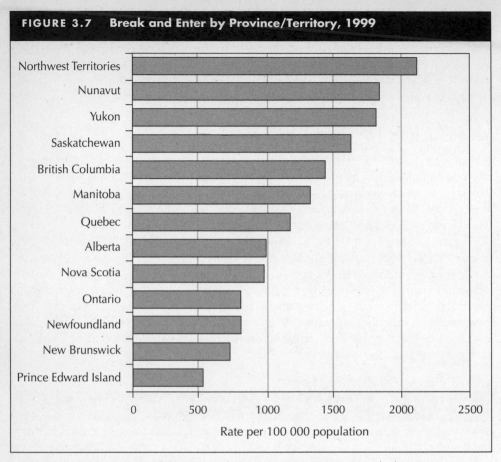

FIGURE 3.7   Break and Enter by Province/Territory, 1999

Rate per 100 000 population

Source: Statistics Canada, "Juristat" Catalogue 85-002. Vol. 20, No. 13, Page 6, Figure 3. Reprinted with permission.

accepting these figures at face value, should we see if there are police practices that could influence these rates? In an earlier study, we found that several police departments near Toronto (Peel, York, Halton, Waterloo, and Durham) had very low B&E rates, as did Toronto itself. Were the police in these cities screening more cases? This suspicion was supported by the fact that two decades ago the Peel police cleared 60 percent of its B&Es (Hackler, Cossins, and Don, 1990). Normally, the police do not know who commits burglaries. Without suspects, clearance rates are low. Thus, clearance rates of 15 percent are reasonable. Sixty percent is not. Vancouver has traditionally had even lower clearance rates for B&Es, suggesting that the police record more cases. These data provide insights into police practices, but they also suggest that B&E rates in Toronto should not be compared with those in the rest of Canada.

Using Victimization Rates

Victim surveys such as the **General Social Survey (GSS)** complement police surveys from the **Uniform Crime Reporting (UCR) Survey**. The GSS is a good way of capturing information on crimes that have been reported to the police as well as those unreported. However, there are

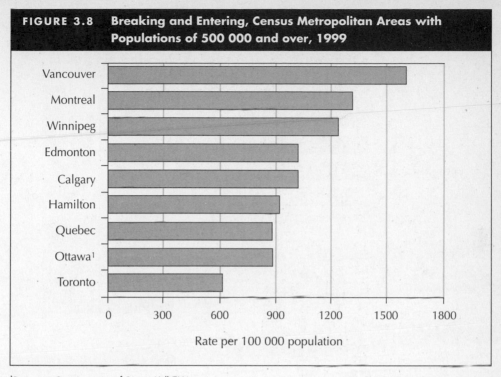

FIGURE 3.8   Breaking and Entering, Census Metropolitan Areas with Populations of 500 000 and over, 1999

Rate per 100 000 population

[1]Represents Ontario portion of Ottawa-Hull CMA.

Source: Statistics Canada, "Juristat" Catalogue 85-002. Vol. 20, No. 13, Page 6, Figure 4. Reprinted with permission.

limitations. Victimization data rely on memory, and only certain crimes correspond to UCR data. For example, B&Es are comparable in both sets of data. Robbery is not. The GSS measures personal robbery, while the UCR data include robberies of businesses and financial institutions.

Although GSS and UCR measures are not directly comparable, the victimization survey may be a better way of making comparisons among regions. Differences in police systems should not matter, and the biases and limitations should be similar from province to province. When we look at Figure 3.9 we can see that the east-west difference still persists but not as much as is indicated by UCR data. Looking specifically at B&Es in Ontario, we note that the rates are low (41) but not as much as suggested by UCR data.

BC still comes out with the highest rates, suggesting that the UCR data and the victimization data generate similar conclusions. Victimization rates for theft for Quebec and Ontario are similar to the Prairie provinces. Earlier we noted that Montreal had a pattern of screening juveniles involved in minor theft. However, there is no indication that adults are being screened the same way. The fact that PEI appears to have a high violence rate has to be viewed cautiously. In a province with traditionally low crime rates, residents could exaggerate incidents of assault. There could also be variations in the willingness to report incidents to interviewers.

When we look at victimization rates by census metropolitan area (Figure 3.10), the general east-west pattern persists. Toronto clearly seems to be a city with less crime than most large cities in North America. Calgary and Edmonton have similar victimization rates, although historically Edmonton has produced higher police-reported rates. As these two cities continually share information, reporting practices may become more similar.

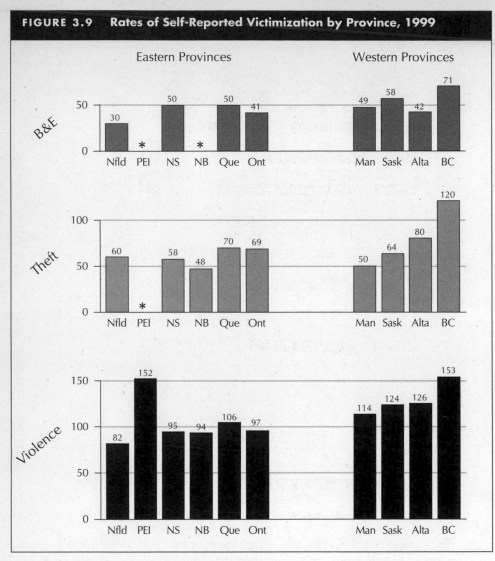

FIGURE 3.9   Rates of Self-Reported Victimization by Province, 1999

*too small to be expressed

Source: Adapted from Statistics Canada, "General Social Survey, 1999."

Because of the difficulty of making international comparisons, I suggested earlier that victimization studies might be useful. When we look at Figure 3.11 there are some surprises. The Philippines and Northern Ireland were on the low end of the scale. The U.S. and Sweden both have victimization rates of 24 percent. Canada has a rate of 25 percent. The U.S. has a lower rate than Switzerland (27 percent) and the Netherlands (32 percent). Some of these findings are inconsistent with what we know about crime in these countries. On the other hand, the victimization rate in the Western industrialized countries was lower, as we would predict, than less-developed parts of the world.

FIGURE 3.10 Rates of Victimization by Census Metropolitan Area, 1999

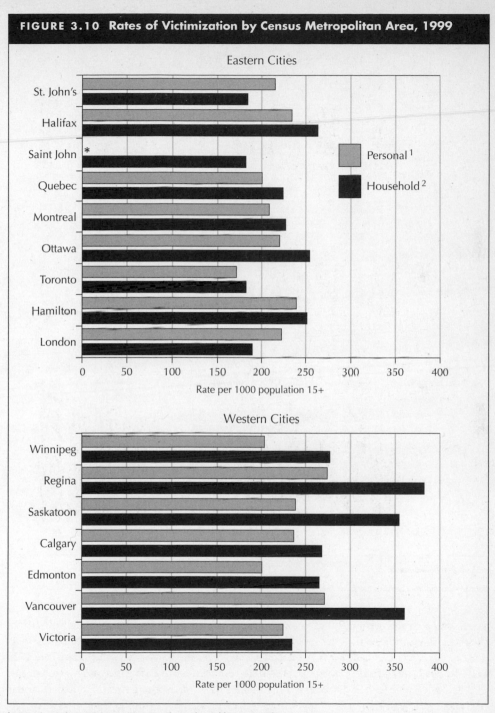

Eastern Cities

Rate per 1000 population 15+

Western Cities

Rate per 1000 population 15+

[1]Personal = Theft personal property + Sexual assault + Robbery + Assault
[2]Household = B&E + Theft motor vehicle/parts + Theft household property + Vandalism
*amount too small to be expressed

Source: Adapted from Statistics Canada, "General Social Survey, 1999."

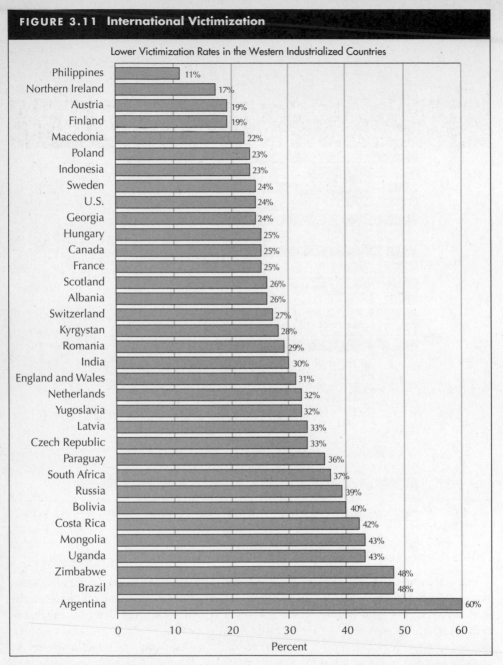

FIGURE 3.11 International Victimization

Lower Victimization Rates in the Western Industrialized Countries

Country	Percent
Philippines	11%
Northern Ireland	17%
Austria	19%
Finland	19%
Macedonia	22%
Poland	23%
Indonesia	23%
Sweden	24%
U.S.	24%
Georgia	24%
Hungary	25%
Canada	25%
France	25%
Scotland	26%
Albania	26%
Switzerland	27%
Kyrgystan	28%
Romania	29%
India	30%
England and Wales	31%
Netherlands	32%
Yugoslavia	32%
Latvia	33%
Czech Republic	33%
Paraguay	36%
South Africa	37%
Russia	39%
Bolivia	40%
Costa Rica	42%
Mongolia	43%
Uganda	43%
Zimbabwe	48%
Brazil	48%
Argentina	60%

Source: Statistics Canada, "Graphical Overview of the Criminal Justice Indicators," Catalogue 85-227, 1999–2000, Page 104. Reprinted with permission.

If we focused on a specific crime, such as break and enter, would we have greater faith in the outcome? Figure 3.12 looks at the fear of break and enter in eleven countries. The comparisons are surprising. The U.S. is relatively low compared with the Netherlands, Scotland,

Switzerland, Canada, England, and France, even though we assume that crime is more common in the U.S. than in these other countries. Do people in different countries perceive victimization differently? At this stage, we cannot be sure. International victimization comparisons are relatively new and we should be cautious in our interpretations at this time.

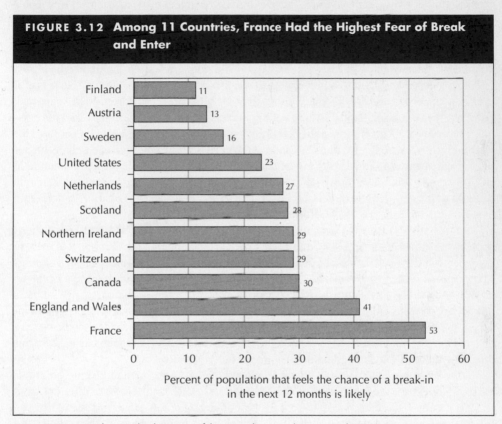

FIGURE 3.12 Among 11 Countries, France Had the Highest Fear of Break and Enter

Percent of population that feels the chance of a break-in
in the next 12 months is likely

Source: Statistics Canada, "Graphical Overview of the Criminal Justice Indicators," Catalogue 85-227, 1999–2000, Page 105. Reprinted with permission.

Police-Reported Property Crime Rates in Canada vs. the U.S.

A look at these international comparisons may make us more cautious about comparisons between Canada and the U.S. Although serious violent crime rates are much higher in the U.S., reported rates for break-ins, motor vehicle theft, and arson were all higher in Canada in 2000. The U.S. reported 11 percent more thefts (Gannon, 2001). Canadians might be tempted to argue that Canadians are reporting more, but the percentage of victims reporting crimes is similar in Canada and the U.S. Admittedly, there are discrepancies in the way break-ins are reported, but motor vehicle thefts are one of the more reliable rates for international and regional comparisons. The Canadian rate first surpassed the U.S. rate in 1996 and in 2000 was 26 percent higher.

We are left with questions: Is Canada overly smug about crime compared with the U.S.? Or should we be cautious about comparative crime statistics?

Is Western Canada More Inclined to Use Agencies of Control?

Most people think of crime statistics as measures of criminal behaviour. They also help us to understand what criminal justice systems do. In fact, this is probably where crime data in their present form are most useful. Although criminal behaviour may vary across Canada, it probably doesn't vary as much as the behaviour of our criminal justice systems. From a policy standpoint, it makes sense to assess our agencies of social control and make deliberate decisions concerning their change. For example, the percentage of young people appearing in youth court tends to be higher in the Prairie provinces. However, Alberta has experienced a 20 percent decrease in court cases from 1992 to 1996 (Hendrick, 1996), a trend which continued in 1998–99 (Sudworth and deSouza, 2001; Moldon and Kukec, 2000). This is useful information, because Alberta has made efforts to divert some of its cases from court. It appears, however, that western Canada is more willing to record crime, use the courts, and use prisons. Measures of incarceration, police reporting, and parole usually indicate higher rates for western provinces. Again we must be cautious about BC. While adult incarceration is higher in BC than in eastern Canada (but lower than the Prairies), the juvenile incarceration rate in BC is lower than any other province except Quebec (Molden and Kukec, 2000), and the rate of cases going through youth court is lower than in the Prairies and Ontario. Victoria and Vancouver Island seem to be an exception to this pattern.

Another possibility is that western Canada simply has a higher percentage of First Nations people who have been marginalized by society. This could apply to the Prairies. It is risky to give a general explanation of crime statistics, but let me hazard the following: *Official responses to crime are a measure of community willingness to reintegrate marginal people back into society*. Conceivably the Atlantic provinces and Quebec are more willing to treat offenders as normal people who made a mistake. They may have done bad things, but they are still members of the community. They should be ashamed of what they did, but then they should be reintegrated into the community. In the Maritimes, the police, as well as the courts, may share this thinking, and thus may be hesitant to cast people out of society.

In the west, particularly on the Prairies, we may be more inclined to give up on criminals. Offenders are not just mistaken, the logic goes, they are bad. They are different from us. We do not wish them in our society. If the police and courts share this mentality and feel that one must use the formal agents of social control to cast out deviants, then crime rates, conviction rates, and incarceration will be higher. This logic would be compatible with Hartnagel's (1997) argument that the greater geographic mobility characteristic of westerners works against informal community control mechanisms. Unfortunately, these characteristics may be part of a *crime-producing society*. John Braithwaite (1989) would also argue that societies that fail to reintegrate those who err create higher crime rates. Has greater mobility and a lack of a sense of community in the west led to a social order that is less tolerant, more willing to cast out offenders and stigmatize them, more eager to use prisons, and thus *create* more crime?

SOME GENERALIZATIONS ABOUT CRIME STATISTICS

Despite this book's cautious approach to crime statistics, a few generalizations are appropriate. Violent crime in North America appeared to be somewhat constant from World War II until the 1960s. Then there was a gradual increase, reaching a peak in the middle 1970s, followed by a gradual decrease in the 1990s. The mass media and politicians exaggerated the increases and ignored the decreases. Compared with the east, western Canada, particularly the Prairies, probably has more violent crime and responds more vigorously to crime. In the future, however, I predict an increase in crime in the U.S. and also in Canada. The gap between rich and poor has widened, social programs have been eroded, and government strategies have favoured the production of material goods and the creation of wealth for those already well off. Official practices have neglected the quality of life among marginal groups. There are, however, counter-forces. The feminist movement has called our attention to domestic violence (to be discussed in Chapter 11, on women's issues), and some governments have taken helpful steps to deal with the issue. Whether gains made by the feminist movement will counteract the crime-producing economic changes remains to be seen.

SUMMARY

1. A variety of factors influence crime statistics, but often we can use them to make comparisons among regions and over time. In addition, these data help us to understand the workings of the criminal justice system. Data have a different meaning at the police, court, or prison level. However, if certain reasonable assumptions are made, they allow us to estimate trends and make comparisons among provinces and cities. In general the west produces higher crime rates than the east.

2. Some measures are more useful for comparisons. Murder rates, although infrequent, tend to be a reasonable way of comparing regions and even countries. Other rates, such as break and enter, can be useful if we understand some of the police practices which might make them less comparable. Many police practices, which may influence statistics, often reflect very intelligent policies. In these cases, the statistics are more useful for understanding the dynamics of the system than understanding the behaviour of offenders.

3. Misperceptions about crime, particularly youth crime, have been created by media coverage. Unfortunately, these myths have sometimes influenced policy-makers more than reliable data.

4. Victimization and self-reported delinquency rates complement data generated by the criminal justice system. Data from different sources usually come to similar conclusions. When victimization studies are used to make international comparisons, methodological issues may still lead us astray.

5. Although violence and drug offences are higher in the U.S., Canadian rates for break and enter, motor vehicle theft, and arson now exceed those in the U.S.

KEY TERMS

census metropolitan areas (CMAs) 39	random errors 35
central city phenomenon 39	systematic errors 35
General Social Survey (GSS) 48	Uniform Crime Reporting (UCR) Survey 48

WEBLINKS

www.statcan.ca/english/Pgdb/State/justic.htm

Statistics Canada, Justice and Crime: current statistics on crime in Canada.

www.scc-csc.gc.ca/index_e.htm

The Supreme Court of Canada: overview of the Canadian judicial system.

www.canada.justice.gc.ca/

The Canadian Department of Justice: general information about Canada's criminal justice system.

EXPLANATIONS
OF CRIME

These chapters follow a predictable sequence. The section moves through the historical and traditional theories of crime, followed by biological, psychological, social-psychological, and social-structural discussions as to why individuals commit crimes. At times we ask what sorts of situations or structural conditions increase the likelihood of crime. Chapter 10, on the ecology of crime, deals with spatial relations, the physical layout of communities, and the impact such features have on criminal behaviour.

Even though theorists have ongoing debates about the importance of various causal factors, the policy recommendations that arise out of the available information are often very similar. For example, providing healthy experiences for families with young children reduces crime. While theorists may offer different explanations as to why this is so, the social policy implications are often in agreement.

These chapters also reflect something of a historical sequence. The themes about individual behaviour were more prominent in the early stages of criminology. The focus on the structure of society came later. Those theories that viewed society as a "given" and as more static could be seen as more "conservative," while later presentations viewing society as more dynamic and made up of components which were in conflict could be seen as more "radical." The reader will also detect a bias with regard to the sort of social intervention which would be most appropriate for Canada: structural changes would yield better returns at present than efforts to intervene at the individual level. The reasons for these recommendations will be clearer in Parts III and IV.

TRADITIONAL AND BIOLOGICAL EXPLANATIONS OF CRIME

This chapter will:

- Review and contrast traditional classical and positive explanations of crime.
- Use one positivistic orientation, biological determinism, to illustrate a persistent and erroneous theme in criminology.
- Note some modern research that utilizes biological research more judiciously.
- Describe recent, misleading racial explanations of crime.
- Emphasize the difficulty of sorting out biological and social factors.
- Warn against the policy implications of emphasizing biological explanations.

THE CLASSICAL SCHOOL AND FREE WILL

Traditional explanations of crime focused on the question, "Why do they do it?" For the **classical school**, crime was a rational, calculated choice; laws could be used to control behaviour. Less thought was given to the possibility that society itself could be a factor. The problem was to understand why some individuals did not conform to the rules of society. To many people, that is still the issue, but today criminologists must also ask questions about the dynamics of different social settings and the nature of the larger society. For now, such questions will be laid aside, as we review these traditional arguments.

Cesare Beccaria and the Assumption of Rationality

Cesare Beccaria wrote an influential treatise in Italy in 1764, which was published in England with the title, *On Crimes and Punishment* (Beccaria, 1963). He placed great stress on humans' rational faculties and ability to make reasonable choices. His thinking was in keeping with the growing concern over individual rights and prerogatives. There was an assumption that society evolved with contractual beginnings; that is, individuals surrendered a degree of sovereignty over their lives in exchange for protection from the hazards of total freedom. This social contract between individuals and the state required that laws be developed to make society viable. The resulting legislation was guided by the principle of creating the greatest happiness for the greatest number of people (Maestro, 1973).

According to Beccaria, punishment should fit the crime. Prior to this period, the severity of punishments bore little relationship to the crime. Beccaria's logic assumed that people acted on the basis of free will. People have a choice between doing right and doing wrong. When they do wrong it is a deliberate choice. Since Beccaria argued that it was better to prevent crime than punish criminals, fear of the appropriate punishment would deter crime. The laws should be clearly written and not be subject to the whims of judges. The roles of legislators and judges were to be distinct. Judges would be bound by the law, while legislators would create it. While rigid, the laws should be impartial and apply to all, regardless of social status. Beccaria's argument for the impartiality of the laws may be his greatest contribution to the study of crime. Writing at the time when North America was just being Europeanized, these ideas were central to the thinking in these evolving societies. Impartiality has still not been successfully implemented in most societies, but the ideal is widely shared.

Jeremy Bentham: A Penal Pharmacy and the Hedonistic Calculus

Like Beccaria, British writer and philosopher Jeremy Bentham disliked the arbitrary, inconsistent, and cruel administration of justice in England during his lifetime (1748–1832). Similarly, he believed that punishment should prevent crime rather than be guided by retribution. He favoured *utilitarianism*, or the "greatest-happiness principle." Human beings were assumed to be *hedonistic*. They chose those actions that would give the maximum pleasure and avoided those that would bring pain. There should be a proper quantum of punishment for each quantum of crime. In his *Introduction to the Principles of Morals and Legislation*, published in 1825, Bentham proposed a "penal pharmacy" prescribing certain punishments for specific crimes. Only enough punishment should be used to achieve the necessary deterrence for potential wrong-doers who use the **hedonistic calculus**. Thus, the potential rapist would calculate the pleasure gained from raping a woman, assess the pain that would be inflicted if he were convicted, and then make a rational decision. This logic assumed that people acted on the basis of free will. In effect, the pain of punishment would outweigh the pleasure gained from the criminal behaviour.

The major criticism of Bentham's ideas was that he concentrated on the laws and neglected human behaviour. He failed to consider criminals as complicated human beings with variegated personalities (Geis, 1972: 53). Consequently, his arguments were based on overly simplistic assumptions about human nature.

The **positive school** (sometimes "positivistic" is used) eclipsed the classical school about a century later, and made assumptions more compatible with the developing thinking in the social sciences.

THE POSITIVE SCHOOL, DETERMINISM, AND THE REJECTION OF FREE WILL

Cesare Lombroso and the Atavistic Criminal Type

While Charles Darwin put together many different facts and observations about the natural world to develop his theory of evolution in *On the Origin of Species* in 1859, the Italian criminologist Cesare Lombroso (1836–1909) also concentrated on measurable facts, assuming this would lead to natural explanations. This approach is somewhat different from scientific theory, as described in Chapter 2. Facts do not speak for themselves. Lombroso was part of a growing school of scientists who assumed that the amassing of data in and of itself would lead to explanations. In contrast, a preferable strategy is to spell out hypotheses, preferably linked together systematically, leading to a *selective* choice of empirical data that would confirm or reject the stated ideas. One needs to be selective in a world that is awash in empirical data.

However, when Lombroso (1911) was publishing his major ideas between 1864 and 1878, the straightforward accumulation of evidence made sense. One cannot propose hypotheses without this background work, but the danger of letting the data dictate explanations is similar to *ex post facto* reasoning. And that is what Lombroso did. His ideas were formulated after looking at the data, but that is typical of most scholarly work.

Lombroso concluded that criminals were different from law-abiding people. They were throwbacks to an earlier stage of evolution, or **"atavisms."** As a physician attached to the Italian army, he examined the physical attributes of many soldiers. These atavistic anatomical characteristics were examined in an intellectual atmosphere in which scientists found it acceptable to view human beings as another animal, without the divine characteristics that had been imputed in the past. Since the breeding of animals to produce various characteristics was a familiar practice, it was reasonable to assume that genetics would influence human behaviour as well. Just as other species are "programmed" from birth to act in certain ways, why not humans? In other words, it made sense to ask if criminals were heavily influenced, if not actually determined, by biological antecedents which they could not control. Criminals were not rational beings with a free will; they were simply "born that way." Just as Beccaria and Bentham were products of their intellectual world, Lombroso was a product of this new intellectual stream a century later.

Enrico Ferri and Continuance of Positivism

Enrico Ferri (1856–1928) continued the positivist thinking of Lombroso. Although trained as a lawyer, he was particularly critical of classicism. For example, he argued that no one could develop a clear standard that would enable us to say a particular punishment would be equitable for a particular crime (Ferri, 1901; Brown et al., 1991: 235). Ferri was also scathing in his attacks on the concept of free will, arguing that "every act of a human being is the result of an interaction between the personality and the environment of man" (1901: 54). Individuals live in different personal, physical, and moral conditions, which lead to a chain of cause and effect that disposes them towards crime. Ferri broadened the range of variables to be considered beyond those considered by Lombroso. He also noted that factors *interacted*, rather than causing behaviour directly. In many ways his thinking was very modern, but his primary argument was that crime was *determined*, not chosen.

Assessing the Early Positivists

Scholars differ on the contribution of the early positivists. A major contribution was to shift the focus of attention from the law and philosophy to the first-hand study of criminals. Empirical evidence began to play an important role. In this respect, they clearly broadened the discussion of crime causation. Marvin Wolfgang argues that Lombroso laid the foundations of modern criminology, by his emphasis on the differences among groups and on the deterministic, or positivistic, approach to explaining behaviour, in contrast to the free will perspective (1972).

Since born criminals couldn't help themselves, a policy for restraining criminals could not rely on a hedonistic calculus. Only through severe social intervention could these atavistic human beings be reformed. Like other animals, they had to be punished until they learned. This was not a matter of justice but "social defence." Society had to be protected. Raffaele Garafolo, a contemporary of Ferri's, argued that it was necessary to eliminate criminal offenders by death, imprisonment, or transportation. Following the thinking of Darwin on natural selection, he recommended that society eliminate those individuals who were too disruptive to social life (Brown et al., 1991). Since the problem was largely one of genetics, such individuals would then no longer produce problem offspring to plague society in the future.

Both Garafalo and Ferri had considerable faith in science as a guide to social policy. They were less critical of the moral values held by scientists, politicians, and those in positions of power. The Italian Fascist party under Mussolini argued for measures that sacrificed individuals for the benefit of the larger society, and Garafalo, like Ferri, finished his life as a Fascist activist (Brown et al., 1991: 236). Adolf Hitler was also able to utilize the thinking of such scholars. Obviously, scholars do not necessarily clarify moral issues or provide ideas for intelligent social policy.

Charles Thomas and John Hepburn are more critical of Lombroso and his followers, arguing that "the rise of the positive school, which quite probably marks the most significant event in criminological history, had the effect of blocking our progress for more than a quarter of a century" (1983: 146). They acknowledge Lombroso's willingness to consider other variables influencing crime as his work progressed, such as climate, race, education, sex, population density, education, and economic factors; however, such factors were secondary to the notion of atavism and to the belief that criminals were inherently inferior. Poverty, for example, was seen as the fault of the individual rather than as a consequence of extreme inequality in the distribution of wealth and legitimate opportunities. "If thieves are generally penniless, it is because of their extreme idleness and astonishing extravagance, which makes them run through huge sums with the greatest ease, not because poverty has driven them to theft" (Lombroso, 1872; cited in Thomas and Hepburn, 1983: 152).

In his book *The Female Offender*, Lombroso also reflected views that were acceptable at the time. Females were considered more primitive than males—naturally vengeful, jealous, insensitive to pain, and lacking any sense of morality. They have lower rates of crime than men because their natural deficiencies are neutralized by piety, maternity, a lack of passion, sexual coldness, weakness, and undeveloped intelligence. Indeed, women were looked on as so monotonous and uniform, when compared with men, that not only did they fail to become artists, scientists, and political leaders, they also lacked the zip to become criminal.

CONTRASTING CLASSICISM AND POSITIVISM

The classical school focused on legal terms. Crime was a legal entity. The positivists rejected this; they viewed crime as a psychological entity—that is, one tried to explain the individual and how he differed from others. The classical school assumed everyone responded in the same way. The classical school emphasized free will; the positivists focused on determinism. The classicists concentrated on the deterrent effect of punishment, while the positivists emphasized the treatment of criminals so as to protect society.

Both themes are still very much alive today. Our criminal justice system is largely a product of classical thinking. Punishments are supposed to be the same, regardless of the individual. However, judges are also influenced by the perceived impact of punishment on future behaviour; that is, they think in terms of the "social defence" logic offered by the positivists. Thus, the respectable person who has done wrong has already suffered by going through the criminal justice system, and only a modest penalty is required to bring about reform. Thomas and Hepburn would probably argue that this "social defence" logic favours the powerful and results in stiffer punishment for the lower classes. The application of classical thinking might justify harsher punishment for the powerful, since they had little excuse.

Neither of these schools serves us well in terms of reducing crime, but for now let us turn to some of the work that emphasized the **biological determinism** pioneered by Lombroso.

BIOLOGICAL DETERMINISM

In a 1950s genetics class, the professor displayed a chart showing the descendants of John Adams, the second president of the United States. This family produced presidents, diplomats, and many distinguished individuals. For some this is evidence of the power of genetics. Others might argue that having famous and powerful parents increases the likelihood of success regardless of genetics. When the genetics professor turned his chart over, the Juke family was displayed. The catalogue of criminals and social degenerates went down through the generations. The original Juke possessed such a miraculous energy in his vicious genes that he transmitted degeneracy for five generations. Let us look at the research that produced this chart.

Richard Dugdale and the Creation of the Juke Myth

The Jukes: A Study in Crime, Pauperism, Disease, and Insanity, by Richard Dugdale, was seen as an authoritative book at the end of the nineteenth century. A well-known publisher, Putnam's, brought out three large editions, which were accepted as sociological gospel. Samuel Hopkins Adams (1955) reviewed the research and pointed out some flaws. Dugdale's qualifications were thought to be peculiar. After three years of schooling in New York, he left to become an assistant to a sculptor. He attended evening classes and won something of a reputation as a debater on social topics. The family then moved to the Midwest to try farming, but failed. The Dugdales returned to New York and Richard turned to manufacturing. The business failed. Richard Dugdale was 23 and had a nervous breakdown. He writes that he could neither earn nor learn. So he became a criminologist.

In 1873, Dugdale was in police court where a youth was on trial. Five relatives were present as witnesses, but the family had a poor reputation. Dugdale invented the name "Juke" for the clan. The fact that the young man was acquitted did not discourage Dugdale. He found that the other relatives had done nasty things, although proof was often lacking. Two girls were listed as harlots. "Under the heading of harlots are included all women who have made lapses, however seldom" (Adams, 1955). Adams goes on to describe how Dugdale continued his precise definition of criminals and degenerates: "With comparatively little inquiry, it was found that of twenty-nine male adults, the immediate blood relations of the six, seventeen were criminals and fifteen others convicted of some degree of offence." Notice the impressive arithmetic. He got 32 out of a possible 29!

As Dugdale went sleuthing back through the generations, he discovered Old Max, an old Dutch reprobate who ran a hostelry in the middle of the eighteenth century. He had a reputation for drinking, gambling, and philandering. He gets the credit for starting the Jukes on their way to ill fame. Nothing criminal appears in his record, however. His two legitimate sons married into six sisters. "One, if not all, of them were illegitimate." Delia is recorded as a "harlot before marriage," and Bell as a "harlot after marriage." Clara was reputedly chaste, but she married a man who shot a neighbour. Notice that Old Max's genetic material seemed to leap over marriages and into his daughters-in-law and even into their husbands.

One sister, Ada, circa 1760, gets credit for the distinctly criminal line of the family. Dugdale changes her name to "Margaret, Mother of Criminals," which does have a better ring to it. But she hardly lives up to her name. A daughter was a "harlot," one son was a labourer, "somewhat industrious," and another was a farmer who had been "indolent" and "licentious in youth." Clearly, some eminent people have had similar backgrounds.

Dugdale developed his "facts" through the generations with a similar attention to accuracy. He created illegitimacy, negative characteristics, and crime when evidence was lacking. He fattened the record with entries like: "petty thief, though never convicted"; "guilty of murder, but escapes punishment"; "supposed to have attempted rape"; "cruelty to animals"; "habitual criminal"; "impossible to get any reliable information, but it is evident that he was a leader in crime." There was also a "contriver of crime," and a hardened character who, in addition to frequenting a saloon, was accused of breaking a deaf man's ear trumpet. Like the Juke who started it all, he was acquitted.

By now the reader can appreciate that Dugdale's work was worthless. However, it was not until after Dugdale's death that prison reformer Thomas Mott Osborne studied the work more carefully and noted that the data Dugdale used were practically non-existent. Tracing legitimate family lines is difficult; illegitimate ones were impossible beyond a generation or two. To put together so much detailed factual information over five generations in one year obviously required the use of "conjectural statistics." It takes a pretty skilled, or imaginative, investigator to learn that, in one branch of the Jukes, 40 women contaminated 440 men.

Dugdale's nonsense, however, was viewed as appropriate sociology, and was still contaminating charts of genetics in college classrooms in the 1950s. The major lesson we might learn is to beware of fads in the intellectual community. One hopes that the intellectual debate that takes place in more mature scholarly circles will avoid the acceptance of such shoddy work.

The Critique of and Debates over Biological Determinism

Charles Goring has been given credit for refuting the atavism theme put forward by Lombroso. A psychiatrist, philosopher, and also a medical officer in various English prisons, Goring (1913) studied 3000 convicts, identifying some 96 traits. These were compared with 1000 Oxford and Cambridge university students, hospital patients, and soldiers. The results refuted Lombroso's work. It is important to note that some of the traits identified by Lombroso characterized Sicilians. At the time, Sicilians were more likely to be in conflict with the rest of Italian society, and were perceived by other Italians to be more criminal. This is the type of error, a spurious correlation, that can lead reasonably careful research astray.

Another illustration of this type of error is the pencil-tapping test used in a study of English delinquents (West, 1969). When asked to tap as rapidly as they could, delinquents were much slower than non-delinquents. Was this evidence of motor coordination and other biological differences? Donald West and his colleague David Farrington were alert to the influence of the social setting. When well-mannered, non-delinquent boys were asked to tap pencils, they performed with enthusiasm. Delinquent boys responded skeptically. "Do *what*? What a stupid thing to do. OK, if you want, I'll tap. How's this?" And with sneers on their faces they leisurely tapped away for the interviewer.

Clearly, careful researchers can be misled as they lay out testable propositions that can be refuted in the future. Other work, such as that by Dugdale, has no merit to begin with. The work on biological determinism is mixed in terms of academic merit. One should not assume that research conducted at universities automatically guarantees superior reasoning. For example, Ernest Hooton, a Harvard anthropologist, claimed that criminals were physically inferior (1939). His massive work contained many errors (Martin et al., 1990: 128)— for example, murderers should look different from rapists, and robbers from thieves; murderers are tall, while burglars tend to be short, squatty men who are also associated with assault, rape, and other sexual crimes. The elimination of crime, then, required the elimination of these physically, mentally, and morally unfit individuals, or alternately, complete segregation from the rest of society. Interestingly, Hooton found that one of the significant characteristics was tattooing. Since one is not born with tattoos, it is difficult to see this as a genetic trait. Perhaps there is a biological tendency for getting tattoos. For such a book to be published in 1939 by a professor at a prestigious university is noteworthy; but it was also ominous that, in one of the most scientifically advanced countries, Hitler had already eliminated 50 000 non-Jewish mentally deficient Germans. The strategy spread to Jews, Eastern Europeans, and others considered to be subhuman (Hagan, 1986: 409).

William Sheldon was influenced by Hooton. He developed the theory of three body types: ectomorph, endomorph, and mesomorph (1940), or, stated more simply, skinny, fat, and athletic. The athletic types were more delinquent. One could argue that Sheldon had tunnel vision. While he measured biological characteristics with great precision, he pointedly ignored the other criminological thinking that was emerging around him (Martin et al., 1990). One might view Sheldon as an excellent illustration of the scholar who looks carefully but has a limited range of vision.

Sheldon Glueck was a professor of law at Harvard, and his wife Eleanor was a professor of social work. They also found that mesomorphs were more likely to be delinquent (1950). Many faults have been found with the work done by the Gluecks, in addition to their arguments regarding the link between crime and body types. For example, studies comparing army recruits, bus drivers, and truckers showed that they were more mesomorphic than delinquents (Kamin, 1986). Since the Gluecks were prolific writers, and their books widely used in schools of social work, one might ask if these biologically deterministic ideas have been leading social workers astray for several decades. In a book focused directly on the many errors in delinquency research, Travis Hirschi and Hanan Selvin found that the work of the Gluecks alone provided them with more than half of their examples (1967).

I have deliberately chosen negative illustrations from scholars at Harvard to reinforce another theme in this book. We should be more suspicious of ideas that come from people who are more insulated from criticism, such as high-status scholars. What is fashionable in criminology is influenced by those who are custodians of intellectual activity. The authors of criminological theories, until the last few decades, have tended to be white, upper-class males. It is not surprising that non-criminals were more inclined to resemble the authors, while criminals were somehow different.

MODERN STUDIES ON BIOLOGY AND CRIME

It is fashionable and "politically correct" to ridicule biological models of crime. In doing so, do I risk making errors similar to those described above? As a sociologically trained criminologist, I openly acknowledge my bias against genetic explanations; but there are arguments *for* some biological studies.

In the 1940s and 1950s, social scientists began to appreciate that genes played a role in determining whether an animal became a turtle or a human being, but once a human was produced, some sociologists began to ignore genetic differences. True, the quality of the work by people like Dugdale deserved ridicule, as did some of the theories of genetic superiority that argued that immigrants, blacks, and others were inherently inferior. But have we developed biases that blind us to considering the role of genetic factors? Some family studies (Robins, 1966) have long shown that one of the best predictors of antisocial behaviour is the father's criminality. There has always been a problem, however, in disentangling hereditary and environmental influences. Karl Christiansen and Sarnoff Mednick have attempted to separate these factors.

Karl Christiansen, Sarnoff Mednick, and the Studies of Twins

Karl O. Christiansen made use of data from the Danish national register of criminal behaviour to trace the fate of over 7000 twins born in Denmark. After Christiansen's death, Sarnoff Mednick and other colleagues continued this work (Mednick and Christiansen, 1977; Mednick and Volavaka, 1980). They attempted to separate the influence of environmental and genetic factors by comparing twins derived from one egg (identical twins) with those who came from two separate eggs (fraternal twins). If criminal traits are inherited, identical twins, whose genetic makeup is the same, would be more likely to have similar behavioural characteristics than fraternal twins, who have many genetic differences. Christiansen found that 35 percent of the identical twins were similar in terms of criminal activity, compared with 13 percent of the fraternal twins. Mednick (1985) notes that these findings point out the importance of both the environment and genes in the development of criminality. The fact that 65 percent of the identical twins did not have similar records of criminality suggests that the environment is very important. However, the identical twins were much more likely than the fraternal twins to be alike in criminal and non-criminal behaviour, suggesting that genetic similarity influences the likelihood of becoming criminal.

Genetic Influences Rather Than Determinants

Doug Wahlsten (1992) makes an argument that is compatible with the reasoning of Sarnoff Mednick (1985). Genes work at the level of molecules. They cannot move up the level of complexity to directly influence something like intelligence, much less a social variable such as crime. However, genes might have an influence on other factors that could eventually be related to antisocial behaviour. For example, people with certain genes have livers that cannot metabolize one amino acid, and this leads to a harmful buildup of the chemical in the blood. The high levels of this amino acid can retard brain development, which will influence intelligence. This, in turn, could influence success in school and a series of events leading to crime. The point to be emphasized, however, is that *there is no gene that codes directly for social behaviour, such as crime.*

J. P. Rushton's Theory of Racial Hierarchy[1]

J. P. Rushton (1988), a professor of psychology at the University of Western Ontario, argues that there are three fundamentally different races of humans (1988). This is in contrast to the more widely accepted view that human characteristics exist on a continuum, with some parts of the world giving rise to groups we crudely categorize as blacks, whites, and orientals. Rushton claims that these racial groups evolved at different times: the African blacks first, then the white Europeans, and finally the orientals (Rushton, 1988). Those who evolved recently were more advanced. According to this theory, life was easy in Africa with lots of fruit to be plucked from trees, thus allowing the Africans to be lazy. They didn't have to evolve to survive, but those who moved north into a cold Europe got a little smarter and showed greater sexual restraint. Things were even tougher for the orientals as they evolved, and they developed still bigger brains and smaller genitals. The result, according to Rushton, is a clear hierarchy of the races with the orientals on top, being more intelligent and less sexually active, and the blacks on the bottom (Rushton and Bogaert, 1987). Thus, the superior orientals committed fewer crimes, while the less evolved blacks committed more.

It is difficult to take Rushton seriously. He uses sources carelessly (Wahlsten, 1992; Weizmann et al., 1990). A detailed critique of Rushton's work is not needed here, but it is healthy to be reminded again that having a PhD or teaching at a university provides no guarantee of clear thinking. For example, in Canada, our Aboriginal population is clearly of oriental origin, but they also are in trouble with the criminal justice system more often than white Canadians. This is inconsistent with Rushton's argument. Most criminologists would argue that those groups, racial or ethnic, that are located towards the bottom of the social hierarchy tend to be viewed as the most criminal.

Race and Genetic Diversity

Anyone watching world-class sports can see that black athletes are over-represented. While only about 10 percent of the world population are of African descent, blacks clearly dominate many professional and amateur sports. If we acknowledge superiority in the physical sphere, should we not consider the possibility that blacks are superior in the intellectual domain as well?

Kenneth Kidd of Yale University has been studying DNA samples from many African tribes to see how much **genetic diversity**, or variation, there is among individuals within tribes and throughout Africa (Dyer, 1997). He found that in almost all of these groupings there was more variation than one finds in the rest of world. The reason seems to be that human beings evolved in Africa about 200 000 years ago. That provided time for considerable genetic variation. When humans began migrating from northeast Africa to other parts of the world, relatively small, homogeneous populations moved into Europe or Asia. They brought with them rather modest genetic variation compared with the much greater variety which remained among those living in Africa. In other words, the rest of the world was deprived of the rich genetic range which had developed in Africa. Over time there were genetic adaptations in Europe and Asia in characteristics such as skin, hair, and eye colour; in terms of height, Africans have the tallest (the Tutsis) and the shortest (the Pygmies) people on the planet.

---

[1] I would like to thank Doug Wahlsten for assistance with this section. For an extended discussion of genetic and environmental factors, see Wahlsten (1990).

Studies in North America show that blacks do poorly in school, but they focus on the offspring of people who were slaves for several generations. Suppose we were to look at Africans who came directly from Africa? Gwynne Dyer points out that Britain has a different mix of African immigrants (1997). Some of them came from the Caribbean and brought with them the crippling cultural baggage of slavery and prejudice that put them at the bottom of the social and economic hierarchy. Only 9 percent of students with this background achieved post-secondary qualifications, compared with 13 percent of the whites. For East Indian young people the figure was 15 percent, and for Chinese it was 26 percent.

But what about the children of immigrants who came directly from Africa, from families who did not suffer generations of degradation and probably were somewhat privileged in Africa? The academic achievement of these children in England was even better than that of the Chinese: 27 percent of them achieved post-secondary qualifications. These British data suggest that black Africans who have not spent generations as slaves are on the top of the intellectual hierarchy.

The greater genetic variation in Africa has probably produced the fastest, the slowest, the strongest, the weakest, the most clever, and the most stupid. Of course, over the years, the slowest, weakest, and most stupid may not have survived as well as the others. We have considerable evidence that Africans are faster and stronger than others; they are probably more intelligent as well. If so, this finding would fit with the general theme of this book: economic and social forces are more powerful than genetic ones. Those with economic power, social privilege, and the biggest guns produce children who do better than those at the bottom of society. Those at the top write the laws, have more control over social institutions, and participate more fully in society. Not surprisingly, they have lower official crime rates as well. But the genetic argument persists. Nicole Hahn Rafter (1997) argues that we need to understand this "born criminal" mentality and recognize the dangers posed by such thinking, which I will now illustrate.

Wilson and Herrnstein: A More Polished Version of Biological Determinism?

In *Crime and Human Nature*, James Q. Wilson and Richard J. Herrnstein (1985) argue that to understand predatory street crime, we must move away from excessive attention to social and economic factors and look more closely at differences among individual people. They acknowledge the importance of interaction between family upbringing and genetic differences, and point out that bad families produce bad children. However, they discount societal characteristics, emphasizing instead the kinds of people and their individual personalities. These views are not new, as the sample of arguments presented in this chapter suggests, but during the 1980s they were endorsed by social critics of a somewhat conservative bent, such as Ronald Reagan.

The book was noted in popular newsmagazines and the press. While it was acclaimed by many, particularly conservative officials, it received very critical reviews by some noted scholars (Kamin, 1986). But why did this book receive so much praise from public officials? Some of the arguments use logic similar to Rushton's. One reason for the different reception may lie in the prestige of the authors. Wilson is a professor of government at Harvard and Herrnstein is a professor of psychology. They claim that their book is interdisciplinary and scientific, citing over 1000 research reports. Were these authors shielded from criticism by their academic status?

Let us focus on some of their arguments. They claim that delinquents are less willing to delay gratification. Unlike non-delinquents, who save money from their paper routes for future goals, delinquents snatch purses and spend their ill-gotten gains in wild abandon. One explanation is that during the 1960s more low-birth-weight babies survived, due to better medical care. The babies were smaller and sicker because of the smoking and drinking of their pregnant mothers. The resulting mental defects made them unable to defer gratification. No one questions the harmful effects of smoking and drinking during pregnancy, but the evidence that sickly children are less able to defer gratification, and hence are more criminal, is less clear. Wilson and Herrnstein discount the *social* conditions surrounding such families that might predict the same results.

Elsewhere in the book, Wilson and Herrnstein suggest that delinquents lie more than others. However, they neglect the studies that show that students studying for law and medicine tend to cheat more than other students. Since there is a tendency for sons of lawyers and doctors to follow their fathers' profession, we could use the biological theories suggested by the authors to conclude that the criminal tendencies of the fathers who became lawyers and doctors have been passed on to their offspring. This explains why pre-law and pre-medical students cheat more than others.

Wilson and Herrnstein use evidence selectively to support their ideas. Kamin (1986) points to their explanation of the low crime rates in Japan. They say that cultural differences may grow out of biological differences. Personality has a biological basis, and the Japanese personality is less criminogenic. In one questionnaire study, the Japanese were classified as introverts. Since introversion tends to be related to lower crime rates, this explained the low Japanese crime rates. Americans tend to be extraverts, and thus more criminal. However, citizens of Uganda are even more introverted than the Japanese, but the authors ignore the high rates of violent crime in that country.

The authors conveniently ignore another aspect of this same study, which measured another criminological trait, psychoticism, which is associated with brutality and insensitivity to others. Which country was the most psychotic? Japan. Which countries were the least psychotic? Canada, the United Kingdom, and the U.S. Thus, these personality tests show the Japanese have low scores on one trait associated with criminality—introversion—but stunningly high scores on another criminal personality trait—psychoticism. However, the authors give us only part of the evidence.

In an earlier article Herrnstein wrote, "as technology advances, the tendency to be unemployed may run in the genes of a family as certainly as bad teeth do now" (Kamin, 1986). However, unemployment, of course, is a social phenomenon, like crime. Explaining it as "running in the genes" illustrates the confusion between correlation and causality. These comments also sound somewhat like Lombroso's comments regarding the poor, cited earlier in this chapter (page 60). Obviously skin colour is strongly influenced by genetics, but must we conclude that unemployment, doing poorly in school, and crime are *explained* by black skin? Is it not possible that a history of slavery, racial prejudice, and blocked employment opportunity has contributed to that correlation?

Wilson and Herrnstein's book was, unfortunately, one of the most influential of its decade, but was its success related to the political thinking of the 1980s? Richard Herrnstein and Charles Murray, in their book *The Bell Curve* (1994), like Rushton, describe a hierarchy of intelligence by race, with Asians on top, followed by whites, and Africans at the bottom. Of course the black youths they studied were the product of slavery, discrimination, and systematic barriers to opportunities. I would argue that *Crime and Human Nature* and also *The Bell Curve* make more polished presentations than Rushton, but the flaws in the thinking are similar.

The Interaction of Environment and Biological Factors: Deborah Denno

The logic and research methodology used by Deborah Denno is superior to that used by Wilson and Herrnstein and leads to more sophisticated reasoning. She followed a cohort of black children born at Philadelphia's Pennsylvania Hospital between 1959 and 1962 (Denno, 1990, 1994). The 500 females and 487 males were almost entirely from low-income families who were socially and culturally isolated. To test different theories of crime, Denno used data on early biological and environmental factors, public school records, and official police records from ages 7 to 22.

As predicted, some of the same factors that influenced crime among males also influenced crime among females. For example, seriousness of delinquent offences predicted adult crime for both males and females. Disciplinary problems and low language achievement in school were related to delinquency. Of particular interest, however, was that some *biological* factors had more impact on females while some *environmental* factors had more impact on males. Among girls, neurological abnormalities predicted disciplinary problems, juvenile crime, and adult crime. Among boys, lead poisoning strongly predicted disciplinary problems, juvenile crime, and adult crime. Although lead poisoning results in neurological and physiological impairment, its origins are environmental. Small children sometimes stick peeling paint, containing lead, in their mouths. Should lead poisoning be viewed as a biological or an environmental factor?

The fact that females appeared to be unaffected by lead, even though they were raised in the same or similar environment as males, suggests that males may be relatively more vulnerable to environmental damage and developmental problems. Males seem to be biologically weaker than females. Males are more likely to experience prenatal and infant mortality, childhood diseases, learning disorders, and retardation. These disorders are most common among the deprived and, to some extent, among criminals. Thus, researchers must ask if boys and girls are influenced in different ways. For example, in an earlier study, Denno (1984) found that low school achievement was linked to delinquency for males but not for females. Again, we have a problem of interpretation. Do males who fail in school turn to crime because social pressures are greater than those on females? Is this a biological or social variable?

The longstanding associations between environmental factors and crime may disguise the significance of biological effects, because researchers rarely incorporate them into delinquency research. To make things more confusing, biological factors can be influenced by the environment. Intelligence has a biological base, but it can be socially altered. It is not clear how social conditions influence physiology, but recent studies of receptor formation in the membranes of cells suggest that environmental factors, even in the womb, may play a far greater role in the development of the individual than previously thought. Other variables, such as disciplinary problems, may be an outcome of both biological and environmental precursors. Much delinquency research offers only sociological explanations. Other researchers focus almost entirely on things like fetal alcohol syndrome or learning disorders.

Overall, however, Denno's work suggests that delinquency is related to family instability and also to a lack of behavioural control associated with central nervous system disorders. It appears that attention deficit disorder and hyperactivity, which are part of disciplinary problems, are associated with learning and behavioural disorders. These disorders inhibit the ability of young children to create social bonds even before the school experience. Academic failure would perpetuate misconduct and impede attempts at future social bonding. Children who show evidence of attention deficit disorder and hyperactivity are more likely to retain antisocial tendencies during young adulthood, a time when most individuals start to show commitments to socially desirable behaviours. While this work does not lead to clear conclusions, it points to the possibility that boys and girls grow up differently, and that it is difficult to separate environmental and biological causal factors.

The better-quality genetic studies being done today do not suggest a direct link between genes and crime; they point instead to the possibility of biological characteristics, such as biochemical abnormalities or neuropsychological defects, leading to behavioural problems—impulsiveness, aggressiveness, and poor school performance. Children with such characteristics are disadvantaged and, if they fail in the traditional routes towards success, are more likely to engage in criminal activity.

With the mapping of the human genome and the cloning of higher animals has come an increased interest in genetic engineering. Like so many panaceas, it is deceptively simple. Tinker with the individual and straighten him out. This lets us avoid more difficult tasks. Genetic findings, however, can lead us astray. For example, blacks suffer from hypertension more than whites. Is this a genetic difference? Studies of blacks in Africa, the Caribbean, and North American cities who have similar genetics indicate major differences in hypertension. In rural African villages, they have low hypertension. In American cities it is high. Is it possible that things are tougher for African Americans than for Blacks living in Africa? Do they face conditions that lead to hypertension as well as situations that increase the likelihood of crime?

Many have argued that First Nations people are genetically predisposed to alcoholism and that there is nothing we can do about it. I do not acccept this argument. When your society crumbles, you may turn to drink. Blaming the genes is a convenient way of avoiding responsibility for reconstructing society.

Those who think the world can be divided into nice people and nasty people who deserve to be punished tend to favour genetic explanations of crime. This book admittedly leans toward the view that criminal conduct is *normal* if society is structured in certain ways.

Dangerous Policies from Biological Explanations

When those in the political arena are influenced by biological explanations of crime, there tend to be predictable consequences:

1. Lower-status citizens are punished more.
2. There is a tendency to ignore the basic flaws in the structure of society.
3. There is less concern for social programs that would help vulnerable portions of the population, which in the long run would reduce crime.
4. There are more jobs for lawyers and prison guards in our booming, but inefficient, criminal justice system.
5. There are more jobs for therapists to identify and correct the deficiencies in individuals.

Countries like Denmark have developed social programs that have "evened the playing field" for disadvantaged parents and their youngsters. Would this make biological variables more visible and more influential? In the U.S., and probably in Canada, lack of such comprehensive social programs means that economic and social factors weigh more heavily on poor families. Thus the *social environment* would explain more variance in crime in societies that have greater disparities in opportunities to achieve acceptance in the dominant society. By contrast, in those countries, such as the Scandinavian countries, that have reduced those disparities—that is, reduced the impact of social variables—biological variables might be more predictive of criminal behaviour.

One might even extend this thinking to sex differences, as demonstrated in Denno's study of 800 black children (1985). The sociological variables were more crucial to the boys. Is it possible that the disparities found in North American society weigh more heavily on boys than on girls? Poor school achievement appears to have more negative consequences for boys than for girls. Is it possible that the socioeconomic factors do not penalize girls as much as they do boys? If that is the case, biological variables might be more predictive of behaviour among girls than boys.

The same argument might be made for people from middle-class backgrounds. When socioeconomic factors become less relevant, genetic factors play a more important role. At present it is difficult to specify just how social and biological variables interact, but it is clear that biological variables cannot act on crime without going through some sort of social filter.

While some people might interpret the twin studies and adoption studies from Denmark as a reason for *neglecting* social programs, I would argue just the opposite. Creating greater opportunities for the underclass in North America to participate more fully in the riches of our society may be a necessary prerequisite to utilizing these genetic studies constructively. A logical public policy would focus first on excellent public health care for children and families and also on social disadvantages; then it would be easier to diagnose physiological factors that persist in influencing behaviour.

SUMMARY

1. The classical school emphasized free will and rationality; the positive school rejected free will and assumed that behaviour was determined.

2. Cesare Lombroso's positivist approach led him to identify criminals as atavistic. This led to erroneous views of crime and criminals, as illustrated by the work of Richard Dugdale and his mythical creations, the Juke family.

3. Modern studies of twins—for example, in countries such as Denmark—have broadened our understanding of biological factors in explaining crime.

4. Recent writings by J. P. Rushton on racial hierarchy show that professors can be rather silly at times. Unfortunately, discredited scholarship can still influence the uninformed.

5. The influential work of James Q. Wilson and Richard J. Herrnstein may suffer from the same inferior logic of past studies. However, the political climate seems to favour such ideas.

6. Doug Wahlsten and Deborah Denno note the interaction of biological and sociological factors and the difficulty of separating them.

7. A society that deals effectively with the social factors that lead to crime is better able to understand, isolate, and deal with biological factors.

KEY TERMS

atavisms   60

biological determinism   62

classical school   58

hedonistic calculus   59

genetic diversity   66

Juke myth   62

positive (positivistic) school   59

WEBLINKS

www.crimetheory.com/
The University of Washington: overview of the predominant criminological theories.

www.home.istar.ca/~ccja/angl/cjc.html
The Canadian Journal of Criminology: abstracts of the journal's current articles.

www.crime-times.org/
The Crime Times: a national, non-profit publication explores the link between biology and crime.

5

PSYCHOLOGICAL PERSPECTIVES

This chapter will:

- Simplify a Freudian approach to crime.
- Note the circular reasoning in some psychological reasoning about crime.
- Emphasize the importance of learning to criminal behaviour.
- Review some of the work on cognitive and moral development and note some of the criticisms of this research.

THE PSYCHOANALYTIC EXPLANATION OF CRIME

Like the explanations offered in the last chapter, psychological views of crime focus on the individual. However, mental processes, personality, and early childhood socialization become the centre of attention. Psychoanalysis is relatively recent and, in a sense, began with Sigmund Freud. As a scholar and researcher, he fits nicely into the positivist tradition, expecting to identify "the causes" of human behaviour. An examination of his own life helps us to appreciate strengths and weaknesses in his theories. He was considered dogmatic and tyrannical by some, showing little tolerance for those who expressed differing opinions (Martin et al., 1990). This led to ardent disciples and others who were rejected from his circle of followers.

According to Freud, humans are born with two basic instincts: the life or love instinct and the death or hate instinct. The complex interaction of these two instincts can lead to much variety in human behaviour. Aggression, for example, which is an innate part of the death instinct, is a *natural* part of human nature. It is not learned, nor is it just a response to frustration of certain needs. In other words, there is a constant struggle going on within the human psyche, and it is common for the bad components to prevail. In general, these instincts make the brain a "seething cauldron of conflict" (Freud, 1965).

The personality of the normal adult is composed of the *id*, *ego*, and *superego*. The **id** is present at birth and is not aware of outside forces, such as morality. It operates at the unconscious level and is intent on immediate gratification. It is governed by the *pleasure principle*, maximizing pleasure while avoiding pain. Although some have portrayed the id as evil, it should really be seen as amoral—morality is simply irrelevant.

As the baby becomes an infant, the **ego** develops as the child faces the real world. There are barriers to some of the id's demands. The ego represents the compromise between the unrestricted wants of the id and the rigid demands of the world. It operates on the *reality principle*, restricting the id when it is unreasonable. One matures with the development of the **superego**, which focuses on ethical concerns. Morality, remorse, and feelings of guilt are produced when the well-socialized person does something wrong. Expectations and standards from parents and others are internalized to produce a *conscience*. For example, a child sees a cookie on the table. Her id demands immediate satisfaction and she grabs the cookie. Father takes the cookie away. Later, when she has developed an ego, she waits until father leaves before taking the cookie. She applies the reality principle and postpones, but does not give up, gratification. If father has made her promise not to take cookies out of the cookie jar, she may or may not obey, depending on the development of the superego. A developed superego would make her feel guilty if she broke her promise. If the superego had not developed, perhaps she could blame the stealing of cookies on her little brother.

The psychoanalytic position would view crime as having several causes:

1. Criminal behaviour springs from within. When the id is uncontrolled, as a result of faulty ego development, the individual has little capacity to repress instinctive impulses. Those dominated by the id are criminal.

2. When the ego fails to develop in the first few years of life, and the superego fails to develop later, the individual is antisocial.

3. An overdeveloped ego may make no provision for the satisfaction of the demands of the id. Crime can result from the compulsive need for punishment to alleviate guilt.

4. Crime can also represent displaced hostility.

Psychoanalytic explanations of crime are obviously more complex than this, but essentially crime is viewed as a symptom of underlying emotional problems. There are differences within this perspective, with some scholars including more family variables. However, psychoanalytic theory does not explain the "normal" crimes of those who learn to commit crime as part of their interaction with others. Peer pressures, the social environment, and social structure are basically ignored.

A major criticism of Freud is that his model of behaviour is not empirically testable (Redl and Toch, 1979). In a theory, concepts should be linked to operational definitions that can be measured. But how does one get a measure of the unconscious? Or of the id, ego, or superego? Admittedly, theories can be tested when some of the concepts are unmeasured, but psychoanalysis offers few handles that would allow the empirically oriented researcher to get a grip on the theoretical ideas.

Freud's insights on women would also be questioned today. Clearly, according to Freud, women are inferior. This is obvious from their sex organs. Women have no penis. Boys and girls both recognize this difference instinctively and thus take male superiority for granted. Dorie Klein (1973) clearly believes that Freud strays from the facts when he argues that:

> Women are exhibitionistic, narcissistic, and attempt to compensate for their lack of a penis by being well dressed and physically beautiful. Women become mothers trying to replace the lost penis with a baby. Women are also masochistic ... because their role is one of receptor, and their sexual pleasure consists of pain. (Klein, 1973: 16)

Is it possible that Freud's view of women influenced a generation of psychiatrists, counsellors, and others so that they developed particular views about rape? Again we see the potential link between ideas and public policy. A "reality" created by a group of thinkers may find a receptive audience in practitioners and policy-makers. One could speculate that Freudian ideas had an impact on the way some people viewed female victims.

THE PSYCHOLOGICAL TEST: A USEFUL TOOL FOR UNDERSTANDING CRIME?

Since World War II, social scientists have spent considerable effort developing a variety of questionnaires related to crime. Psychologists have created intelligence tests and measures of personality types, and a number of such devices have been used in the hope of identifying criminals and delinquents. In general, they have shown that there are correlations between different types of test scores and criminal behaviour. However, it is less clear that the tests measure what they claim to be measuring. For example, a well-known psychological test developed in California asks juveniles which president they prefer, Lincoln or Washington. Those who choose Lincoln are more delinquent. Since Lincoln did away with slavery, he has been more popular with Blacks in the U.S., while Washington has been favoured by Whites. It is not surprising that a test item that distinguishes Blacks from Whites in California is also correlated with crime.

While this type of error can trap researchers rather easily, those who are in the business of producing psychological tests are resistant to change. In the 1980s, I was told by a psychology student in Ontario that the question asking which U.S. president one preferred, Lincoln or Washington, was still being asked of *Canadian* young people on the same standardized test. Clearly, one must question the use of such an instrument for studying delinquency in Canada.

Circular Reasoning in Psychological Testing

A major weakness of some psychological tests is that they contain built-in **tautologies**, or **circular reasoning**. The items in the test are basically the same as the thing they are trying to measure. For example, the Minnesota Multiphasic Personality Inventory (MMPI) is a widely used diagnostic tool with ten clinical scales. Some of the scales differentiate criminals from non-criminals. However, Gordon Waldo and Simon Dinitz (1967) pointed out that the item, "I have never been in trouble with the law," is an illustration of circular reasoning: a test item identifying people who have been in trouble with the law, not surprisingly, is related to people who have been in trouble with the law.

This sort of faulty reasoning is illustrated in Canada by the psychopathic checklist popularized by Robert Hare (1980, 1985), presented as "reliable and valid" in a popular Canadian criminology text edited by Rick Linden (1987: 131). Among the 22 items on that checklist one finds, "juvenile delinquency" and "poor probation or parole risk." It is difficult to be on probation or parole without having committed a crime. Thus, when Wong (1984), using this checklist, finds that 22 percent of the inmates in eight federal penitentiaries were classified as psychopaths, it is very difficult to see how one could avoid such a finding.

Hare has defended the scale in public discussions by claiming that the other items on the checklist also predict criminality, but let us look more closely at some of the other items: previous diagnosis as psychopath; pathological lying and deception; parasitic lifestyle; short-tempered/poor behavioural controls; promiscuous sexual relations; early behavioural problems; impulsivity; many types of offence. If one were asked to describe a criminal, isn't it likely that the adjectives used might be those on the checklist? While some psychologists claim that their measuring devices "work" on the basis of a number of sophisticated statistical analyses, they seem to forget that they are not measuring concepts that are independent. Instead of measuring psychological constructs that *predict* crime, they may, in fact, simply be *indicators of* crime. The ritualistic use of statistical techniques has obscured the *thinking* that must also be applied to the question of explaining crime. In all fairness, this type of problem is not rare in scientific work. Circular reasoning and undiscovered factors that lead to spurious relationships are often deeply embedded in the most careful research. Once these are recognized, however, scholars are obligated to take them into account.

Lee Robins (1992), famous for her psychological studies of crime, recognized the frequent tautologies—circular arguments—in many psychologically oriented criminological studies. She has also pointed out factors that have trapped psychologists and has suggested how we might make better sense of the available data. For example, Whites who are arrested are more likely to have antisocial personalities than Blacks. In the general population, Blacks and Whites have similar rates of antisocial personality. Thus, other (social?) factors seem to lead to the arrest of Blacks. If social policies and societal change could reduce differences due to race, then personality differences might become more meaningful.

Since science tends to be self-correcting, why have some psychologists persisted in the use of faulty test instruments for such a long time? Is it because a "psychological test industry" has a vested interest in the continuation of some of these measuring devices? This book cannot engage in a balanced debate on this issue, but the reader should again be aware that the creation of knowledge in criminology is influenced by the dynamics of the professional traditions of the involved researchers.

LEARNING AND CRIME

By deliberately beginning with some criticisms of certain research procedures, I hope to sensitize the reader to the fallibility of some of our thinking; but these cautions should not let us overlook the major contributions that have been made in this area, including the extensive and significant work by Robert Hare, whom I have criticized above (see, for example, Hare, 1970; Hare and McPherson, 1984). A major premise shared by psychologists and sociologists is that crime is learned. Different personalities may respond to situations in ways that lead to crime, but criminal behaviour, or the failure to behave in a criminal manner, is learned.

Classical Conditioning and Instrumental Learning

Many people have heard of Ivan Pavlov's famous experiment with dogs who learned to salivate at the sound of a bell. Pavlov paired a neutral stimulus (in this case a bell) with a meaningful stimulus (food), which led the dogs to associate the bell with the food. In **classical conditioning**, animals or people have no control over the situation. The learning that took place in the situation created by Pavlov was not because of a reward but because of the association between the bell and the food. Gordon Trasler (1962) used these principles in arguing that learning experiences early in life influence the probability of crime at a later time. If parents punish a child for breaking rules, the child will experience anxiety. This will become a conditioned response, similar to the salivation of Pavlov's dogs. To avoid situations that cause anxiety, people will avoid certain types of behaviour. Essentially, conforming behaviour is escape or avoidance of that which is painful or stressful. The inhibition of criminality is learned through conditioning. The inhibition persists, or resists extinction, because it continues to reduce anxiety. As long as one conforms, one doesn't get punished.

Trasler notes that some people are more resistant to this conditioning. Those who are outgoing and crave excitement (extraverts) are more resistant to such conditioning, while quiet, self-controlled, introspective individuals (introverts) are susceptible to conditioning. Some individuals learn *not* to be criminals more than others; that is, they are more amenable to *passive avoidance conditioning*. Those who learned early in life that improper behaviour led to anxiety-producing punishment, physical or psychological, are inhibited from improper behaviour later in life. They would still experience anxiety if they even considered committing a crime, even when the likelihood of punishment is negligible. In other words, learning has become coupled with a response from the involuntary nervous and glandular system, and these reactions create a barrier to criminal behaviour.

Instrumental learning or **operant conditioning** is different. The learner must *do* something in order to obtain a reward, or alternatively, to avoid being punished. An important distinction between instrumental learning and classical conditioning is that when the former is operating the individual anticipates a reward (or punishment). Classical conditioning is the result of an association with a stimulus and takes place without a reward. In the book *A Clockwork Orange*, by Anthony Burgess, a psychopathic individual "learns" to decrease his aggressive behaviour by aversive conditioning. During his treatment something unpleasant happens to him each time he thinks antisocial thoughts. After a while, the aggressive behaviour automatically recalls the aversive stimuli (such as feeling sick or receiving an electric shock). The character in the novel learns that there are consequences for his behaviour. The environments, of course, may differ. A two-year-old boy may learn that a temper tantrum can be used to manipulate Dad but not Mom. Thus, he uses them when Dad is in charge, but abandons that strategy with Mom.

The best-known name in this area is the late B. F. Skinner, whose ideas influence the use of **behaviour modification**, that is, the application of operant conditioning to eliminate undesirable patterns of behaviour and strengthen desirable alternatives. Like other psychologists with a behaviourist orientation, Skinner believes that humans follow the same basic natural laws as other animals (Bartol and Bartol, 1986: 78–83). He is also a *situationalist*. Individuals have no control or self-determination. Free will is a myth. Humans do not control their environments; they react to them. When a pigeon pecks in a certain way to get food, this is a reaction to a stimulus to receive a certain reward. It is not self-determination. The behaviour is moulded by *reinforcement*, which can be positive or negative. Societal members must learn at an early age that they will be rewarded if they do good things, and not be rewarded (or even punished) if they do bad things. A major problem in this scheme is understanding how to provide adequate reinforcement. If a young man gains status among his peers, increased self-esteem, and feelings of competence for bringing off a daring theft, it is difficult for society to provide competing positive reinforcement for avoiding such behaviour.

Social Learning Theories

While Skinner and the behaviourists emphasize external factors as determining behaviour, learning theorists underscore thought processes, perceptions, and the way the environment is assessed. Social learning accentuates cognition, which we might simplify as thinking and remembering. In addition to conditioning, people learn by watching and listening to those around them. Reinforcement would be necessary to maintain behaviour, but criminal behaviour might be first acquired through association with others and through observation of others. The experience can be direct, or it can be based on modelling. For example, a boy watches his older peer (who acts as a model) steal something, so he tries it himself. If a store clerk spots the boy and grabs him as he leaves, the aversive experience may inhibit future theft. But if the theft is successful and if others applaud his skill and daring, the reinforcement could be positive.

Ron Akers (1985) has elaborated this argument as **differential reinforcement theory**. He and many other scholars have tested these ideas to explain delinquency and drug use, and find considerable support. People first learn behaviour, including criminal behaviour, through imitation or through observing what happens to others. Depending on the nature of the reinforcement, whether the behaviour is rewarded or punished, the pattern will be maintained or will be extinguished. The family, peers, and other significant others, such as teachers, are important as role models and as differential reinforcers.

Learning Aggression: Albert Bandura

Violence on television can clearly influence violence in children and adults. Even a recent study sponsored by the National Cable Television Association acknowledges this fact (Wilson et al., 1997). Several theories link the mass media with crime, but I will concentrate on the work of Albert Bandura and his work on aggression (1973). Bandura's classic work with children notes that they can learn how to shoot a gun from watching TV, not in a skilled manner, perhaps, but enough to pull triggers, just as adults "know" how to use a pistol even if they have never done it before. Thus, when children watched a film showing adults beating an inflated rubber doll, they imitated the behaviour. When cartoons were used in which a cat bashed Bobo the doll, children imitated the aggression. Not only did they hit Bobo more frequently than children who watched a peaceful film, they also used dart guns, peg boards, and tether balls in a more aggressive manner than the control groups. Thus, we should not automatically view the Road Runner cartoons as harmless entertainment. Not many seconds pass before a violent message is delivered. The coyote, who is stalking the road runner, is crushed by rocks, blasted by dynamite, or flattened by a steamroller in a variety of ways. Despite the claim that all children know that these cartoons are fantasy, the potential for increasing aggression is there, since, as Bandura also notes, adults who observe aggressive acts also become more hostile.

In recent years, objections by the public may have led to some reduction in the portrayal of violence, but the level is still excessive. Wilson and her colleagues (1997) noted that only 15 percent of the violent programs provided warnings; programs rarely emphasized anti-violent themes; in 73 percent of violent scenes the perpetrators went unpunished; characters who engaged in violence showed little remorse; and the long-term consequences of violence were underemphasized. A study of a small British Columbia logging town that was recently introduced to television found that after the introduction of television, there were more frequent displays of physical aggressiveness (Joy et al., 1986). On the other hand, policy-makers should not ignore television's constructive potential. There is evidence that prosocial cartoons, for example, can increase the likelihood of prosocial behaviour (Forge and Phemister, 1987).

Cognitive and Moral Development

Are honesty and other moral characteristics something we learn early in life and internalize so that they operate in all situations? Most of us tend to believe that people have "character," which makes them act consistently under different conditions. Another argument is that people respond to the *situation*. Thus, the individual's honesty and moral behaviour are determined by circumstances. This chapter focuses on studies that view moral behaviour as a characteristic of the individual. In the next chapter, we will note dynamic group situations that lead to behaviour that would not be anticipated from our knowledge of the individuals concerned.

In their classic work, *Studies in Deceit*, Hartshorne and May (1928–30) generated a debate on some basic questions regarding the consistency of behaviour. They found that children who were dishonest or ruthless in one situation acted differently in other types of situations. However, Burton (1963, 1976) re-analyzed these data, omitting some that were unreliable, and found a general tendency for children to be somewhat consistent in terms of honesty or dishonesty. This general disposition was related to the social status of the child's family, with higher-status children displaying more honesty. Similarly, more intelligent children tended to be more honest and displayed more consistency in their honesty than those who were less bright. Of course, one might ask: do intelligent, higher-status children live in a less difficult world?

Consistency is what one would expect from the work done by Jean Piaget (1952), a Swiss psychologist who pioneered studies of how children organize social rules and make judgments. He argued that morality develops in a series of stages, depending on the intellectual or cognitive skills of individuals, as well as on their social experiences. Kohlberg (1976) continued this train of thought when he argued that the individual grows in an undeviating sequence through six stages of moral development. The individual must develop the skills and insights in sequence, building on each step before moving to the next. People progress through these stages at different speeds, and some do not progress as far as others.

There are three primary stages: *preconventional, conventional,* and *postconventional* morality, each of which is divided into early and late substages. At the *preconventional* stage, individuals act entirely out of self-interest. They have not developed notions of right or wrong. They defer to those in power, but the rules and expectations are external to the "self" of the individual. During the *late preconventional* stage, individuals become more practical. They learn to use others and understand that they must adapt in order to meet their own needs.

With the *conventional* stage, which characterizes the average adolescent, the individual strives for social approval and acceptance, particularly from peers. One's good behaviour is designed to receive social rewards and avoid negative experiences. One's image of what the peer group expects is somewhat stereotyped, but the rules of society have been internalized. Those rules have been determined by those with the power to reward or punish. At the *late conventional* stage the conscience develops; a sense of duty to the society emerges, but the individual does not question the morality of the authorities or the society at this stage.

At the *postconventional* stage, one begins to appreciate larger principles and rights of individuals. Customs are critically examined. A minority of adults after age 20 begin balancing rights of individuals with demands of society and the consideration that some laws may be unjust. The late *postconventional* individual is oriented to decisions of conscience and ethical principles that appeal to comprehensiveness and consistency. These principles may be abstract and reflect universal principles of justice (Jennings, Kilkenny, and Kohlberg, 1983).

Kohlberg argues that people pass through these stages at different rates, with many never going beyond a certain level. Criminals, like children, tend to remain at the *preconventional* stage. Although the stages represent a progression, Kohlberg acknowledges that individuals can display a wide range of moral judgments. However, they would cluster around a single stage. In addition, these judgments would be related to the individual's perspective. If the delinquent displays loyalty to his gang or the Mafia member adheres to the code of his society, he may be behaving in a manner consistent with higher levels of morality. One can see the problems with applying these arguments to criminals if someone has been socialized into criminal lifestyles. Can we assume that morality has a single dimension, or do different subgroups create different moralities?

A number of questions arise regarding the acquisition of moral character. Kohlberg suggests that it is something that is internalized and then remains fairly constant. Bandura's experiments, such as those mentioned above, suggest that *situations* lead to the imitation of others. Peers also exert a strong influence on criminal behaviour, particularly during adolescence. There are also situations in which people *know* what is morally correct, but for other reasons do not behave accordingly. Our theories select certain factors as explanations for criminal behaviour when, in reality, many things are happening at once, or possibly are coming into play at different times or under different circumstances.

Doubts about Kohlberg's reasoning have been raised as part of the discussion of President Clinton's affairs in the White House. Kohlberg believed that a few great individuals, Mahatma Gandhi and Martin Luther King Jr., for example, achieved the highest level of principled morality. But even honourable people are inconsistent. Gandhi treated his wife, family, and followers rather badly. He loved humanity, but was harsh with real human beings. Martin Luther King Jr. died for the civil rights movement, but he was a womanizer. Heroes in battle who exhibit great bravery and save their fellow soldiers from death have been known to be cruel with others. It is wrong to assume that moral failure in one domain—and former President Clinton seems to have failed badly in some areas—accurately predicts behaviour in other situations.

Psychological explanations focus on the individual, but clearly individuals do not operate in a vacuum. While many psychologists tend to concentrate on characteristics of individuals and the immediate environments in which they are socialized, it is difficult to explain criminal behaviour without looking at other forces in the community and in the larger society. Theories of offenders' attributes, personalities, or social background and conditions do not explain why others with the same traits, same personality type, or similar upbringing do not persist in criminal careers. The terrorist attacks on the World Trade Center in 2001 have generated some psychological explanations for the actions of the perpetrators, but they clearly are inadequate. Criminological theories that stress individual traits or offender pathology also fail miserably at explaining spatial patterns of crime, regional variations, intercity and intracity differences, or changes in crime over time.

A murderer, after savagely killing a woman and robbing her house, took the utmost care to feed the victim's dog and cat (Fattah, 1971). He even left them enough food, for fear that nobody would come to the scene of the crime for some time. Violent offenders who exhibit extreme cruelty and callousness towards victims sometimes show tender love and compassion for others, and even for animals. In other words, concentrating on attributes of the individual alone cannot yield an adequate explanation of crime.

SUMMARY

1. A Freudian or psychoanalytical approach to crime argues that when the id, ego, or superego are not functioning properly, crime is more likely.

2. While psychological testing has been a frequent tool in studies of crime, some of the best-known ones have been flawed by circular reasoning. With circular reasoning we have trouble separating *explanations* from *descriptions*.

3. Learning theories are central to psychological theories of crime. Classical conditioning is involuntary. The response is automatic. Instrumental learning or operant conditioning requires the learner to *do* something to obtain a reward or avoid punishment.

4. Piaget and Kohlberg argue that morality develops in stages as children grow. According to this perspective criminals are those who do not develop past a certain stage.

KEY TERMS

behaviour modification   77

circular reasoning   75

classical conditioning   77

cognitive and moral development   79

differential reinforcement theory   78

ego   74

id   74

instrumental learning   77

operant conditioning   77

superego   74

tautologies   75

WEBLINKS

www.digeratiweb.com/sociorealm

SocioRealm: on-line sociology resources from the University of Minnesota with links to crime-related topics.

www.hare.org/

Web page of Dr. Robert Hare, prominent researcher in the area of psychopathy.

Chapter 6

GROUP DYNAMICS, COLLECTIVE BEHAVIOUR, AND CRIMINOGENIC CIRCUMSTANCES

This chapter will:

- Attempt to describe situations that are conducive to or discourage criminality.

- Describe how individuals can "mutually excite" each other and create reactions that have unintended consequences.

- Describe the role of authority in making people do things they know they should not do.

- Note that some settings, such as prisons, can cause otherwise normal people to behave in an antisocial way.

- Examine research which tries to understand why some people in some circumstances come to the aid of others.

- Summarize how the "attributions" we make or assumptions about causes can influence criminal behaviour.

- Note the importance of friendships for increasing prosocial behaviour.

BOX 6.1

The researchers left the automobile on the streets in an eastern U.S. city across from the campus of a large university; the licence plates were removed and the hood was raised. Then the researchers unobtrusively observed the car for 64 hours. Within ten minutes the first visitor arrived. One observer noted: "family of three drive by, stop. All leave car. Well dressed.... Mother ... stands by car on sidewalk keeping watch. Boy, about eight years old, stays by father throughout, observing and helping. Father (neatly) dressed ... opens trunk, rummages through, opens car trunk which is full of tools, removes hacksaw, cuts for one minute. Lifts battery out and puts in his trunk."

Another thief was a distinguished-looking, middle-aged man pushing a baby carriage. He stole something from the trunk and put it in the baby carriage. After 26 hours the car was stripped of the battery, radiator, air cleaner, radio antenna, windshield wipers, chrome strip, hub caps, a set of jumper cables, a gas can, a can of car wax, and its only good tire. Nine hours later random destruction began when teenagers tore off the rear-view mirror.

SITUATIONAL DYNAMICS

While the experiment described in Box 6.1 was being conducted in an eastern U.S. city, a similar procedure was followed in California near the Stanford University campus. After 64 hours the car in Palo Alto was untouched. In fact, when it began to rain, one passerby lowered the hood so the motor would not get wet (Zimbardo, 1970).

Why did those in the eastern city act more criminally? Attempts to explain such behaviour, as characteristics of individuals, ignore many dynamic factors. For example, several adults observed the family of three stealing the battery but did nothing. Furthermore, most of the vandalism was done in broad daylight by well-dressed, apparently middle-class people. One can focus on the setting, but clearly there seems to be considerable **interaction** among a number of factors. The setting is dynamic rather than static, and outcomes are somewhat different from what would be predicted by looking at isolated factors.

The Setting and Deindividuation

Some settings and circumstances appear to encourage **deindividuation**, whereby people lose their identity and become part of a group. Zimbardo (1970) predicted that the large concentration of population in the eastern U.S. would mean that people would be more likely to lose their identity and feel less responsible for their actions. In addition, the anonymity in the larger city, in combination with situational cues, suggested that no one else cared what the "thieves" were doing. In the setting near Stanford University, people could be more easily identified. Somehow, this explanation seems incomplete to me. What is it that makes someone take the first step towards a criminal act?

Robertson Davies, in his book *The Manticore* (1972: 150), provides a description of how the central character in the book, while a teenager, joined other boys in breaking into a cabin owned by elderly people. The leader began damaging things and goaded the others into following his lead. Their appetite for destruction grew with feeding. The leader piled photographs on a table, jumped up on the table, stripped down his trousers, squatted over the photographs, and defecated on them. At that point, the central character in the book came to his senses and tried to understand what was happening. The scene dramatically captures the transition from normal boys to destructive criminals. In this case, it is difficult to view the boys as being inherently criminal or the setting as criminogenic; instead, the *dynamics* of the group play a more important role.

Mutual Excitation and Circular Reactions

Andrew Wade (1967) provides an explanatory argument for vandalism that is quite compatible with these ideas. Wade describes the damage done by a group of boys in a feed mill warehouse. The boys explained how they originally gained entry to play tag among the stacks of feed bags. Soon the motorized fork-lift trucks were discovered, and the boys began having fun driving them. They didn't *deliberately* drive them into the feed bags, but they were unskilled pilots of the fork-lift trucks. The first time the grain sacks were damaged, the boys may have hesitated, perhaps a bit anxious about what they had done; but they may have also wondered how deeply you could drive the forks on the trucks into a bag of grain if you really took a run at it. The challenge, the dare, the competition, and the perverse pleasure in the destruction stimulated others to go further than they had earlier planned. This is *mutual excitation.* In earlier studies of collective behaviour, Blumer suggested the term **circular reaction** (1951). This is the type of interstimulation whereby the actions of one individual stimulate another, which in turn is reflected back to the first person, providing reinforcement. Soon there is group contagion. Wade documents five stages in this process:

Stage I: Waiting for Something to Turn Up
The actors are poised for some action-provoking suggestion. Sometimes "games" are being played, such as trying to shoot bottles with a BB gun. It doesn't take much of a shift, however, to find that street lights and windows can be exciting targets.

Stage II: Removal of Uncertainty (the Exploratory Gesture)
The unstructured situation changes when an action-provoking suggestion is offered. The exploratory gesture, the first deviant step, is sometimes made cautiously, sometimes boldly, but it provokes interest in contrast to what might have been prevailing boredom. Of course, the exploratory gesture could be rejected. In the above description of the boys vandalizing the cottage, the process might have failed to develop if the exploratory gestures had been rejected, if the circular reaction had been stifled initially. But let us postpone such thoughts until later, when we consider antidotes to this type of crime. Assuming, however, that the exploratory gesture is not rejected, how does the uncertainty change into direct action?

Stage III: Mutual Conversion
A number of pressures may be operating to cause the individual to go along with the actions implied in the exploratory gesture: challenges to one's self-image related to courage, manliness, or daring. One does not want to be viewed as "chicken." There can be a struggle between the internalized norms of the larger social system, norms that favour prosocial behaviour, and the demands of loyalty to the peer group, which may favour deviant behaviour. When the peer group wins in this struggle, **mutual conversion** has taken place. Obviously, the likelihood of conversion depends on background factors. Highly delinquent boys will not need much encouragement to engage in vandalism. On the other hand, those who perceive that others in the group would think badly of them if they responded favourably to an exploratory gesture to do something wrong would resist such conversion.

Stage IV: Joint Elaboration of the Act
In this stage there can be large-scale property destruction. The *circular reaction* and **mutual excitation** accelerate the potential for reckless behaviour, so that a veritable orgy of vandalism can take place. Any impact of favourable family socialization must be submerged and replaced, at least temporarily, by pressure from peers to conform to new norms. The individual must respond to challenges and call the bluff of the others. The deindividuation described by Zimbardo appears to fit these other situations. The temporary loss of identity and sense of security in the peer group reduces feelings of individual responsibility. Cautious individuals, who would normally be very reluctant to engage in criminal behaviour, now feel they can hide behind the perceived anonymity. An **impression of universality** is created, giving the appearance of group solidarity.

Stage V: Aftermath and Retrospect
In a **retrospective view of the act**, the participants may redefine the criminal behaviour as "getting even" with someone who did them wrong: this is not a meaningful "explanation"

but instead an *ex post facto* rationalization. Most of the boys thought the vandalism was simply "fun" at the time and were carried away by events, rather than seeing any reasoned attempt to get revenge against some real or imagined enemy. Feelings of shame and guilt will depend on the importance of other reference groups. If the primary source of self-definition comes from prosocial elements, such as parents, guilt will be strong, but even so, Wade found that some boys still expressed some malicious delight at having been participants in these wild acts. Adult males, holding respectable positions, often delight in retelling stories of past misdeeds. The passage of time makes the description of their previous daring more status-enhancing than the shame they might exhibit for such thoughtless behaviour.

Breaking the Chain of Events

The sequence of events is not inevitable. In the scene above, in which the boys were trashing the cottage, what event would have interrupted the process? Jack Katz (1988) used the behaviour of soldiers as an illustration of mutual excitation and other group dynamics, which led from routine interrogation of Vietnamese peasants to brutality. A soldier was beating a woman when she had a spontaneous bowel movement. "The soldier stopped. I'm beating up this girl, for what? What the fuck am I doing? I just felt like a shit" (1988: 7). Crime prevention involves making potential deviants "feel like a shit," preferably before the behaviour takes place. In Victoria in 1997, Reena Virk was beaten by seven young females and one young male. They tortured her, burned her with cigarettes, and left her by the water to be drowned by a rising tide. Nothing broke the chain of events.

The Definition of the Situation

In addition to the group processes operating as Wade described above, people perceive situations differently. In the abandoned-car experiment referred to earlier, the reader will recall that the automobile near the Stanford campus was not vandalized. Zimbardo (1970) argued that it was not clearly identified as abandoned. The experimenters decided to damage it somewhat to see if others would follow suit.

> There is considerable reluctance to take that first blow, to smash through the windshield ... but it feels so good after the first smack that the next one comes more easily, with more force and feels even better. Even though the sequence was being filmed, the students got carried away. (Zimbardo, 1970: 290)

Everyone was eager to use the sledge hammer. One student jumped on the roof and began stomping it in, two were pulling off the door, another broke all the glass he could find. They later reported that the experience was stimulating and pleasurable. Observers, who were shouting to hit it harder, finally joined in and turned the car completely over on its back. This was another illustration of mutual excitation. The experimenters realized that they had gone too far and that there was little likelihood that such a badly wrecked car would be vandalized further. However, that night three men with pipes and bars were pounding away at the carcass. The situation had been redefined. The car was clearly "abandoned." Sometimes it is not clear when a car has been abandoned, as the following anecdote suggests:

> A motorist pulled his car off the highway in Queens, New York, to fix a flat tire. He jacked up his car and, while removing the tire, was startled to see his hood being opened and a stranger starting to pull out the battery. The stranger tried to mollify his assumed car stripping

colleague by telling him, "Take it easy buddy, you can have the tires; all I want is the battery." (Zimbardo, 1970: 292)

It appears that circular reactions and mutual excitation can make people go further than they had originally intended, but there is often the need to have the situation defined as "okay" before people begin to commit questionable acts. Having a person in authority define things as "okay" has considerable impact on this process.

The Role of Authority in Producing Wrongful Behaviour

Group members do not all have the same influence. People defer to others even when they encourage actions contrary to what they feel is right. Soldiers kill when ordered to do so. People at the bottom of hierarchies sometimes do things because they assume that the people above them have superior knowledge that enables them to see consequences not visible to those who must do the dirty work. This makes the questionable acts acceptable. At times, the underling feels she has no choice. At other times conscience wins out.

The Milgram Experiment on Obedience to Authority

Stanley Milgram (1963) did a controversial study in which the subjects gave electric shocks to others to "teach" them. The subjects were told they were studying the effects of punishment on memory. They would be the "teachers" who would administer the punishment, but they did not know the "learners," who pretended to feel the electric shocks, were part of the experiment. When the subjects met the learners, a coin was flipped to see who would be the teacher and who would be the learner. In fact, the naive subject always "won" the toss and became the teacher. The learner was then taken into an adjacent room and strapped into an "electric chair" in front of the naive teacher. The teacher would then go into the next room, containing the "shock generator," which had labels indicating different levels of shock from 15 to 450 volts. The labels also provided descriptions, such as "slight shock" and "danger: severe shock" and further on the scale "XXX." Each time the learner gave a wrong answer, the researcher told the teacher to administer a stronger shock. The confederate learner, of course, gave wrong answers, displayed increasing discomfort, finally screamed in agony, banged on the wall, and pleaded with the teacher to stop.

How far would people go in administering painful shocks when told to do so by the authority figure (the researcher)? Milgram was surprised that two-thirds of the subjects went past the danger level, all the way to the extreme level. While obeying the instructions, many of them displayed considerable discomfort, sweating profusely, biting their lips, and so on, especially when the victim began pounding the wall (Milgram, 1963; 1974).

Milgram varied the physical distance between the teacher and learner, and by varying how much the teacher could hear, varied the "psychological" distance. For example, in the closest physical and psychological distance, the teacher sat next to the learner. In general, the subject resisted the instructions of the experimenter more when close to the victim.

However, the nearer the *experimenter*, who remained calm, got to the teacher, the higher the rate of compliance. While compliance was similar for male and female subjects, female teachers displayed greater discomfort. These distance factors may be relevant to violent crime. The more *impersonal* the weapon, the greater the likelihood of damaging behaviour. Is an individual more likely to shoot another at twenty feet than stab someone at two feet?

Is stabbing easier than strangling someone with bare hands? Can a manufacturer run a factory, using poisonous substances that hurt workers, if she does not know the workers in the plant? Is it easier for a terrorist to crash an airplane into a skyscraper if he does not know the people in the building? On the other hand, Serbs and Croats grew up together, worked together, and later tried to kill each other. This may seem a digression from the theme of this chapter, but there are implications for social policy in these experiments.

The subjects rationalized *after* having administered the severe shocks. They were sure the experimenter would not permit the victim to be harmed, thinking that "He must know what he is doing." Still others had faith, perhaps unwarranted, in the merit of social science research: the knowledge gained justified the method. However, as cautioned above, these rationalizations may reduce guilt after the fact, rather than "explain" the behaviour.

This work by Milgram and others who have investigated the pressures of group dynamics raises questions about the nature of society. One thing is abundantly clear: personality factors or levels of moral development are simply not enough to explain many types of antisocial or criminal behaviour. Let us look more closely at group processes, not only for more complete explanations, but for insights into intelligent social policy.

Criminogenic Settings

A number of factors described above come together in the prison experiment initiated by Zimbardo (1973). Student volunteers were screened and paid 15 dollars a day. The experiment required two roles, guard and prisoner, assigned by the flip of a coin. The next day, "prisoners" were unexpectedly "arrested" and brought in a police car to a simulated prison at Stanford University, where they were handcuffed, searched, fingerprinted, deloused, issued a prison uniform, and placed in a 1.8 m by 2.7 m cell with two other "inmates." The guards wore uniforms and mirrored sunglasses and carried night sticks, whistles, and handcuffs. They drew up formal rules for maintaining order in the "prison."

Both guards and prisoners took on their roles completely by the end of six days. Previous socialization and values seemed to count for little, as the guards treated the prisoners as if they were animals, taking pleasure in cruelty. The prisoners became servile, thinking only of their own survival, with mounting hatred towards the guards. Three prisoners had to be released during the first four days when they became hysterical and depressed. Others begged to be "paroled," willing to forfeit the money they had earned from the experiment. None of the prisoners simply said, "I'm quitting the job, and if anyone tries to stop me I'll have you charged with kidnapping." Instead, they continued to play their role as inmates, trying to escape or get better treatment by following the artificially created rules. Even Zimbardo, as prison director, got caught up in his role. Suspecting a "prison riot," he had taken some precautions. When another professor dropped by to see how the experiment was going and began asking questions about psychology, Zimbardo was annoyed. Here he was with a potential prison riot on his hands, and this ivory tower type was asking questions about dependent variables. Zimbardo had *become* a prison director instead of a psychologist.

A third of the guards abused their power, but even those who were seen as fair but tough never supported the prisoners against guards who were treating the inmates badly. The exercise of power was self-aggrandizing and self-perpetuating. The most hostile guards moved spontaneously into leadership roles and became role models for others. The situation became so bad that Zimbardo terminated the experiment in six days instead of proceeding through the planned two weeks.

In less than one week normal young males learned to behave in a pathological and antisocial manner. It has been said that prison guards tend to be recruited from those with a lust for power and other antisocial characteristics. An alternative argument is that, when a situation is created in which some have power and others are powerless, everyone learns to despise lack of power. Prisoners and guards learn to admire power for its own sake. Real prisoners learn how to gain power through informing, gaining sexual control of other prisoners, or forming powerful cliques.

This experiment suggests that prisons cannot avoid doing damage, but *calls into question some of the assumptions about incarceration.* It also fits into the larger issue of pathological behaviour being raised in this chapter. The *characteristics of individuals* are often insufficient to explain antisocial behaviour. Criminogenic situations exist that will increase the likelihood of violence and physical abuse. By the same token, different situations could be created that make people more caring, more altruistic, and more inclined to come to the aid of someone in need. Criminologists tend to ignore this constructive side of the coin. On this note, let us turn to studies that involve the role of bystanders.

BYSTANDER BEHAVIOUR AND COMING TO THE AID OF OTHERS

In February 1981, a young University of Alberta student was stabbed and clubbed to death by six men, as his horrified girlfriend looked on. Bystanders watched curiously, but made no effort to help (*Edmonton Journal*, February 23, 1981). In July of the same year, several people waited for a bus while an elderly man lay at their feet, dying of a heart attack. "The guy was lying in front of the bus stop and his face was turning blue, but nobody even glanced at him" (*Edmonton Journal*, July 29, 1981). The man was pronounced dead on arrival at the hospital.

Upon hearing of such events, it is tempting to offer explanations in terms of moral depravity or lack of humanity on the part of the non-intervening onlookers. It is unlikely that Edmonton is much different from other cities in Canada. These sorts of situations, unfortunately, occur regularly in many different types of communities. If we attempt to explain these phenomena in terms of the characteristics of the bystanders, our reasoning is often deficient in that it fails to explain criminal acts. Characteristics of communities, the dynamics of the situation, and other factors also influence the likelihood of crime or antisocial behaviour and, in addition, influence the bystanders or observers of crime. It is reasonable to argue that bystanders can make a difference. Therefore, it is worthwhile to review studies of bystander behaviour, and expand on the principles reviewed in the earlier part of the chapter to those people who have a potential for intervention. We could ask, "In what type of setting do antisocial acts take place?" For now, however, we will ask, "What type of stimuli do people need to act in a prosocial or antisocial way?"

The Willingness to Help and the Diffusion of Responsibility

The Smoke-Filled Room

This experiment placed undergraduate males in a room to complete a questionnaire. The experimenter began to introduce "smoke" into the room. When a subject was alone in the room, he would glance up from his questionnaire. Most subjects would get up from their chairs and investigate. No subject showed any sign of panic, but three-quarters of the men reported the smoke. However, when a naive subject was in the room with two "stooges" who were instructed to ignore the smoke, the behaviour of the subject was quite different. Only one in ten reported the smoke; "the other nine stayed in the waiting room as it filled up with smoke, doggedly working on their questionnaire and waving the fumes away from their faces. They coughed, rubbed their eyes, and opened the window—but they did not report the smoke" (Latané, Darley, and Darley, 1968: 218).

In a third test situation, three naive subjects were placed in the room. To a large extent, the three naive subjects acted like the single naive subject placed with the two stooges. In general, *the presence of others led to a delay in noticing the smoke, and inhibited prosocial action*. This leads us to question the assumption that the presence of many people at an emergency will increase the likelihood that aid will be provided.

The "Woman in Distress"

Perhaps there was no real danger in the smoke-filled-room study. Individuals might respond differently if someone were actually in pain. In a related study, naive subjects were ushered into a room by a young woman to fill out a questionnaire. A few minutes later, they heard the young woman fall in the next room and cry out for help. "Oh, my ankle. I can't get this thing off me" (Latané and Rodin, 1969). Of those who heard the fall while *alone* in the waiting room, 70 percent offered to help the victim. When an inactive stooge was present, only 7 percent of the subjects intervened. Similarly, a second naive subject, instead of the stooge, tended to inhibit the action of the subjects. However, one of the test situations included two persons who were friends, rather than strangers. They were more inclined to offer help than subjects who were strangers. The researchers suggest that friends are less likely to worry about looking foolish in front of one another than in front of strangers.

Asking the Wrong Questions

Criminologists may not have been asking the best questions when it comes to explaining crime. "Why do some *individuals* commit crimes? Why do some *individuals* object to antisocial behaviour in others? Why do some *individuals* come to the help of others in distress?" They sound like reasonable questions, but the characteristics of individuals—their moral development, their socialization, and their personalities—may play a smaller role than has previously been thought. Situational factors, particularly those factors that influence the dynamics of the immediate social environment, may be more crucial in determining whether a person will take part in criminal behaviour or interfere with others when they observe acts of deviance.

Helping Models

It would be inappropriate to leave the reader with the impression that the interesting experiments by Bibb Latané, John Darley, and their colleagues provide the definitive answer to certain types of behaviour. In the "flat-tire" study by James H. Bryan and Maryanne Test (1967), a woman stood by an automobile with a flat tire. An inflated tire was leaning on the car. The young woman, flat tire, and inflated tire were conspicuous to passing traffic. A quarter of a mile towards the traffic another car had a flat tire. This time a young man had pulled his car off the road and appeared to be changing the flat tire for the woman. Of two thousand vehicles that passed the automobile where the young woman was being helped, 58 stopped at the second car where the second woman was alone.

In a second experiment, there was no "helping model" to be seen shortly before coming upon the woman with the flat tire. If one uses the "diffusion of responsibility" model, one could argue that the evidence of someone helping would *decrease* the obligation on a passerby to help. If others are willing to help, there is less need to do so. But the flat-tire study indicated the opposite. Only 35 cars stopped when there was no helping model to remind drivers of the social responsibility norm. It seems, then, that we are encouraged to act in a prosocial manner when we have seen others acting in a prosocial manner.

ATTRIBUTION THEORY

Attribution is the process of explaining causes of behaviour. A friend steals your car. You might attribute this act to characteristics of the person, *internal causes*, or to an unusual situation, *external causes*. Which alternative you choose is important for you to understand your friend's behaviour.

Attribution theory might help to explain the beginnings of some of the dynamics described above. For example, a person with some potential for criminal behaviour observes a potential victim. Let us assume that a few youths are observing someone who is sleeping on the sidewalk. The youths may believe the man is drunk. If they attribute the drunkenness to faults in the man, they may identify him as responsible for his problem (internal causes). They may feel disgust and fail to help him. Or they may see him as worthless and undeserving, and therefore an appropriate victim of theft.

They may view a well-dressed businessman, who is walking towards them, as someone who lives by exploiting others, a person not worthy of respect (internal causes). He may also be seen as partially to blame for the type of system they live in that makes it hard for them to find jobs. Thus, robbing him becomes acceptable. In a similar manner, they may attribute certain characteristics to the owner of a store. He cheats his customers, so it is easy to dislike him. Once having shared this dislike with peers, robbing his store becomes a more likely response.

Of course, the reasoning of the youths could proceed along different lines. The man lying on the street may remind the young men of someone they know; they may believe that he is having a heart attack. At any rate, they may attribute the situation to circumstances beyond the victim's control (external causes). It is not his fault that he is lying there; therefore he is deserving of sympathy. Providing help might be the final response.

Similarly, the well-dressed businessman may be someone to admire. The boys might attribute his successful manner to the fact that he worked hard, displayed intelligence, was honourable in his business relations, earned the trust and respect of others, and as result now has an important position. If he were to slip on the ice, the young men might go to his aid.

The owner of the store might have been someone who came to North America from the old country with the grandfather of a friend of one of the boys. He worked hard, got ahead, treated customers well, granted credit to deserving people facing tough times, and gave jobs to kids in the neighbourhood. He and his store have been welcome in the area, so if the youths pass the store at night and see someone trying to break in, they might frighten the burglar off and call the police.

People also attribute internal and external causes to their own behaviour. The battered wife might believe she was at fault. The drug addict could attribute his behaviour to his parent's behaviour or stress from the outside world. Males are more likely than females to attribute their criminal behaviour, or personal failures, to external factors. When they fail exams, males are more likely to blame inadequate study time or stupid teachers (Burns and Seligman, 1989). Females are more likely to blame their own lack of ability. This may help males to maintain self-confidence. It may weaken self-confidence in females.

We often commit the **fundamental attribution error**: the tendency to attribute most behaviour to internal factors. For example, one could say that terrorists fly airplanes into buildings because they are vicious, unprincipled, insensitive cowards. In doing so, one fails to take into account other factors. It also works the other way. You may develop great confidence in a friendly, helpful, and reliable friend. Thus, it is hard to understand the variability in behaviour created by external causes. When you learn that he secretly robbed banks to support his lifestyle and mistress, you are surprised. When a polite, well-to-do, apparently normal Muslim student in Hamburg travelled to the U.S., hijacked an airplane, and flew it into New York's World Trade Center, even his family was amazed.

The *fundamental attribution error* often leads people to blame victims of unfortunate circumstances: women get raped because they wear seductive clothes; unemployed workers are seen as lazy. The working-class East Germans I met were constantly annoyed by the West German opinion that they had not learned to work under the Communist system. Instead, the Germans from the East attributed their unemployment to factories being purchased and closed by West German firms.

Other biases occur when people explain their own behaviour. When my students do not respond well to my lecture it is because either they are not listening, it is too hot, or the jack-hammer outside the building is too noisy (external factors). By contrast, the politician giving a talk at a meeting I intended was just plain stupid (an internal factor). We tend to take credit for success, attributing it to personal characteristics or efforts, but blame external factors for failure. These attributions influence crime, particularly in small groups.

The Dynamics of Cooperation, Competition, and Conflict

The prisoner's dilemma: Two men are separated immediately after being arrested. The prosecutor believes they are guilty but does not have enough evidence to convict them. If both refuse to confess, each will be convicted for a minor crime and jailed for six months. If both confess and give information about the other, each will get five years. But if one prisoner remains silent and one confesses, the confessing prisoner goes free while the other gets ten years. Each prisoner faces a dilemma. The best mutual outcome, short sentences, is to be achieved through cooperation: neither should talk. But remaining silent is risky. If the other prisoner talks, hoping to go free, the silent one gets a long sentence. If they both compete—that is, confess—they both go to jail for longer than if nothing was said.

This is a common game. In North America particularly there is a strong tendency for people to exploit each other and respond competitively. For 50 years the U.S. and the former Soviet Union spent enormous sums on military budgets. Each side could save enormous sums if they reduced their spending. Does competition lead to more crime? Does cooperation reduce crime? Does exploiting others lead to cheating?

Intense competition leads to interpersonal conflict, which can lead to revenge. Some people who feel exploited or aggrieved may spend years plotting how to get even. Employees who feel wronged may steal or disclose company secrets. In extreme cases, fired employees have murdered their bosses.

Failure to Cooperate Encourages "Groupthink"

Competitive group dynamics can separate groups from others and give extreme leaders more influence. A religious cult in Waco, Texas, saw itself in extreme competition with the rest of the world. They shot and killed four FBI agents executing a search warrant. Groupthink operated on both sides. Cooperation became impossible. Confrontation was violent. The resulting fire killed all but nine of the eighty cult members, including 25 children.

Was groupthink operating when George W. Bush decided to bomb Afghanistan? Under some conditions group members have difficulty evaluating new options and alternatives realistically. People in groups will have such difficulty: (1) when under great stress and expected to *do* something, (2) when there is time pressure, and (3) when the leader is biased and has a limited vision of the past and future. There are enormous pressures to "close ranks with the leader." When the U.S. Congress was asked to give the president extensive authority to go to war, only one member of Congress, Barbara Lee, a Black woman from California, spoke for a more cautious role. She received criticisms and even death threats. Under these conditions, groups become close-minded and rationalize their decisions. Irrational attributions about the character of others are accepted to create unity. The group dismisses other options and suppresses dissenting voices and becomes convinced that its attributions are correct.

Groupthink also characterized some of the "politically correct" movements at universities in the 1990s. Certain topics were not acceptable for discussion in class. Anyone expressing "incorrect" views was assigned negative attributes. In a sense, people were charged, tried, and punished for expressing ideas that did not fit a certain mould.

What has this to do with crime? How did I get from the subject of deviance in small groups to the subject of war? I argue that *conditions that create cooperation and consideration of options in small and large groups reduce crime*. When a gang of boys discuss the attributes of a store owner (perhaps he is a nice guy), the gang is less likely to rob it. When people in a group assess their future actions and openly debate the validity of their attributions, they are less likely to hurt others. When a factory owner dumps toxic waste into a river, it is not just a crime: it is an attempt to gain something while others lose. When all factory owners cheat, we ruin the environment. When cooperation is the norm, small and large groups create an anti-criminal and prosocial ethic. False attribution errors are reduced. In the long run the small groups benefit as well as the rest of society.

There are ways to avoid groupthink and some of its unfortunate consequences. Earlier in this chapter we spoke of "breaking the chain of events." The role of a "devil's advocate" in a group, always challenging a group consensus, or a tradition of inviting contrasting views, encourages the consideration of options. These anti-groupthink factors didn't operate in the Reena Virk case. They rarely operate among street gangs, prisons, boys considering vandalism, university students, or among politicians who feel compelled to advocate punitive legislation for juveniles. The same dynamics operate when a coalition of leaders under pressure say, "we will hunt down those responsible and punish them."

This is not a sophisticated explanation of crime, but group dynamics make a difference. The way people perceive and interpret the world around them influences their actions, but the factors that influence those perceptions and interpretations are not always of their own making. It is appropriate to end this chapter with a study that links some of these ideas to other elements in the society.

SOCIAL TIES AND THEIR IMPACT ON NORMS AND EXPECTATIONS

In order to control children, or adults for that matter, and see that they are following the norms of society, we have to know what they are doing. We audit books of a company to be sure it is behaving properly, and we reveal certain aspects of our lives to assure others that we are not doing something wrong. Similarly, if parents are to socialize their children properly, they need to know where they are and what they are doing. Based on this last assumption, Barth, Watson, and Blanchard (1966) did a survey in which they asked the following hypothetical question:

> Suppose that a young girl, about fourteen, was seen by some neighbours climbing out of her first floor bedroom late at night, after her parents were in bed, to keep a date with a boy who picked her up in a car.

The respondents were then asked:

> In this situation, (1) what do you think the neighbours *should* do? (2) What do you think most of the people actually *would* do? (3) What would you, yourself, do in this situation?

The first question represented the preferred norms, what *should* people do? This is the *right* thing to do. Of course, people do not always do what they should. We expect them to fall short of the mark some of the time. The second question represents the *expectations*, the sort of thing people would do in reality. Finally, what would you do? Would you do the *right* thing? Or would you hold back somewhat?

The respondents were also asked to answer these questions depending on their relationship to the girl's parents: (1) friends, (2) acquaintances, or (3) strangers. The results are summarized in Table 6.1.

The data show that, under conditions of close friendship, there was a very high consensus on the proper course of action. If the neighbours were friends, 95 percent of the subjects thought they should tell them that their daughter was climbing out of windows at night. This was the *right* thing to do. Telling other neighbours was clearly wrong; that would be gossiping. Only 5 percent thought you should say nothing to anyone. As the social ties or degree of intimacy with the neighbours decreased, so did the obligation to tell the parents, dropping to 74 percent for acquaintances and 48 percent for strangers. However, it was clear that one should *not* gossip with neighbours, even though, in the case of strangers, telling no one came close to the norm of telling the parents (44 percent compared with 48 percent).

Having established the norm, the *right* thing to do, one might ask what is likely to happen in reality. Would your neighbours do the right thing? The expectations fell short of the norms. The respondents thought that people who were friends of the girl's parents would fol-

TABLE 6.1	Norms, Expectations, and Predicted Behaviour in Reporting a Deviant Act		

	Tell Parents	Tell Neighbours	Tell No One
Norms: What *should* the neighbours do if they were:			
Friends of the parents	95%	0%	5%
Acquaintances	74%	3%	23%
Strangers	48%	8%	44%
Expectations: What *would* the neighbours do if they were:			
Friends of the parents	85%	7%	8%
Acquaintances	40%	38%	22%
Strangers	11%	47%	42%
Prediction of *own behaviour* if parents were:			
Friends	94%	0%	6%
Acquaintances	68%	4%	28%
Strangers	34%	13%	53%

Source: Barth, Tom, Walter Watson, and Wayne Blanchard (1966). "Parent-Child Relations in Mass Society." In Jeanette R. Folta and Edith S. Deck (eds.), *A Sociological Framework for Patient Care*. New York: Wiley.

low the norms fairly well, reporting the behaviour 85 percent of the time; but the respondents expected acquaintances and strangers to fall below the norm. In fact, they were expected to do what one should not do—that is, gossip, or tell other neighbours. Thirty-eight percent of the respondents expected that acquaintances, and 47 percent expected that strangers would tell the neighbours (i.e., gossip). In other words, with the decline of intimacy the respondents felt that others would violate the norms.

When asked to predict their own behaviour, the respondents reported a pattern similar to the norm. Of course *they* would follow the proper course of action. If the parents were friends, the respondents said they would tell the parents in 94 percent of the cases. Absolutely none of them said they would tell the neighbours. Even if the parents of the 14-year-old girl were strangers they would tell the parents 34 percent of the time, much higher than the 11 percent they would predict for others. They confessed they might gossip in 13 percent of the cases, but certainly they were much better than other neighbours, who would gossip 47 percent of the time.

How much faith should we put in the respondents' assessment of their own behaviour? I can't speak for you, readers out there, but of course *I* would certainly do the right thing. If Morris Milgram asked me to move a lever, sending a shock to the person in the next room who began groaning in pain, *I* would quickly tell Dr. Milgram to take his shock generator and stuff it. If *I* were with those teenagers who broke into the cottage as described in Robertson Davies's book, *I* would have strenuously opposed their vandalism. You wouldn't catch *me* driving fork-lift trucks into grain sacks the way those detestable boys did. *I* would certainly not become a nasty guard in the Stanford Prison Experiment. A young lady in distress, yelling to get a table off her, would assuredly find *me* quickly at her side. On my honour as a Canadian criminologist, *I* would have done what was right … Or would I? … Or would you? And would the respondents in the survey above have really acted according to the norms they expressed in the first portion of the survey? It is probably more realistic to assume that people would act according to the *expectations* expressed in the second portion of the survey, rather than according to the *norms* expressed in the first part. In fact, some of the studies reviewed above suggest even poorer performance on the part of most people. Surely, we were surprised at how many people were willing to give severe shocks on the instruction of the experimenter. It is surprising that, under certain conditions, people did nasty things or failed to do the "right" things. However, the Barth, Watson, and Blanchard study suggests that *when people are friends, they are more likely to follow the norms.*

It appears that friends communicate more accurately with each other. Assuming that most of us respect the norms of society, is it important to have conditions where people form more genuine friendships? To what extent are groups of boys *really* friends? When they are unsure of themselves and less confident in the quality of their relationships, are they more inclined to respond to dares, to do something outrageous? One might argue that, when people are comfortable and secure in their relations with others, they may be freer to disagree, to express values that are consistent with their convictions. They may be under less pressure to portray themselves according to expectations they assume other people have. Is "pluralistic ignorance" reduced? That is, do we make fewer false assumptions among friends about others' expectations for us? At times those expectations, especially among male groups, could lead to conditions and situations that are criminogenic.

Students of criminology should be asking what makes people do the *right* thing as well as the wrong thing. Characteristics of the individual, including socialization, will not always provide adequate explanations of criminal behaviour. What the individual brings into a group situation can make a difference, but the group dynamics also matter.

Sorting out these factors is not easy. Why did some people help Jews escape from the Nazis during World War II (Fogelman and Wiener, 1985)? While some made deliberate decisions to rescue Jews, others got involved accidentally. One person reluctantly agreed to let his secretary's husband hide from the Nazis in his office. Having been drawn into the situation, he became more compassionate, eventually rescuing about 200 people. Some who helped were very religious, others were atheists, and surprisingly, a few were even anti-Semitic.

Understanding group dynamics can help us make better policy decisions regarding crime. Although the arguments about television raised in the last chapter have not been resolved, current media practices can influence group dynamics in a way that increases crime. There are ways to structure some of our activities, settings, and communities to increase the likelihood of prosocial behaviour in groups.

SUMMARY

1. Criminal behaviour is increased by *deindividuation* and anonymity and also by mutual excitation and circular reactions. Certain dynamic conditions can have unintended consequences.

2. When directed by those in authority, people sometimes do antisocial things.

3. Some settings, such as prisons, tend to cause otherwise normal people to behave in antisocial ways.

4. People are more likely to come to the aid of others when they are alone. The presence of others seems to inhibit prosocial behaviour. In addition, watching someone else acting in a prosocial way increases the likelihood of additional prosocial behaviour.

5. Attributing negative characteristics to someone increases the likelihood that such a person will be treated badly, such as being robbed. The *fundamental attribution error* is the tendency to attribute most behavior to internal factors. This leads to a failure to take other factors into account.

6. People who are friends are more likely to intervene when antisocial behaviour is witnessed than if they are strangers.

KEY TERMS

attribution theory   90

circular reaction   84

deindividuation   83

fundamental attribution error   91

impression of universality   84

interaction   83

mutual conversion   84

mutual excitation   84

retrospective view of the act   84

WEBLINKS

www.iir.com/nygc/

The National Youth Gang Center: provides comprehensive statistical and legislative information about American gang activity.

www.crime-prevention.org/english/main.html

National Crime Prevention Council of Canada: provides information on federal government crime-prevention projects.

SOCIAL INTERACTION: FAMILIES,FRIENDS, AND SCHOOLS

This chapter will:

- Summarize control theory and the importance of the "social bond."

- Note that social support theory broadens control theory and can also be combined with differential association.

- Extend the central idea of social control theory by looking at "turning points" over the life course.

- Contrast control and learning theories.

- Offer one explanation for lower crime rates among females.

- Consider how interaction among peers can give rise to criminal subcultures.

- Note how certain school strategies can utilize these ideas, especially if they can sort out the causal sequences.

TIES TO CONVENTIONAL SOCIETY: CONTROL AND SUPPORT THEORY

Criminology books organize ideas into compartments, even though the borderlines between explanatory arguments are fuzzy. This chapter focuses on theories that emphasize families, friends, and schools. Many of the recent feminist issues have expanded these theoretical discussions. Some of these, such as power-control theory, will be discussed in Chapter 11, on women's issues. More traditional orientations are discussed here.

Francis Cullen pulls many of these ideas together in "social support theory," which argues that emotional support (love, nurturance, the understanding ear) and also instrumental help (money, information, contacts for a job) have a meaningful impact on crime (Cullen, 1994; Cullen and Wright, 1997). Many of the elements of support theory have historical roots in **control theory**, in which the family plays a central role. The notion of "social control" arising out of social bonds that link young people to families and significant others

has been part of the thinking of many criminologists. To provide background, we will summarize the work of four American authors.

Walter Reckless: Containment Theory

Walter Reckless was an early contributor to "control theory" (Reckless, Dinitz, and Murray,
1956). His version was called "containment theory" and contributed insights into crime committed by relatively normal people. Reckless asks: What makes people conform? He suggests
that there is an inner control or containment system, as well as outer containment.

Inner containment focuses on components of the self: self-control, good self-concept,
high frustration tolerance, sense of responsibility, goal orientation, ability to find substitute
satisfactions, tension-reducing rationalizations, and other characteristics that have become
internalized.

Outer containment represents characteristics of the surrounding world that provide restraints:
a consistent moral front presented by family and others, institutional reinforcement of norms
and goals, a reasonable set of social expectations, effective supervision and discipline, opportunities for acceptance and identity, as well as safety valves for dealing with crises.

These containments act to restrain the tendency of juveniles to get into trouble because
of *internal pushes*, such as restlessness, hostility, anxiety, and the need for immediate gratification (Reckless, 1967: 469–83). There are also *external pressures* arising out of poverty,
unemployment, racial minority status, and limited opportunity. *External pulls* would include
delinquent companions, membership in deviant groups, and the mass media. To a large
extent, Reckless attempted to synthesize current knowledge in a comprehensible manner,
but his attempts to test these ideas have been criticized for a variety of reasons (Schrag,
1971: 84; Schwartz and Tangri, 1965).

Travis Hirschi: The Social Bond

Like other control theorists, Travis Hirschi does not ask "Why do they do it?" Instead, he
assumes that most people would commit crime if they dared, particularly children. Thus
Hirschi focuses on why people do *not* commit crime, what prevents them from becoming
lifelong criminals. An individual's *bond* to society, largely through the family, ties individuals to social groups. We are moral beings to the extent that we have internalized the
norms of society and have become sensitive to the needs of others. What others think is
important to us. On the other hand, if an individual does not care about the opinions of
others, is insensitive to them, he is free to deviate.

Hirschi also makes certain assumptions about society—for example, the members of
society are tied together by a common value system. Morality is self-evident. Having conflicting value systems within a society is contrary to Hirschi's assumptions. Being loyal to groups
that have different values would mean that a person could be tied into a group that is deviant,
but Hirschi rejects this view for the bulk of crime. In a stable society, *almost everyone* agrees
on what is improper behaviour, and those who are bound by the **social bond** to society will
be constrained from deviant behaviour.

The social bond consists of four major elements. *Attachment* refers to the ties of affection
and respect to people like parents, teachers, and friends. A strong bond with all three will be
a major deterrent to crime. Parents are the most important. If families are broken by divorce

or separation, the attachment can still remain strong and help children internalize the norms of society, and also have more respect for people in authority, such as teachers. Alienation from parents increases the likelihood that the children will also be alienated from others.

The second element of the social bond is *commitment*. To the extent that children are committed to the ideal requirements of childhood, they will be less likely to engage in delinquency. Spending time and energy on education, saving money, and other conventional activities increase one's stake in the conventional world. One avoids risk-taking behaviour and postpones drinking and other adult activities to avoid risking that stake.

Involvement in school, family, and recreational activities doesn't leave much time for delinquency. Idleness and boredom make one consider disapproved activities. Finally, *belief* in a shared moral worldview includes sensitivity to the rights of others and respect for the laws of the land.

Francis Cullen: Social Support Theory

Social support theory encompasses elements from the control theories. Cullen and Wright (1997) draw from a large body of research (for example, Pierce, Sarason, and Sarason, 1996) which shows that the delivery of social supports early in life contributes substantially to a child's healthy psychosocial development. Social supports also counter structural factors, discussed in the next chapter, that create strains toward deviance.

Social learning and modelling, which were discussed earlier, are also influenced by social supports. The impact of the models provided by parents and non-deviant adults, as well as attempts to control youth, are more effective within supportive relationships (Wright and Cullen, 1996). Sophisticated, experimental tests of these ideas are underway under the direction of Richard Tremblay at the Université de Montréal. Systematic attempts are made to help parents create supporting relationships starting when children are very young. Many, probably most, attempts to prevent delinquency have failed, but the work by Richard Tremblay and his colleagues, which will be discussed in Chapter 13, on violence, demonstrates some of the more promising attempts to apply criminological knowledge to the reduction of crime.

Terence Thornberry: Interactional Theory

Interactional theory challenges the unidirectional causal order that is inherent in many theories of crime (Thornberry, 1987). That is, factors are viewed as exerting a causal influence on delinquency, without taking into account that delinquency may, in fact, influence these very same factors. Arguing that human behaviour develops dynamically over time as people interact with one another and as the consequences of prior behaviour are felt, interactional theory posits that delinquent behaviour may also have reciprocal causal influences on such variables as attachment to parents and commitment to school (Thornberry et al., 1991). As a result, there is a potential for spiralling a person along an increasingly delinquent behavioural trajectory. Thus, delinquency is viewed as part of a larger causal network, affected by social factors but also affecting the development of those social factors over time.

Some scholars in Canada have combined variables from control theory and differential association. That might be seen as moving towards integration (Linden and Fillmore, 1981; Linden and Hackler, 1973), but what makes the work of Thornberry and his colleagues different is that it specifically calls attention to developmental issues and the reciprocal, or looping, effect of these interactions. Such interactions are complex, and one must ask if this complexity is worthwhile. Since this book is interested in the policy implications of criminological theories, how might interactional theory provide some guidelines? Delinquency contributes, in a very real sense, to its own causation. That is, it causes a deterioration in the attachment and commitment to family and school, which further erodes the restraints on delinquency. Thus, comprehensive, holistic treatment strategies are required, rather than the search for a single key variable (Thornberry et al., 1991). This means that effective interventions will be expensive and difficult to manage. On the other hand, successful intervention in one part of the system will have a ripple effect throughout the system, helping intervention efforts targeted at another factor. Family interventions that improve attachments to parents should also indirectly improve commitment to school, thereby making the efforts of teachers a little easier.

Another implication is that family interventions should start early, because the impact of parents on the behaviour of their children weakens as they become adolescents. In addition, schools must attempt to break the cycle of alienation from education early. Enjoying the classroom during the early years has an impact on other factors that are related to delinquency. By late adolescence, the focus should shift and aid in a smooth transition from school to meaningful work. If the early problems are left unattended, a behavioural trajectory is established, which increases the likelihood of adult crime. By the same token, if early problems are dealt with successfully, the same reciprocal quality of the system works to *decrease* crime.

TIES TO UNCONVENTIONAL SOCIETY: SUTHERLAND—DIFFERENTIAL ASSOCIATION

One of the most influential explanations of crime—**differential association**—was offered by Edwin Sutherland in 1939. In some respects Sutherland's explanation fits with learning theory, which was discussed in Chapter 5, on psychological perspectives, but it also provides a link between psychological and sociological thinking, which characterizes control theory. Sutherland revised his ideas in various editions of a popular criminology text, with a final version appearing in the 1947 edition. It has appeared in each revised edition since (Sutherland and Cressey, 1978). Most of the nine points in the theory can be summarized as follows:

Criminal behaviour is learned in interaction with others in intimate personal groups. A person becomes criminal because of an excess of pro-criminal definitions. Associations with different types of others will vary in: how often exposure takes place (frequency), how long each exposure lasts (duration), whether it takes place during the early, impressionable stage of life (priority), and how close the personal bond is with the message sender (intensity). Learning crime is like other learning. While crime is an expression of general needs and values, it is not explained by them since non-criminal behaviour is an expression of the same needs and values.

This argument cannot be summarized simply by saying that crime is caused by having bad companions. Rather, it leads us to study the ratio of messages for and against criminal behaviour being sent from associates. These messages do not necessarily have to come from individuals who are criminals, nor do all criminals always present criminal definitions to children and friends. For example, some gangsters have been known to present very prosocial messages to their children, even though different messages are sent to their criminal colleagues. Similarly, a non-criminal mother may say that it is all right to steal bread if her family is starving. This theory also differs from some of our previous arguments with regard to the impact of the mass media. Sutherland emphasized interaction in *intimate* personal groups. The mass media may make a person receptive to criminal behaviour, but the message has more weight when delivered by a friend. When the TV hero corrects problems around him by leaving a trail of blood and gore, it is not the same as having a loving father send a similar message.

When differential association was first proposed, it broadened explanations beyond the personal pathology arguments that dominated criminology in the 1930s. It explained why normal, sociable, gregarious, active males in slum areas could easily become criminals, while similar boys taking part in Boy Scout activities in middle-class neighbourhoods did not. Isolated individuals would also respond differently. These ideas helped to explain why certain minority groups, lower-class individuals, and males, in contrast to females, were more likely to become criminal. Sutherland also applied his ideas to white-collar crime. Those in positions of power, who interacted regularly, reinforcing messages about the appropriateness of certain activities that were, in reality, illegal, would be systematically engaged in corporate criminal behaviour (Sutherland, 1949).

There are problems with the theory, including the difficulty of measuring certain elements. For example, how does one *know* when there has been an excess of pro-criminal definitions? If one uses the commission of a crime as the indicator of such an excess, one commits the same tautological mistake we accused psychologists of making in the chapter on psychological perspectives (Chapter 5). Despite these problems, differential association has been one of the most influential attempts to explain crime.

Combining Differential Association with Control Theory: Eric Linden

One of the criticisms of control theory is that it assumes that all of us would be criminal if we were not restrained. It does not account for separate *motivations* to commit crime. This doesn't square with our knowledge of human interaction. Crime is not necessarily attractive to everyone. In addition, some people "go along with others," even though they have reservations. Rick Linden combines differential association with control theory to provide a more complete explanation (Linden, 1987; Linden and Hackler, 1973; Linden and Fillmore, 1981). For differential association, the *presence* of ties with others is crucial to provide definitions and messages that encourage crime. For control theorists, the emphasis is on the *lack* of ties with others which would restrain antisocial behaviour. Originally, Hirschi felt those who had ties with peers, even deviant ones, would be less delinquent than those with no ties at all. Linden argues that the *direction* of the tie, conventional or unconventional, is also important. Lack of ties with the conventional order not only frees the individual to deviate, it also increases the likelihood of association with deviant peers who define crime as desirable and provides a source of definitions favouring crime. This extension of control theory explains more of the variation in delinquency than can either of the parent theories alone (Linden and Fillmore, 1981; Linden and Hackler, 1973). The relationship among the interacting variables is shown in Figure 7.1

Gillis and Hagan (1990) note that the nature of the social bond may differ for delinquents. On self-report questionnaires, delinquents do not express the same willingness to be good samaritans as conventional juveniles. However, in crisis situations involving direct and instant intervention on behalf of family or friends, the delinquents expressed a greater willingness to intervene. It appears that the notion of delinquency as simply being produced by a lack of social ties does not adequately take into account the nature of the networks that link delinquents to others.

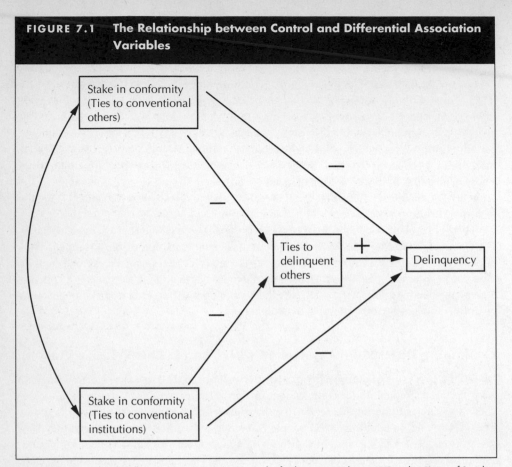

FIGURE 7.1   The Relationship between Control and Differential Association Variables

Source: Linden, R., and Cathy Fillmore (1981). "A Comparative Study of Delinquency Involvement." *Canadian Review of Sociology and Anthropology* 18: 343–61.

Turning Points through Life: John Laub and Robert Sampson

John Laub and Robert Sampson (1993) extend the central idea of social control theory, the social bond, to situations that vary over the life course. The first building block of their "sociogenic" developmental theory focuses on the mediating role of informal family and school social bonds. The second building block emphasizes the continuity that extends throughout adulthood across a variety of experiences. This may include incidents that involve crime, alcohol abuse, divorce, military experience, or unemployment. Although continuity of experiences influences social behaviour, salient life events and social ties in adulthood can counteract, to some extent, the trajectories of early child development. Thus a third and major thesis offered by Laub and Sampson is that social bonds in adulthood, especially attachment to the labour force and a cohesive marriage (or cohabitation), explain criminal behaviour regardless of prior differences in criminal propensity.

In other words, pathways to crime and conformity are not fixed in childhood, but are modified by key social control institutions in the transition to adulthood. Laub and Sampson blend continuity and change. Living is a dynamic process in which trajectories interlock and transitions generate **turning points** in the life course. The way individuals adapt to these events is crucial because the nature of the adaptation influences the next trajectory and can "redirect paths."

To test these ideas they reanalyzed an older data set of 500 delinquents and 500 control subjects matched on age, IQ, ethnicity, and neighbourhood deprivation (Sampson and Laub, 1993). These data included official records, observations, and personal interviews with subjects, parents, spouses, neighbours, and employers, and were gathered originally by Sheldon and Eleanor Glueck (1950). These findings are useful for policy-makers. Conditions that influence turning points later in adolescence or adulthood can modify future criminal behaviour. The ideas offered by Sampson and Laub fit nicely with anomie, or strain, theories which will be discussed in the next chapter.

Turning points can be dramatically influenced by opportunities that are available throughout the life cycle (Agnew, 1997a). In addition, the nature of these turning points may differ in childhood and adolescence. One study using New Zealand data indicated that childhood antisocial behaviour was related more strongly than adolescent antisocial behaviour to low verbal ability, hyperactivity, and negative/impulsive personality, whereas adolescent antisocial behaviour was related more strongly than childhood antisocial behaviour to peer delinquency (Bartusch et al., 1997). This suggests different strategies for younger children and for adolescents. The study further indicated that childhood antisocial behaviour was more strongly associated with convictions for violence, while adolescent antisocial behaviour was more strongly related to convictions for non-violent offences.

Gradual Drifts into Crime: Del Elliot, David Huizinga, and Scott Menard

University of Colorado researchers (Elliot and Menard, 1996; Menard and Huizinga, 1994) report gradual transitions from non-offending to minor offending and then to serious delinquency. Similarly, the sequence of events varies. However, for those who enter adolescence with conventional friends, there appears to be a dominant sequence: exposure to minor illegal behaviour comes first, followed by minor offending, exposure to more serious illegal behaviour by friends, more serious illegal behaviour, and finally involvement in highly criminal groups.

This approach is compatible with the "turning points" argument offered by Laub and Sampson. Not only do many individuals stop their delinquent involvement at some point, their turning points do not necessarily have to be dramatic events.

Extending Control Theory and Differential Association to Economic and Political Elites: John Hagan and Rick Linden

Social control theory is typically applied to lower-class adolescents, but John Hagan (1991: 100–3; 1985: 170–74) notes that economic and political elites often find themselves relatively free of the ties that restrain most of us from criminal behaviour. Some powerful individuals feel that they are above the law. They operate in areas in which the general public has difficulty assessing their "badness." Robbing a bank is clearly wrong, but when corporate leaders appoint each other to serve as directors on the company boards, and then vote themselves many privileges, it is harder to evaluate their wrong-doing. They have fewer ties to ordinary

people. The powerful rationalize their behaviour. Without being constrained by the disapproval of intimates who would be shocked at their actions, such individuals are psychologically free to pursue their interests without moral or legal constraint. Hagan uses the Watergate
affair in the United States as an illustration. After an unsuccessful break-in at the Democratic
National Headquarters in Washington's Watergate complex, it became clear that powerful
people were regularly committing crimes during the early 1970s. These events finally led to
the resignation of President Richard Nixon and the imprisonment of some of his aides.

Hagan asks a basic social control theory question: why aren't all upper-world citizens
criminal? One might answer that inner and outer restraints operate to keep most of them, to a
reasonable degree, in line. However, the inner restraints, such as morality, seemed to be lacking in the Watergate affair. The principal actors were not ashamed of their criminal behaviour. Thus, only outer restraints, the risks imposed by other institutions and their representatives,
needed to be assessed. Since these external control mechanisms also seemed to be weak, violating public trust became more likely as the main actors perceived clear rewards and low risk.

In his reading of the transcripts of the case, Hagan notes that there were few references
to societal values, to those internal constraints that arise from an uneasy conscience. Instead,
there were discussions of the rights and obligations of the executive branch and the limits
of executive privilege. In addition, the criminals in this case were also the people who
controlled the institutions of social control. It is ironic, however, that the criminals of
Watergate had a high stake in conformity. Control theory argues that people calculate the
costs of breaking the rules, but it appears that Richard Nixon miscalculated those costs over
and over again. The price paid by the criminals in the Watergate affair was clearly much
greater than they had anticipated.

One could argue that the way Linden combines differential association with control
theory offers an even better explanation of the Watergate affair and upper-world crime than
the use of control theory alone, as suggested by Hagan. Powerful members of the economic
and political elite *learn their behaviour in interaction with others and provide consistent
definitions which favour "bending" certain rules*. When Hagan reviews white-collar and
corporate crime in Canada (1987), he does not explicitly use the social control model he
has offered elsewhere, nor does he consider the combined model suggested by Linden and
Fillmore; but the conditions Hagan describes in his chapter on white-collar and corporate
crime appear to fit the combined theory suggested by Linden and Fillmore, summarized
above. If Edwin Sutherland were alive today, he would approve of this use of differential
association, since he clearly saw adequate explanations of crime as part of broader theories
of behaviour. Linden and Hagan have carried on this tradition.

Contrasting Control and Learning Theories

Theories call attention to different factors and sometimes suggest social action. This point
is illustrated by contrasting social control and learning theories, which underscore modelling. While learning theories emphasize what the role models *do*, control theory emphasizes
the *nature and quality* of the social bond. Let us consider tobacco use—the most dangerous drug, as far as health is concerned, currently being used in North America. Our discussion of drugs will be postponed until later, but we can all agree it would be desirable that
young people grow up as non-smokers. The question is: which is more important, the close-
ness of the bonds that parents establish with their children or the role model they present?

According to control theory, parents who smoke, but who also have close ties with their children, should be able to inhibit drug use on the part of their offspring. Many of us are aware of children who nag their parents extensively about their smoking, sometimes because of the close ties of affection. The parents agree that their behaviour is unwise, convey the message that the children are correct to oppose it, but plead human frailty. The message and the social bond can be more important than the role model.

Learning theory would make a different argument. Close ties with drug-using parents might not inhibit juvenile drug use. Modelling may be more important. The desire to imitate parents may make juveniles decide that smoking is the proper thing to do. In fact, close ties with the parent may increase the likelihood of imitation.

Clearly, a combination of a good role model and close parental ties would be preferred, but in a complex social world it may be important to ask which variable is more important—the social bond or modelling behaviour. In addition, we may also wish to condition young people to respond to drug users, such as smokers, in a tolerant way.

Family Factors and the Low Rate of Female Criminality

Questioning the Traditional Female Stereotypes: Ngaire Naffine

In his well-known work on control theory, Hirschi (1969) excluded females from his analysis, even though he had collected data from them. Since women have higher levels of conformity than men, they are seen as having stronger attachments to the conventional world. In addition, they experience higher levels of parental supervision than boys. Ngaire Naffine offers a different view of female criminality (1987). She is critical of the view that females are passive, compliant, and dependent, and thereby bonded to the conventional order. Nor does she share the view that "liberated" females become more criminal. Law-abiding women are not helpless and insipid, clinging to conventional society. Rather, they are responsible, hard-working, and immersed in conventional activities. They are rational in their decision not to place the gains achieved by the feminist movement in jeopardy by committing crimes. Being involved in both work and childrearing, modern women already have more powerful attachments to conventional society. Thus, Naffine would argue that increases in female crime, if there are any, should be seen as a response to the increased economic marginalization of women, rather than as a result of liberation from traditional female roles.

This argument would fit with the preceding discussion if we assume that economic marginalization leads to less social support, fewer social bonds, and also more turning points that lead to a crisis. Central to this issue is whether or not women face more economic marginalization or, by contrast, greater opportunities.

INTERACTION AMONG PEERS

So far, theories have been reviewed that link individuals to society. However, peer groups can create **subcultures** of their own, which may develop norms contrary to the dominant society. These subcultures may then influence behaviour and also the ties with others. But how do subcultures evolve?

Albert K. Cohen: The Subculture of the Gang

When Albert K. Cohen presented his influential ideas about the "subculture of the gang" (1955), few efforts had been made to link group dynamics and social ties. Cohen argued that the middle class establishes certain standards for behaviour in school, a "middle-class measuring rod." This includes an emphasis on having good appearances, selling oneself, restraining aggression, being sophisticated, displaying respect for authority, and deferring gratification. Until recently, theories ignored female delinquency on the assumption that juvenile crime was primarily a male problem and that girls did not face the same type of problems. The proper middle-class boy works hard at his paper route, saves money to go to college, and so on. Adherence to these standards makes one popular with teachers and leads to success in school.

Lower-class children may not be socialized in the same way. They are told to stick up for their rights, not to let others push them around. Adult role models from the lower classes also provide a different set of norms. Winning a few hundred dollars at bingo may lead to buying drinks for all your friends at the pub, displaying generosity rather than putting money away for a rainy day. These lower-class standards of behaviour may serve to integrate one into male peer groups, which probably have chauvinistic attitudes towards females and a somewhat devil-may-care outlook towards life, but such a worldview rarely makes boys popular with their more strait-laced, middle-class teachers. These boys do not do well against the middle-class measuring rod and achieve relatively little status in the classroom.

Reaction Formation and Mutual Conversion

What can the young male do when things are going poorly in school? One possibility is to change—adopt behaviour consistent with the middle-class measuring rod. This is not easy. The teacher may not even recognize such efforts. There may be little support from home, in terms of facilities, such as encyclopedias, quiet rooms for study, or in attitudinal support from parents. A second possibility is to withdraw and become isolated. A third option is to alter one's immediate social world. This might be achieved through **reaction formation**, a psychological mechanism for redefining standards from those that cannot be achieved to standards that are achievable. The middle-class norm is to defer to authority. This can be changed to: don't let people push you around. The middle-class student is polite to the teacher. This can be changed to: don't suck up to the teacher. The middle-class student dresses in a presentable way: the gang wears jeans at half-mast, unique hairdos, and leather jackets ripe with many months of sweaty wear in hot weather. And so it goes. The middle-class rules have been reversed, turned upside down. These new norms are now achievable for those who failed in the past.

However, reaction formation does not come into existence spontaneously. It evolves through collective action brought about by **mutual conversion**. It is a gradual process. Imagine that a boy who has done poorly in school is on his way home to the wrong side of the tracks. He is walking with another boy who also finds school unattractive. "How did you like school today?" asks the first. The second responds cautiously, "How did you like it?" "Not much," says the first. "Neither did I."

Each boy tests the waters carefully. "How did you like the teacher?" … "Not much" … "She isn't always fair" … "I think she stinks" … Each boy sticks his neck out a little further. They respond as most of us do, cautiously sending out signals when we are not sure of the feelings of others. Gradually, however, the boys find that they have similar ideas. Or they mutually convert each other towards norms that are contrary to the middle-class measuring rod. It is also possible that the final convergence is more extreme than the views held by the individual boys.

Certain individuals can also be defined in new ways. "What do you think about the little girl who sits up front and wears pink ribbons?" "You mean the one who brings an apple for the teacher?" "Yeah, the one whose father is a professor." (The first boy asks himself: Could the other boy like this little girl? I'd better be careful.) "She always does her assignments." "I think she's the teacher's pet." (OK, he doesn't like her either.) "I think she's a kiss-ass." "She's really stuck on herself." Notice that the boys do not offer firm opinions at first, but lead up to them. Again, the final conclusion may be more extreme than the original opinions held by either. Cohen argues that when this process goes on among a number of boys who are losing out in the conventional school system, they can create a delinquent subculture and a gang with values contrary to those of the dominant society.

Once the subculture is established, the new norms make the action of the gang very visible. Their toughness is advertised. Fighting is a way of gaining status. Having a "rep" and "heart" provides prestige within the gang. As the gang members increase their solidarity and loyalty to one another, they become more isolated from the conforming society. In control theory terms, the bonds with conventional institutions, such as school, and possibly family, become weakened. In differential association terms, their interaction with deviant peers provides many definitions favourable to violating the law. Even pluralistic ignorance, as discussed earlier, adds to the criminal norms. Each youth may *assume* that others hold more criminal norms than he does. Thus, more extreme members of the gang may be perceived as expressing universal standards.

Some Implications of Criminal Subcultures

As losers in the dominant system turn to the deviant subculture for support, status can only come from the gang. Cohen warns us that this phenomenon can occur when societies go through certain crises. Hitler rose to power with the Nazi party, which gave young males who were unemployed and unsuccessful a chance to define themselves as superior. Today, similar pressures appear to be operating, particularly in the former East Germany. Since reunification, crime rates have been rising in East Germany. Immigrants of a different skin colour have been attacked. The racist young males in East Germany today may be responding to factors similar to those facing German youth more than half a century earlier. Under communism there was pressure to belong to socially approved groups. Young people belonged to the Young Pioneers. There was full employment. Now many are unemployed. They might be seen as "losers." Joining others in the same situation allows them to redefine the world. The outside world is wrong. The deviant subculture they have joined becomes more extreme. Some religious cults become ostracized by others and turn inward to their own group. They become more alienated from the larger society. Unsuccessful young men may interact more with others who are out of step with dominant social norms. The negative opinion of conventional members of society becomes less important to them.

Imagine the plight of young males growing up in refugee camps in the Middle East. With few educational and employment opportunities, would a holy war be attractive? Being a suicide bomber or flying an airplane into a building to kill perceived enemies may have more appeal for those who have not been well integrated into society.

As long as societies can provide opportunities for the vast majority of their young people to succeed in conventional society, these gangs may recruit relatively few members; but in pre–World War II Germany, the high unemployment rate provided potential members for Nazi organizations. Similar conditions exist today and may encourage the creation of subcultures with fanatical views. Cohen's ideas should be reconsidered for the current period. The link between failing in school and/or the workplace and criminal subcultures and extreme political parties should not be forgotten.

SCHOOL ATTACHMENTS: WHO NEEDS THEM THE MOST?

Learning who benefits the most from a successful academic experience may be useful, but the growing evidence that school programs can make a difference argues for reasonably comprehensive efforts to change social behaviour in the early grades.

The Johns Hopkins Research Center targeted specific antecedents that have been shown to predict later problem behaviours (Dolan et al., 1993; Kellam et al., 1994). The Good Behaviour Game focused on reducing aggressive and shy behaviours, which are predictors of later antisocial behaviour and heavy drug use. Children were placed in teams, and good behaviour was rewarded at the team level. The Mastery Learning intervention consisted of an extensive and systematically applied enrichment of reading materials. It emphasized reading achievement that would reduce psychiatric symptoms such as depression.

Not only are programs that teach social behaviour worthwhile, but reading enhancement pays off directly in reducing psychiatric symptoms, such as depression, as well as providing skills that change opportunities. After four years, first graders who took part in the Good Behaviour Game were more successful at adapting to their new school and the demands of social tasks than those who did not participate. Those who took part in the Mastery Learning program read better but showed no significant change in terms of aggressive behaviour, suggesting that the programs had independent effects. However, improved reading did reduce depression. Male low achievers benefited more than high achievers. For females the opposite was true, since high achievers benefited more than low achievers.

Psychologists have demonstrated modest success in many types of school experiments (Tremblay and Craig, 1995), and these successes reinforce factors central to control theory. Sociologists such as Allen Liska and Mark Reed (1985) call attention to the *reciprocal* impact of many of these relationships—that is, not only does reading ability influence depression, but depression in turn influences reading ability. One factor influences a variable, which, in turn, has a counter-influence, either directly or indirectly. For example, attachment to school affects delinquency, but delinquency, in turn, influences school attachment. Figure 7.2 suggests that parental attachment affects delinquency, which affects school attachment, which, in turn, affects parental attachment. In other words, the bonds with parents reduce delinquency but influence school attachment less. In fact, being delinquent is more inclined to reduce attachment to school than the reverse. Being delinquent could threaten relations with parents as well, but Liska and Reed suggest that attachment between parents and their children is less conditional on behaviour. Even when juveniles act badly, parents still support them. By contrast, the link that ties teachers to their students is more dependent on behaviour. The social bond in the other direction, from student to teacher, may be overrated, at least for white boys. The notion that students control their delinquency in order to curry the good opinion of teachers is questioned. Perhaps bonding with their teachers is more relevant for younger students, but for adolescents, the good opinion of teachers is less important than that of their parents.

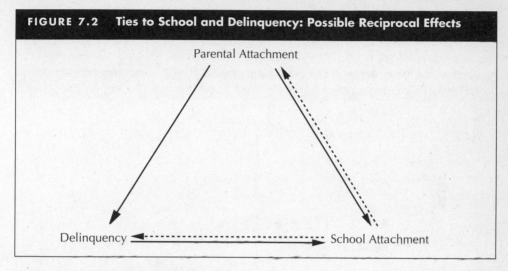

FIGURE 7.2   Ties to School and Delinquency: Possible Reciprocal Effects

Parental Attachment

Delinquency   School Attachment

This pattern may be appropriate for white, male youths but not for black, male youths. The arrow from School Attachment to Delinquency appears to be stronger for black, male youths.

Source: Based on material in Liska, Allen E. and Mark D. Reed (1985). "Ties to Conventional Institutions and Delinquency: Estimating Reciprocal Effects." *American Sociological Review* 50: 547–60.

For black students, however, Liska and Reed found a strong effect of school attachment on delinquency. Is it possible that school is the only link to conventional institutions that is available to many black youths? If so, black youths who aspire to college and decent jobs may place more importance on relationships with teachers; avoiding crime might also be part of their thinking.

Would these ideas have merit in Canada? Do minorities see the school system as offering opportunity? Families from Hong Kong view success in the schools as an important step towards success in the larger society. It is less clear how the Native peoples of Canada or black youths in Halifax and Dartmouth view our school system.

The causal structure of psychosociological forces is much more complex than the simple models that have been offered by most social control and related theories, but policy implications are evident. Liska and Reed suggest that making schools attractive to marginal youth may also deter delinquency. These ideas are not original, but they are frequently put aside while more politically expedient ideas prevail. For example, punishing parents of delinquent children is a popular theme expressed by many indignant citizens from time to time. However, there is little evidence that parents who are struggling with problems of their own benefit from further harassment. While most of the theories offered here are crude, they offer guidelines superior to the sort of comments frequently offered by politicians in the press.

A Developmental Theory of Delinquency

Many of the recent theories on crime are explicitly stated in causal sequences. While this makes it more difficult to test some of these theories, there are clear advantages to clarifying time sequences. If one is hoping to launch a delinquency prevention program, it helps to know if one's efforts are directed towards conditions that *precede* potential delinquency. The Opportunities for Youth (OFY) Project in Seattle, which was supported by the Ford Foundation, the Boeing Corporation, and some U.S. federal agencies, produced a theory to guide the strategy of a delinquency prevention program (Hackler, 1978: Ch. 3). The theory came from my PhD dissertation (Hackler, 1970). Figure 7.3 spells out the sequence.

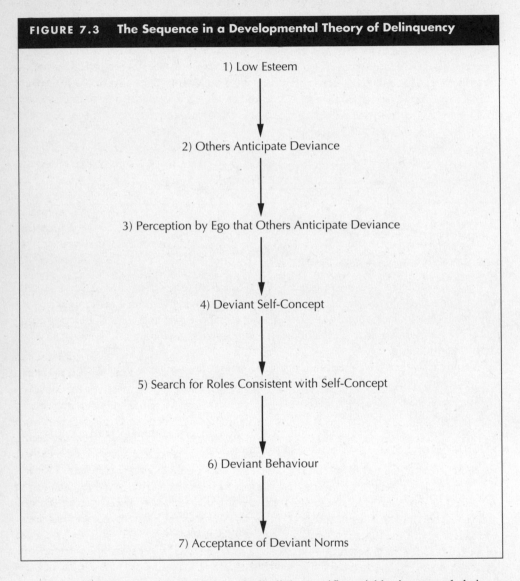

FIGURE 7.3   The Sequence in a Developmental Theory of Delinquency

1) Low Esteem

2) Others Anticipate Deviance

3) Perception by Ego that Others Anticipate Deviance

4) Deviant Self-Concept

5) Search for Roles Consistent with Self-Concept

6) Deviant Behaviour

7) Acceptance of Deviant Norms

The developmental sequence systematically links specific variables in a causal chain, as follows: (1) having low esteem leads to (2) the anticipation on the part of others that ego will act badly or at least not be able to act properly; this leads to (3) ego's *perception* that others anticipate improper behaviour if (a) opportunities to play conforming roles are perceived as blocked by those in dominant positions, such as teachers, and if (b) ego views the self-rele-vant responses from primary and non-primary significant others as valid; this would lead to (4) the development of a delinquent self-concept, which leads to (5) the search for roles compat-ible with a delinquent self-concept; this leads to (6) delinquent behaviour and finally to (7) the selective endorsement of delinquent norms through dissonance-reducing mechanisms.

While these ideas are similar to many other sociological arguments, they treat the role of norms differently. Traditionally, we assume that people have certain norms and attitudes which guide behaviour. The above formulation argues that such norms and attitudes are the *product* rather than the *cause* of behaviour. That is, people get involved in activities and then justify that behaviour by rationalizing and by adopting new norms. Admittedly, the relationship between norms and behaviour is more likely to be of a reciprocal nature, as described by Liska and Reed above. However, if the dominant causal direction is for deviant norms to develop *after* actual deviance, it would have certain implications for intervention. With the above model, one would not attempt to change delinquency by changing the atti-tudes or norms of youth. To be effective, one should start at the *beginning* of the causal chain. It is difficult, however, to change the esteem of a boy or of his family (Step 1 in Figure 7.3). We assume that certain groups will be held in low esteem in certain communities, and that changing that status would be far beyond most delinquency-prevention programs. Step 2 is also difficult to alter. Teachers and others who are in contact with children frequently anticipate that children from "the wrong side of the tracks" will be more delinquent than those from higher-status families. Ideally, we would like to change teachers, police, and other representatives of societal institutions, so that they do not anticipate deviance from low-status groups, but in the Opportunities For Youth Project, we felt it was more realistic to focus on Step 3. Could we change the boys' *perception* that other people thought they were delinquency-prone? The experimental program focused on this particular variable. The main experimental techniques utilized (1) a procedure in which boys tested teaching machines in a structured setting, guaranteed to make them successful, and (2) a supervised work program that made success very likely.

The portion of the program using teaching machines asked the boys to evaluate the machines. Teachers sent a message that *assumed* the boys were capable. We wanted them to perceive that we anticipated competent behaviour. Similarly, the work experience conveyed the idea that the boys were good workers and that we naturally anticipated that they would succeed. In general, the program aspect of Opportunities For Youth was carried out success-fully, but did it have a measurable impact on delinquency? Four thousand computer tables, using 49 different criteria for success suggested that, as far as delinquency was concerned, we were irrelevant. Our project did not have an impact on delinquency (Hackler, 1966).

Nor could we determine accurately whether the various activities led to changes, as predicted by the theory. Despite the fact that the program activities appeared to be success-ful, the actual impact of the experiment on the boys was so negligible that it was not possi-ble to test any of the theoretical possibilities (Hackler, 1978: Ch. 3). What does one make of such a result? One possibility is that most of our programs have little impact on the lives of young people. Opportunities for jobs with real futures may have permitted a test of se ideas, but one day a week for a year did not make a great deal of difference.

However, the data gathered in the study were used for less direct tests of causal se (Hackler, 1970). The data analysis supported the causal theory somewhat, but was ularly convincing. In addition, Hagan (1973) points out that the patterns of re displayed were compatible with the proposed causal sequence, but that they were equally compatible if the anticipations of others, such as teachers, were *accurate* in their predictions of deviance. The causal model argues that various adults in the community, such as school teachers, *anticipate* deviance on the part of juveniles who come from low-status families. The assumption made in the OFY project was that boys from low-status families were really just like everyone else, and it was the *anticipation* of their deviance by their teachers, correctly perceived by other boys, who then developed deviant self-concepts, etc., which finally led them to delinquent behaviour. But as Hagan points out, if boys from the wrong side of the tracks were *in fact* more delinquent, and if teachers correctly predicted that delinquency, the data would appear the same as those predicted by the causal model. In other words, simply using a causal format for a theory of delinquency does not necessarily lead to clear tests that support or reject a theory. Of course, if a theorist simply states that certain variables are related, without stating a causal sequence, the tests become even weaker. An even wider variety of plausible explanations will be consistent with the same set of findings. The OFY project illustrates that even well-conceived research projects do not always yield clear results.

Causal Theories and Implications for Policy

This proposed causal, or developmental, theory of delinquency, like the other theoretical ideas discussed here, is not offered as a particularly adequate explanation of deviance. Causal theories may suffer from a variety of weaknesses, but they provide more opportunities for rigorous testing, modification, and rejection. If they are supported, they give clearer indications to policy-makers. They show what might happen if certain changes are made. For example, if the causal theory of delinquency had received more support, teaching machines and supervised work might be promising delinquency-prevention tools. Actually, the project produced mixed findings (Hackler and Hagan, 1975).

Another policy implication implicit in the causal model is expressed by the sequence of Steps 6 and 7 in Figure 7.3. The claim is that deviant attitudes and norms will *follow* deviant behaviour. In other words, boys become deviant not because of the attitudes they hold, but because they are striving to play a coveted role. After engaging in deviant acts, boys will justify their behaviour by endorsing deviant norms, thereby reducing dissonance which would result from discrepancies between behaviour and the attitudes they hold (Festinger, 1957). For example, when a well-socialized Mormon is offered a drink, he usually refuses because this behaviour would be incompatible with deeply held norms. However, if the Mormon finds himself in a situation where the social pressures lead to drinking, he faces a dilemma: his behaviour and his norms are at odds. If the pressure to continue drinking persists, it is quite possible that the Mormon will begin to rationalize and finally come to believe that drinking is not so bad after all.

What does this discussion have to do with crime- and delinquency-prevention programs? Many programs assume that if they can just change boys' attitudes, their behaviour will change. If, in fact, the sequence goes from behaviour to attitudes, instead of from attitudes to behaviour, then such programs would be similar to bolting the barn door after the horse has run away.

The Difficulty of Applying Theories of Social Interaction

Why have criminologists been unable to produce scientific theories that lead to effective crime-prevention programs? So far I have reviewed models that concentrate on individuals, families, and small groups. These ideas neglect the structure of society itself. The individual and the family are only part of the crime picture. Thus, tinkering primarily with individuals, as Correctional Services Canada does, will not lead to effective anti-crime programs. Focusing on many of the factors mentioned in the last three chapters may have some impact, but unless changes are made in the structure of the larger society as well, the potential for crime reduction will be limited.

SUMMARY

1. Most of us are tied to conventional society by various "social bonds." Delivering social support early in life helps prevent crime.

2. Differential association is also compatible with control theory. These ideas can be applied at various "turning points" in life and influence the direction in which a young person might go.

3. Control theories emphasize the social ties to family members and others rather than the message that is being delivered. Learning theories emphasize the message. Modelling good behaviour is particularly important. Obviously, strong ties *and* providing good models and messages would be best, but which factors are most important is still being debated.

4. One explanation of lower crime rates among females is that they are more strongly attached to conventional society.

5. Criminal subcultures are more likely to arise if young males have few opportunities for legitimate success.

6. Attachments to school may be more important to minority students. Close attention to the sequential or causal order of factors would probably lead to better explanations of crime.

KEY TERMS

control theory 97	social bond 98
differential association 100	social support theory 99
mutual conversion 106	subcultures 105
reaction formation 106	turning points 103

WEBLINKS

www.crcvc.ca/
Canadian Resource Centre for Victims of Crime: a national, non-profit victims' rights advocacy group.

www.canada.justice.gc.ca/en/ps/voc/index.html
The Policy Centre for Victims' Issues: a Department of Justice site providing information on federal government initiatives concerning crime victims.

www.hc-sc.gc.ca/hppb/familyviolence/index.html
National Clearinghouse on Family Violence: a Federal Department of Health site providing links to international, national, and provincial information.

FOCUSING ON THE STRUCTURE OF THE SOCIETY: THE CONSENSUS TRADITION[1]

This chapter will:

- Review the structural-functional perspective and apply it to several situations.
- Argue that crime is more frequent when social cohesion is weakest and when anomie or normlessness exists.
- Show how Merton modified the idea of anomie to emphasize the gap between goals and the means to achieve those goals.
- Note that communities and situations offer different types of opportunities, including criminal ones.
- Raise the question of whether marginal opportunity structures are better than none at all.
- Point out that complex societies may have multiple goals and only deviance can make it possible to meet most of them.
- Assess these traditional theories and look at their policy implications.

SOCIAL STRUCTURE AND CRIME

Previous chapters focused on individuals in a variety of small-group settings. It is not possible to develop a complete explanation of crime by looking at a single level of abstraction, that is, by focusing on individuals or on small groups. Nor is it possible to explain crime by looking only at the characteristics of societies. However, for those interested in social policy, theories that deal with the structure of society provide particularly useful suggestions for reducing crime.

Theories that integrate psychological and sociological levels of thinking into an integrated theory will eventually be needed. At present, such attempts are still in their beginning stages, and therefore it is useful and more understandable to review explanations at a single level. Some important sociological traditions look at the structure of society. Before these

---

[1]This chapter is based in part on Hackler (2000).

characteristics of society can be translated into crime at the individual level, several links are needed. Thus, theories of crime that focus on the structure of society are inevitably somewhat crude. On the other hand, policy-makers may find this level appropriate for introducing change. When attempting to reduce crime, it is unrealistic to talk about cures. Rather, we should be asking if we can achieve a modest reduction in crime. Changes at the social level, then, may be practical even though they are difficult to control.

THE CONFLICT-CONSENSUS DEBATE

It is convenient to think of two major orientations toward explaining crime. The older tradition can be viewed as the **consensus** perspective. This approach assumes that the vast majority of the population holds similar views regarding right and wrong. Morality is universal, with values being shared by all members of the society. Customs persist, and the laws represent a codification of societal values. This perspective assumes that criminals are those who go through the criminal justice process and are convicted. Thus, adjudicated offenders represent the closest possible approximation to those who have, in fact, violated the law. They are the people whose behaviour needs explaining. Although most citizens acknowledge that powerful, upper-class lawbreakers are less likely to be arrested, tried, and convicted than lower-class offenders, a traditional perspective would agree that those who have been convicted of crimes are more criminal than those who have not been convicted.

The *conflict* perspective on what is crime and who is the criminal questions such assumptions, and argues that criminal law may be regarded as part of a body of rules that prohibit specific forms of conduct and indicate punishment for violations. The character of these rules, the kind of conduct they prohibit, the nature of the sanctions, and so forth, depend on the character and interests of those powerful groups in the population that influence legislation. In other words, the set of rules that represents criminal law does not necessarily represent the moral values of the majority, but will vary depending on which groups are in a position to create and enforce those laws. The social values that receive the protection of the criminal law are ultimately those that are treasured by the dominant interest groups. It is not the *majority*, but rather the most *powerful*, whose values and concerns will be represented in the justice system. Ronald Hinch has organized these conflict theories into categories (1994), and we expand on these ideas in Chapter 9. By contrast, this chapter reviews the more traditional consensus perspective.

THE CONSENSUS PERSPECTIVE: STRAIN THEORIES

Consensus theories assume a reasonable degree of agreement on things that matter in society. One assumes that large portions of the population share these views. Crime occurs when people are subjected to unusual influences. Those special, crime-producing influences come from strains, frustrations, or stresses generated by the way society is organized. The term **strain theories** has been used to describe these ideas since the 1970s, even though the ideas are much older. They emphasize adaptive processes that arise from barriers to success or the failure to achieve widely held expectations.

While it is convenient to separate our discussion into the consensus and conflict perspectives, the reader should be aware that this arbitrary classification oversimplifies reality. It may be more appropriate to think of particular crimes as being of the consensus or the conflict type. In most societies, there is a high level of agreement that robbing someone and doing bodily harm are crimes. Other activities, such as smoking marijuana and committing adultery, will lead to less agreement regarding the need for criminalization. Laws regarding homosexuality illustrate not only varying attitudes, but changes in attitudes and laws over time. Thus, elements of consensus and conflict are always present in modern societies.

Durkheim: The Functions of Crime and Anomie

In his book *Division of Labour in Society*, first published in France in 1893, Émile Durkheim argued that social solidarity—that is, social groups working together towards agreed-upon goals—was an essential characteristic of human societies (1933). In preliterate societies, social groups were isolated and self-sufficient. There was little division of labour outside of the family. All men had similar skills and all women did similar work. Such societies had *mechanical solidarity*.

Modern industrialized societies, by contrast, have a highly developed division of labour, with individuals specializing in unique tasks. Since individuals are dependent on others, group solidarity evolves because of this diversity. We need each other to satisfy our needs. This type of interdependence Durkheim called *organic solidarity*.

Crime was normal, even necessary, to define the boundaries of that which was acceptable, and for the creation of laws that would identify certain behaviour as criminal (1933). The process varied in different types of societies. In societies with mechanical solidarity, crime served several functions. Since everyone was so uniform, deviance was easy to spot and reaction against the offender strengthened social bonds. Crime is also functional in that it reminds members of a community about the interests and the values they share. Community bonds are strengthened. The deviant act inspires indignation. And, even more importantly, deviance reassures the "good" members of a community that their morality is the acceptable one. Since crime is functional, society encourages, or at least permits, a certain amount of deviance.

In addition, crime tested the social limits, making groups evaluate social norms. In complex societies, pushing the legal limits led to change. When Judge Emily Murphy pushed for legal rights for women, she was not content with laws as they were. The same could be said when Louis Riel led a revolution in Manitoba. Mahatma Gandhi and Martin Luther King Jr. clearly opposed the established authorities, and Jesus Christ was a deviant in his day.

There must be a balance between the functional and dysfunctional aspects of deviance. Excessive crime and deviance would destroy a society, but if there were none at all, society would be compelled to create some. Even in a society of saints, someone must push the limits of proper behaviour. For Durkheim, every society needs its quota of deviants.

The Dilemma of Diversity

If a society is made up of many different elements, social cohesion is more difficult to achieve. There will be less consensus on what is good, and a higher rate of crime. This simple explanation has been generally supported in many different situations. It also presents us with a dilemma. If we believe in a heterogeneous and diversified society in which people with different cultures, languages, and tastes can mix, there will be more problems of social cohesion and crime. Some of us are not happy with the implications of such explanations. We feel that diversity makes for interesting societies, leads to expanded ideas, and helps us to be tolerant. For example, the Canadian prejudices against the Chinese and the Japanese during the first 50 years of the twentieth century have gradually given way to tolerance, acceptance, and finally the appreciation of valuable cultural traits which enrich Canada. Similarly, adapting to both English and French cultures leads to stress, but it also generates mechanisms for dealing with diversity. There is a price, however. Diverse populations have more crime.

Anomie and Normlessness

Durkheim popularized the concept of **anomie** to explain crime in more advanced and differentiated urban societies. Heterogeneity and increased division of labour weakened traditional societal norms. The resultant changes loosened the social controls on people, allowing greater materialism and individualism. When social cohesion breaks down and social isolation is great, society loses its traditional social control mechanisms and crime increases. In his classic work on suicide, Durkheim argues that individualism leads to a lack social cohesiveness (1951). Suicide, crime, and general deviance are inhibited in cohesive communities. Of course, homogeneous, cohesive, and less individualistic communities may be less able to change and adapt.

Durkheim's theory may have merit, but I am not content with a theory that tells me that we have to be more homogeneous to reduce crime. Instead, I want a theory that tells me how to attain a diverse, multiracial, multilingual society which still has a reasonable degree of social cohesion and a reasonably low rate of crime. In other words, I want theories that provide policy guidance in directions that fit my values.

Merton: The Gap between Aspirations and Means

In the 1950s and '60s the most cited article in criminology was one by Robert K. Merton (1938), in which he discussed social structure and anomie. Crime was viewed as a symptom of the *dissociation*, or gap, between **culturally prescribed aspirations** and the **socially structured avenues** for realizing those aspirations. The culturally prescribed aspirations are the *goals* held up for all members of society. Merton argues that in America the accumulation of money, and the status that results from material wealth, is a universal goal. Socially structured avenues, such as schooling, are the accepted **institutionalized means** of reaching these goals. Socially structured avenues to achieve these universal goals are no problem for well-off members of the society. If a father is a medical doctor, it is more realistic for the son to aspire to the same occupation and social status. One attends schools that condition students towards thinking about a college education, and the home environment encourages reading and getting good grades. Although certain individual characteristics, such as minimal intelligence, may be required, the means to achieve culturally prescribed aspirations is available to many middle-class youths.

By contrast, the son of an immigrant family, or a member of a racial minority, could find things more difficult. If a father has abandoned the family, if an older brother has been in trouble with the law, and if a mother has been on welfare, the means to achieve success are not readily available. A youth coming from such an environment may not respect the school system, his grades may be poor, and his likelihood of entering college could be minimal. However, he might also like to be a doctor and have both the material and social rewards that accrue to that occupation.

The gap between goals and means is small for certain portions of the society but large for others. The strain resulting from the gap between goals and the means to achieve those goals could result in "innovation," often criminal in nature. In simpler terms, when society encourages people to want things, but makes it difficult for certain groups to get them, those groups are more likely to steal, sell drugs, cheat on their taxes, or go into prostitution.

Merton's argument seems to fit many forms of lower-class crime particularly among marginally employed people. Robert Crutchfield (1995) points out that the lack of work influences crime. In addition, if these marginally employed people reside in concentrations of similarly underemployed people, the propensity to engage in crime is greater. This description fits certain ethnic groups in the U.S. and Canada. The argument may also fit certain upper-class crimes in which people aspire to great wealth. The legitimate avenues to success may not be sufficient because of severe competition; other businesspeople may be "cutting corners" in a variety of ways. Thus, if there is a gap between the desired goals and the means, innovation or illegitimate tactics are more likely.

Institutional-Anomie Theory: Messner and Rosenfeld

Steven Messner and Richard Rosenfeld (1997a, 1997b) extend this argument. American culture emphasizes monetary success, but in addition there is a weak emphasis on the importance of legitimate means for the pursuit of that success. This combination of strong pressures to succeed monetarily and *weak restraints on the means* is intrinsic to the "American Dream." It contributes to crime directly by encouraging people to use illegal means to achieve culturally approved goals, especially monetary goals. It also exerts an indirect effect on crime through its links with and impact on the institutional structure, or "the institutional balance of power." One institution—the economy—dominates all others (Rosenfeld and Messner, 1997). Other important institutions—the family, schools, and the political system—are relegated to secondary roles. Although these other institutions traditionally curbed criminogenic tendencies and imposed controls over the conduct of individuals, economic factors overwhelm those institutions which socialize people into prosocial behaviour. In other nations, such as Japan and India, the family appears to rank higher on the hierarchy of institutions and to be more influential vis-à-vis economics. Thus, North America produces higher levels of serious crime than those countries where the institutional balance of power leans toward non-economic institutions.

The recent targeting of the economic sector and the application of anomie theory has led several scholars to offer new insights into upper-class and corporate crime (Cohen, 1995; Vaughn, 1997). Summarizing this work is difficult, so I will concentrate on simpler discussions of anomie theory. In addition, I am less concerned with fairness to Merton's original ideas than with the utility of various interpretations and the extension of these influential ideas.

Opportunity Structures and Their Influence on Crime

Durkheim argued that human aspirations had to be regulated and channelled. Since human aspirations are boundless, and people cannot always have what they want, they must be persuaded to accept what they receive. When people are not persuaded, society becomes anomic, and moral guidelines are unclear. Social control breaks down and some people violate the norms of those in power.

While Durkheim emphasized the restraints that control crime, Merton focuses on opportunity structures. He begins his argument similarly to Durkheim's and suggests that American society has an overriding dominant goal, material success, but that guidelines for achieving that success are not always clear. If this type of anomie is so widespread, however, why isn't crime distributed evenly throughout society? Merton accepts the argument that crime is distributed unevenly, that it is higher in the urban slums, for instance. To explain this social-class-specific crime by anomie, he redefines anomie as the disjuncture between the cultural goal of success and the opportunity structures by which this goal might be achieved (Box, 1971: 103–6). This is another way of explaining the gap between culturally prescribed aspirations and socially structured avenues, as described above. Anomie was shifted from normlessness, according to Durkheim, to *relative deprivation*. Instead of viewing an entire community as anomic, specific individuals felt deprived: committed to the goal of wealth, but barred from the means that would lead to the realization of this goal.

Interpreting Merton

A frequent application of Merton's work has been to explain delinquency. Many scholars have worked to translate these ideas into measures that could be tested empirically. Debates arose over what Merton meant. Were his ideas intended to explain the behaviour of individuals or, as Thomas Bernard would argue, the behaviour of aggregates or groups (1987a)? Bernard argues that it is not correct to interpret *strain* or *anomie* in psychological or social-psychological terms; instead, these are properties of social structures. Merton uses the word *anomia* as the sociological counterpart of the psychological concept *anomie*. According to Bernard, Merton's theory suggests that societies whose cultures overemphasize monetary success and underemphasize adherence to legitimate means will have high rates of instrumental (in contrast to irrational, impulsive) crime. If legitimate opportunities to achieve those monetary goals are unevenly distributed, then instrumental crime will be unevenly distributed.

One must note the distinction between *cultural* factors and *structural* factors in a society. In societies in which structural features create an uneven distribution of legitimate opportunities—that is, in which there are many blocked opportunities—there will be pockets of instrumental crime, regardless of cultural values. *Individuals* facing blocked opportunities are those who are more criminal. If, by contrast, the culture emphasizes the ruthless pursuit of wealth and everyone has equal opportunities, then crime will be widespread, and such a *society* will have a high rate of crime. Both elements could be operating, and one might argue that the United States is the best illustration of such a society today.

Perhaps Bernard is correct in his warning that Merton's ideas should be applied only at the societal level, but many of us find it useful to apply Merton's ideas to individuals. As one applies strain theory to individuals one can see a convergence with differential association and control theory. An attempt in this direction, using strain theory as a base, is offered by Robert Agnew (1992). Adolescents located in unpleasant environments, such as school, from which they cannot escape, are more likely to be delinquent. Although strain has usually been defined in the past in terms of blocked opportunities in education and jobs, Agnew reminds us that other negative experiences also lead to stress and hence a search for illegitimate alternatives. In addition, different types of strain are more relevant to different subgroups (1991, 1992). There is also empirical support for the interaction of strain variables and social-psychological ones, such as having delinquent friends (Agnew and White, 1992). Bonds with both delinquent and non-delinquent friends can lead to other stresses.

As more sophisticated measures of strain/anomie were developed, these ideas have been applied to different populations (Agnew et al., 1996). Recent empirical studies suggest that strain, or anomie, theory is more complex than the simplified versions presented here. We are learning more about the sources of individual strain and the macro-level determinants of such strain (Agnew, 1997b; Jensen, 1995).

Some Criticisms of the Concepts Used by Merton

Gwynne Nettler is critical of the clarity of Merton's concepts (1984). Is what people *say* they want out of life an adequate measure of their *aspirations*? When asked what we would like, it is easy for us to answer "money and status." But Nettler questions the uniformity of wants or values in society, at least in terms of acting on those wants. The serious offender may have a philosophy that is different from the majority, in terms of being cynical, hedonistic, hostile, and distrustful. According to Hy and Julia Schwendinger (1967), the philosophy of serious offenders might go something like this: "Do unto others as they would do unto you … only do it first," and "If I don't cop it … somebody else will" (98).

Nettler also feels that the concept of "opportunity" is vague. Is there a difference between *perceived* opportunities and *real* ones? "*Opportunities are by their nature much easier to see after they have passed than before they are grasped*" (1984: 209). If people do not end up equally happy and rich, is this due to differences in opportunity? We must avoid the tautology, or circular argument, of explaining the cause by using the outcome. Problems over the meaning of these concepts have led to considerable debate, as scholars have tried to develop operational definitions to test these ideas.

Merton's strain theory is also unhelpful in explaining lower crime rates for women. Merton takes into account differences in opportunity that arise out of social class, but does not apply the same reasoning to blocked opportunities based on gender (Comack, 1992). Women, like disadvantaged lower-class males, might be expected to be more criminal as a means to achieve universal goals. While many conventional theorists have assumed that women experience less strain than men in the struggle to achieve through institutionalized means, many feminist scholars reject these statements as assumptions and biases rather than facts (Morris, 1987; Naffine, 1987). While the strains women are subject to may differ from those experienced by men, they may be just as severe. Unless one assumes women have more modest goals, strain theory does not explain why women are less criminal.

Despite these arguments, or perhaps because of them, no theory of crime has engendered as much work by criminologists. For decades, sociologists found support for these ideas. Critics joined the debate during a later period. Recently there has been renewed interest in strain theory, but an analysis of the debate would be too complex for our purposes. Instead, let us summarize some original ideas by Sol Kobrin, who noted that communities differ in the availability of opportunities (1951).

Kobrin: Opportunity Structure in Different Communities

Although there may be strains that create a pressure towards criminal behaviour, there are also different opportunity structures that facilitate breaking the law. Some communities, or some situations, may not provide opportunities for crime even though individuals are discontented. In one of the seminal articles in criminology, Sol Kobrin (1951) argues that opportunities differ in various communities, which could be organized in the following typology suggested originally by Clarence Schrag in class.

Kobrin points out that we live in communities that sometimes offer a variety of opportunities, both legitimate and illegitimate. The means available to attain aspirations within these communities are, in actuality, not just present or absent; rather, they offer a range of possibilities. Table 8.1 simplifies those possibilities to make the theoretical point, and treats opportunities as simply available or not. If communities have legitimate opportunities and/or illegitimate opportunities, four types of communities are possible. No community actually fits the pure examples illustrated in the figure, but there are approximations.

Table 8.1	Typology of Community Opportunity Structures Implicit in Kobrin (1951)			
	Type I	**Type II**	**Type III**	**Type IV**
Type of Community	"Stable Slum"	"Transitory Slum"	"Suburbia"	"Unlikely"
Legitimate Opportunities	Present	Absent	Present	Absent
Illegitimate Opportunities	Present	Absent	Absent	Present

In Type I communities, there are illegitimate opportunities as well as legitimate ones. One might call this type of community a "stable slum," where prostitution, gambling, and a variety of other illegal activities are well organized. The organized criminal element may concentrate on certain activities and avoid, or even discourage, violence and other types of crime that would upset the community and the forces of control. In such stable, lower-class neighbourhoods, one would expect a number of legitimate opportunities that reflect the normal, ongoing activities of a city. These would include restaurants, stores, repair shops, and the like, and the normal economic activities that would arise to meet the needs of any urban society. In fact, well-organized illegitimate activities might provide the capital for legitimate economic enterprises. This typology oversimplifies reality. In actuality, there will be gradations in terms of opportunities, but it is useful to think in terms of ideal types.

The Type II community might be called a "transitory slum," as typified by a decaying housing project. In such a disorganized community, there is extensive unemployment. No business dares to establish a store in the neighbourhood, because of the fear of robbery. Newspaper carriers do not deliver in the area, because customers would lose their papers, the carriers might be attacked, and newspaper publishers would find it unprofitable. Restaurants are not established; thus, there are few opportunities for waiters, dishwashers, or cooks. In other words, it is an area with very few legitimate opportunities for earning money. Even the illegitimate opportunities are unprofitable, because the neighbourhood is poorly organized. Prostitutes find it dangerous to work there; those who wish to gamble go to the more stable slum areas. And although the residents may frequently attack each other, the pickings are slim: the people are poor. In these disorganized areas, crimes are more likely to be predatory and vicious. There is little community life and families are poorly integrated. Minimal opportunities exist in either the legitimate or illegitimate world.

The Type III community, "suburbia," has legitimate opportunities but no illegitimate opportunities. Teenagers can find work mowing lawns, especially if the neighbour knows that the teenager comes from a reliable family. Paper routes are available, and because of various contacts in the community, juveniles may learn of opportunities for summer work and other part-time jobs. The adult and adolescent worlds are involved in economic activities which create opportunities for work and the anticipation for future work. On the other hand, illegitimate opportunities are rare. If a person wanted to become a prostitute, she or he might have difficulties wandering about a suburban community, approaching customers.

Even if they went downtown to the appropriate streets, their middle-class background would leave them unskilled in this business, and the competition might make them unwelcome. Similarly, college students from middle-class homes may be unsuccessful selling an armful of stolen hubcaps door-to-door in suburbia. In other words, suburbia may be lacking in illegitimate opportunities.

What about the Type IV community? Although such a combination is theoretically possible, it is unlikely that any neighbourhood could develop a wide range of profitable illegitimate opportunities without also spawning some legitimate ones. If the illegitimate opportunities were well organized, we would expect restaurants, stores, laundries, and other facilities to develop, to provide those stable lower-class communities with normal services. If either organized crime or the citizenry had things fairly well under control, the community could become viable. Control mechanisms may differ in such neighbourhoods, but a community with well-organized illegitimate opportunities alone is very unlikely.

Kobrin (1951) emphasizes the *dual* characteristics of lower-class communities. Both legitimate and illegitimate opportunities exist together to a greater or lesser degree. How these two structures interact and what draws people to one versus another has generated considerable debate among sociologically oriented criminologists. Policy-makers must take community characteristics into account and be aware that a uniform strategy is unlikely to work, because of the different nature of communities.

Richard Cloward: Illegitimate Opportunity Structures

Just as there are differences between legitimate and illegitimate opportunities, there are different *kinds* of illegitimate opportunities. Francis Cullen points out the importance of "structuring variables" (1984: Ch. 3). Richard Cloward asserts that simply being subjected to socially generated strain does not enable a person to deviate in any way she chooses. People can only participate in a given adaptation if they have access to the means to do so (Cullen 1984: 40). Even though lower-class persons may be under a great deal of strain, they are less likely to engage in violations of financial trust, political corruption, and other white-collar crimes in order to achieve their goals. Such opportunities are simply not available.

In an article (1959), and then in a book with Lloyd Ohlin entitled *Delinquency and Opportunity* (1960), Richard Cloward extended Merton's ideas by combining them with themes found in Sutherland's "differential association." Sutherland argued that criminal behaviour is learned through associations with others who define criminal activity favourably. While Merton emphasized *legitimate* means, Sutherland called attention to the concept of *illegitimate* means (Cullen, 1988). People under strain cannot become any kind of criminal they choose; they are limited by the opportunities available to them. Dealing in drugs is not automatically available to a "square" college professor as a means of supplementing her income; she probably lacks the skills and contacts. In other words, illegitimate means are not readily available to anyone simply because they lack legitimate means. While Durkheim and Merton developed plausible theories of structurally induced pressures, they did not explain the resulting adaptive behaviour as Cloward tried to do.

Merton appreciated Cloward's insights and extension of his ideas. The editor of the *American Sociological Review* persuaded Merton to write a commentary on Cloward's 1959 manuscript, which appeared immediately after that article. Merton noted that earlier research indicated five times as many criminals convicted of fraud in Texas as in Massachusetts. Perhaps it was more difficult to sell someone a dry oil well in Massachusetts than in Texas. Illegal opportunities for certain types of fraud are clearly more available in some areas than others.

Opportunity theory fits many different types of deviance, but Cloward and Ohlin are best known for the application of these ideas to juvenile delinquency. Although undergoing "strain," juveniles face different barriers to resolving that strain. The way they respond to social barriers for achieving goals could lead to three different types of gangs or subcultures, namely, *criminal*, *conflict*, or *retreatist* gangs. Herbert Costner, in lectures at the University of Washington, used the diagram illustrated in Figure 8.1 to explain how these gangs are formed.

FIGURE 8.1   Barriers to Legal and Illegal Opportunities Implicit in the Work of Cloward and Ohlin (1960)

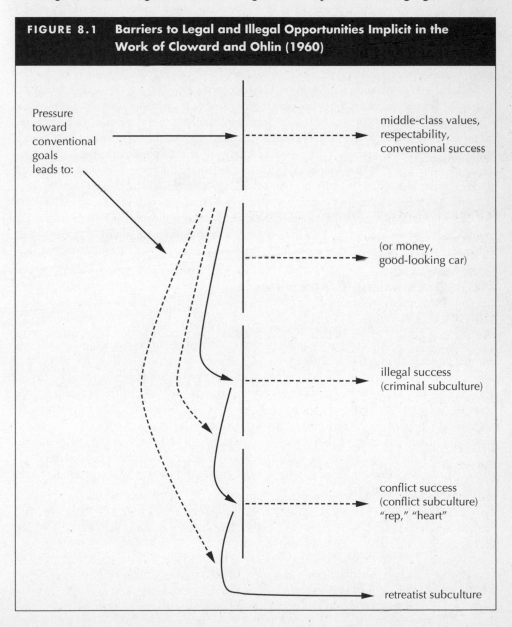

There are barriers to conventional goals and middle-class values, such as respectability and conventional success. If one overcomes those barriers, as most middle-class juveniles do, there is little crime. However, the lower-class male may actually have different goals. Instead of respectability, he may be more interested in money, a car, and, assuming he shares the chauvinistic views of many of his peers, having a "good-looking chick" on his arm. Under certain economic conditions, this might be achieved by working in areas in which his skills are scarce, working in a hazardous occupation, or possibly being fortunate as an athlete. In other words, it is possible to be successful in a working-class style of life. These ideas differ somewhat from Merton's in that aspirations are not *universal* as Merton had argued. Striving for success can mean different things to different people.

Cloward, however, emphasizes the barriers to lower-class goals as well as to middle-class goals. Even if certain working-class people aspire to different things, the means to achieve them, even working at unskilled jobs, are not necessarily available. But crime has an opportunity structure of its own. If legitimate opportunities are blocked, the next step may be to search for illegal success, but even here there are barriers. Without contacts with certain subgroups, it may be difficult to get into illegal gambling or learn the skills of a successful safecracker. Many juveniles will have difficulty learning the skills necessary to succeed. However, if there are barriers to profitable property crime, juveniles can still turn to a conflict subculture as a means of attaining status, at least among their peers. Juveniles unskilled as thieves can show their bravery by fighting for their "turf." This demonstrates "heart," and their courageous behaviour will give them a "rep." But even conflict success has barriers. Not every juvenile is keen on wielding a bicycle chain in a gang war. One may lack strength or courage or both. These juveniles may employ a third delinquent alternative: the use of drugs. In the drug or "retreatist" subculture, there are practically no barriers.

Marginal Opportunity Structures

Francis Cullen (1988) feels that many scholars have not fully appreciated the extensions made by Cloward, because they focused on the gap between aspirations and perceived opportunity. In fact, other deviant adaptations become apparent when one looks beyond traditional types of crime and at different settings. Fred Desroches describes the way some men adapt to pressures related to homosexual activity in public restrooms in Ontario (1991). The "tearooms," those public toilets where homosexual activity takes place, provide an opportunity structure for those under certain types of strain. Desroches does not attempt to explain why these men engage in the activity, but he adds Canadian content to ideas put forward by Laud Humphreys (1970a, 1970b). Whatever it is that drives men to the public restroom for homosexual activities, alternatives do not seem to fill the need; thus, this marginal opportunity structure is used, with the risk that police action will create additional problems in their lives.

Street life offers another type of marginal or illegitimate opportunity structure (Hagan and McCarthy, 1997a, 1997b). Youth in families that are functioning well do better in school as well as in finding work. Negative family experiences increase the likelihood of "hanging out" on the street. The interaction among parental unemployment, weakened marital ties, neglect, and abuse increases the likelihood of crime directly, but it also exposes such youth to additional new stresses when they leave one negative environment for another. Seeking food and shelter on the street, these vulnerable youths meet seasoned offenders, who coach the newcomers in criminal activities. The police will also view them as criminally inclined.

Street life increases exposure to networks of seasoned offenders, who offer tutelage in offending and a means of acquiring "criminal capital," that is, information (e.g., where to sell stolen goods) and skills (e.g., how to use burglary tools). Physical and sexual abuse have conditioned them to respond to police confrontations with defiance and rage. Hagan and McCarthy show how employment, a source of social and human capital, in contrast to criminal capital, can reduce involvement in crime and street life.

Another marginal opportunity structure is illustrated by the oil company spy. In Alberta, many oil companies drill wells in wilderness settings and try to keep their findings secret. Spies from rival companies sometimes pose as hunters or fishers to observe drilling operations without being detected. This activity can be hazardous, but it highlights the presence of particular opportunities and particular barriers to potentially profitable tasks. Kobrin and Cloward have applied these ideas to conventional crime, but there may be a much wider range of marginal behaviours that might fit these models.

Figure 8.1 indicates a number of barriers or "structuring variables" that influence the choice of activities. If all opportunities are blocked, skid row may be the alternative. P. J. Giffen describes the "revolving door" in Toronto, whereby skid-row alcoholics go in and out of jail on a regular basis (1966). If the retreatist subculture is the end of the line for certain types of delinquents, we might argue that skid row represents a similar situation for those who find other barriers insurmountable.

Which Is Better: Marginal Opportunities or None at All?

The question of opportunity structures, including illegitimate ones, poses an interesting policy question for society. Which is more desirable: having skid-row alcoholics with no opportunities, or having people engaged in marginal criminal activities? Prostitutes and gamblers engage in activities that are seen as deviant by society. Is this better than a skid-row lifestyle? While legitimate opportunities are clearly preferable to illegitimate ones, is it possible that the integration of some borderline, or even obvious, deviance would be better than the total breakdown represented by some of society's rejects? In a society that must sometimes choose between levels of evils, would policy-makers be wise to consider the nature of different opportunity structures and assess the impact of selected illegitimate opportunities on society?

Empirical Evidence for the Theory of Illegitimate Opportunity Structures

Cloward's theory of illegitimate opportunity structures suggested that specific types of subcultures would develop. According to Figure 8.1, he predicted three distinct types of gangs, corresponding to the criminal, conflict, and retreatist subcultures. However, there has been little empirical evidence for three distinct types of gangs corresponding to these adaptations (Short and Strodtbeck, 1965). It seems that stealing, fighting, and drug use are more likely to be found in combination rather than in distinct subcultural forms. Even though specialized subcultures are not readily apparent, the idea of barriers to illegitimate success has been a major contribution. Other characteristics, such as race, may be related to some of these barriers. Thus, Asian youths in Vancouver may have opportunities to work with Asian gangs who extort money from restaurant owners, while black youths in Toronto and Montreal may be more represented in drug subcultures, finding it more difficult to overcome barriers to both legitimate and certain illegitimate success. Violence and drugs may be the only things left. In Canada, Native people's abuse of alcohol may also be influenced by barriers to both legitimate and illegitimate opportunities.

Do certain groups assess opportunities correctly? According to one study, young black males in Chicago seemed quite aware that they would face financial problems if they got married and raised children (Short and Strodtbeck, 1965: Ch. 2). In periods of depression, Native people in Canada, blacks who have lived in Nova Scotia since the American Revolution, Jamaican immigrants in Toronto, Haitian immigrants in Montreal, and others probably have a realistic view of the barriers to material success, both in the short and the long term.

Scott Menard (1995) tested anomie theory using a national sample of American adolescents, and extended the analysis (1997) to include additional measures of illegitimate opportunity structures. Exposure to delinquent friends was used as an indicator of an illegitimate learning environment, and neighbourhood criminal activity was used as a measure of an illegimate performance environment. These indicators improved the ability of the model to predict illegal behaviour.

The reader should note that similar measures are used as part of other explanatory arguments. Delinquent peers, for example, are central to control theory and to most social-psychological theories. Thus, the "theories" created by researchers are oversimplified and are created to measure concepts that are really quite complicated. The concept "delinquent peers" is easy for us to understand, but its true meaning and impact are complex. Control theorists focused on some aspects of peers, but Menard used peer influence somewhat differently in strain theory.

Menard found that female respondents were more likely than males to abandon or scale down their aspirations. Interestingly, the profile of the individual most likely to be a "conformist" was a non-white individual from a lower-socioeconomic-status family *who believed that it is possible to succeed without breaking the rules.* One must be careful with oversimplified "lower-class-status-causes-crime" arguments. This conclusion is also consistent with social control and rational choice theories: individuals who have the most to lose by breaking rules are the least likely to reject the rules. Menard also found that anomie theory predicted illegal behaviour better at older ages, probably reflecting success or frustration in the labour market.

At first glance, one might argue that good job opportunities would automatically lead to reduced crime. However, Matthew Ploeger (1997) found that youth employment may increase criminal networks and actually increase crime. Some German research has also found that apprentices in work programs leading to stable jobs still found crime attractive.

Educational versus Financial Goals

Some critics, such as Hirschi (1969), argue that the gap between aspirations and expectations is not as meaningful as the aspirations themselves. He believes strain is redundant as an explanation of delinquency; goal commitment is enough (Kornhauser, 1978). Margaret Farnworth and Michael Leiber (1989) provide evidence of the potency of educational aspirations but, in addition, find that the *disjunction* between economic goals and educational means is an even better predictor of delinquency. That is, those who want lots of money but don't anticipate college are more likely to be delinquent. As opportunities for education decrease in Canada, along with less employment, the criminogenic conditions described by Farnworth and Leiber seem to be increasing.

THE POSSIBILITY OF MULTIPLE GOALS: CRIME IN THE FACTORY

So far we have been viewing crime as something disruptive. Is it possible that complex societies have multiple goals that are often in conflict? Is crime necessary as a way of achieving a balance among these goals? Bensman and Gerver (1963) describe a factory in which one task was to assemble plates of metal that utilized recessed nuts and bolts. At times the plates got out of line, and it was not possible to get the bolt to turn into the recessed nut. Under these conditions, a tap was sometimes used. A tap is a cutting tool of extremely hard steel which can be used to re-thread the recessed nut. When this is done the holding power of the bolt is weakened, and the improper work cannot be seen by an inspector. In this factory, the use of such a tap was "illegal" and provided grounds for immediate firing. However, the tap was used from time to time.

New workers were socialized into the way the tap was used. It was not to be used carelessly or unnecessarily; but despite the dangers of getting caught, there were times when the tap expedited the flow on the assembly line. The new worker was constantly reminded of the dangers: "If it snaps, your ass is in a sling." New workers who displayed the appropriate caution and followed the informal rules regarding the use of the tap eventually bought their own and occasionally lent them to others in need. When a foreman asked him to perform a tapping, the worker had established his identity.

The agencies of "law enforcement" in the factory had several levels. The purchaser of the product had the ultimate control, but there were only two inspectors from the purchaser in the plant. The second level of control came from the 150 plant quality-control inspectors. They fraternized with the workers and hoped they would not "louse them up." The inspector could not maintain quality simply by his efforts alone. Thus, he counted on the willingness of the workers to do good work. Since the penalties for the use of the tap were severe, an inspector was hesitant to report a violation. There were subterfuges: the tap was not to be used in the presence of an inspector; an inspector may move a tap to the bottom of a tool box, expressing his good will and his awareness of what goes on; at times the inspector may catch a worker and issue a stern reprimand.

The third level of enforcement lay with the foreman. Like the inspectors, the foreman gave a tongue-lashing to the occasional new man caught using the tap. The foreman usually made it clear that it was only his intervention that kept the man on the job. One learned not to use the tap unless it was absolutely necessary. The worker was obliged to accept the reprimand. If he took it lightly, then the foreman genuinely got angry. The worst crime was to take the rituals surrounding the use of the tap lightly.

Note the contradictions in behaviour. On the one hand, the foreman taught the use of the tap and assisted in evading rules; on the other hand, he performed rituals of punishment. A certain "double-think" was necessary. The foreman was primarily concerned with production, not quality. Despite the emphasis on the illegality of the tap, and the fact that its use was grounds for immediate firing, no workers were ever fired when they were caught.

The taps were also brittle and could break, leaving the telltale piece in the recessed nut. Naturally, the company tool room did not supply taps, but it did supply tap extractors to remove the piece of a tap that had been left behind.

As we attempt to explain the persistence of tapping in this factory, deviance, in the sense of rejecting the norms of the social system, does not fit here. Tapping is intrinsic to the system. The "crime" is as central to the system as the norm it allegedly violates. It is difficult to say what is functional and what is dysfunctional. If one attempts to use the Mertonian scheme, what are the goals of the *system*? It may be possible to locate the goals for *individuals* in a system, but the goals of the system are much more difficult to specify.

There seems to be a multitude of goals, which have different meanings for different people in the system:

- The company wants to earn profits.
- The purchaser wants a high rate of production, good quality, and low cost.
- The foreman wants production and promotion. Maintaining his production quota is the means for his private goals.
- The inspectors want to get along, to avoid "buying" jobs that might be rejected later. The tap represents a compromise.
- The worker needs to get the work done and stay out of trouble.
- The semi-secret use of the tap represents a way of bringing these diverse goals together.

What may be a means for one group may be a goal for someone else. Production is the goal for the worker and for the foremen, but it may be the means to achieve profitability for the company. "It is the plurality of ends (goals) that accounts for 'deviant behaviour' rather than the conflict between means and ends (goals)" (596). Different goals become more salient for different persons in the system. If you accept the dominance of the ultimate goal and view crime as a conflict between means and goals, you overlook the possibility that this conflict is really conflict between the means to one goal and the means to another. Crime is not a form of anomie here. The use of the tap is not innovation, but rather a permanent part of the organization. The major result of this conflict of goals is a form of double-think in which the major crime is to show lack of respect for the ceremonials surrounding the use of the tap. The major crime is the violation of the rules of criminal behaviour. It is important to note that the use of the tap is rigidly controlled. A careless worker is ridiculed and sent elsewhere but is never fired. This would expose the practice.

Another Definition of Crime

Bensman and Gerver's study led them to a very conservative definition of crime:

> A "crime" is not a crime so long as its commission is controlled and directed by those in authority towards goals which they define as socially constructive. A violation of law is treated as a crime when it is not directed and controlled by those in authority or when it is used for exclusively personal ends. (598)

This study calls our attention to the fact that, in a complex society, the goals and means to achieve goals differ for various groups and various individuals. At times, the system will not fit together very smoothly. Bensman and Gerver have tried to give us a new definition of crime; but when we look at the above statement more carefully, four situations are possible, as described in Figure 8.2.

In Figure 8.2 we have the use of the tap falling in Cell 1, directed by those in authority towards goals defined as socially constructive. The opposite diagonal, Cell 4, is clearly a crime

FIGURE 8.2	A Classification of Questionable Behaviour		

		Directed by People in Authority	
		Yes	No
Goals Defined as Socially Constructive	Yes	No Crime	?
	No	Probably Crime	Crime

according to Bensman and Gerver. But what about the other two cells? If the activity is directed by people in authority but the goals are defined as unconstructive (Cell 3), is it a crime? Who is going to define the activity as unconstructive? If the manager of a furniture factory is having a crew make furniture privately for him on the side, that would probably be defined as criminal. If an auto manufacturer decides not to shift the position of a gas tank, despite being aware that many deaths and injuries will result, should this be defined as a crime? (In the case of the Ford Motor Company, a court decided it was not.) If the province of Alberta refuses to pass seatbelt legislation that would protect children, should this be seen as criminal? While one might agree with Bensman and Gerver that breaking rules in society under the conditions existing in Cell 1 might not constitute crime, other combinations are less clear. Furthermore, crimes by the state have no place in this formulation. In fact, it seems to assume that authorities cannot be criminal.

The other diagonal (Cell 2) provides different problems. When environmentalists or peace advocates protest in ways that are illegal, such activity is not directed by people in authority; yet some would argue that the goals are socially constructive. To what extent can people who lack authority break the law without being considered criminal? It may depend on how many people they can convince that their goals are shared by the larger society.

Crimes by Those in Authority

When the MacDonald Report described how the RCMP broke the law many times in Quebec, breaking into buildings and stealing property belonging to certain political parties (Canada, 1981), how did the public respond? The activity was directed by people in authority; and the goals, at least as defined by those in power and by much of the general population, were probably defined as socially constructive. Thus, can the RCMP activities be considered crimes?

The ideas offered by Bensman and Gerver would clearly not be acceptable to many criminologists today, but they call attention to the *structure of society* and to the multiplicity of goals in the various segments of society. They point out difficulties in using the structural-functional approach to explain crime as a response to striving towards a common universal goal.

REINTEGRATIVE SHAMING

John Braithwaite (1989) offers an integrated and general theory of crime, particularly those predatory acts that are seen by the community as reprehensible. Central to his own thinking is the concept of *reintegrative shaming*, in which both negative and positive responses of community members must be considered. The key to crime control is to shame offenders in ways that are "reintegrative." Braithwaite builds on control theory, labelling, opportunity, subcultural, and learning perspectives.

Crime is committed more frequently by young, unmarried males who live in large cities and who experience high residential mobility. They differ from married people and females in the degree of their *interdependency*. The employed are also more interdependent than those who are unemployed. Interdependent people are less likely to commit crime because they are more susceptible to shaming. Societies in which people are interdependent are more likely to be *communitarian*, and shaming is more widespread and potent. Urbanization and high residential mobility undermine communitarianism. Japan is communitarian, even though it is modern and highly industrialized. The U.S. provides a stark contrast in that it espouses individualism.

Shaming can become stigmatization or can be followed by reintegration. Community disapproval ranges from mild rebuke to severe degradation ceremonies, which may or may not be followed by gestures of reacceptance and ceremonies that bring the offender back into the fold with other law-abiding citizens. Reintegrative shaming is more likely to bring the wrong-doer back into line. In communitarian societies shaming is likely to be reintegrative and crime rates low, because disapproval is dispensed without the deviant rejecting those who disapprove. Thus, the potential for, and the power of, future disapproval remains intact.

Stigmatization, by contrast, is a form of disapproval that often drives offenders to further acts of criminality. Stigmatizing shaming casts the deviant out of the circle of supporters and makes other groups, such as criminal subcultures, more attractive. When shaming becomes stigmatization, for want of reintegrative gestures and ceremonies that decertify deviance, the deviant is attracted to criminal subcultures and cut off from non-deviant interdependencies. To the extent that shaming is stigmatizing rather than reintegrative, and that criminal subcultures are accessible, higher crime rates will result. High levels of stigmatization encourage subculture formation by creating outcasts with no stake in conformity.

In societies where individualism is the prevailing ideology, citizens are more inclined to shun and isolate offenders and endeavour to control crime through stigmatizing punishments, which push offenders into interdependencies with other violators. Systematic blockage of legitimate opportunities, exacerbated by the stigmatization, fosters criminal subcultures. Although such blockages are most evident for those trying to climb out of poverty, Braithwaite points out that these principles apply to white-collar offenders as well. When affluent corporations see barriers to even greater wealth accumulation, they look to each other and develop corporate criminal subcultures as a means of achieving certain goals. To counter such corporate crimes, Braithwaite argues that punitive measures against white-collar crime should emphasize direct adverse publicity, so that the offences and the people who commit them are known to the rest of the community.

ASSESSING CONSENSUS, FUNCTIONALIST, AND OPPORTUNITY THEORIES

Despite renewed debate over strain theory, there is considerable agreement that the contributions emerging from Merton, Kobrin, and Cloward are still useful (Agnew, 1991, 1992, 1997a, 1997b; Agnew and White, 1992; Bernard, 1987a, 1987b; Cullen and Wright, 1997; Farnworth and Leiber, 1989). Traditional theoretical perspectives do not have to be seen as distinct and competing explanations. There has been a convergence of ideas that permits strain theory, differential association, and control theory to complement one another. In addition, the policy implications of the different theories can be similar. For example, enabling the disenfranchised to participate more fully in what society has to offer is probably related to greater social bonding with others, and a stronger belief in the rules that guide the larger society. However, if social bonds are primarily with people who condone or rationalize criminal behaviour, and with those who face similar blocked opportunities, criminal behaviour is likely. In such situations, control theory, differential association, and strain theory complement one another.

Nikos Passas (1997) suggested such a blend when he linked together anomie, reference group, and relative deprivation theory. For structural strains to translate into individual deviant behaviour, it is necessary that people *experience* the gap between means and ends. The culture of the American Dream and high rates of social mobility foster *non-membership*, that is, unrealistic reference groups. For example, it would be unrealistic for me to aspire to the lifestyle of the chief executive officer of the Royal Bank of Canada. Wealthy business executives are a non-membership reference group for me. Symbolic interactionists have noted that people falsely identify with groups even when they obviously do not belong. This leads to unfavourable comparisons, *feelings* of relative deprivation, and deviant responses. Such experiences, interactions, and responses may crystallize into deviant subcultures and thereby produce *deviance without strain*. Thus, businesspeople engaged in white-collar crime, which they feel is necessary in order to compete, may be able to rationalize their behaviour without feeling guilty. Using *reaction formation* and *mutual conversion*, as suggested by Albert Cohen in the last chapter, they translate a structural strain into a personal response.

When Durkheim introduced his ideas, the scholars of the day were explaining crime primarily by genetics and inner psychological forces. Durkheim turned the attention towards social forces, a radical idea at that time, but now the dominant view for explaining crime. His attempts to explain the link between crime and modernization may not be completely accurate, but the basic ideas have had broad applicability. They make considerable sense for patterns of crime that have evolved in Western Europe, and also in Eastern European socialist countries and the emerging nations of Asia, Africa, and Latin America as they move towards modernization (Shelley, 1981).

Durkheim was less accurate in his description of pre-modern nations as stable, crime-free societies. In fact, many had, and still have, high levels of violence. Furthermore, there seems to have been a long-term decline in crime over the last few hundred years in Western countries (Gurr, 1981). Despite the continual complaints we hear today, during the seventeenth century the average citizen in most cities in Western Europe would rarely leave the security of a locked home after dark.

Do Strain Theories Deal with Gender and Race Effectively?

A long-standing deficiency of most strain theories is their neglect of the gender issue. Differential rates of crime for men and women have frequently been discussed by criminologists, and some strain theorists might argue that women are less concerned about educational and economic opportunities, or that the female role is not as subject to stress as the male role. Such assumptions have clearly been questioned. Traditional thinking in this area illustrates male biases and ignores the stresses and frustrations that women face in the workplace and in the family. Opportunities appear to be more limited for women; stresses may actually be greater than those faced by men. Why aren't they more criminal? It remains to be seen whether strain theories can be recast to explain the continuing lower crime rate for females.

Other evidence that questions strain theory comes from a study that showed that blocked opportunities were more associated with delinquency among whites than among blacks (Cernkovich and Giordano, 1979a). Blacks may develop an attitude of resignation towards future occupational goals. It is also possible that strain and delinquency are the result of degradation and loss of status that occur when juveniles fail in school. They may not be viewing school as a means to an end, but failure in itself is demeaning and frustrating. In a broader sense the whole notion of opportunity structures may not take into account the fact that people can find satisfying roles in life that do not emphasize material success. The skilled craftsperson may take pride in his or her work, the academic may be comfortable in her or his role, but material success could be modest. Merton's contribution overlooks the broader notion of simply having a niche, even a modest one, as part of being a conforming member of society. Thus, strain theory draws attention to some characteristics of society that create situations that increase the likelihood of deviance, but it might be wiser to view these ideas as heuristic, as useful and revealing perspectives, rather than as complete explanations. They call our attention to *settings* that might be potentially criminogenic.

POLICY IMPLICATIONS OF THE CONSENSUS TRADITION

According to the thinking just reviewed, wars on poverty and unemployment should reduce crime, but have these efforts instead served the interests of poverty-serving agencies? Do we tend to reward agencies and professionals who work with the disadvantaged, without necessarily changing structural opportunities for such clients? If so, there is little reason to expect our expanding bureaucracies to reduce crime.

However, scholars do not have to be in complete agreement regarding strain theory before applying many of these principles to public policy: decreasing the gap between rich and poor makes sense. Nor should we ignore the warning Merton voiced in his 1938 article: *the ruthless pursuit of profit creates a criminogenic society*. Unfortunately, continued "economic growth" seems to be a basic premise for both Canada and the U.S. This is not the same as increasing opportunities for the less privileged. Rewarding the wealthy in the hope that some of the wealth will trickle down to the poor is a self-serving philosophy advocated by the powerful. According to any version of strain theory, this would lead to more crime. There has been a dramatic increase in the wealth available to the upper classes, but the frequent visual display of a luxurious lifestyle, especially on television, creates all the more strain for those who aspire to a share of that material wealth.

SUMMARY

1. Durkheim argued that crime was more frequent when social cohesion was weak, when there was anomie or normlessness. Merton modified the idea of anomie to that of relative deprivation caused by the gap between goals and means. The focus on opportunity structures grew out of these ideas.

2. Kobrin showed that communities offer different types of opportunities, and Cloward suggested that juvenile gangs also provided opportunities and support. Opportunity

structures make sense for other types of crime as well. Governments can influence these opportunity structures.

3. It is not clear whether marginal opportunity structures are worse than no opportunities at all. In addition, in a complex society many goals may be in competition. Various forms of deviance may allow for some adaptation among these competing goals.

4. While these consensus theories are static, ignore questions of gender, and may overemphasize material success, they call attention to settings and conditions that are criminogenic. Despite many criticisms, consensus (or strain) theories can be applied to a number of policy-relevant issues.

KEY TERMS

anomie   117

consensus (strain) theories   115

culturally prescribed aspirations   117

institutionalized means   117

socially structured avenues   117

WEBLINKS

www.ccla.org

The Canadian Civil Liberties Association: a lobbying, non-profit organization concerned with human rights issues.

www.icclr.law.ubc.ca/

The International Centre for Criminal Law Reform & Criminal Justice Policy: a non-profit institution located in Vancouver, British Columbia, affiliated with the United Nations, providing an extensive list of research publications.

FOCUSING ON SOCIETAL REACTIONS: MARXIST THEORIES AND CONFLICT

This chapter will:

- Question the assumptions about consensus in modern societies and trace the beginnings of explanations of deviance that emphasize societal reactions, which, in turn, can lead to labelling individuals as criminal.

- Trace the links between labelling, conflict theories, and Marxist theories.

- Express concern about the "victory of capitalism," which ignores many of the warnings expressed by the conflict theorists, and the implications this has for crime.

- Note different forms of conflict theory at the macro and micro levels and note their importance for criminal justice reform.

ASSUMING CONFLICT RATHER THAN CONSENSUS

The traditional emphasis on structural functionalism was fairly accepting of societies as they were. Cultures and societies evolved into something that was imperfect but reasonably workable. Conflict theorists do not assume that the societies that result are necessarily desirable. In this chapter we use the term *conflict theorists* to include a variety of critical thinkers who differ from liberal-humanitarian thinkers who hope to "do good" within the framework of the current society. The liberal-humanitarians want changes, but they worry that revolutions are often disappointing. Conflict theorists are less satisfied with capitalist societies and more willing to see dramatic changes. Instead of viewing societies as stable entities, conflict theorists view modern, complex societies as collections of competing elements, each struggling to make gains, usually at the expense of others. They see evidence of economic disparity and inequalities in the distribution of power. Conflict theorists bring criminology back to some of the broader themes that are part of other sociological thinking. They are critical of the assumptions made by business and political leaders during the period

134

of unrestrained capitalist expansion in the nineteenth century, assumptions still accepted by many people today.

In actuality, the distinction between consensus and conflict thinking is quite arbitrary. John Lowman (1992) points out that most critical criminology concerns itself with the social construction of consensus as much as with conflict. The oversimplifications and categories used in this chapter distort many of the elaborate arguments made by those whom I lump together as "conflict" criminologists. For example, most of the feminist theorists would be considered "conflict" criminologists, but I present their ideas in the chapter on women and crime rather than here. A sample of Canadian thinking in this area can be found in a collection edited by Ronald Hinch (1994).

These ideas had only a modest impact on criminology until after World War II, even though they were raised by previous social thinkers. Robert Ratner (1984) points out that the impact was even slower in coming to Canada. A number of developments in mainstream criminology, however, led to conceptualizing crime and criminality differently, and cast doubt on ideas that had been taken for granted. For example, what did criminal statistics mean? For years many criminologists assumed that crime and delinquency statistics were good measures of criminal behaviour, but now we know that the dynamics of the agencies, as well as a variety of other factors, influence those numbers tremendously. To avoid this type of bias, Nye and Short (1957) led a minor methodological revolution by asking people (usually school children) to report on their own crimes and delinquent acts. These studies found that the relationship between crime and lower-class status was much weaker than anticipated (Nye, Short, and Olsen, 1958). Middle-class juveniles also committed many crimes, although admittedly few of them were serious. Other studies found that the relationship between race and crime, which existed when official statistics were used, diminished considerably with self-reports.

LABELLING CRIMINAL BEHAVIOUR: A SOCIETAL REACTION APPROACH

Some criminologists began to argue that the over-representation of the poor and others at the bottom of the social hierarchy was the result of discriminatory practices of agencies of social control (Tannenbaum, 1938). It was not that they stole more, but that when they did steal, the system reacted more strongly, hence generating biased statistics. This type of thinking led to research focusing on the agencies themselves. The **labelling** theorists concluded that attempts to punish or even treat individual offenders were likely to increase subsequent illegal conduct, by stigmatizing them as criminals and by modifying their self-concepts. This *labelling approach*, and its attention to the role of *societal reactions* to deviance, has raised additional questions, which have provided fuel for conflict thinking. Labelling theorists were **symbolic interactionists**, who saw society as the product of the everyday interaction of individuals. Symbolic interactionists raised questions neglected by the structural functionalists discussed in the last chapter.

Several scholars have summarized the labelling approach, but Clarence Schrag (1971) shows how it breaks with traditional thinking and develops links with conflict theories:

1. No act is intrinsically criminal. It is the law that makes an act a crime. Crimes are defined by groups that have the power to influence laws.

2. Criminal definitions are enforced in the interest of power groups through their official representatives.

3. A person is designated a criminal by the reactions of authorities, who confer upon him the status of outcast.

4. Dividing people into criminals and non-criminals makes little sense. Most of the time criminals conform with the law, while some of the behaviour of supposed conformists violates the law.

5. Although many people violate the law, few are caught and singled out for special handling. This processing in the criminal justice system subjects the individual to unique experiences, which "tarnish" his image in his own eyes as well as in the eyes of others. If convicted, he is condemned not only for what he has done but also for the evils attributed to other criminals. He becomes a scapegoat.

6. Penalties vary according to characteristics of the offender. Recidivists are usually treated more harshly than first offenders, reflecting the view, "Once a criminal, always a criminal."

7. Sanctions also vary according to non-criminal characteristics of the offender. Males, the unemployed, the poorly educated, members of minority groups, transients, and residents of deteriorated urban areas are treated more severely. These categories are precisely the ones who continue to have high offence rates.

8. Criminals are assumed to be pariahs—willful wrong-doers who are morally bad and deserving of the community's condemnation. This status is achieved by status-degradation ceremonies. Attempts on the part of the offender to change this status by changing behaviour and attitude are likely to be unsuccessful. The public will probably not recognize such changes because the justice system dramatizes evil people rather than acts. If the former offender mends his ways, his efforts may be viewed as a devious device for concealing criminal inclinations. If he continues his criminal activities, his behaviour confirms the community's previous verdict.

9. Being labelled criminal makes it difficult to maintain a favourable image. Initially, one may blame a criminal's low status on discrimination or other things beyond her control, thus resisting the negative opinion others hold. However, she will also be inclined to reject her rejectors and develop antagonism towards the community, especially its officials, increasing the probability of further offences. Eventually she acquires the traits first imputed to her and becomes the criminal person she was labelled.

Empirical Evidence for the Labelling Approach

Obviously, it is important to know which of the claims made by labelling theorists are correct, or at least to what degree they are correct. The empirical evidence is mixed, because people in different situations differ in their resistance to deviant labels. In addition, it is difficult to tell if a teacher, for example, has been giving a child a negative label or has simply been perceptive in identifying characteristics that would later lead to delinquency. Clearly, higher-status people can resist negative labels even when their behaviour is reprehensible.

The term "teflon man" has recently entered our vocabulary, referring to important people to whom "the mud doesn't stick." The former premier of British Columbia, William Vander Zalm, was charged with illegal acts in connection with the sale of his Fantasy Gardens. Although Vander Zalm was acquitted, the judge felt that the former premier exercised poor judgment. Will the acquittal change the label of *criminal* created by the charge? Powerful people can resist negative labels more effectively than those who are weak.

One reason the labels do not stick is because laws have been formulated to benefit powerful groups (Williams, 1980). Laureen Snider's study of corporate crime in Canada addresses this issue (1978, 1993). While Snider does not claim that her study offers overwhelming proof for this general argument, she concludes that those who control the major economic resources have been able to use their power to prevent the introduction of laws that threaten their positions. At the least, they have resisted being classified as criminal, despite the clear criminality of some of their behaviour.

Lower-status people may face discrimination and differential processing in the criminal justice system, but it is more difficult to document, possibly because it is hard to separate out so many causal factors. Williams (1980) concluded that over 80 percent of both racial and socioeconomic studies failed to support differential processing. Similarly, Wilbanks (1987) concluded that there was insufficient evidence to support the charge that the system is racist today. Coramae Mann (1993) and others argue that Wilbanks is simply wrong (Reiman, 1990). Mann argues that racial discrimination is endemic in the U.S. and permeates social institutions, including the criminal justice system. Native people in Canada probably face similar experiences.

The criminal justice system may be less biased against the poor and minorities than it was in the past, but it still functions to *weed out the wealthy* (Reiman, 1990: 84). Agents of social control may not deliberately discriminate, but in Canada, as in the U.S., social control comes down more heavily on the weak (Ericson, 1982; Ericson and Baranek, 1982). In addition, Canadians should not be smug about contrasts with the United States. While Canadian police have better reputations than their U.S. counterparts, increasing Canadian research on agencies of social control demonstrates more similarity than difference.

It is not clear if our systems simply *reflect* societal biases or *contribute* to the criminalization of those at the bottom. If courts, for example, make decisions on the basis of a prognosis for the future, middle-class defendants are clearly a better risk. If the playing field is uneven before people enter the system, it may be unrealistic to expect the system to even the odds. If a child from a stable family appears in Youth Court, it is unlikely that she will spend time in an institution. However, if the child comes from a badly disorganized home, the likelihood of institutionalization is much greater, even if the offence is the same. Statistically, this will appear to be a bias, but the judge may have fewer options for some juveniles. Any serious attempts at crime reduction must influence situations and lives *before* people come into contact with agents of social control.

Improving Labelling Theory

Early labelling theories were somewhat oversimplified, but recent formulations take into account some of the subtle ways in which the reactions of agencies amplify or stabilize patterns of deviance. It is not just the public labelling, but also self-labelling that may amplify deviance. Bruce Link and his colleagues (1987; Link et al., 1989) note that when individuals are socialized, they learn that people in general see the "mentally ill" in a certain way. If an individual becomes a mental patient, these beliefs become very relevant and begin to apply in very personal ways. The more patients believe that they will be devalued and discriminated against, the more they feel threatened as they interact with others. They may try to keep their treatment a secret, and withdraw from social contacts they perceive as rejecting. This can lead to the loss of social support networks, problems with employment, and loss of self-esteem.

Bruce Link has focused on mental illness, but one can see possible parallels with criminal justice. If someone is convicted of a crime, that person can feel devalued and may hesitate to interact with others whom she believes will reject her. Unlike the mentally ill person, a person labelled as a criminal may be able to find others who will reward her for her criminal label. In other words, this reformulation of labelling theory might be even more potent for crime than for mental illness.

The Link between Labelling and Conflict Theories

One aspect of labelling theory that is particularly suspect is the claim that labelling *causes* criminal behaviour. Obviously, high-status criminals did not commit their crimes because they had been labelled criminals. For conflict theorists, the labelling approach is primarily important because it emphasizes the other side of the coin—instead of focusing on criminals, it looks at the functioning of bureaucracies, such as police units, courts, and probation offices that come into direct contact with potential criminals. Conflict theorists are inclined to view these bureaucracies as merely pawns acting on the wishes of powerful members of society, but one can study these units without this assumption and gain insights that are relevant to criminology. Studies of agents of social control suggest that they are often not particularly benign, and that the dynamics involved in these bureaucracies can lead to agendas that differ from publicly stated goals. However, it is not clear to what extent agents of social control are simply extensions of those in power.

Labelling theorists look at the dynamics of specific agencies, but most conflict theorists concentrate on power relationships among different elements of society. This is probably where conflict theory makes its most important contribution, even though these issues are not new. Social scientists, philosophers, journalists, and others have made similar points in the past. Edwin Sutherland called attention to white-collar or corporate criminality (1949), and Frank Tannenbaum (1938) saw crime as related to the activities of an entire community, not just selected members from a certain social stratum. In the 1930s, Thorsten Sellin (1938) presented arguments very similar to those made by later conflict theorists, but the major expansion of this thinking in criminology began in the 1960s and 1970s.

One of the influential documents of this period was produced by the American Friends Service Committee (1971). In a very coherent report, they argued that actions that bring the greatest harm to the greatest number of people should be labelled criminal. This would apply most frequently to official actions of government agencies. For example, the greatest number of murders in this century have been committed by governments in wartime. The greatest theft of property in the U.S. was the theft of lands belonging to Indian tribes. The evacuation and internment of Japanese Americans during World War II was carried out by the government with the approval of the courts. (Canada's record in this area may be even worse.) Civil rights demonstrators, exercising constitutional rights, have been beaten by police.

By the 1970s, the conflict perspective was a major force in criminology. Robert Ratner describes the growth of radical criminology in Canada as in competition with "entrenched foes" (1984: 159), and the ongoing debates were at times acrimonious, but there is little doubt that the "mainstream" of criminology was taking these arguments into account. It is difficult to present a short overview, but I will begin with Karl Marx and Friedrich Engels. They called attention to economic factors. While "conflict" theory, as used in this book, covers a number of somewhat different perspectives, the Marxist views provide a convenient starting point. Ron Hinch (1994) argues that Marxist theories should not be grouped with other conflict theories, but in this chapter we join with others who do so.

MARXIST THEORIES

By the middle of the nineteenth century, the Industrial Revolution had led to mechanized factories, coal was being used to drive steam engines, and a variety of economic activities had become integrated. Cottage industries were replaced by large factories. Wealthy owners had great power over workers and were rarely concerned about the terrible working conditions. Trade unions began challenging that hegemony but were ruthlessly suppressed.

Marx and Engels concentrated on the means of economic production and its influence on social life. Capitalism led to unequal distribution of property and power, which, in turn, led to the inevitable class conflict that characterized most complex societies. Ron Hinch (1999) warns us that there are several Marxian theories of crime and criminality, and that debates over *economic determinism* continue among Marxist scholars. However, many claim that class conflict is a major factor influencing the definition of crime and who gets criminalized. These arguments can be grouped into *instrumental* and *structural* perspectives.

An Instrumental Perspective on Marxism

From a historical perspective, instrumentalists argue that Canada evolved as a colony providing resources for England and France (Panitch, 1977). The leaders of society felt that what was good for those on top was also good for those on the bottom. When Canadian Pacific built the railroad across Canada, it received extensive amounts of public lands and money on the assumption that this would eventually benefit everyone. Similarly, providing tax concessions to the West Edmonton Mall, giving public support to companies refining oil in the Tar Sands of Alberta, or drilling in the Hibernia oil field off Newfoundland were viewed by those in power as appropriate government investments. Charles Reasons (1984) contends the government apparatus served the interests of the capitalists. From the perspective of conservative governments at least, what was good for Imperial Oil was good for everyone.

Brickey and Comack (1986: 17–21) summarize these ideas succinctly. The **instrumental perspective** is that the state acts at the behest of the capitalist class, those with the power. The institutions within the state, including the police, the courts, and the prison system, are the tools of the capitalists. One view of the creation of the North-West Mounted Police was that it was designed to control workers and Native peoples, that is, serve the interests of those in power (Brown and Brown, 1973). Concepts such as "the rule of law" and "equality before the law" are means of obscuring the reality of *lack of equality* in most situations. Taken to its extreme, the instrumentalists would view capitalists as immune from legal sanctions (Quinney, 1975; Chambliss, 1975). The capitalists not only make the law but control those who enforce it.

Such a view offers a "conspiracy theory" involving all powerful people, which ignores structural restraints on the influence of the capitalists. It also fails to recognize that laws are often passed that restrict the interests of the capitalist class, such as anticombines legislation and right-to-strike legislation. Powerful individuals clearly have advantages, but they are not immune, as evidenced by the conviction of Donald Cormie with regard to the Principal

Group fraud; Colin Thatcher, Saskatchewan cabinet minister and son of a former premier, in connection with murder; Charles Keating as an outcome of the Savings and Loan scandal in the U.S.; Michael Miliken with his criminal involvement in finances; and Leona Helmsley, the New York hotel queen, as a result of her income tax evasion. In addition, the law does not serve the powerful alone—at times it serves the weak as well.

A Structuralist Perspective on Marxism

Nicos Poulantzas (1973) sees many of the descriptions of the state as an instrument of the capitalists as oversimplifications. The state is neither completely free of control by the dominant classes nor simply dominated by them. Instead, it is relatively autonomous, allowing it to serve as a "factor of cohesion" and help regulate the overall equilibrium of society. Brickey and Comack note that, in contrast to instrumentalism, the **structuralist perspective** argues that the state acts on *behalf* of capital rather than at the *behest* of capitalists. The state acts as an "organizer"; it mediates between capital and labour, usually to the advantage of the former. It creates the conditions that will aid in the process of capital accumulation. It also tries to maintain and create conditions of social harmony by convincing the economically oppressed classes that this is for the good of all. Clearly, during the 1980s in Canada and the United States, many of the "lower" classes bought into this argument and elected governments that generally accepted this position. At the beginning of the 1990s, there was fairly wide acceptance of the view that if those at the top prosper, so will those at the bottom.

To achieve these goals, the state requires a certain degree of autonomy from direct manipulation by many elements of the dominant class. The state must be able to resist the specific demands and *immediate* interests of certain dominant individuals or groups, in order to ensure the *long-term* interests of capital. The state evolves out of the constraints and contradictions inherent in the capital-labour relationship. Thus, laws that favour workers, such as the length of the working day and health and safety regulations, also protect the long-term interest of capitalistic enterprise. Smandych (1985) notes, for example, that Canadian anti-combines legislation arose in the late nineteenth century to mediate the conflicts between large capitalistic forces, which were attempting to eliminate competition, and small businesses, which were trying to maintain competition.

Similarly, the police, courts, and other systems of the state need to maintain the appearance of neutrality in order to win the acceptance of the dominated classes. Despite the formal equality that is maintained in law, the economic inequality of reality frequently compromises the ideal. One might argue that the instrumentalists exaggerate discrimination in the operation of the law, while other critics claim that structuralists err in the opposite direction by minimizing it.

Testing Marxist Hypotheses

Tony Platt's book, *The Child Savers* (1969), might be said to reflect the instrumentalist view. He claimed that the juvenile justice system was created to serve capitalist interests. New categories of youthful deviance were "invented." Child savers (mainly middle-class women who had the psychological need to do good) and other representatives of the powerful recommended increased imprisonment or other control systems, in order to rehabilitate juveniles. The entire "juvenile court system was part of a general movement directed towards developing a specialized labour market and industrial discipline under corporate capitalism by creating new programs of adjudication and control" (1974: 377).

Hagan and Leon (1977) used data from Toronto to test this argument, and found that juvenile justice in Canada evolved without the apparent concern of the industrial elite. The key proponents of the Juvenile Delinquents Act of 1908 seemed to be a crusading news reporter, J. J. Kelso, and a philanthropist, W. L. Scott. Opposition came primarily from the police, who saw no reason to "kiss and coddle" delinquents. The developing role of probation seemed to be crucial to the new legislation and, as a result, imprisonment rates went down as informal methods of dealing with delinquents and the family became more popular. Hagan and Leon suggest that capitalism may not be particularly relevant to some aspects of criminal justice, such as the evolution of responses to juveniles.

Platt's work assumes that corporate capitalism *directly* influenced the juvenile court. The work by Hagan and Leon illustrates the type of micro-level work that reveals a number of processes operating within these agencies of social control. *The link with dominant powers in society remains a hypothesis to be tested.* The workings of agencies of social control will be influenced by external and internal factors, but Hagan and others would argue that it is an oversimplification to assume that the wishes of the power elite are transmitted directly to and through elements of the criminal justice system.

A more benign view of the agencies of social control is that a lot of the people involved mean well but, because of bureaucratic demands *for a variety of structural reasons*, serve their clients poorly (Hackler, 1991b). To summarize, many criminologists probably accept that portion of conflict theory that argues that the powerful have undue influence in the creation of legislation, and that they successfully resist laws that interfere with their perceived well-being; but there is less agreement on the levers of power that guide the agencies of social control in their dealings with troubled and troublesome people.

The Future Impact of Marxist Theory on Crime Policy

With the break-up of the Soviet Union and the failure of communism in Eastern Europe, some people assume that Marxist theorists have lost all credibility. It is a mistake to believe that radical thinkers in the West were unaware of the deficiencies of communist dictatorships. Like the rest of us, conflict theorists knew that crime was common in Russia and that these states lied about their social problems. In addition, changes recommended in the *Communist Manifesto* in the nineteenth century have, to a large degree, become the reality in most Western nations, thanks to the efforts of progressive thinkers and others who saw the need for change. Nor are Marxist theorists unaware of some of the benefits of reasonably free enterprise, and of their good fortune in living in a society in which they can criticize the powerful. Their contributions to an understanding of crime, and hopefully its eventual reduction, will continue to be important simply because economic factors and power relations have a crucial impact on human behaviour. While some criminologists will not appreciate all of the arguments coming from the far left, the Marxian conflict theorists turn the spotlight on criminogenic conditions that cannot be ignored in modern complex societies, by calling attention to deficiencies in capitalist societies.

Of much greater concern is that the so-called "victory of capitalism" will lead North American governments in particular to ignore some of the dangerous consequences of the shift to the right since the early 1970s. Galbraith (1992) talks about a "culture of contentment," in which reasonably well-off Americans represent such a powerful voting block that they prevent governments from taking important steps which directly influence the quality of life. For example, the "contented majority" may not be interested in universal medical care (Hackler, 1993). The infant mortality rate is acknowledged as the best measure of a country's medical care. The U.S. ranked about 28th in 1992. Most European countries have long had medical programs superior to those in the U.S. In 1996, the World Population Data sheet showed additional countries with lower infant mortality rates: Hong Kong, Ireland, Macoa, Netherlands Antilles, Slovenia, Spain, and Brunei.

The deterioration of inner cities in the U.S. suggests that the brand of capitalism espoused by many leaders in the U.S. offers an unattractive option. Galbraith's message seems particularly appropriate for Canada. Our "contented majority" is more concerned with protecting individual wealth than with creating a society with less crime. Eastern Europe and developing nations unfortunately look only at the material successes, particularly in the United States. They ignore the failures in the social area. The emphasis on a single yardstick of goodness, material wealth, coupled with uneven access to such wealth and the perpetuation of myths about social equality, leads to conditions conducive to crime. The break-up of the Soviet Union might be viewed as an illustration of the deficiencies of corrupt dictatorships, but there is no evidence that unrestrained free enterprise, particularly the American model, reduces crime and other social problems.

When the majority of the people are told that everyone should be treated equally, but those in the working classes are convinced that certain elites are favoured by the law and by the agencies of government, *criminogenic* conditions exist. Obviously, this is an oversimplification; but when people believe that many others are cheating, they see less reason for being honest themselves. The basic assumption of capitalism and free enterprise, that greed for individual profits leads to the greatest social good, simply tears at the fabric of society. Traditional criminologists also agree with conflict theorists that this leads to crime.

Bob Ratner (1998) suggests that capitalism is incompatible with many of the movements which try to utilize local neighbourhoods to prevent crime. His thinking has been influenced by Stephen Schneider (1997), who studied the ability of a disadvantaged neighbourhood in Vancouver to mobilize effectively to prevent crime. Schneider argues that such efforts are hampered at the community level by ethnic and income heterogeneity, at the organizational level by inadequate resources and leadership, and at the structural level by the effects of dominant institutions and ideologies. In addition, these levels are critically interconnected. Capitalism itself is the main obstacle to community mobilization as it accelerates centralization within the metropolis, distorting any sense of a humane set of relationships. He argues that capitalism destroys neighbourhoods and communities.

Schneider offers "radical planning theory" as an alternative. This would involve decentralizing power and increasing communication among formal agencies, such as the police and community-based organizations. Schneider's argument may have seemed idealistic, as his doctoral examiners urged him to be more "realistic" in his recommended reforms. But Ratner (1998) speculated that the examining committee of university professors (of which he was one) may represent institutional structures which are "pragmatic" and willing to adapt to the world as it is. In other words, universities may be part of the structures which inhibit the sort of thinking that would lead to the creation of communities capable of reducing crime.

Having also been a somewhat pragmatic criminologist, I notice that some ideas that seemed terribly radical and idealistic in the past appear more practical today. One of the major contributions of some radical thinkers has been to challenge accepted assumptions, many of them reinforced by the current love affair with globalization and free enterprise.

Bernard Schissel (1997) also asks if the current political climate increases crime. He argues that the moral panic that scapegoats youth is a coordinated, calculated attempt to nourish an ideology that supports a society stratified on the basis of race, social class, and gender. The war on youth is part of a state-capital mechanism that continually reproduces an oppressive social and economic order (Herman and Chomsky, 1988).

The Crimes of the Powerful

One of the major contributions of the Marxist theorists and others with a radical perspective is to call attention to the crimes of the powerful. A rich literature has been produced (Barak, 1991; Chambliss, 1988; Goff and Reasons, 1978; Reasons, Ross, and Paterson, 1981; Snider, 1993), but this discussion will be postponed to those chapters dealing with specific forms of criminal behaviour. It is appropriate, however, to end a discussion of Marxist criminology with a comment on whom and what criminologists should be studying. Friedrich Engels (1958), writing in 1844, summarizes the point rather well:

> If one individual inflicts a bodily injury upon another which leads to death ... we call it manslaughter; ... if the attacker knows beforehand that the blow will be fatal we call it murder. Murder has also been committed if society places hundreds of workers in such a position that they inevitably come to premature and unnatural ends. Their death is as violent as if they had been stabbed or shot.... Murder has been committed if society knows perfectly well that thousands of workers cannot avoid being sacrificed so long as these conditions are allowed to continue. Murder of this sort is just as culpable as the murder committed by an individual.

Today there are many illustrations of laws that regulate occupational health and safety designed by those with power that produce profit while creating risks for workers. It is often suggested that occupational health and safety risks are inevitable, but Baere (1996), McMullan (1992), and Snider (1997) note that many deaths and injuries are the direct result of employers' failure to comply with the law. In addition, the laws themselves, sometimes designed, at least partially, by those who would profit by them, have sometimes led to more, rather than less, illness and injury (Chambliss and Seidman, 1982).

CONFLICT THEORIES, CRIMINOGENIC CONDITIONS, AND THE POSSIBILITIES OF CRIMINAL JUSTICE REFORM

Organizing conflict theories into meaningful categories depends on how one wishes to use them. It is a convenient simplification to say that some focus on macro-level arguments—that is, the larger structure of society—while others concentrate on micro-level arguments—that is, on the agencies that define crime and handle those identified as criminals. By the 1950s, a number of scholars were finding consensus theories limiting. Dahrendorf (1959), Sellin (1938), and Vold (1958) offered suggestions to supplement and extend some of the traditional theories.

Various groups in society interact; that interaction is not always peaceful. In fact, modern societies are characterized by a constant state of conflict. Groups ally themselves with others in defence or for advancement within society. Such interaction includes groups involved in making or enforcing the law, as well as groups that are required to obey the law. Legislation represents the triumph of a particular group, or an alliance of groups, over other groups. Naturally, those who succeed in having a law passed are likely to conform to it, while those who oppose it, or whose actions were the target of the new law, are least likely to obey the law and most likely to get in trouble with the enforcers of the law, usually the police.

During the 1970s, many radical thinkers rejected the possibility of participating in criminal justice, arguing that crime problems could not be solved within the capitalist system, that band-aid solutions would not change a corrupt system. Other well-known radical thinkers, such as Nicole Hahn Rafter (1986), disagree. It is incorrect, she believes, to claim that laws prohibiting serious kinds of rule-breaking, like homicide, rape, and robbery, are expressions of class conflict and instruments of class oppression. Radical criminologists must also address the mundane problems of crime causation, look at empirical evidence objectively, and not be concerned if they occasionally find their thinking compatible with mainstream researchers. Rafter states, "dirty hands are preferable to having no hand at all in the formulation of criminal justice policy" (1986: 18).

One of the bridges between conflict theorists such as Nicole Rafter and middle-of-the-road liberals is the hope that research will lead to reforms in the criminal justice system. Thus, those conflict criminologists who focus on specific agencies of social control offer insights into changes that might produce improvements. For example, Richard Ericson and Pat Baranek (1982) bring a critical perspective to the processing of defendants through the criminal justice system. In my own work on juvenile justice, I am critical of Canadian practices (Hackler, 1996), and argue that our failure to be aware of juvenile justice systems in other countries limits our vision and imagination (Hackler, 1988b). Conflict theorists might focus on what keeps authorities in a position to continue this situation; those of us with a liberal perspective criticize the workings of the system *without* assuming it is necessarily entrenched in relationships of dominance which the authorities are striving to maintain. Liberals also assume those in authority are concerned with their own self-interest, but this assumption is not limited to capitalism. Rather, self-interest characterizes groups and individuals in all societies, including those with benign and humanitarian orientations.

Although it is clearly an oversimplification, the liberal non-conflict theorists are more optimistic about making changes *within* the present system. Some of us, perhaps naively, assume that many people in positions of power mean well and, given the right set of conditions, would help to modify the system and make it "better" for the more disadvantaged members of the society. We liberals do not expect heroism or great self-sacrifice from those in dominant positions, but as we criticize the system we cling to the notion that many people are somewhat noble and that virtue brings about its own psychological rewards. This faith sometimes persists even when we are continually confronted with evidence to the contrary.

Conflict theorists are less charitable, less sanguine, more cynical, less optimistic, and perhaps less naive. They see the need for more basic and sweeping changes in the structure of society. In addition, they point out that some supposed reforms may be initiated by those in authority as a smokescreen to conceal other agendas which, in fact, serve the status quo. Maeve McMahon and Richard Ericson (1987) illustrate this perspective with the example of the development of the Citizens' Independent Review of Police Activities (CIRPA), an organization established to reform the police in Toronto. They argue that the reform group was co-opted by the authorities. This allowed the issues to be redirected by the police. In reality, the reform effort may have solidified the power of the authorities by providing the appearance of change. As one CIRPA board member stated, the police "have to be a bit more careful about what they say. It doesn't mean they have to be more careful about what they do, but at least they have to keep a facade" (65). Thus, the intended reformers assist in maintaining the status quo, and the police give the impression that they are willing to be accountable and take heed of civilians who criticize. According to this view, reformers working from within the systems always attempt to co-opt, neutralize, or use the "true" outside reformers to achieve their own goals.

Here again, ideology and explanation become somewhat confused. Traditional supporters of the system are puzzled by the criticisms levelled by McMahon and Ericson because, from their traditional standpoint, the main goal of criminal justice is to protect society. Co-opting recommendations from outsiders is reasonable because it may improve the system for the average citizen as well as those who are disadvantaged.

A Liberal Perspective on Reform

Ezzat Fattah, of Simon Fraser University, has written on reform from liberal and critical perspectives. His arguments against capital punishment are among the most influential in Canada. He also points out that reform efforts should not be judged from a radical or critical perspective alone (1997). Reforms that perpetuate authoritarian social control, as described above, may yield an unanticipated negative result, but that does not mean that this was a carefully thought-out strategy of the power elite. At other times, something quite different happens: relatively minor attempts at reform lead to positive changes that are even greater than what was anticipated.

Fattah (1987) also criticizes an approach that often characterizes radical criminology: the elite are thought to be eager to criminalize the weak and the poor, while the lower classes are assumed to be benevolent. In fact, Fattah states, it is not the elite who consistently demand harsher penalties, more severe police powers, and so on, but members of the middle and lower classes. They, rather than the elite, persistently complain about the lenient treatment of offenders, the country club–like conditions in penal institutions, and the "bleeding hearts" who wish to help wrong-doers. It is the middle and lower classes, not the elite, who are the strongest advocates of stigmatization and exclusion of offenders and who call for an extension of the powers of social control authorities.

In addition, Fattah (1987) points out that the distinction between inside and outside reformers is not appropriate, because those who are genuinely interested in reform do not care if it comes from within or without, or whether it is achieved by confrontation or cooperation. Fattah's thinking would be compatible with the **left realists**, those critical criminologists who point out that radicals should broaden the scope of their thinking and consider a wider range of reform efforts. Such an orientation leads to considerable overlap with the reform efforts of liberal criminologists, and the border between conflict and liberal reform becomes blurred. For many criminologists with reform inclinations, less concern with ideological purity is preferred.

One should not exaggerate the differences between conflict theorists and other criminologists. Most criminologists agree that crime reflects the way society is organized, and even conflict theorists admit that there are "bad" individuals. Many of these points of agreement appear in what Jock Young (1986) refers to as "left realism."

Left Realism and the Potential for Reform

Some radical criminologists have a tendency to romanticize crime, or to assume that the only serious crimes are those committed by the powerful. While income tax evasion certainly involves more stolen money than bank robbery, the majority of direct victims of crime are poor people victimized by other poor people. Crimes of violence usually involve one poor person attacking another, and half of the time it is a man hitting his wife. Conflict theorists such as Nicole Hahn Rafter (1986), David Greenberg (1981), and Jock Young (1986) criticize some of the conflict theorists for ignoring the fact that crime really is a problem, particularly for poor people. Brown and Hogg (1992) review left realism in England and Australia and note some promising new directions. For example, some left realists devote considerable attention to police–community relations (200). Heavy-handed, proactive policing often alienates communities plagued with crime problems. In fact, these concerned communities can be the most important resource in helping to reduce crime. Instead of just seeing police as oppressors, the left realists recommend that the police be responsible to, and responsive to, the communities being policed.

Left realism does not ignore the impact of crimes of the powerful, but notes that people who are more vulnerable economically and socially will be caught in compounding problems which create criminals and victims. While left realism argues that crime illustrates the antisocial fruits of capitalism, it also takes seriously the specific risks to vulnerable people: the dangers of a woman being in a public place at night, the widespread occurrence of domestic violence, and the fears of working-class people in crime-prone areas. Official statistics, despite their flaws, provide insights that help us understand the risk of crime in working-class areas. In general, left realists share with liberal humanists a practical concern for the day-to-day damage crime does to the most unprotected part of the population.

Following the Fads

To understand current theoretical thinking, one must take into account the fads that come and go in criminology. Those who work with statistical techniques are aware of the rise and fall in popularity of certain analytical tools. In the 1960s, for example, it was a rare data set that escaped being "factor analyzed." Some psychologists ask if every correlation is "significant at the .05 level of probability." Often, these tools reflect the latest fad and may be irrelevant to the intellectual question at hand. Theorists go through similar fads. The tendency to emphasize single causes of crime has weakened the contributions of some theorists. Examples include: capitalism is practically the only cause of crime; unemployment automatically leads to crime; poverty leads directly to riots; and increases in crime are simply the consequence of greater criminalization on the part of the police (Young, 1986; Greenberg, 1981). Simplification and generalization are necessary, but we must be ready to modify, specify, and reject. Rigidity based on ideology, rather than caution based on evidence, has characterized the work of some conflict theorists, just as the ritual and unthinking use of statistical techniques has characterized other criminological work.

In summary, left realism recognizes and criticizes faddishness and extremism and attempts to develop a balance between two themes. The first theme states that we should not underestimate the problem of conventional crime, but must resist the hysteria that exaggerates certain types of crime. The second theme is illustrated by the systematic distortion of images of crime, victimization, and policing by the media (Ericson, Baranek, and Chan, 1987, 1989;

Cohen and Young, 1981). Despite overwhelming evidence that most violence takes place among acquaintances, the media exaggerate the role of the dangerous stranger. This provides ammunition for repressive and ineffective social-control tactics. For example, headlines about sexual abuse in day-care centres have shocked the public but probably misled policy-makers. Such abuse is rare in day-care centres; it is much more frequently committed by parents. Thus, our concern should still be with families. Hysterical reactions to distorted images of crime lead to political and popular support for law-and-order campaigns that do little to protect victims in the future.

Left realism resists the hysteria, but does not deny the severity of crime as a problem. It is skeptical of official statistics and agencies of control, without rejecting figures and data out of hand. Nor does it automatically reject the possibility of reform. For a period, radical criminology concentrated only on the crimes of the powerful, the state, and its agencies, noting the impact on those at the bottom of the hierarchy (Chambliss, 1988, 1989). These themes are still important, but the left realists, in contrast to the "left idealists," argue that one cannot ignore the structural determinants of everyday crime. Nor can one accept uncritically that every action of the police and other agencies, such as school teachers, social workers, and so forth, is a deliberate act pursued and directed by the agents of capitalism.

Perhaps the main contribution of the conflict theorists has been to bring criminology back to broader societal themes. Among the developed countries, those that are the strongest advocates of free enterprise are likely to have more crime. Among third world countries, those where the powerful exploit the weak seem to have more crime. It is difficult to test many of these ideas—to know which ones are true compared with those that are statements of faith—but the empirical data that support many of the propositions made by conflict theorists appear to be growing.

Colvin and Pauly: An Integrated Structural-Marxist Approach

Earlier I noted that Thornberry integrated social-psychological, or microsociological factors. Macrosociological-level variables may be more amenable to social action if we recognize the erosion of certain structural supports in society. Mark Colvin and John Pauly (1983) developed an integrated structural-Marxist theory which incorporates social-psychological factors into a macrosociological framework. They argue that lower-social-class employees who work in environments where there is coercive control are more likely to become hostile and alienated. The capitalist system creates social relations in the workplace that do not inspire loyalty and respect for authority. This hostility and alienation comes home with the disgruntled worker, and is reproduced in the family. Children of alienated workers, particularly boys, are socialized differently than boys who live in families in which the parents are more satisfied with their work and with the system. The attitudes in the workplace influence the attitudes in the home, and shape the initial bond or ties to authority. Lower-class parents who face coerciveness at work transfer this to their children. This influences the way children relate to other adults, the school, and peer groups.

Legitimate opportunities are more available to those who belong to the higher social classes and who have the appropriate socialization, whereas illegitimate opportunity structures will attract those who see barriers. The resulting association with delinquent peers, and the interaction that follows, would fit the models described above. In terms of policy, this structural-Marxist model suggests that changes are needed in the workplace. This theoretical model predicts that, due to the increasing numbers of North American companies that are "downsizing" and laying off workers who are already vulnerable, there will be more discontent among lower-class families, more criminogenic conditions, and more crime in the future.

SUMMARY

1. This chapter examines a variety of views that fall under the general category of conflict theories. Such theories view capitalist societies as having little consensus. Instead there are many competing elements, with great disparity in the distribution of wealth and power. This is linked to the question of who gets labelled as criminal.

2. Marxist theories emphasize economic factors. An *instrumentalist* perspective argues that the state acts at the behest of the capitalist class, those who are in power. The institutions of the state, including the police, courts, and prison system, are the tools of the capitalists. A *structuralist* perspective views the state as more autonomous, allowing it to regulate the equilibrium of society. It acts on *behalf* of capital rather than at the *behest* of capitalists. Thus, laws might favour workers in order to ensure industrial peace and enhance the long-term interests of capitalism.

3. The recent "victory of capitalism" throughout the world and the failure of communism in Eastern Europe have allowed traditional thinkers in the West to underestimate the impact of the corrupt dictatorships in these countries. The criticism of socialist principles, usually advocated by conflict theorists, leads to reinforcement of the idea that "individual greed leads to the greatest social good." This notion tears at the fabric of society and leads to crime.

4. Some conflict theories could be grouped into macro-level arguments—those that focus on the larger structure of society—and micro-level arguments—those that concentrate on agencies, such as the police, who handle those identified as criminals.

5. Reform strategies and responses to crime vary with different types of conflict theories. The left realists, for example, warn against romanticizing crime. The majority of crime victims are poor people victimized by other poor people.

6. Finally, we should be aware of fads that focus on narrow themes. These fads plague many different perspectives within criminology.

KEY TERMS

instrumental perspective   139

labelling   135

left realists   145

structuralist perspective   140

symbolic interactionists   135

WEBLINKS

www.crimetheory.com/

Resources offered through the University of Washington provide an overview of radical criminology.

www.amnesty.org

Amnesty International: a worldwide organization that campaigns to promote human rights.

THE ECOLOGY OF CRIME: THE COMMUNITY AND SPATIAL RELATIONS

This chapter will:

- Offer explanations of why some communities become "dangerous" and note the policy implications of these ecological theories.

- Note that ecological arguments may counter some of the racist explanations of high-crime-rate areas.

- Show that crime can be prevented by creating "defensible space" and suggest that routine activities in people's lives influence predatory crime.

- Illustrate how social planners can "design out crime" in areas of high public use.

- Note the steps in the thinking of a potential criminal as he or she considers targets.

- Explore the nature of neighbourhood integration in various cities.

DANGEROUS PLACES: RODNEY STARK AND THE ECOLOGY OF CRIME

Some areas have more crime than others. Is it because of the "kinds of people" who live there? Or is it possible that certain "kinds of places" produce a disproportionate amount of crime? A school of thought evolved at the University of Chicago prior to World War II that saw some neighbourhoods as disorganized. Using this framework, Norman Hayner (1942) described a high-crime-rate area in Seattle in the 1930s. He recounted the social and cultural shortcomings of the residents, largely Italians of Sicilian origin. The businesses of the area were run down, and vacant and dilapidated buildings were common. Fifty years later the district remained a high-delinquency area, but very few Italians lived there. Instead, it became the heart of the black community.

Rodney Stark (1987) asks how neighbourhoods remain high-crime areas *despite a complete turnover in their populations*. Those who grow up in those neighbourhoods and leave do not necessarily commit excessive amounts of crime elsewhere. Stark concludes that there must be something about places that sustains crime. Criminologists have focused on why individuals commit crime, but Stark reviews the findings from studies of human or urban **ecology**, the study of the link between the physical and social dimensions of cities. He notes that there are five characteristics, or essential factors, that distinguish high-crime-rate areas: (1) high population density, (2) poverty, (3) mixed use of buildings for residential and commercial purposes, (4) transience, and (5) dilapidation.

In addition, these factors influence the way people respond. These responses can be grouped into four categories: (1) moral cynicism among residents, (2) increased opportunities for crime, (3) increased motivation to deviate, and (4) diminished social control. These responses further amplify deviance by attracting crime-prone people and criminal activities to the neighbourhood; by driving out the least deviant; and by further reducing social control.

Stark spells out thirty propositions to form a theory of dangerous places. The following is a summary of his most salient propositions:

1. *The greater the density, the more association there is between those most and least disposed to crime.* In low-density neighbourhoods, it may require an effort for one 12-year-old to see another. Thus, kids and parents can limit contact with bullies and those in disrepute. In dense urban neighbourhoods, the "bad" kids are close by, dominate the playground, and are difficult to avoid. All young people living there will be under peer pressure to deviate.

2. *The greater the density, the higher the level of moral cynicism.* In low-density suburban neighbourhoods people keep up good appearances in public. In dense urban neighbourhoods, this is harder—discreditable information is more likely to leak. Teenage peers will know more embarrassing things about one another's parents. This colours their perceptions of what is normal, reducing respect for conventional moral standards. People in dense neighbourhoods become inferior role models—these same people would *appear* to be more respectable in less-dense neighbourhoods.

3. *Where homes are crowded, there will be less supervision of children.* Parents may be relieved if children are out of the house; supervision is thus reduced.

4. A reduced level of supervision results in poor school achievement, with a consequent reduction in stakes in conformity.

5. *Poor, dense neighbourhoods tend to be mixed-use neighbourhoods.* The encroachment of commercial use leads to neglect of residential buildings and dilapidated conditions.

6. Poor, dense, mixed-use neighbourhoods have high transience rates.

7. *Transience weakens voluntary organizations, thereby reducing informal and formal sources of social control.* If neighbourhoods are transient, there is less of a commitment to the area, which leads to dilapidation. As areas get stigmatized, an individual's stake in conformity is reduced.

8. *The most successful and potentially best role models will flee stigmatized neighbourhoods whenever possible.*

Policy Implications of Ecological Theories

Rodney Stark's ecological theory of crime has some interesting policy implications. A single social variable does not provide an explanation. Take poverty, for example. The ecological theory predicts less crime in poor families when their neighbourhood is less dense, homes are not crowded and dilapidated, there is less transience, the police are not permissive of vice, and the unemployed and demoralized are not concentrated. Effective action against crime would probably require *many changes at once*, but it is important to note that each change would increase the effectiveness of other changes.

S*ocial support theory*, discussed in the chapter on social interaction (Chapter 7), illustrates this interlinking of several types of support. Cullen and Wright (1997) emphasize the importance of supports supplied by a loving family, but they also point out that other supports come from the community. Financial support can come from a government program, helpful information can come through local networks, and job contacts can be provided by neighbours. In general, Cullen (1994) argues that crime rates will be lower in communities and nations that are supportive rather than mean-spirited toward their citizens (see also Chamlin and Cochran, 1997).

Two housing projects in France illustrate both ends of the continuum of supportive communities in terms of criminogenic conditions. The housing project I observed west of Paris had "matured" into a supportive community. The one near Marseilles had deteriorated into a ghetto for crime. In the community near Paris, many people living there no longer qualified for low-income housing. However, the authorities did not require these people to move. Schools and other facilities were good, because they shared facilities used by wealthier neighbourhoods. With more successful and better role models remaining in the neighbourhood, there was admittedly less opportunity for demoralized residents to move in. With less transience, there were more voluntary organizations. One could argue that fewer poor and demoralized residents were being provided with low-cost housing, but from society's standpoint is it not wiser to offer a larger number of housing projects containing smaller percentages of poor and demoralized residents, rather than concentrate such residents in one area? A few formerly poor people were getting subsidized housing, but were they not adding something to the community that would be expensive to replace?

By contrast, not far from Marseilles, I observed the type of disorganized slum that characterizes some urban areas in the United States. The high-rise apartment building was impressive architecturally, and the residents were almost entirely Arab-speaking and on welfare. Successful Arab-speaking migrants had moved out, and other welfare families refused to move in. The police avoided the place. Not only did these factors contribute to crime, but this type of residence also increased the friction between the French and Arab populations.

Ecological Arguments As an Antidote to Racist Thinking

I chose an illustration from France because what happened there could happen in Canada. Some French arch-conservatives believe their crime problem is caused by the presence of immigrants. Right-wing politicians in France are willing to state the nature of the crime problem in a way that is rarely expressed, in public anyway, in North America. At least, not yet. For the right-wingers in France, crime is a "kind-of-people" problem—that is, they believe crime is a characteristic of individuals, ignoring the possibility that situations and conditions contribute to crime. Many Canadians feel the same way.

In the U.S., when American social scientists talk about poor central-city neighbourhoods, they mean black neighbourhoods. In Canada, when we talk about problem neighbourhoods, we sometimes mean areas where there are large numbers of Native people. Social scientists are not comfortable trying to explain crime rates of blacks or Natives. While poverty plays a role, it is only part of the explanation. Stark argues that, to a large degree, high black crime rates are the result of where they live. Can we extend this argument to Native populations in Canada? to Haitians in Montreal? to Jamaicans in Toronto? to the many generations of blacks living near Halifax? Although the reserves for Native people may not be densely populated, many of the other characteristics described by Stark would apply there.

Sampson and Wilson (1995) suggest that the roots of urban violence among youth in the 1990s may have stemmed from childhood socialization that took place in the late 1970s and early 1980s. This cohort spent its childhood in a rapidly changing urban environment. The concentration of urban poverty and other social dislocations began increasing in about 1970 and continued into the 1980s. The proportion of black families headed by women increased over 50 percent from 1970 to 1984 (Wilson, 1987: 26). Thus, the poverty, racial segregation, population turnover, and joblessness among blacks created more severe social dislocations compared with the relative stability that existed earlier.

To summarize, community settings have a powerful influence on behaviour which cannot be explained by individual characteristics. For example, we know that sex is an individual characteristic that influences behaviour, including crime, but males behave differently in all-male groups than they do if they are the only male in a group of females. Similarly men or women, blacks or whites, Natives or non-Natives will be more or less criminal, depending on the social settings in which they live.

DEFENSIBLE SPACE AND ROUTINE ACTIVITIES

Another type of ecological study has concentrated on crime prevention through environmental design. Oscar Newman (1973) is an architect who believes that citizens can be involved in crime prevention through the construction of residential complexes that deter crime by creating **defensible space**. Housing can be designed that allows residents to notice and identify strangers, and encourages them to have an interest in the protection of their territory. For example, the area enclosed by the wings of a building often becomes the focus of surveillance and informal control by residents of the facing apartments, particularly if the building is not very tall. Children playing in such areas are often under the watchful eyes of neighbours. Having play equipment and benches in such areas attracts people and keeps children closer to home. Residents feel safer if they can see and be seen, hear and be heard. When people are less anxious they spend more time in "shared" space, thereby increasing surveillance and informal control. Such settings increase the willingness of residents to intervene when deviance is observed, as suggested by some of the studies of bystanders discussed in the chapter on group dynamics (Chapter 6).

It is unlikely that defensible space design can dramatically reduce crime, but studies in the UK suggest that it has had an impact in public housing areas in England (Baldwin, 1979). It is possible, of course, that crime is merely displaced from well-designed areas to nearby targets that are more vulnerable. In addition, the emphasis on the design of space may ignore social and demographic characteristics. For example, a project with many teenagers may have a higher crime rate, whereas one with many older people who observe enclosed areas may have higher surveillance and reduced crime. Areas with residential mobility may fail to develop a community spirit, whereas stable neighbourhoods may become more cohesive and reduce crime. High-population-density areas may attract more police officers, leading to an increase in formal control of crime (Gillis and Hagan, 1982). In general, the physical environment interacts with other factors associated with formal and informal social control. The concept of defensible space has been broadened by some scholars, and combined with other factors. The routine-activities approach, for example, could be viewed as an expansion of this concept.

Routine Activities: Lawrence Cohen and Marcus Felson

It is difficult to steal something if there is little to steal. The increased availability of consumer goods in stores and in homes has provided new opportunities for crime. There was a fundamental shift in lifestyle after World War II. Personal affluence and the accumulation of household property increased, providing opportunities for theft. This pattern appeared in Europe as well. The availability of consumer goods in Sweden was related to theft (Stack, 1982). Several scholars have observed the relationship between the availability of criminal opportunities and the amount of money in banks (Gould, 1969) and the availability of cars in Canada (Giffen, 1976). The **routine activities** perspective builds on these findings, but combines them with other factors to provide a more complete explanation.

The routine activities approach treats the motivation to commit crime as a constant. Thus, Cohen and Felson (1979) explain the volume and distribution of predatory crime as related to the routine activities of people's everyday lives. These elements can be grouped into: (1) the availability of suitable targets (such as homes containing goods that can easily be resold), (2) the absence of capable guardians (homeowners, watchful neighbours, friends, and relatives), and (3) the presence of motivated offenders (such as unemployed teenagers). Thus, when motivated offenders are located around suitable targets that are not protected, there is a greater likelihood of predatory crime. This approach has been used to examine trends in crime and to make suggestions for criminal justice services and programs (Cohen and Felson, 1979; Cohen, 1981; Cohen, Kluegel, and Land, 1981).

With increased affluence, people spend less time in home-based "routine" activities. People are more at risk outside of the home, especially if they go to bars or other places that generate "excitement." Similarly, their unguarded residences are more likely to be targets of crime. In addition, since 1960 more women have been working outside the home. With children in day care, homes are left unguarded and therefore become more suitable targets for crime. Similarly, suburbia usually does not have as many neighbours who are relatives or close friends and who could serve as effective guardians of nearby homes.

The more wealth a home contains, the more likely it will be victimized, especially with the increase in easily transportable wealth, such as TVs, VCRs, computers (Massey, Krohn, and Bonati, 1989). Other research suggests that a large supply of youths competing for a smaller number of jobs and educational opportunities provides a surplus of "motivated offenders" (O'Brien, 1989).

In Canada, Leslie Kennedy and David Forde (1990) have used the routine activities approach to look at different *lifestyles*, using victimization data from seven Canadian cities. Young, lower-class males who went out late at night to bars, work, classes, or for a walk or a drive were the most likely to become crime victims. Sacco and Johnson (1990) also used Canadian data to support a lifestyle/exposure theory. Those who averaged 30 or more evening activities outside the home per month were more than twice as likely to be robbed. One might conclude that it is safer to stay at home. However, these arguments apply to victimization from strangers; those who stay at home are more likely to be killed by family or friends (Messner and Tardiff, 1985).

While the routine activities perspective helps to identify high-risk situations, Kennedy and Forde note that one must also take into account such factors as the setting and other parties who interact with the victims. They also point out the need for conflict-resolution tactics to resolve problems beyond the simple avoidance of high-risk conditions (1990: 150).

Designing Out Crime: Hong Kong's Mass Transit Railway

Although ecological models of crime are still relatively selective, the knowledge that is available can be of use. Mark Gaylord and John Galliher (1991) describe how the Mass Transit Railway (MTR) in Hong Kong utilized an awareness of defensible space in order to "design out crime." Unlike governments in many North American cities, the Hong Kong government took seriously the knowledge that automobiles stifle cities. They were also aware that subways are potentially dangerous places in some cities. Therefore, the achievements of the MTR in Hong Kong are somewhat remarkable. The MTR is the world's busiest subway in terms of passenger density per mile. It is also the world's cleanest, and enjoys the lowest accident and crime rate. Passengers are safer *within* the MTR than when they are at street level. In Paris, some residents avoid the Metro late at night, because of concerns for their safety.

Mark Gaylord, a sociologist who does research and teaches in Hong Kong, spent many months studying the way the police and MTR authorities monitor the system. He and his co-author also describe the interaction between the police and those who planned the system. Stations were designed to minimize alcoves, dog-leg passageways, and columns, thus denying would-be criminals hiding places (Gaylord and Galliher, 1991: 19). Where this was not possible, mirrors and closed-circuit television were installed. There are no chairs, public toilets, fast-food facilities, or left-luggage lockers where bombs or drugs can be planted. Loitering is discouraged.

Every police officer is in constant contact with headquarters. Each station is equipped with closed-circuit television cameras that are monitored in a central control room. The MTR police claim that, for spotting criminals, the TV is better than foot patrols.

Each subway car has a Passenger Alarm Plunger which permits passengers to talk directly to the train operator, who may then request that police meet the train at the next stop. The operator will keep all doors closed until the police are ready to enter the train. Over the years, both passengers and criminals have learned that a police officer will be at the scene within 90 seconds of notification. Trains are built with a "straight-through" format, allowing passengers and police to walk freely between cars. One can often view the entire length of a train from either end. At the coupling that connects the cars, there is a slight rise which permits police to gain a good view over the heads of standing passengers. Stations offer a limited number of entrances and can be sealed off quickly, but since this can interfere with traffic flow, risks must be balanced. Since most stations are nearly a hundred feet below surface level, the chance of a suspect reaching the street without being captured is very low.

Hong Kong provides some other important insights to some of the principles discussed earlier. Some of our notions of population density must be considered within the context of a specific culture. Hong Kong has the highest population density in the world: 13 600 people per square mile. It also has a low crime rate, compared with other international cities: in 1986, New York City had 1582 murders, London registered 210, and Hong Kong, with 5.7 million people, recorded 67. Obviously, the low rate of crime in the MTR is related to the relative safety of residents on the streets of Hong Kong.

Under some conditions transit systems can become "crime attractors" (Brantingham and Brantingham, 1995). A study of nine stations of the Vancouver Sky Train found that public transit does attract crime (Robinson, 1998). It is possible that these crimes are the result of opportunities existing in these areas rather than being directly related to public transit.

Designing in Crime: The Destruction of Public Transportation in the U.S.

Most people would agree that public transportation and other aspects of urban design have an impact on pollution and other environmental problems. Fewer people would extend that thinking to crime. Governments can improve this aspect of city life. Public transportation is particularly important to that portion of the population most likely to be affected by crime. Some transportation specialists argue that urban sprawl and auto dependency generate alienation and encourage problem neighbourhoods like those described by Stark. These ecological factors, which seem to plague U.S. cities more than European ones, reflect the ineffectiveness of city planners and government officials. Admittedly, some economic interests find urban sprawl to be profitable, even though it damages the environment and probably contributes to the weakening of the social fabric that helps to control crime.

The U.S. love affair with the automobile has obviously been encouraged by automakers. In the 1930s, General Motors, in league with Standard Oil of California, Firestone Tires, and some cement companies, secretly purchased over a hundred public transportation systems in the U.S. and systematically destroyed them (Fischer, 1979). When they took over the Los Angeles system, the GM cartel destroyed the largest electrified transportation system in the world. The electric streetcars were replaced by GM buses, using Standard Oil diesel fuel and Firestone tires; the expansion of freeways was profitable for the cement companies in the cartel. Auto sales increased, and bus companies (owned by the cartel) lost money and petitioned for subsidies as public transportation declined and more people purchased cars. Los Angeles has become an ecological disaster. Many more lives are lost on freeways than on public transportation. But, in addition, has urban sprawl created criminogenic communities?

The San Francisco–Oakland Bay area has also suffered from the activities of the General Motors cartel. A light rail system could have been accommodated under the Bay bridge, but it was many years before it was discovered that the GM cartel controlled the bridge and had sabotaged public transportation plans. The tunnel under the San Francisco Bay was a much more expensive option. By the time a congressional investigator discovered the activities of the GM cartel in the 1970s, public transportation in much of the U.S. was in a state of shambles.

The point to be made here is that in Hong Kong public transportation is not only *profitable*, it reduces crime *directly* and provides service to working-class residents that *indirectly* influences criminogenic conditions. Most Canadian governments neglect public transportation, despite the inevitable concentration of populations in large urban centres. The application of ecological theories can create safer ways to move people about, contribute to community cohesiveness, and reduce crime. Let us turn now to the perspective of the potential offender.

The Criminal's Viewpoint

One study used 23 ex-burglars, who examined a series of slides and visited the sites of some burglarized apartments (Phelan, 1977). For the ex-burglars, familiarity with an area was critical, and techniques used to promote territoriality, as suggested by Newman (1973) and others, did not seem to be as important. Instead, Phelan found that the burglars emphasized surveillance as the major deterrent: could they be seen and reported by residents, passers-by, or patrol personnel?

On the other hand, different groups may have different strategies for choosing or avoiding targets. Sarah Boggs (1965) noted that crimes committed by blacks were committed most often in neighbourhoods where the offenders lived, but crimes committed by whites were more dispersed. Similarly, Carter and Hill (1979) studied the way offenders viewed Oklahoma City, and found that black and white offenders saw the city differently. Black offenders avoided areas that had good crime targets, because they were not familiar with them. White offenders, on the other hand, moved about the city more freely, and were aware of a greater range of targets.

Carter and Hill are cautious about the ability of policy-makers to use this knowledge to control crime effectively. They came to conclusions similar to those of Jane Jacobs, a perceptive observer of neighbourhoods, who has become well-known in Toronto. Her influential book, *The Death and Life of Great American Cities* (1961), argues that neighbourhoods are not protected primarily by the police, necessary though they may be. Rather, it is the intricate, almost unconscious, network of voluntary controls and standards among the people themselves that keeps the peace. No level of police enforcement can prevent crime if this informal mechanism is working badly (33).

Patricia and Paul Brantingham are aware of these dynamics, but they start from the perspective of the potential offender (1981). They argue that the actual commission of an offence is the end result of a multi-staged decision process, which identifies targets positioned in time and space. The potential offender uses cues to locate targets. He begins close to home because of familiarity, but he is also more likely to be known there and therefore discovered. For simplicity, the Brantinghams focus on the "routine activities" of the potential offender. The figures that follow simplify the stages of exploration that might lead to crime. Figure 10.1 shows the search area of a cluster of potential offenders. Although conscious of surveillance in the immediate neighbourhood, offenders may look for potential targets fairly close to home, and also explore areas adjacent to their neighbourhoods.

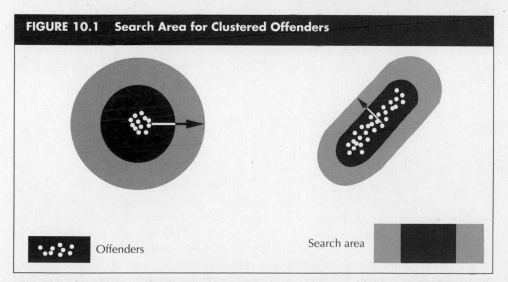

FIGURE 10.1 Search Area for Clustered Offenders

Offenders

Search area

Source: Brantingham, Patricia L. and Paul J. Brantingham (1981). "Notes on the Geometry of Crime." In Paul Brantingham and Patricia Brantingam (eds.), *Environmental Criminology.* Beverly Hills, CA: Sage. Reprinted by permission of Sage Publications.

Like other citizens, offenders move about the city and acquire knowledge about other parts of an urban area through work (even sporadically), school, shopping, or recreation. Criminals develop an **awareness space** about parts of the city. In general, offences occur within the criminal's awareness space (see Figure 10.2).

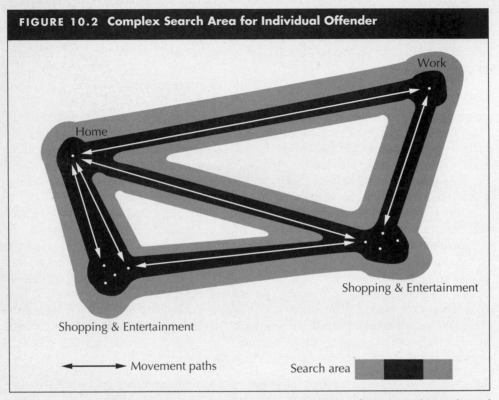

FIGURE 10.2 Complex Search Area for Individual Offender

Work

Home

Shopping & Entertainment

Shopping & Entertainment

Movement paths

Search area

Source: Brantingham, Patricia L. and Paul J. Brantingham (1981). "Notes on the Geometry of Crime." In Paul Brantingham and Patricia Brantingam (eds.), *Environmental Criminology*. Beverly Hills, CA: Sage. Reprinted by permission of Sage Publications.

Depending on how a city is arranged, the awareness space of criminals may be larger or smaller. If shopping, recreation, and work locations are dispersed, awareness spaces will be larger. The way one moves about the city will also influence awareness. If an offender is travelling on the subway in Toronto, it is very hard to examine nearby targets in apartment buildings—it would be easier by car or on foot. Opportunities to observe shops and other targets would be greater at the subway station, while the offender is waiting for a connecting bus. Figure 10.3 suggests a more complex search area for a cluster of offenders, perhaps a gang.

Although the search area may be large, the sub-area that contains good targets is smaller. For an individual offender, Figure 10.4 illustrates additional areas with good potential targets. Some of these additional targets, however, are outside the individual's awareness space, so only the cross-hatched areas are places of likely crime.

As with other routine activities approaches, the above ideas only deal with a limited aspect of crime; but they may help to explain changes in crime patterns in cities. For example, newer cities with a mosaic of shopping centres, work areas, and entertainment locations

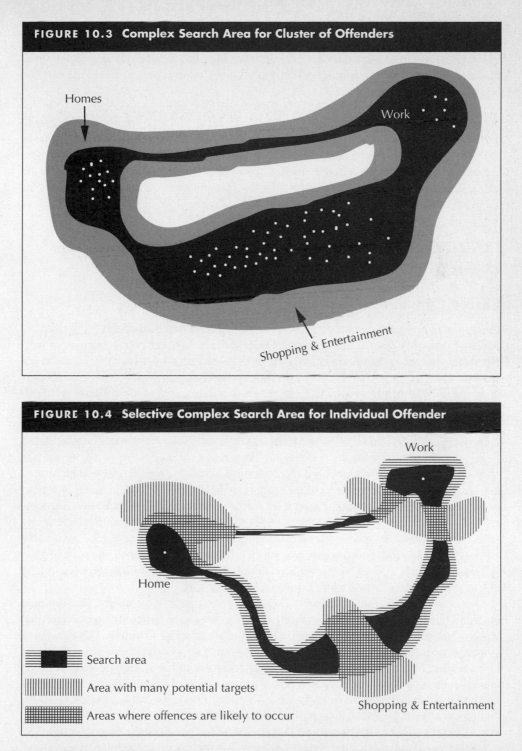

FIGURE 10.3 Complex Search Area for Cluster of Offenders

Homes

Work

Shopping & Entertainment

FIGURE 10.4 Selective Complex Search Area for Individual Offender

Work

Home

Search area

Area with many potential targets

Areas where offences are likely to occur

Shopping & Entertainment

Source (both figures): Brantingham, Patricia L. and Paul J. Brantingham (1981). "Notes on the Geometry of Crime." In Paul Brantingham and Patricia Brantingam (eds.), *Environmental Criminology*. Beverly Hills, CA: Sage. Reprinted by permission of Sage Publications.

will have dispersed crime patterns. Potential offenders travel more and have broader target search areas. This has obviously been influenced by the widespread use of automobiles. In Canada, cities in the west are newer than cities in the east and probably have poorer public transportation systems. Is this a partial explanation for lower crime rates in the east and higher crime rates in the west?

An interesting and useful application of these spatial mapping techniques has been devised by Kim Rossmo and the Vancouver Police Department. By using geographic profiling—identifying areas where crimes take place, the distances from the site of the crime to the site of other crimes, the characteristics of those areas, and the areas where offenders are likely to live—Detective Inspector Rossmo has been able to suggest areas where the police should direct their efforts (Rossmo, 1997). This strategy is particularly important for serial killers, who tend to follow certain patterns.

LINKING ECOLOGICAL STUDIES WITH OTHER SOCIO-LOGICAL STUDIES

Shared Communication Networks

In Chapter 6, on group dynamics, I discussed experiments that studied the "collective behaviour" that takes place in small groups. Under some conditions, people were more willing to intervene when deviance was observed. When participants knew each other, it increased the likelihood of intervention. One might assume that in *integrated, cohesive* neighbourhoods people would know each other. Therefore, it is necessary to look at situations in different cities and neighbourhoods that might increase integration.

Vienna, Austria, seems to provide evidence for and against some of the ecological arguments presented so far. I once lived in an area of Vienna that was densely populated, but during my year of residence the crime on my street that generated the most discussion was dogs defecating on the sidewalk. At the beginning of this chapter, Rodney Stark argued that dense populations could encourage crime. But in Hong Kong and in many European cities, property- and violent-crime rates were perceived to be low. Like the Swiss, Austrians carried large amounts of cash, merchants displayed goods on sidewalks without exercising excessive guardianship, and bicycles were often seen without locks. One quickly noticed the informal networks in the neighbourhoods, which provided social cohesion, the societal glue. Windows at the street level were often open during the summer. A walk to the store usually meant several conversations with neighbours along the way.

A century earlier, when apartments did not have their own water supply, people would meet and talk at the common water faucet. The term *Bassenagespräch* (basin conversation) arose, which referred to the gossip that developed while standing around the water fountain. Although the term has negative connotations of gossiping about neighbours, it also illustrates how a physical characteristic of a building brought people together to share information. With modern plumbing in each apartment, it is now easier to isolate oneself from the communication network that existed at the water fountain. This lack of privacy may have made it more difficult to present a better moral front, but it also created pressures to conform. Minding everyone else's business may be viewed as an advantage or disadvantage to North Americans who live in Vienna, but a communication system that spreads information probably reduces crime.

In one sense, the communication network, as well as cultural factors, may be more important than the factors emphasized by Rodney Stark and may make the routine activities perspective less relevant in parts of Europe.

In Glasgow, one term for neighbourhood gossip was "havin' a hangin'." That is, you hung out the window to talk to your neighbour across the narrow street. Naturally, with modern apartment buildings this is harder to manage if you are on the thirtieth floor and the neighbouring apartment is a hundred metres away. The conditions I am describing in Glasgow and Vienna obviously mean that in those cities there are more people watching what goes on in the street.

Eyes on the Street

Years ago, a bridge crossing the North Saskatchewan River in Edmonton was occasionally the scene of an accident that blocked traffic. No residences were close to the bridge, but when an accident occurred, someone immediately called the police. No one ever learned who the caller was, but when those involved in the accident, or someone trying to help, finally walked to a telephone, they were often surprised that the police had already been notified. In fact, the police often arrived before anyone got to a phone.

To what extent do eyes on the street deter crime? In some areas of Quebec, front porches are common: residents often sit on them, and sometimes chat with people as they go by. How does one assess this type of architecture in Quebec in terms of its impact on social cohesiveness and crime deterrence? As we saw in the chapter on collective behaviour, observing events does not necessarily mean that someone will act. Not only do we need conditions that encourage people to watch, we also need the type of community integration that increases the likelihood of action. In planning apartment complexes, architects thought that they could create inner courtyards and grassy areas where people would congregate. But these somewhat private inner courtyards are not where the action is. In some apartment complexes, mothers take their small children out next to the parking lots in playpens, and sit in their chairs because the comings and goings of people in the cars provide topics of conversation (who is driving a new car, who bought a new dress, etc.). The asphalt and auto exhaust fumes win out over the shade and green grass of the courtyard because the parking lot provides more interesting subject matter.

A man was standing by a bus stop. After a few minutes a woman opened a window and called to the man, asking where he was going. When he explained, the woman said that the bus he wanted didn't stop there anymore. He needed to go around the corner. How is this sort of activity related to crime prevention? If a stranger were doing something suspicious in the neighbourhood, would she be noticed? With the advent of television, it is possible that many "eyes on the street" have been lost. The violence and crime on television are more intriguing than observing the rare real thing out the window.

Imagine a little girl playing on a sidewalk. A car drives up. The man in the car tries to get the little girl to get into the car. She shakes her head and refuses. The proprietor of the small hardware store behind the girl has been watching. He now steps onto the sidewalk holding a hammer in his hand. The butcher in the shop next door has also been observing the scene. He comes to the doorway with the meat cleaver still in his hand. Let us ruin the suspense by mentioning that the man in the car is the little girl's father, but the point should be clear. Jane Jacobs and others argue that busy sidewalks with many interested observers looking on make for safer environments. We would add that the social-psychological studies described in the chapter on group dynamics suggest that when people know each other in the community, they are more willing to intervene.

In a study of the community cohesiveness in a dozen census tracts in Edmonton, we found ourselves referring to one section of town as the "Jane Jacobs Area" (Hackler, Ho, and Urquhart-Ross, 1974). It was low in socioeconomic status, but it had characteristics that suggested social cohesion. From one street corner we could see six small churches on one street. This suggested the possibility of smaller organizations where people could communicate more easily.

Fences can be barriers to communication, or they can expedite it. In this area, the lots were small, perhaps 25 feet wide, with small houses. Many fences were three to four feet tall, topped by a two-by-four with heavy wire used as the fencing material itself. One could lean on such fences and chat with a neighbour, perhaps about the vegetables in the front yard. In the home where I grew up, the fence separating the two back yards made communication between neighbours fairly easy. It was a wire fence with large openings. Many years ago, when my sister was about four years old, she was given a bone to take to the dog next door. When she did not return, we looked out the window. My sister was putting the bone through the fence so the dog could take a bite; then she would take the bone back and chew for a bit while the dog waited patiently for his turn. Surely, such a fence was no barrier to neighbourliness.

Regional Differences in Crime

Characteristics of neighbourhoods provide understandable suggestions regarding differences in crime, but why do provinces differ? Why does British Columbia always have higher crime rates than the Maritime provinces? Hartnagel's (1997) suggestion that geographical mobility breaks down community cohesiveness would be compatible with ideas about stress offered by Linsky, Bachman, and Strauss (1995). Using data on each of the United States, they developed a stress index. This included fifteen measures of stress such as business failures, unemployment, mortgage foreclosures, high-school dropout rates, divorce, infant mortality rates, and so on. This stress index was correlated with "self-destructive" behaviour, such as smoking, drinking, and suicide. The index was also correlated with "other-destructive" behaviour, such as domestic homicide and rape. However, homicide among strangers was not related to the stress index.

Admittedly, it may not always make sense to link state-wide measures to individual stress, and one could argue that it would be more meaningful to compare metropolitan areas rather than states; however, the findings do support some of the concerns stated in this book. *A highly individualistic society may work against a sense of community.* It may also produce greater stress at the individual level. As governments buy into the current free-enterprise philosophy, as indicated by the free trade arguments, they may also be accepting high stress at the individual level. If North America is, in general, a place where stress is high, is self-destructive and other-destructive behaviour also a normal result? Within Canada, does British Columbia produce communities with more stress than the Maritimes?

Clearly the physical environment can influence social relations. Spatial factors are related to characteristics of the neighbourhood and create circumstances that influence crime. Even if the impact of these factors is small, it behooves policy-makers to take them into account. Modest gains can sometimes be achieved with relatively little cost. The Hong Kong Mass Transit Railway offers an excellent illustration of intelligent public planning that can reduce the level of crime.

SUMMARY

1. Rodney Stark argues that crime is more likely when communities have certain characteristics that influence the way people respond. Some responses amplify deviance. These ecological explanations suggest that many things are happening at once. Thus, crime-prevention strategies need to change many factors so that they will reinforce each other.

2. Oscar Newman demonstrated the feasibility of crime prevention through environmental design that creates "defensible space." Routine activities in people's lives suggest that the availability of suitable targets, the absence of capable guardians, and the presence of motivated offenders explain the volume and distribution of predatory crime.

3. "Designing out crime" has been demonstrated in some high-public-use areas such as the Hong Kong and Washington, DC, subway systems.

4. Patricia and Paul Brantingham suggest that criminals develop an "awareness space" in which potential targets are noted.

5. Neighbourhood integration and the willingness to intervene are greater in cities where there is more interaction among residents.

KEY TERMS

awareness space	158		ecology	151
defensible space	153		routine activities	154

WEBLINKS

www.statcan.ca/english/Pgdb/State/justic.htm
Statistics Canada, Justice and Crime: current statistics on crime in Canada.

www.canada.justice.gc.ca/en/ps/rs/index.html
The Canadian Department of Justice: general information about Canada's criminal justice system.

MODERN CRIME PATTERNS

Instead of using conventional categories of crime, the chapters in Part III focus on certain patterns that generate a variety of social responses. Women's issues, the subject of Chapter 11, have changed criminological thinking considerably in recent decades. Chapter 12, on drug crimes, emphasizes the blatant hypocrisy that characterizes drug legislation and practices, particularly in the U.S. The results of this hypocrisy have created problems for society that outweigh the damage from the drugs themselves.

Chapter 13, on violent crime, spends less time on murderers and more time on murderous situations. We often forget that corporate violence harms more people than muggers do. In addition, families provide the most common setting for violence. Although schools are one of the safest settings, school boards use scarce educational funds to respond to rare incidents with metal detectors and security guards as if schools are common targets of terrorism. In Chapter 14 we look at both a rational approach to property and one that emphasizes the thrills involved. The chapter also calls attention to corporate and occupational crime, which, in dollar terms, far exceeds the damage from conventional property crimes.

Chapter 15, on the criminalization of sex, questions whether society should respond to certain sexual activities as crimes or as "order maintenance problems." Organized crime and gangs are reviewed in Chapter 16, which asks if society is structured in such a way as to create opportunities for, and pressures toward, illegal behaviour.

Chapter

WOMEN'S ISSUES AND CRIMINOLOGY

This chapter will:

- Note the neglect of feminist perspectives on crime.
- Review traditional explanations of female crime, the biases they contained, and the implications for women in the justice system and in prison.
- Debate the merits of power control theory and other arguments regarding trends in female crime.
- Examine the role of victimization, legal responses, and police responses to assault in the family.
- Caution the reader of the dangers of false accusations against men.
- Use other countries to illustrate more enlightened ways of responding to young females in trouble.

THE NEED FOR A FEMINIST PERSPECTIVE ON CRIME

Recent feminist perspectives have led to new insights into the way society should respond to women as offenders and as victims of crime (Chesney-Lind and Bloom, 1997; Chesney-Lind, 1997; Chunn and Menzies, 1996; Comack, 1993, 1996; Johnson, 1996). For a time there was a focus on the way the criminal justice system responded, but, as Holly Johnson (1996) points out, that approach is limited. The criminal justice system

> is cumbersome and unpredictable and can take control away from those whom it was designed to help. It cannot, nor should it, be expected to provide the entire solution to social problems. Wife battering and sexual violence, like many other criminal justice issues such as youth crime and prostitution, are not only legal issues—they are also issues for educators, health professionals, religious leaders, and community organizations. (1996: 226)

Until feminists looked carefully at this issue, however, scholars using traditional perspectives were simply not asking appropriate questions.

Marie-Andrée Bertrand (1969, 1979, 1983), at the Université de Montréal, is one of the better-known Canadian criminologists to emphasize the male bias in criminology. There has been an intellectual sexism in theories of female crime. This typically resulted in an emphasis on biological factors, which "naturally" had certain consequences. Men were innately more aggressive and females were naturally more nurturing. Social inequality was often ignored and economic forces were overlooked. Furthermore, the criminal justice system was characterized by institutionalized sexism in its response to females in trouble. A double standard was frequently applied. Sexual deviance and "immorality" were included with criminality. Traditional theories ignored the way agencies of social control reinforced women's place in a male-dominated society (Chesney-Lind, 1995).

Historically, most criminologists have been men. Thus, it is not surprising that traditional theories of crime pay little attention to gender or the impact of patriarchal power relationships. When women became producers of knowledge, the new ideas were not always well received by those who had had a monopoly on the creation of wisdom. New issues were raised that have largely been ignored by traditional scholars. Such transitions take place in all disciplines, but it is appropriate to describe how a male-dominated discipline has responded to feminist views in criminology over the past three decades.

Admitting Females to the Bastions of Male Criminological Thinking

More than other academic areas, criminology has probably resisted feminist thinking and suffered from what Chesney-Lind and Bloom (1997) call the "stag effect"—that is, men joust for position at the top of hierarchies. Similarly, women have been slower to move into positions of influence in criminological academic organizations. In academic associations in anthropology, psychology, sociology, and even medicine, women have become members of boards of directors, have served as presidents, and so on, for several decades. The process was slower in the American Society of Criminology (ASC), the most influential organization for Canadian and American criminologists. Few women served in leadership roles, and a woman did not become president of the ASC until Joan McCord was elected in 1988.[1] By contrast, Canadian male criminologists have been able to participate in the American "old-boy network" for some time, even though they represent a much smaller proportion of the ASC membership than do women.

While one should not use election to office as the only measure of intellectual acceptance, it is reasonable to argue that, compared with other areas of academic endeavour, criminology has been slow to utilize female talent to expand certain areas of knowledge. The Society for the Study of Social Problems (SSSP) recruited females for leadership positions in the 1960s, and by the late 1970s competent female scholars were easily winning elections and leading the society. The old-boy network broke down more quickly in the SSSP than in the ASC. Feminist thinking has broadened sociological perspectives on social problems. In criminology, feminist thinking has been more isolated from other areas of interest.

---

[1] Women had served as presidents of the Canadian Association for Criminological Research and the Canadian Criminal Justice Association from a much earlier date.

The abilities of women in the American Society of Criminology were not readily appreciated, nor were their intellectual contributions incorporated into programs to the extent they were in the Society for the Study of Social Problems. In response, women in the ASC organized a division on Women and Crime. By 1997 things had changed considerably: the majority of the Executive Board of the ASC were now women. In other organizations, such as the SSSP, intellectual interaction among male and female scholars had started earlier. Admittedly, some members of the Division of Women and Crime may have felt a need for a "sisterhood" as an understandable response to the situation in the American Society of Criminology, but the major thrust of the division has been to expand intellectual horizons. It is my impression that male criminologists, compared with other social scientists, have found it more difficult to interact with female colleagues who are bright, young, strong-minded, and who challenge traditional ideas. As a result, in criminology the fertilization of ideas that comes with the infusion of feminist thinking has come later than it has in other disciplines.

Male-Generated Myths of Feminism

Feminism has dramatically challenged criminology (Chesney-Lind and Bloom, 1997; Heidensohn, 1996; Stanko, 1995). When you are "one of the boys," it is easy to develop a certain perspective on feminist views of criminology. Part of that masculine bias might be summarized by three myths:

1. Feminist analyses of crime are not objective.
2. Feminist analyses focus narrowly on women.
3. There is only one feminist perspective.

Kathleen Daly and Meda Chesney-Lind (1988) address these myths. Their ideas are paraphrased here.

Myth No. 1: The Lack of Objectivity

Until recently, depictions of the differences between men and women have been made almost exclusively by white, privileged men. Men have no monopoly on objectivity, and, as a consequence, biased interpretations of human evolution and behaviour are offered as authoritative. For example, theories of the evolution of "mankind" emphasize how bipedalism and expanded brain size resulted from men's toolmaking and tool use in the hunting of large game. Some feminist anthropologists asked, "Have only men evolved?" (Hubbard, 1982). Although other new ideas have arisen in the past that offer alternative accounts of social life, feminist ideas are assumed to be biased, while the dominant and traditional modes of inquiry are *a priori* accorded greater legitimacy. Of course, symbolic interactionists question the entire concept of objectivity.

Myth No. 2: The Narrow Focus on Women

Feminists do not ignore men, although they give more attention to women. Obviously, traditional criminology focuses more on men, but whose social reality is worthy of explanation and who can be trusted to get it right? Much feminist work has focused on the way men think, theorize, collect, and marshal evidence. This contributes to a broadened awareness of how knowledge is created. Eleanor Miller's *Street Woman* (1986), for example, provides a vision of the world from the perspective of its subjects, street prostitutes. It not only provides insights about women, it makes us aware of other marginal people who struggle to survive in a society that claims to care about the weak, but has allowed practices that fall short of that goal. Traditional non-feminist criminology is more likely to be narrow, focusing on the lives of men, with minimal attention to gender relations. Although feminists will also make mistakes, the movement has broadened, not narrowed, the discipline.

Myth No. 3: The Single Feminist Perspective

Feminist scholarship includes a variety of views. It would be more accurate to say that it includes a *set of perspectives*, based on certain common assumptions about gender inequality. The dominant voice of American feminism is admittedly white, middle-class, and heterosexual, but other voices are beginning to reflect different social concerns. In addition, men are also engaged in feminist investigations, although criminology may lag behind other social sciences in this respect.

FEMINISM AND LAW IN CANADA

Elizabeth Comack (1993) reviews several of the theoretical frameworks that are relevant to the abuse of women. Several Canadian scholars use a socialist feminist perspective (Chunn and Menzies, 1996; Currie, 1990). These authors claim that the state, and particularly the legal system, is a major player in the process of organizing and reproducing a sexist, racist, and class-based social structure. This points to the importance of power, who wields it, and the role of the state in the dynamics of distributing that power.

Marxist and Socialist Feminism and Radical Feminism

Feminist views that utilize Marxist thinking have noted inequalities arising out of the structure of society. Women's unpaid labour in the home was undervalued; rape was seen as more serious when the woman "belonged" to a man or had not been "married off" by parents. Traditional Marxism ignores the fact that women give birth and are the primary caregivers of children. Historically, family, labour, and welfare laws let men control women. Shelley Gavigan (1986) contends that the law provides the medical profession with authority over women's reproduction. **Radical feminism** rejects liberal and socialist perspectives in favour of a more direct attack on patriarchy—the systematic male domination of women that permeates society. Laws governing reproduction and sexual assault are seen as extensions of patriarchal control over women.

Feminist views are broadening, rather than narrowing, criminological inquiry. They may shed light on certain puzzles, such as the fact that those who are repressed and disadvantaged are more criminal or at least become officially labelled as criminal. Women are disadvantaged in our patriarchal society. Why aren't they more criminal? True, disadvantaged women are more criminal than those who are not, but it is still difficult to explain the low rate of female crime. Feminist questioning goes beyond women and crime to include basic questions about the structure and function of the larger society and the dynamics of institutions that influence our lives.

TRADITIONAL EXPLANATIONS OF FEMALE CRIME

A short review of some of the thinking about female crime is useful to set the stage for both criticism and change. The traditional approach to female crime tends to focus on sex, and is almost oblivious to the fact that "it takes two to tango." Clearly, males who have sex are not deviant but unmarried women who have sex are. This double standard permeates the traditional, earlier "studies" in criminology.

The Sexualization of Female Crime

In *The Unadjusted Girl* (1923), William I. Thomas used case studies and equated female criminality with sexual delinquency. Thomas was influenced by biological models of crime. The reader will recall from Chapter 4, on traditional and biological theories, that Lombroso and Ferrero (1895) viewed women as less intelligent, more passive, and morally deficient, compared with men. Unless carefully supervised, women's sexual instincts, it was believed, would get them into trouble. Thomas also emphasized instincts and assumed that the need for love was more intense for women than for men. Prostitutes did not receive enough love in a socially approved manner. The double standard is blatant, in that unmarried men seeking sex are "normal," but unmarried women doing so are "unadjusted." According to Thomas, the differences between good and bad girls are often due to their social-class position and upbringing. Middle-class females are socialized to treasure their chastity. Lower-class girls lack this socialization. Good women sell their bodies for marriage, bad ones trade their bodies for excitement.

While these ideas are clearly sexist, they reflected a common view of female crime and had a great deal of impact on academia, the police, and other agents of social control. This basic theme persisted in criminology up to the 1960s, when Otto Pollak, in *The Criminality of Women* (1961), still saw women as basically inferior. He argued that official crime data under-reported the criminality of women. He emphasized the "chivalry hypothesis": The male-dominated justice system is lenient with women. But women are also deceitful. The deceitfulness of women is biologically based and socially induced. Men are less deceitful, because they must have an erection in order to have sex and cannot hide their failure. Men cannot pretend. A woman's body, however, permits pretence, and lack of orgasm does not prevent her from having sex. With the assurance gained from deceiving men, women can commit crimes that go undetected. It is hard for me to imagine how having sex without orgasm provides training for crime, but Pollak was considered an expert in the 1960s. Women's social roles as homemakers also provide cover for other crimes: sexually abusing young children and poisoning the sick. In addition, women mastermind the crimes and men carry them out. Pollak's ideas suggest that, compared with other areas of intellectual endeavour, criminology lagged behind. Such thinking persisted, however, even among women. Edith de Rham writes that females have an "inordinate talent for concealment and deception which characterizes the feminine style and makes the female lawbreaker harder to catch" (1969: 5). We are assured that most husbands are aware of this.

The reader can recognize the drift of the argument, so there is no need to summarize the many other scholars who wrote in this vein. However, it is important to note the consequences of this thinking. The agents of social control were imbued with this logic and applied the double standard; thus, the institutional reinforcement of these "explanations."

By the 1960s many criminologists were suspicious of biological models and favoured socialization to explain female crime, especially their tendency to commit fewer crimes than males. Essentially, boys and girls learn different roles. Boys learn to become breadwinners and girls learn to be homemakers and caregivers. Boys are taught that they must take risks and be assertive, while girls are instructed that they should be passive, cautious, and dependent (Bertrand, 1969; Naffine, 1987: 43–47). Thus, we tolerate boisterous and aggressive behaviour among boys but not among girls. The attributes compatible with crime are those that characterize masculinity. When women commit crime, then, they are seen as poorly socialized or as having taken on masculine traits.

The chapter on psychological perspectives (Chapter 5) reviewed Lawrence Kohlberg's ideas on moral development (Kohlberg, 1976; Jennings, Kilkenny, and Kohlberg, 1983). According to Kohlberg, females do not move up the same levels of moral maturity as males. They develop concern for and sensitivity to others, but they are less inclined to develop insights into the abstract and universal rights that are part of the final stage of moral development. Carol Gilligan (1982, 1987) questions this conclusion. If women operate at a lower level of moral development, she asks, why do they commit less crime than men? She goes on to point out the masculine bias in Kohlberg's work, and in psychology in general.

Invalidating Women's Experiences

Liz Kelly and Jill Radford (1996) explore the processes by which women's experiences of sexual violence are invalidated. Such events are less likely to be reported to the police if they are not seen as "real crimes." They conclude that the law defines sexual violence very narrowly, thereby trivializing women's experience with sexual abuse.

Women themselves often downplay abusive situations because the alternative of taking action may be seen as even more undesirable. Unfortunately, this "nothing really happened" response, as a way of rationalizing their failure to take official action, may lead to the denial of services that might help them in the future. When the law says "nothing really happened," it implies the woman was not abused. Thus, women who withdraw a complaint of rape or other abuse are not referred to counselling services. The way women define situations and their expectations of help arise within an institutional framework that is unsupportive.

Institutional Support for the Sexualization of Female Crime

Meda Chesney-Lind (1997) and Holly Johnson (1996) draw on considerable empirical research which shows that the justice system not only has been a means for controlling females who do not conform to certain expectations, but has been part of the pattern of patriarchal power that has put females at a disadvantage in society in general. Psychiatric institutions also play a role in controlling women. Women are placed in the "sick" role when they do not perform in traditional ways. Diane Hudson (1987) contends that women are more likely than men to be lobotomized to solve behavioural problems. A bias on the part of psychiatrists is illustrated by the following case history:

> C was diagnosed as "reluctant to accept authority" when she found it difficult to relate to a male psychiatrist after disclosing … a long-term stable lesbian relationship. Her lesbianism was interpreted as a personality disorder for which she received drugs. She was diagnosed as "hostile and aggressive" towards the stepfather who had sexually assaulted her when she was

thirteen … She confided, just before she died, that a "brain operation" to help her had been discussed. She perceived this as a threat rather than as a mode of treatment and the fear instilled by this threat probably contributed greatly to her suicide. (Hudson, 1987: 117)

The "sick" role is also used to "explain" women who kill their children. Psychiatrists have trouble viewing such women as "normal." Similarly, if a woman were to attempt suicide, that would confirm the diagnosis that the dysfunction was with her, not with her situation. Dorothy Chunn and Shelley Gavigan summarize this point rather well:

Criminalization is the control mechanism reserved for the few women not constrained by fear and medicalization, that is, those who directly attack male power. Historically, men have frequently used criminal law against women who attempt to assert control over their own reproduction and sexuality. (1991: 291)

Menzies, Chunn, and Webster (1992) summarize much of the research that has been done on the processing of women vis-à-vis men by clinicians. When accused of crime, females are more likely than males to get a clinical evaluation. Those males who are remanded for clinical assessment are more likely to have criminal records than the women, who are more likely to have a psychiatric history. Men who commit serious crimes of violence are more likely to be seen by psychiatrists as legally and morally guilty and deserving of lengthy prison terms (Allen, 1987a, 1987b). Female offenders are transformed into pitiful victims who lack moral culpability.

When Menzies and his colleagues analyzed data from the Metropolitan Toronto Forensic Service, gender did not play as important a role in predicting outcomes as one might antic-ipate from previous research. Instead, the dominant characteristic of both the females and their male counterparts in this study was their marginality. They tended to be homeless, unemployed, and isolated, and were repeatedly involved with criminal justice, welfare, and mental health agencies. As research looks at the impact of gender more closely, we may find that the interaction of a number of factors must be taken into account.

In the past, however, privileged women supported a general pattern of patriarchy during periods of reform, such as those that led to the creation of children's and family courts, which came into existence in South Australia in 1895, Illinois in 1899, and Canada in 1908. These middle-class women typically supported the stereotypes of the model female, and were active in the creation of monitoring systems designed to keep young girls from engag-ing in inappropriate behaviour (Feinman, 1980; Messerschmidt, 1986).

Although most reformers probably had a genuine desire to help young females, the insti-tutional response by police and other agencies usually victimized women. For example, physical examinations for venereal disease and pregnancy were typically given to women, regardless of the charges against them. The results could then be used as evidence that these women were promiscuous (Chesney-Lind, 1973, 1989). Sanctions were also severe. Traditional views of women placed them in one of two categories: madonna or whore (the word *madonna* has been redefined in recent years). While chivalry may have been extended to the madonnas, it was not available to the whores (Feinman, 1980).

In Chicago in 1899, where the family court was introduced to North America shortly after it had been founded in South Australia, girls were more likely to be sent to reformatories than boys. A similar pattern has existed in Canada. In the 1960s, Barbara Nease (1971) found that even though girls in Hamilton, Ontario, seemed to be screened out of the system somewhat by the police, once they appeared in court, they were more likely to be incarcerated than boys.

Caution is appropriate here, however, since other Canadian studies indicate more favourable treatment for girls and women than for boys (Chunn and Gavigan, 1991).

Sexual behaviour, however, is still more likely to be noted for females when sentencing or charging is being considered. Dorothy Chunn studied the Toronto Juvenile and Family Court before World War II, and found that status offences were twice as likely to lead to court hearings for girls as for boys (Chunn, 1992). In Australia, Linda Hancock (1981) found that 40 percent of the referrals of girls to court specifically mentioned sexual and moral conduct, while such comments were made in only 5 percent of the referrals of boys. Christy Visher (1983) examined 785 police-suspect encounters in three American communities, and found that younger females received harsher treatment than their older counterparts. The police adopted a more paternalistic and harsher attitude to deter future inappropriate sexual behaviour. Furthermore, female suspects who violated typical middle-class standards of traditional behaviour did not receive chivalrous treatment.

Chesney-Lind's work in Hawaii provides a useful illustration of how the morality of one culture was imposed on another, creating particular hardships for the females. In Honolulu, during 1929–30, over half of the girls were charged with "immorality." Another 30 percent were charged with "waywardness." Girls were twice as likely to be detained as their male counterparts. Even in the 1950s, girls constituted half of those committed to training schools in Honolulu (Chesney-Lind, 1989).

Similar practices existed in England. Lorraine Gelsthorpe (1986) noted that English police were concerned about the sexual behaviour of girls. In the case of a 14-year-old girl, the police pursued a truancy application over objections from parents and social services, and despite a written medical report that the girl was pre-menstrual. The reason was, in one officer's words, "I know her sort … I'm still suspicious that she might be pregnant. Anyway, if the doctor can't provide evidence we'll do her for being beyond the care and control of her parents, no one can dispute that. Running away is proof " (136).

A word of caution is appropriate here. While perceived sexual behaviour influences the treatment of women in the criminal justice system, in Canada women appear to receive more lenient treatment for crimes of violence and property offences (Chunn and Gavigan, 1991). This may be due to the double standard, by which one assumes that a woman who is "acting that way" must be sick and irrational. In addition, women may be viewed as the unwilling accomplices of men. Clearly, the double standard and the "chivalry hypothesis" influence the way laws are administered, but the results are mixed. Men and women are treated differently, but the debate over who gets treated worse by the system may obscure a more important point: what type of criminal justice system marginalizes *both* men and women, and decreases the likelihood that they can participate more adequately in normal society?

Women in Prison

This sexualization of female crime continues through the justice system into prison. Margaret Shaw (1991) and her colleagues (1992) have examined the situation of female inmates in the Canadian federal prison system. Sentences under two years are served in provincial facilities, but sentences over two years are served in the federal system. In 1992, of the 12 000 federal prisoners in Canada, about 250 were women. Because of the relatively small number of women in Canada receiving long sentences, a single federal penitentiary for women was built in Kingston, Ontario, in 1934.

Although Aboriginal women make up only 2 percent of the population, they represent 23 percent of the female federally sentenced population. Both Aboriginal men and women are over-represented in prison in Canada, but the discrepancy is greater for Aboriginal women than for men (LaPrairie, 1987, 1990). The majority come from the Prairie provinces. Thus, when they are sent to prison in Kingston, they are effectively cut off from family visits. Women are also now serving longer sentences. With the abolition of the death penalty in Canada in 1976, women (and men) sentenced for first-degree murder must serve 25 years before they can be considered for parole. For second-degree murder, the period is ten years.

This has created more hardship for women than for men, because of their removal from homes and families. Recent programs have allowed some federally sentenced women to serve time in provincial institutions closer to their families. Unfortunately, serving time in separate wings of provincial institutions may mean that programs and facilities are unavailable to federally sentenced women. When provincial institutions are co-educational, it may be an improvement for both men and women; but there are risks. Usually, security concerns about the men take priority over co-educational programming. The use of minimum-security institutions for women is often not considered because of the long sentences. However, the risk to the public may not be as high as the length of the sentence suggests.

Some of the problems faced by female offenders in Canada may be exacerbated by geography, but others are similar to problems in other countries (Rafter, 1990). Although females make up a small proportion of prisoners in Western countries, there has been a dramatic increase in the use of imprisonment for women in the United States. By contrast, Australia and England and Wales show less dramatic increases. Scotland seems to have very few women in prison (Carlen, 1983). Canada tends to fall between the U.S. and other English-speaking countries: we imprison women at a higher rate than England (Shaw et al., 1992) but at a lower rate than the United States.

From the standpoint of understanding women and crime, what can we learn by studying this small group of long-term female offenders in Canada? How different are they from the 8800 women sentenced for less than two years in provincial prisons? Three-quarters of the federal offenders studied by Shaw and colleagues had not been convicted of a criminal offence before, nor had they been convicted of minor offences. What purpose is being served by these long sentences in prison? Shaw argues that most of these women did not come from caring and protective environments. Over half of these women said they had injured themselves or attempted suicide at some stage in their lives. Can they be expected to respond without anger in a prison environment? Should, for example, a woman with a history of depression, found crouched under a wash basin, crying, be punished for hiding? Is rehabilitation possible under the present prison circumstances? While acknowledging that these women have committed crimes, they are often victims of abuse, violence, or poverty. Ongoing research by Elizabeth Comack (1993) on 727 women imprisoned between 1988 and 1993 in a provincial prison in Manitoba presents a picture of female offenders as victims. Seventy-eight percent had been sexually and/or physically abused. For Native women, it was 81 percent. Interviews reinforced the image of women who had gotten a poor deal in life, but Comack found these heart-wrenching stories were really about survivors rather than simply victims. She saw incredible strength in these women, reinforcing her doubts about applying such concepts as "learned helplessness" to women in abusive relationships.

Margaret Shaw recommends a shift in strategy that is more compatible with John Braithwaite's reintegration argument, discussed in Chapter 8, on the consensus tradition. It involves changing the basis of sentencing to one that focuses on the effects on the victim and the community, and how these might be redressed, rather than on the breach of the law itself. A number of mediation schemes have demonstrated the scope of such an approach, even for offences involving violence. Canada has been slow to use mediation programs (Nylund, 1991), but there is reason to believe that more emphasis on dispute resolution, mediation, and group processes, along with treatment and support, rather than on punishment and control, would yield a better return for the society as well as for female offenders. In her book, *Partial Justice*, Nicole Hann Rafter (1990) presents a similar perspective for the United States. She examines prisons for women in the U.S. from 1800 to 1935, and notes that in one New York prison for women at least half of the inmates were convicted of sexual misbehaviour, including such "crimes" as premarital pregnancy. Rafter argues that although prisons have changed, women still suffer from sexual stereotyping.

Reorienting Thinking about Females and Crime

Feminist theories of crime focus on the consequences of the roles women are expected to play, including problems caused by racism and poverty. This includes the impact of the agencies of social control, which respond to males differently than they do to females. For example, parents use these agencies to resolve conflicts with daughters. In 1929 and 1930 in Honolulu, 44 percent of the girls who appeared in court were referred by parents (Chesney-Lind, 1989). Other research shows that juvenile courts have traditionally received referrals for females more often than for males for "deviant" activities that differ from regular crime. In other words, parents, the agents of social control, and society in general "control" the behaviour of girls differently than they do the behaviour of boys, and *these differences in the control process must be incorporated in explanations of deviance*. "Anyone seriously interested in examining women's crime … must carefully consider the role of the contemporary criminal justice system in the maintenance of modern patriarchy" (Chesney-Lind, 1986).

Radical theorists have long called attention to such differences in power relationships. Sometimes referring to themselves as "critical" criminologists, they now include women in their categories of disadvantaged. Similarly, feminists who look at agencies of control make arguments similar to the arguments of those who have examined these agencies critically for years. The gap between feminist thinking and much other work done in criminology is not as great as some people imagine. Perhaps feminist authors have not made the link with the larger issues concerning marginal people in general as often as they should, but many of them certainly do (Daly, 1990; Daly and Chesney-Lind, 1988).

The Desexualization of Female Crime

Traditional images of female roles and female crime obviously influence the response of the agencies of social control. However, the behaviour of the agencies persists, even when evidence indicates that those traditional images and explanations are faulty. Even before feminist scholars introduced innovative thinking in this area, empirical research was pointing out that the similarities in criminal patterns between men and women were greater than the differences, except that the frequency and seriousness of female crime are less (Cernkovich and Giordano, 1979b; Canter, 1982). Female delinquency was not particularly specialized, but tended to parallel that of male delinquents. The sexualization of female crime may be understandable, in that many marginal women are struggling for survival. Selling and using sex may be one of the few areas in which they have an advantage over males. Female crime is closely connected to the fact that females are more vulnerable as victims. Girls are more likely than boys to be abused in the family, and their abuse begins earlier and lasts longer (Finkelhor and Baron, 1986). Females from disadvantaged settings, particularly juveniles, require more protection, and admittedly it is difficult to know how to provide effective protection.

However, the crimes they commit tend to be similar to those of males, but of a lesser volume. Instead of sexualizing female crime, feminist thinking calls our attention to the needs of marginal people and less powerful groups in a patriarchal and hierarchical society.

Power Control Theory: Hagan, Gillis, and Simpson

At the University of Toronto, Hagan, Gillis, and Simpson have developed **power control theory** to explain different rates of female crime (1985, 1987). The focus is on the relative positions of power held by husbands and wives. Power in the workplace is translated into power relations in the household. These relations influence the way boys are controlled, as distinct from girls. In a *patriarchal family*, the husband is employed outside the family, with a wife not working outside the family. In such families, husbands tend to be dominant and daughters are expected to be like their mothers; that is, they should prepare to enter the "cult of domesticity." The sons are expected to prepare for participation in the external labour force.

In the *egalitarian family*, both parents work in positions of influence outside the home. Therefore, consumption and production activities are shared by males and females. In egalitarian families, parents produce sons *and* daughters for entry into the production sphere of the labour force.

In the patriarchal family, females are more controlled. Both father and mother exert more control over daughters than sons, but daughters are even more controlled by their mothers. In egalitarian families, parents treat sons and daughters more equally. In general, mothers gain power relative to husbands, and daughters gain freedom relative to sons. The result is that, in patriarchal families, girls are less inclined to take part in risk-taking activities, which are acceptable for boys. In egalitarian families, risk-taking is more acceptable for girls. Thus, *differences in delinquency by gender are greater in patriarchal than egalitarian families*.

As females become more "empowered," their risk-taking and offending should increase. Chesney-Lind (1989) feels that power control theory offers a limited definition of patriarchal control, which focuses on parental supervision and variations in power, primarily economic, *only within the family*. When mothers participate in the work force, particularly in high-status occupations, they provide "egalitarian" models for their daughters, which leads to increased risk-taking and hence delinquency. This is a variation on the earlier liberal feminist approach, only it is the mother's "liberation" that causes the daughter's crime. Chesney-Lind argues that there is no evidence that as women's labour-force participation and female-headed households have increased, girls' delinquency has increased. Instead, it appears to have declined or remained stable (Ageton, 1983). Merry Morash and Meda Chesney-Lind (1991) partially tested power control theory, and found that identification with a nurturing mother was a more important variable than control.

Power control theory is generally compatible with liberal feminist thinking. Freda Adler's book *Sisters in Crime* argues that by striving for social and economic independence, women have begun to alter social institutions that protected males in positions of power (Adler, 1975).

As women successfully compete with men, they will also be exposed to similar opportunities to achieve, but also opportunities to cheat. Thus, the women's liberation movement will produce increased amounts of female crime, because it creates an environment in which the roles of males and females converge. Similarly, Rita Simon, in *The Contemporary Woman and Crime* (1975a), analyzed changes in arrest rates for females, and concluded that increases in arrest rates are a function of the changing role of women. James Messerschmidt (1993) combines a number of these ideas by arguing that power, in terms of gender and social class, is central to understanding why men commit more crimes and more serious crimes than women. The interaction of gender and class creates positions of power and powerlessness, which give rise to differing opportunities for crime. One criticism of power control theory is that it focuses on the formal threats or controls in patriarchal families and ignores the informal controls from shame and embarrassment. Understanding the impact of these factors is difficult. For example, Blackwell (2000) reported that females were more threatened by shame than males, but this was true for both patriarchal and egalitarian families. Thus, shame may be an important control factor for girls in general. The impact of embarrassment was not what Blackwell expected—there were no gender differences in the patriarchal families. In fact, in the egalitarian families females perceived lower threats of embarrassment than males. Does this suggest that girls, compared with boys, can be controlled more by shaming but less by embarrassment?

Summarizing the complexity of this research is not possible here, but as mothers take on more important roles and as fathers play a larger role in the social development of their children, these changes may influence girls differently from boys.

TRENDS IN FEMALE CRIME: THE LIBERATION HYPOTHESIS

With more empirical research focusing on women, different theories have arisen to explain female crime. One aspect of this work was that it sharpened the use of official criminological data and the assessment of trends. Central to this debate was the question, "Are women committing more crime?"

Feminist criminologists disagree over the **liberation or convergence hypothesis**, which suggests that as women become more liberated and have greater job opportunities, they will also engage in more crime. Male and female behaviour will converge (Adler, 1975; Simon, 1975b; Smart, 1976). Women now have increased opportunities to commit larceny, fraud, and embezzlement. Fox and Hartnagel (1979) examined trends in Canadian female conviction rates for theft from 1931 to 1968. Conviction rates increased, along with female labour-force participation and post-secondary education rates. Although there were changes in female work patterns during this period, it preceded the strong feminist movement that developed in the 1970s in Canada. Rita Simon and Jean Landis (1991) revised Simon's 1975 theme, adding more recent data. They again argue that the data support an "opportunity thesis," which asserts that, as women assume positions of greater authority and prestige, they will use the new opportunities to commit white-collar crime.

Criticisms of the Liberation Hypothesis

Correlation is not the same as causation, and some scholars have criticized the interpretations of data offered to support the liberation perspective. Shelley Gavigan (1983, 1987) notes that the increase in female crime does not support the liberation hypothesis. Paul Maxim and Carl Keane (1992) likewise found little support for the hypothesis when they looked at violent deaths in Canada between 1950 and 1986. Meda Chesney-Lind (1986) points out that since the 1800s, criminologists, as illustrated by Otto Pollak (1961), have issued warnings that the emancipation of women would result in dramatic increases in female crime. In reality, female offenders are not liberated professional women but are still minority women from backgrounds of poverty.

Peggy Giordano and her colleagues (1981) state that although women are more likely to enter the labour force, they occupy disadvantaged positions with poor security and pay. Thus, the increase in female property crime rates is the result of the economic marginalization of women, rather than an expansion of opportunities. Steffensmeier (1981) notes that the amount of female crime is so small, it does not take much to show an increase. For example, there was an increase of 600 percent in Canada in the number of women charged with first-degree murder between 1976 and 1984. This shocking figure is less menacing when we realize that the increase was from two to fourteen offenders (Johnson, 1986: 8). Police decisions to use first-degree instead of second-degree charges might also have played a role.

Another view is that the chivalry response is fading, in terms of the sanctioning of women. Instead of seeing actual increases in female crime, the greater equalization of gender roles leads to a less lenient treatment of women (Steffensmeier, 1981). Others argue that the chivalry hypothesis is still operating, particularly for juveniles (Chunn and Gavigan, 1991).

Most of these studies analyze data at one point in the criminal justice process, and thus it is very difficult to detect the effect of small but incremental influences that operate at many levels. We need studies of actual offenders, but obviously this poses problems for researchers. Such studies are rare for either male or female criminals. Thus Jody Miller's (1998) study comparing active female and male armed robbers is unique. The motivation for the female robbers is complex, being both similar to and different from their male counterparts.

Female Crime as a Product of Victimization

Holly Johnson (1987) argues that prostitution thrives in a society that values women for sex more than for their labour. Entry into prostitution often follows running away from home, frequently to escape abuse. The street, unfortunately, puts women at greater risk of violence. They tend to become psychologically and economically dependent, often on males who abuse them. Comack (1992) points out that women are concentrated in jobs in which the wages are the lowest. Canada has a "feminization of poverty." Single mothers are especially at risk. "As many as 85 percent of single-parent families are headed by women. In 1987, 57 percent of these families were living below the poverty line" (142).

Jill Rosenbaum (1989) studied the records of women who had been sentenced as girls to the California Youth Authority (CYA) in the 1960s. Approximately twenty years later, it was clear that these institutional programs to help girls did not help much in avoiding crime. All but 6 of 159 cases (96 percent) were arrested again as adults, even though two-thirds of these women had earlier been sentenced to the Youth Authority only for status offences, mostly running away. The girls (now women) uniformly came from extremely troubled homes and received little help after contact with authorities, even though the majority were not initially convicted of delinquent acts.

The mothers of these girls also had very troubled lives. By the time they were sixteen, their mothers had been married an average of four times, experienced abuse at the hands of another, and, in turn, abused their children: 37 percent of them had been charged with child abuse and/or neglect. These mothers of CYA wards tended to marry young. The girls in this study, who became wards of the state of California in the 1960s, were running from miserable family situations and, as Rosenbaum states, they were double victims: victims of their families and of the criminal justice system. However, she also makes it clear that to say the system was primarily at fault is simplistic. It is impossible to disentangle system effects and family effects in the adult criminality of these girls, and the options for the system to deal with runaways were limited.

Recent work on child abuse also suggests that girls are more likely to be victimized than boys. Moreover, Cathy Widom (1986) notes that abused or neglected females are more likely to have records of adult crime. Interestingly enough, men with abuse backgrounds are more likely to commit violent crimes as adults, but with women who have suffered abuse, the link is not specifically with violence. *Females are more vulnerable, both in their families and in the agencies that respond to their difficulties.* They run away from home, only to find that the streets are also unsafe. They use the only commodity they have to sell that men are always willing to buy.

Domestic Networks among Disadvantaged Women

Eleanor Miller's *Street Woman* (1986) goes beyond individual case histories of prostitutes and describes the social networks that support street hustling. She provides a strong argument that the bulk of women's crime—and prostitution is only one expression—usually evolves out of the severe social and economic problems confronted by teenage girls. Women of colour are particularly vulnerable. Recruited by older males with criminal records, these women organize into **domestic networks**. These networks secure a semblance of financial and emotional security among impoverished and alienated segments of a highly stratified society. Carol Stack first used the term "domestic networks" in her book *All Our Kin* (1974). Female kin who share in the care of children, sometimes including the father's female kin, as well as friends, chip in for rent, and sometimes act as safety nets for the poor in the event of a late welfare cheque, robbery, or some other disaster.

The downside of the domestic network arrangement is that it is difficult for individuals, through hard work or good fortune, to become upwardly mobile. To disentangle oneself from the network would mean withdrawing one's resources from others in need. I saw a similar situation within Australian Aboriginal communities. In a society that was expected to share, your food pantry, refrigerator, and other belongings were always available to relatives and friends. Any aspirations to "get ahead" were easily frustrated in such an environment.

Miller (1986) further points out that these circles of domestic networks intersect with deviant social circles primarily engaged in hustling of different kinds, which she calls "deviant street networks." It becomes easy to understand how involvement with drugs, prostitution, and a variety of crimes is an almost inevitable consequence. It is also easy to see why the criminal justice system is completely ineffective, and why these women hold it in disdain.

A Superior Justice System Response to Marginal Females in France

One might sympathize with judges and social workers who must choose between sending girls back to dysfunctional families or to an institutional facility. However, a case that I witnessed in France illustrated a more flexible approach. The 14-year-old wished to take a hairdressing course, the mother disapproved, the girl ran away and stole food. In almost all juvenile cases in France, the youth appears in the judge's office *the same day as police contact*. The judge must decide if a trial is appropriate. In this case, the judge predictably brushed the offences aside and concentrated on the basic problem. I interviewed the girl in a group home, where children could leave very easily. The judge did not attempt to impose a solution. The social worker was to attempt family reconciliation; the girl could go home at any time, but she could clearly also choose to stay in the group home while things were being resolved. If the girl had been older, 16 or so, the judge might have considered establishing the girl independently in an apartment, but 14 was rather young.

What impressed me was that the French girl viewed the judge differently from the way girls view the system in North America. She had considerable input into the decisions, saw the judge as flexible, and was aware that she could call upon "her" judge in the future. If there is no trial, French judges cannot impose incarceration. In 80 to 90 percent of the cases, the judge forgoes trial. Thus, the relationship between judge and children is almost always seen as helpful, from the standpoint of the juveniles.

But certainly, I thought, some girls pose more serious problems. Therefore, I found a residential facility for really "difficult" girls. I was surprised to learn that 40 percent of the girls connected with this residence were living in apartments independently, so they could attend specialized schools or work in a variety of settings. In the residence itself, the girls each had keys to their rooms, but the staff did not. In response to my question, "Can they go home on weekends?" the answer was, "Of course, but we won't pay the train fare every week." When the staff was organizing a bike ride, I noticed that no one was counting noses. The response was, "they will be able to find their way back." I was concerned that they might run away; the French staff did not recognize this as a problem. Preventing girls from leaving was simply not their concern. Running from a residence or not obeying a judge is not a crime. It can be annoying, and the judge will probably be unhappy the next time the juvenile wants help, but punishment is not an alternative. Of course, girls have to obey the rules of a residence or they will not be allowed to stay. These girls had more control over their destinies than their North American counterparts.

In North America, judges and others simply impose decisions on juveniles. The clients of the system often feel powerless. The logic of the American mentality, in contrast to the French, was expressed by Judge Milligan, representing the National Council of Juvenile Court Judges, when he argued in Congress that the current legislation allows a child to decide for himself whether he will go to school, live at home, run away from home, or even obey orders of the court (Chesney-Lind, 1988: 158). Compared with other countries, we punish people, not just for committing crimes, but for disobeying those in authority. We have no trouble rationalizing this practice, but in fact, the continual harassment of people who have done wrong, but who are no longer committing crimes, increases the likelihood that some of these former offenders will be criminalized.

French judges are also concerned about such issues as school, running away, and where children live, but *it is not a crime to disobey administrative rules*. The judge can scold and complain, but punishment can only be justified if there is another actual crime. The French practice lets girls explain their situations. When I asked one judge what she would do if a girl refused to follow the judge's recommendation, she replied, "My choice may not have been the best either, but I will still be here, ready to help, while the girl is working through her problem." But, I asked, what if the girl is potentially suicidal? The judge responded, "There are risks in helping young people make their decisions versus imposing our own, but in the long run we accomplish little if the juvenile isn't willing."

The French system is certainly "parental" but it uses strategies that increase the likelihood of rapport between juveniles and judges, enhance the possibility of genuine help, and *decrease the likelihood of girls being victimized a second time by the agents of social control.*

The Dangers of False Accusations

Feminist writers have not devoted much attention to false accusations against men. Dr. Robert Ross of the University of Ottawa was charged with offences against female inmates at Grandview Training School in Cambridge, Ontario. After four harrowing years, he was acquitted. In April 1992, before any charges were laid, the CBC television series *The Fifth Estate* broadcast a program on the training school, calling it a story of "brutality and betrayal" (LaFramboise, 1997). Although Ross was acquitted, he was not compensated for the $600 000 he had spent on legal fees, for income lost when he was prohibited from teaching, or for the irreparable harm done to his reputation as an international expert on offender rehabilitation.

In the concern for helping female victims, have we sometimes neglected principles of justice? A self-help book, *The Courage to Heal*, by Ellen Bass and Laura Davis (1997) suggests that clear memories of sexual abuse are not prerequisites for concluding one has been victimized. If you think you were abused and your life shows the symptoms, then you were. Such claims are being made even as we become more aware of the "false memory syndrome." It is possible to create memories of something which did not happen, especially with the help of a therapist making suggestions, and use them to "explain" current feelings of inferiority and so on. It also takes little imagination to envision situations in which self-interest might lead females to falsely accuse a husband, a teacher, a counsellor in a youth custody centre, a boss, or someone in authority. Political correctness can also be intimidating. Preventing female crime certainly involves issues of poverty, abuse in the home, and negative environments in custodial institutions, but the important contributions of feminist scholars, which often link female crime with victimization, can be weakened if others use these ideas to make indiscriminate attacks on men.

At present, our justice system is poorly designed to deal with such situations. Fear of accusations can inhibit staff at youth custody centres and make them less effective in their efforts to work with girls. Nor does an acquittal necessarily protect the innocent. *The cause for protecting women from abuse will be poorly served if attempts to correct past injustices against women lead to future injustices against men.*

SELECTING APPROPRIATE EXPLANATIONS OF FEMALE CRIME

None of the current theories satisfactorily answers basic questions. For example, the disadvantaged usually commit more crimes than the advantaged. However, women seem to be disadvantaged but are still less criminal. (Ngaire Naffine gives a plausible explanation in Chapter 7, on social interaction and families.)

Another debate concerns whether or not theories should be **gender-neutral**—that is, the same reasoning should explain crime for all human beings. Doug Smith and Ray Paternoster (1987) tested some of the conventional theories in order to predict marijuana use among males and females. They concluded that the factors that influence marijuana use are similar for males and females. They suggest that the sex differences in the amount of deviance reflect *differential exposure* to common factors that precipitate deviant behaviour.

Thus, Smith and Paternoster favour "gender-neutral" theories of crime, as do other scholars (Canter, 1982; Figueira-McDonough and Selo, 1980). They find **gender-specific theories**, which emphasize one set of factors to explain the deviance of males and another to account for the deviance of females, to be based on the doubtful assumption that men and women are influenced by different underlying processes and motivations. Such a gender-specific approach would perpetuate the sterile sexist origins of theories of deviance.

Some might respond by asking: can you have a gender-neutral theory if neither the social order nor the structure of crime is gender-neutral? There are also times when it is difficult to know if you are being gender-neutral or gender-specific. For example, one extension of power control theory (Keane, Gillis, and Hagan, 1989) argues that boys are more willing to take risks than girls. Therefore, contact with police may deter girls but amplify deviance for boys. Being identified by an agency of social control is embarrassing, given the socialization of girls, but the same experience may enhance status for boys, given their socialization. Does this indicate similar or distinct processes?

At present, there is a healthy debate over the explanations of female crime. The simplistic theories of the past have given way to a broader range of issues, which have been stimulated by feminist thinking. The lack of agreement is not only healthy but introduces new directions. Systematic and critical thinking from a feminist perspective is very new; perhaps we are still not asking the best questions.

SUMMARY

1. Feminist perspectives have been slower to influence criminology than other disciplines partially because of myths about feminist explanations.

2. Traditional explanations of female crime tended to sexualize such crime and to contain biases that had implications for women in the justice system and in prisons.

3. Power control theory argues that "patriarchal" families expect daughters to be like mothers whereas "egalitarian" families expect daughters, as well as sons, to enter into the labour force. Thus, in patriarchal families females are more controlled and less delinquent.

4. The "liberation hypothesis" explains increased female crime by pointing to greater job opportunies and greater freedom for women. Critics say that women are still disadvantaged in the labour force. Others point out that the increase in female crime is actually very small. With a fading of the chivalry response, authorities may be responding to females less leniently.

5. Other countries offer strategies for more enlightened ways of helping vulnerable young females by offering better services and by decreasing the likelihood of girls being revictimized by the justice system.

6. The feminist movement has not been particularly effective in dealing with false accusations of sexual abuse against men.

KEY TERMS

domestic networks   179

gender-neutral theories   181

gender-specific theories   182

liberation or convergence hypothesis   177

power control theory   176

radical feminism   169

sexualization of female crime   170

WEBLINKS

www.voices4children.org/

Voices for Children: a group working with organizations and individuals to strengthen public commitments to the healthy development of children and youth.

www.caveat.org/

Canadians Against Violence Everywhere Advocating its Termination (CAVEAT): an organization that is concerned with public education and the justice system.

DRUG CRIME: THE CONSEQUENCES OF HYPOCRISY[1]

This chapter will:

- Challenge some of the pharmacological assumptions about drugs and call attention to the social environment.
- Note the discrepancy between drug use, conviction rates in the courts, and the coverage of these topics in the press.
- Compare the evolution of drug policies in Canada, England, and the U.S. and note the renewal of repressive measures in Canada.
- Offer a strategy for reducing drug use.
- Discuss decriminalization, legalization, and harm reduction and note the hypocrisy that limits responsible policy-making.

HYPOCRISY AND DRUG POLICY

Unlike former President Bill Clinton, I have never smoked pot, let alone inhaled. Nor have I attended, or even been invited to, a marijuana-smoking party. As my wife and Mormon friends would testify, I am rather square. Thus, the liberal views expressed here, and my tolerance for those with other lifestyles, are not the product of a reckless personality. I am, however, disgusted by the hypocrisy displayed by politicians and bureaucrats, particularly in the U.S., who continue to support policies that make no sense in the light of current evidence. It is difficult to decide whether these leaders are ignorant, or if it is to their advantage to continue to support current strategies.

---

[1] This chapter owes a great deal to Patricia Erickson of the Addiction Research Foundation.

THE PHARMACOLOGY OF DRUGS

Decisions regarding the criminality of drug use are supposedly related to the damage that the drugs do. But this is not the case; otherwise tobacco and alcohol would be the first on any list of forbidden substances. However, potential damage is cited as a reason for making a specific drug illegal. Let us use cocaine as an illustration.

We have all heard the debate over pregnant mothers who use cocaine. In some places, such mothers have been treated as criminals and their children taken from them at birth. What is the evidence against the use of cocaine by pregnant mothers? If you wish to get attention at your next social gathering, simply state that there is no evidence available that shows that cocaine use during pregnancy hurts the fetus. You will probably get a variety of disagreements. Let us look at the state of current knowledge.

Cocaine-using mothers are almost invariably tobacco smokers and alcohol users, and have poor nutritional practices. The illnesses of children of such mothers are all related to tobacco and alcohol use. We know that mothers who smoke during pregnancy are more likely to produce children with medical problems. Even if smoking mothers quit during pregnancy but resume smoking while the children are small, these children will have more medical problems than children raised by non-smoking parents. Since cocaine-using mothers are almost inevitably smokers and drinkers, how does one separate the distinct impact of cocaine on fetuses? We need to find a reasonably large population of pregnant mothers who do not smoke or drink, keep in top physical shape, eat nutritious foods, are never around others who smoke, follow the medical advice of their obstetricians, have supportive husbands who contribute to their psychological well-being, and then, in addition, use cocaine regularly. Such pregnant mothers are very rare.

I am not advocating the use of cocaine. Personally, I favour healthy lifestyles; however, the reader should be aware that the societal demand to punish, stigmatize, and exclude users of certain substances is *not based on pharmacological evidence*. Cocaine-using mothers are usually poor, black, on welfare, unmarried, and less able to resist demands of the society that they be punished (Noble, 1997). Upper-class women who smoke and drink during pregnancy are dangerous to their children. They may be scolded by their doctors and others, but they do not receive the attention of the police and other criminal-justice agencies. These examples illustrate the difficulty of determining the pharmacological damage of various drugs, but they also demonstrate that such evidence plays a secondary role in drug policy. Instead, hypocrisy characterizes North American drug policy.

Addiction: Pharmacological, Psychological, and Social Aspects

"Junkies" have been viewed as fools who toyed with irresistible pleasure and got "hooked." Some researchers working with animals argue that there is a natural affinity for the pleasure drugs produce. In experimental settings, rats and monkeys consume large amounts of opiate drugs with little encouragement. If opiate addiction is so powerful, then it cannot be cured or even prevented. It is like sex or eating. But suppose the experimental animals' affinity for opiate drugs existed precisely *because they were isolated in laboratory cages.* Who wouldn't want to be stoned during a life of solitary confinement? Alexander, Hadaway, and Coambs (1988) decided to compare opiate consumption of rats in radically different environments. "Rat Park" was spacious, pleasant, with peaceful forests painted on the walls.

Tin cans and other "toys" were strewn about the floor. It was also friendly; the sixteen to twenty rat groups consisted of both males and females. The other environment was the traditional laboratory cage, where individual rats could not see or touch one another. The rats were offered opiates in three ways, analogous to the ways they become available to people. In the Easy Access procedure, the drugs were freely available, but rats in both environments avoided the narcotic solution. The impact of the environment could not be tested.

In the Seduction mode of presentation, the narcotic solution was sweetened, and the pure tap water was not. Since rats have a powerful sweet tooth, the experimenters gradually (and diabolically) increased the level of sweetener in the narcotic solution. Rat Park rats resisted the narcotic solution very successfully, but the rats in steel cages drank plenty of it. Finally, in the Kicking-the-Habit procedure, the rats were given nothing but the narcotic solution for 57 days, long enough to make them physically dependent. Then the two sets of rats were given free choice between water and the narcotic solution. The rats in Rat Park again resisted the narcotic solution, while the caged rats continued to drug themselves.

Like humans, rats are gregarious, active, and curious. The experimenters suggest that in a "rich" environment, rats (and people) resist narcotic use because it interferes with playing, eating, mating, and engaging in those active behaviours that make life rewarding. Chein and his colleagues (1964) noted that in areas where heroin is freely available, most people simply ignore it. The public has also been misled by the media, which have sensationalized a few experiments in which monkeys have been addicted to cocaine (Morgan and Zimmer, 1997). On the other hand, the press ignores the evidence that methylphenidate—a drug commonly prescribed to children with attention deficit disorder—seemed to be more addictive and damaging to monkeys than cocaine.

Box 12.1

If only it were legitimate, there would be much to admire about the drug industry. It is, to start with, highly profitable. It produces goods for a small fraction of the price its customers are willing to pay. It has skillfully taken advantage of globalization, deftly responding to changing markets and transport routes. It is global but dispersed, built upon a high level of trust, and markets its wares to the young with no spending on conventional advertising. It brings rewards to some of the world's poorer countries, and employs many of the rich world's minorities and unskilled.

Source: *The Economist* (July 28, 2001).

The "Once an Addict, Always an Addict" Myth: Environmental Conditions and Policy Implications

Much evidence explodes the popular myth of inevitable and irreversible addiction, even though some programs, such as Alcoholics Anonymous, are based on the notion that "Once an alcoholic, always an alcoholic." People can, and do, leave drug dependence behind, even in the case of tobacco, one of the most addictive substances. American soldiers in Vietnam had access to large amounts of heroin, combined with a decidedly unpleasant environment. This may have increased the likelihood of regular heroin use; but only 12 percent of these regular heroin users relapsed to addiction within three years of returning to the United States (O'Brien et al.,

1980). Over 90 percent of those who become physically dependent on hospital medication do not crave opiates upon recovery from their illness and release from the hospital.

The policy implications of the information presented above should be obvious: we should be striving for interesting, fulfilling, and rewarding lives for all members of society. Instead, we have experienced a decade and a half of policies designed to take those who have had the most barren experiences and stigmatize and exclude them even more. This does not imply that medication is irrelevant. For example, taking pills of buprenorphine, which erases the craving for opiates, may be an important tool in helping addicts (Cloud, 1998).

Understanding the Subculture of Street Addicts

In order to devise strategies that would actually make a difference to marginal people who think of themselves as "dope fiends," it is important to view the world through their eyes. Drug researcher Philippe Bourgois and his colleagues immersed themselves in the homeless encampments of a network of heroin addicts living in the bushes of a public park in downtown San Francisco (Bourgois, Lettiere, and Quesada, 1997). These network members invariably exaggerate their levels of physical dependence on heroin. In fact, they are both proud of and aghast at being heroin addicts. They panhandle, work at temporary jobs, recycle, shoplift, and steal from cars. They also understand the risk of sharing needles; but the well-meaning street worker distributing clean needles, bleach, and condoms probably does not understand the power relationships that overcome the "rationality" of the medical world. Network members share paraphernalia almost every time they inject heroin. When Bourgois and his co-workers warned them of the risks, they were usually disregarded.

Heroin comes primarily in twenty-dollar units of "Mexican black tar" about half the size of a pencil eraser. The awkward consistency of black tar heroin makes it difficult to divide. Thus it is heated in a communal cooker using a measured quantity of water. The solution is then drawn into separate syringes so that portions can be carefully calibrated and compared. Each injector receives the precise amount proportional to the amount of money contributed. If one person draws too much, the extra contents of the unclean syringe go back into the cooker. Storing the ready-to-inject solution is difficult, making it hard to prepare when the addict is overwhelmed by a desire for the drug.

By injecting small quantities, the addicts avoid becoming "dope sick," but also avoid for several hours a heavy heroin "nod," which would interfere with their capacity to hustle effectively. Thus, the sharing network provides knowledge and the means for survival. The pragmatics of income-generating strategies shape risky behaviour. Like everyone else, they construct complex visions of their own moral authority, but they recognize that a dope fiend in withdrawal has the right to use any means necessary to obtain a dose of heroin.

Agents of the medical establishment morally rebuke street addicts and offend them:

Philippe Bourgois (the researcher): What about sharing? You know of the risk?

Hogan: Ain't no dope fiend out here gonna turn down no forty units [a syringe filled with 40 units of heroin] if he's sick.

Philippe: But don't you worry about HIV?

Hogan: ... You give any motherfucker out here a motherfuckin' taste of forty units, and even if the man has any kind of knowledge about you having AIDS or something, he ain't gonna give a fuck ...

Philippe [turning to Butch]: Has that happened to you?

Butch: Oh, c'mon man, you know! Don't ask me that question. [Angry] You know damn well it has, man!...

Philippe: Sorry man ... didn't mean to offend you.... Just trying to get our AIDS prevention rap out ...

Butch [putting his hand on Philippe's shoulder and calming down]: Yeah, yeah.... We know you're in the health AIDS business ... I mean most of us try to be careful most of the time. (161)

Later in this chapter I emphasize harm reduction as an intelligent response to drug use. Needle-exchange programs fit in this category and in the mid-1990s were the most useful public health modality for curbing dirty needle use (Bourgois, Lettiere, and Quesada 1997: fn. 3).

The Discrepancy between Drug Use, Convictions, Media Coverage, and Policies

A minority of our population, youth as well as others, search out chemical highs. While many others use drugs occasionally, usually as part of a social setting, they rarely become dependent and do not suffer much harm. The greatest health risks to this population still come from the highly addictive and dangerous legal drugs, alcohol and tobacco. Although the perception of a drug "epidemic" among the general population is overstated, and cocaine use is relatively rare compared with alcohol, tobacco, and cannabis, cocaine use is prevalent among certain high-risk groups (Smart and Adlaf, 1992). "Street" youth use more cocaine, crack, alcohol, and other drugs than normal youth. They probably use more tobacco as well. Unlike students and adults who use drugs for social or recreational reasons, do street youth use them to cope with problems? Are they like the rats imprisoned in steel cages? The "problem" is not a specific drug, but rather the circumstances that leave youth adrift in the community. A repressive drug-enforcement policy does not alleviate the conditions that encourage young people to turn to drugs, legal or illegal. Nor will it reduce the crimes that are an obvious byproduct of such situations (Cheung and Erickson, 1997).

It would be comforting to believe that factual information would have some impact on the media or on politicians. However, we are constantly told that drug use is becoming an epidemic, and that young people are out of control. Politicians continue to pander to a misled population. Thus, it is not surprising that cocaine *conviction* rates have increased fivefold in Canada between 1980 and 1988, despite declining use (Smart and Adlaf, 1992). Enforcement agencies are influenced by the perceptions of those in authority, and by the "needs" of those in charge of agencies to find an "enemy" against whom they can use their resources. This may not be a deliberate strategy, but "drug crimes" are created, to a large degree, by the actions of those in authority. Other crimes against property and against individuals are spawned partially as a result of the creation of the "drug crimes." When the Netherlands decided to decriminalize some forms of drug use, there was a reduction in other types of crime (Leuw, 1991; Grapendaal, 1991). Despite the fact that the proportion of street-dwelling junkies among heroin users in that country is low, their conspicuous presence has etched a highly undesirable image of heroin on the public mind (Grapendaal, Leuw, and Nelen, 1995).

THE FORMATION OF DRUG POLICY IN CANADA, THE UK, AND THE UNITED STATES

Scientific evidence and rational thinking have had little influence on drug policies. Historical factors provide better explanations of drug policies. Drug strategies in the U.S., the UK, and Canada have been influenced by somewhat different forces. In the case of the U.S., neither public opinion nor medical opinion played an important role in shaping drug policies.

U.S. Drug Policies and Moral Entrepreneurship[2]

Drug policies in the U.S. have been heavily influenced by the Treasury Department. Andrew Mellon, the Treasury Secretary from 1921 to 1932, was banker to DuPont, and sales of hemp threatened the firm's effort to build a market for synthetic fibres. Spreading scare stories about cannabis was a way to give hemp a bad name (*The Economist*, July 28, 2001).

Moral outrage is more effective when it is backed by a few vested interests. Thus, the U.S. Federal Narcotic Laws were originally, in theory, revenue measures. The Harrison Act was passed in 1914 to make the process of drug distribution a matter of record. Supposedly, there was no intent to deny addicts access to legal drugs, or to interfere with medical practice. The act stated that a registered physician would be able to administer drugs "for legitimate medical purposes," as long as they were "prescribed in good faith." Thus, the Harrison Act did not make addiction a crime, nor did it forbid doctors from prescribing drugs for addicts. It simply required that the handling of drugs become a matter of record.

Court decisions, however, influenced policy. In 1915, a U.S. Supreme Court decision (in the *Jin Fuey Moy* case) ruled that possession of illegal drugs by an addict was a crime. A new category of criminals had been created. This decision meant that a medical doctor was the only legal source of drugs left to the addict. Future court decisions against doctors eliminated that source. The *Webb* case in 1919 and the *Behrman* case in 1922 involved physicians who prescribed large quantities of drugs to addicts. These cases concluded that a physician may not provide narcotics for a drug user "to keep him comfortable by maintaining his customary use." This made it almost impossible for a medical doctor to claim that he had acted in good faith.

In 1925, Dr. Charles Lindner received an addict in a state of partial withdrawal. He provided four tablets to be used at her discretion. She was a police informer who reported the incident, and Dr. Lindner was prosecuted. Lindner was convicted by a lower court, but after prolonged litigation, which cost him $30 000 and caused him to be without a medical licence for two years, the decision was overturned by the U.S. Supreme Court. This important decision established two principles. First, drug addiction should be viewed and treated as a disease, and second, a physician acting in good faith could give an addict a moderate amount of drugs to relieve withdrawal stress. However, the Treasury Department and its subsidiary, the Federal Bureau of Narcotics, which was established in 1930, acted as if the Supreme Court decision had never taken place. The risk of arrest was a fact for any physician who attempted to treat drug addicts. Very few physicians cared to risk their careers by challenging the practices of the Federal Bureau of Narcotics.

The lower courts in the United States influenced the punitive pattern for dealing with the drug problem, and the medical profession in the U.S. saw no reason to support its mem-

---

[2]Although many sources provide a history of drug legislation, my main source for the U.S. has been Lindensmith (1965).

bers. Since drug addicts were typically poor and low in status, there was little inclination for doctors to risk their careers. Physicians of integrity continued to be arrested. The claim that drug addiction was a disease, according to the Supreme Court, seemed to have no impact on the lower courts. Two 1936 cases illustrate the situation. Three physicians were asked by the city of Los Angeles to take over the treatment of addicts who were former patients in that city's narcotics clinic. All three doctors were then convicted in federal court for violations of the narcotic laws. While the conviction of one was reversed, the appeals of the other two were rejected. One of the ironies in this trial was that the informer who testified in court admitted that he was being regularly supplied with drugs by government agents, as was the informer in the *Lindner* case. Although this practice has been deplored, government agents continue to supply informers with drugs.

Harry Anslinger: Moral Entrepreneur Extraordinaire

The Federal Bureau of Narcotics was founded in the Treasury Department in the early 1930s by Harry Anslinger, who was appointed by his wife's uncle, Andrew Mellon, the Treasury Secretary. Anslinger had a definite image of drug addicts. They were bad people, clearly criminal, and should be prosecuted. He was the most influential person in the United States, possibly in the Western world, in terms of moulding drug policy.

Laws do not come into existence because they are "needed" or "wanted." Rather, rules are created when people are afraid, concerned, or have something to gain (Becker, 1963: Ch. 8). Someone takes the initiative of translating that fear or concern into a law or rule, which then becomes the norm for the society. These **moral entrepreneurs** are of two types: *rule creators* and *rule enforcers*. Some people create the rules, such as those who campaign to get legislators to pass laws; others, such as the police, enforce them. Some rules are rarely enforced, or enforced selectively. Moral entrepreneurship is not automatically bad. I would be happy to outlaw power boats on lakes in the national parks and many other areas as well, feeling that pollution and noise detract from an appreciation of the outdoors. We have moral entrepreneurs for the anti-abortion movement; others might campaign against smoking. A moral entrepreneur is someone who attempts to sell her version of morality to the general public. Harry Anslinger had his version of morality, and, using the Federal Narcotics Bureau, sold his version to the legislators and the authorities.

This principle was illustrated by the Marijuana Tax Act of 1937. The Bureau provided the necessary feeling of urgency and alarm to get the legislation passed. They held themselves up as experts in the area of drugs. The Bureau prepared the wording of the bill and provided the principal witnesses at the hearings of the Congressional Committee considering the bill. Marijuana smokers sent no delegation. The only potential obstacle was the objections of the Hemp Seed Oil and Bird Seed industries, but these were neutralized by minor changes in the bill, which swiftly became law (Cohen, 1966: 35).

The United Kingdom: Treating Drugs as a Medical Issue

In the United Kingdom during this same period, a similar dispute arose between enforcement authorities and British physicians concerning the physician's right to prescribe drugs for addicts. The Rolleston Committee was established, and, after extensive testimony from medical personnel with specialized knowledge, the committee recommended that doctors be permitted to treat addicts as ill persons. When this report was published in 1926, it became the official interpretation of the Dangerous Drug Laws of 1920.

In reality, the English and U.S. legislation were similar. It was legal for a physician to provide drugs for medical purposes, and the drug addict was defined as a person in need of medical care, rather than as a criminal. The dramatic differences in the way the drug problem has been handled in England and the U.S. are not based on legislation, but on the behaviour of certain agencies, such as the Federal Bureau of Narcotics.

In the 1950s, the U.S. pressured the United Nations to demand an international ban on the use of heroin. In 1955, Britain complied, but opposition from the medical profession led to a gradual shift towards a compromise pattern utilizing public clinics (Boyd, 1991). More intrusive controls and policing followed. The number of known addicts grew in England, and government policies of the last few decades have been controversial. However, one thing is very clear: the illegal drug problem in England is nowhere near as severe as it is in the U.S.

Canada: The Bias against Asians

Shirley Small (1978) points out that the first anti-opium legislation was passed in 1908, as a result of Mackenzie King's investigation of the use of opium in Vancouver, As deputy minister of Labour, King was sent to supervise the compensations to be paid the Chinese and Japanese after the anti-Asiatic riots of 1907 in Vancouver. Much to his surprise, he received claims from Chinese opium-manufacturing merchants, whose stock had been destroyed. One could purchase opium over the counter, in spite of a provincial law against it. King submitted his report, and the Opium Act of 1908 was passed with little discussion. Not surprisingly, the type of opiates used by the Chinese became illegal, but opiates in medicine, with the ingredients on the label, were legal.

King soon acquired the reputation of being a specialist on opium. He read alarmist testimonials concerning drug abuse during debates in the House of Commons. Public concern became apparent in the 1920s, and harsher penalties for drug users were being demanded. *Maclean's* magazine ran five sensationalist articles in 1920, written by Mrs. Emily Murphy, a juvenile court judge in Edmonton. Her book, *The Black Candle*, expanded on these views in 1922.

The opiate users were primarily Chinese, and the early legislation was directed against them. The House of Commons debates in 1907 and 1908 illustrated the antagonism Canadians displayed towards Asian immigration. Each article in *Maclean's* magazine written by Judge Emily Murphy included a cartoon caricature of a Chinese opium smoker, slanted eyes closed, with puffs of smoke coming out of each ear. Small (1978) quotes Murphy as follows:

> It is hardly credible that the average Chinese pedlar has any definite idea in his mind of bringing about the downfall of the white race, his swaying motive being ... greed, but in the hands of his superiors he may become a powerful instrument to this very end ... whatever their motive, the traffic always comes with the Oriental, and ... one would, therefore, be justified in assuming that it was their desire to injure the bright-browed races of the world ... Some of the Negroes coming into Canada ... have similar ideas, and one of their greatest writers has boasted how ultimately, they will control the white man. (Murphy, 1922: 186–89)

A few objected to the growing tide of prejudice. Small (1978) quotes a portion of a speech by Senator J. H. Wilson, a physician who strongly objected to making addiction a crime. A political decision was being made when the Chinese, rather than the medical profession, were singled out as offenders:

The indiscriminate use of opium is a very deleterious habit, yet there is no justification for making the use of it a criminal offense. This habit is principally among the Chinese. Have we the right to make criminals of people, because they have learned the habit in their younger days and now desire to continue it? They give no offense except by injuring themselves. Much of the habit of using opiates, morphine or cocaine has been brought about by its indiscriminate use as authorized by physicians…. Why not punish the physician? (Small, 1978: 32)

Some medical doctors insisted on treating drug addiction as an illness, but the general public assumed that addicts were dangerous persons. Authorities were allowed to harass Asians, while treating medical doctors, druggists, and other "honest citizens" quite differently.

The Role of Law Enforcement Interests in Shaping Drug Prohibition

Organizations tend to expand. Bureaucracies seek new worlds to conquer, new ways to be of service. Universities, industrial firms, and government bureaus utilize the equipment and expertise they have, to convince the powers that be that they should be given new tasks and expanded roles to play. Law enforcement agencies fit into this picture. In Canada, the Division of Narcotic Control was a branch of the Department of Health in 1919. The first two men to occupy the position of Chief of the Division acquired the status of experts on narcotics. Like Anslinger in the U.S., it was difficult to challenge their views. Colonel C. H. L. Sharman, who headed the Division for eighteen years until 1945, had his version of reality. There were three types of addicts: medical addicts suffering from painful disease; professional addicts, usually doctors and nurses; and criminal addicts or members of the underworld (Small, 1978). Although professional addicts used drugs illegally, they neither deserved nor received criminal treatment.

Small also points out that the RCMP was facing a precarious existence during this period. It had been criticized for its role in labour disputes, such as the Winnipeg General Strike. Fortunately for the survival of the RCMP, there was a new world to conquer. They convinced others that they could wage a war on drugs and, incidentally, save their jobs. Just as Harry Anslinger expanded his power and influence in the U.S. by finding a convenient enemy, the Mountie drug squads became leaders in the moral crusade in Canada. Their enthusiasm varies with the political climate.

One might deplore the nature of the leadership provided by the U.S., but there was also an American impact on those countries with more progressive social programs. Jorgen Jepsen (1988) laments the pressures for international solidarity and cooperation in drug-control practices, which are heavily influenced by American thinking. He worries that even the Scandinavian countries may be caught up in "magical thinking and unrealistic, but powerful moral imperialism" (11).

Differences among Canada, the UK, and the U.S. in Responding to Drugs

In terms of their responses to drugs, England went the medical route, the U.S. went the law-enforcement route, and Canada followed a path somewhere in between. This is a vast oversimplification, and Canadian scholars have recently produced considerable sophisticated and detailed analyses of early and recent drug policies (for example, Giffen, Endicott, and Lambert, 1991; Blackwell and Erickson, 1988). Canada's early entry into drug prohibition may have influenced the U.S. in the period prior to the formation of the Federal Bureau of Narcotics (Erickson, 1992). My argument that Canada has been less repressive than the U.S. is illustrated by the handling of a documentary film done by the National Film Board of Canada in cooperation with the police. The film used drug addicts as actors, won a National Film Award, and, in 1948, was taken to the United Nations in New York for a showing before the Division of Narcotic Drugs. The *U.N. Bulletin* called it "the best technical film relating to the control of narcotic drugs which has yet been shown to them. The enlightened treatment of the problem of the drug addict must receive specially favourable criticism." Anslinger, however, was not pleased, and attempted to prevent it from being shown in the United States. He was generally successful. One showing was cancelled, despite great interest, because Anslinger did not feel it was appropriate for the susceptible minds of the people in this group: the American Psychiatric Association (Lindesmith, 1965: 252–54).

The hegemony of the United States in the United Nations enabled Anslinger to become influential internationally. This made it more difficult for enlightened approaches to be adopted at the international level. However, research agencies and government organizations in other countries, such as the Home Office in England, have maintained a more objective approach. Here in Canada, the Addiction Research Foundation in Toronto has consistently produced well-balanced research.

The Le Dain Commission (Commission of Inquiry into the Non-Medical Use of Drugs) produced four reports in the early 1970s which were more enlightened than the official practices of the Canadian government and in marked contrast to the punitive policies of the U.S. government. In its final report, the Commission recommended against any further extension of the criminal sanction. "We should gradually withdraw from the use of the criminal law against the non-medical user of drugs rather than extend its application" (Commission of Inquiry into the Non-Medical Use of Drugs, 1973: 129). One of the commissioners, Marie-Andrée Bertrand of the Université de Montréal, has long favoured the controlled, legalized sale of opiates to drug-dependent persons (Erickson and Smart, 1988), a view that has come to represent a majority position among North American criminologists. The majority of the Commission, however, favoured the treatment approach of methadone maintenance over heroin maintenance, in most cases. Despite the positive reception in the academic world to the Le Dain Commission's findings, the formal reaction to the Commission's legal recommendations, in terms of legislation and policy-making in Canada, was negligible (Erickson and Smart, 1988; Giffen and Lambert, 1988; Giffen, Endicott, and Lambert, 1991: Ch 18.). No government wants to "concede that the line between legal and illegal drugs is a rather arbitrary by-product of our social history, rather than a matter of moral consequence" (Boyd, 1991: 11).

Two Ways of Conceptualizing Differences between Canada and the United States

The **cultural lag model** assumes that the differences between Canada and the U.S. in terms of their responses to the drug issue are only a matter of degree; it is simply a matter of time before Canada imitates the pattern of its larger neighbour. The media favour this argument (Erickson, 1992). Each drug bust, each case of drug-related violence or cocaine overdose, indicates that we are destined to achieve American levels of urban disorder and decay. The **distinct society model** holds that the two countries are fundamentally different in terms of values, culture, and social institutions. Canada values social order over individual rights and places greater faith in the discretion of legal authorities. The broader social net in Canada may have helped reduce levels of poverty and deprivation, and may provide less fertile ground for drug use. I hope this second view will prevail.

The Resurgence of Prohibitionism: From Malign Neglect to Renewed Repression, 1986–1992

Despite the apparent decrease in drug use in Canada and the U.S. in the 1980s, Pat Erickson (1992) notes that policies became more punitive by the mid-1980s. In 1986, when U.S. President Ronald Reagan declared a new crusade on drugs, Prime Minister Brian Mulroney followed suit two days later, when he departed from a prepared text. Government officials were caught off guard. As one high-ranking official noted, "when he [the PM] made that statement, then *we* had to make it a *problem*" (Erickson, 1992: 248). Drug professionals attempted to respond to new government initiatives by emphasizing prevention and treatment and by including alcohol, legal drugs, solvents, and even tobacco in their efforts.

A number of factors encouraged the renewal of prohibitionism and repressive strategies. The American media portrayed cocaine as a "demon drug," representing it as highly dangerous and addictive (Akers, 1991). Evidence that demand for cocaine and cocaine derivatives was declining (Bachman, Johnston, and O'Malley, 1990) had little impact on the media's need to sensationalize and distort this issue. The drug panic over cocaine was imported from the U.S. and helped to justify further repression, even though evidence from Ontario showed a decline in cocaine use among students after 1985 and a stable level of use among adults (Erickson, 1992). While Canadian journalists produced "scare" stories, a more balanced view was provided by David Suzuki's *Nature of Things* special on CBC, "Dealing with Drugs."

Before suggesting alternatives, we might ask if the harsh strategies used in the U.S. have resulted in reduced drug use. *Pulse Check* is a publication of the Office of National Drug Control Policy (2001). It attempts to put together information from ethnographers, epidemiologists, law enforcement officials, and treatment providers throughout the U.S. Although not based on systematic research, it provides a snapshot of about twenty sites in different parts of the U.S. At the end of 2000 they concluded:

- Heroin use is increasing. Supply and purity are up and prices have gone down. Young people in suburbia have increased their use, primarily through snorting.

- Marijuana availability appears to be stable with increases in potency due to improved cultivation techniques. Sellers are usually users but tend not to be involved in violence.

- Crack and powder-cocaine supplies are stable; treatment sources in ten cities report an increase in novice use. The sellers tend to be users and are inclined to be involved in violence.

- The use of ecstasy has increased at almost every site.

- Of the more than 30 sites surveyed over 90 percent think that marijuana is widely available. For cocaine the figure is about 75 percent and for heroin about 62 percent.

With a U.S. drug policy that absorbs over 35 billion dollars each year, locks up a disproportionate number of young blacks and Hispanics, corrupts local police, and distorts foreign policy, these statistics point to a failed strategy. In addition, this policy has not reduced drug use. Moral outrage is simply a poor basis for policy. The U.S. should have learned this lesson when it attempted to prohibit alcohol in the 1920s. Prohibition increased bootlegging, encouraged the spread of guns and organized crime, and corrupted many federal and local enforcement officers.

Like the U.S., Canada usually ignores most of its drug professionals when developing policy. Researchers at the Addiction Research Foundation favour harm-reduction strategies and the inclusion of drugs like tobacco and alcohol in the "drug problem." Compared with the U.S., Canadian professionals probably have a greater impact on the thinking of those who influence public policy than do their American counterparts. Thus, Canada may be more likely than the U.S. to adopt some of the strategies used in the Netherlands, Australia, and elsewhere, which focus on health factors rather than on simple prohibition. Let us now turn to some strategies that might be incorporated into future policies.

Reducing Drug Use by Aiming at a Broader Target

There are links between legal drug habits and illegal substance abuse. The logic for the argument presented here is borrowed primarily from empirical work done by Canadian alcohol and drug researchers (Popham, Schmidt, and de Lint, 1976; Schmidt and Popham, 1978; Whitehead and Smart, 1972). For example, the distribution of alcohol use is one in which most drinkers are light users, fewer consumers are moderate users, and even fewer are heavy users. It is impossible to draw a clear line between abusers on the one hand and normal drinkers on the other. The distribution of alcohol consumption is characterized by the curve as described by the solid line in Figure 12.1.

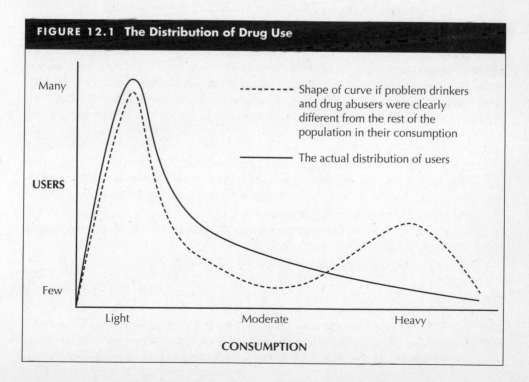

FIGURE 12.1 The Distribution of Drug Use

- - - - - - - Shape of curve if problem drinkers and drug abusers were clearly different from the rest of the population in their consumption

———— The actual distribution of users

USERS — Many / Few

CONSUMPTION — Light / Moderate / Heavy

Drug use also fits the pattern described above. Minor offenders are common; as drug abuse becomes more serious, offenders are less common. If we lump all sorts of drug use together, it seems that many people drink coffee and ingest the occasional substance that is not very healthy. Relatively few, however, are hooked on heroin or alcohol, or smoke six packs of cigarettes a day. While the news media call attention to specific exotic substances from time to time, the general phenomenon of drug abuse remains fairly stable: minor abusers are common, serious abusers are rare. However, we respond to the serious abusers and ignore the minor abusers. While this seems reasonable at first glance, the shape of the curve described by the solid line remains constant. One cannot chop off the right side of the curve. With cigarette smoking, for example, marginal smokers have quit and heavier smokers have cut down on the amount they smoke. The curve is a smooth one, but it has been shifted to the left. In other words, a successful, *uniform* response to all substance abuse is accompanied by decreases among moderate as well as heavy users. It also suggests that there are common factors that influence all drug use, and thus one might conclude that a single sort of prevention strategy is possible.

Who are the logical targets for bringing about change? Typically, we assume that the real problem lies only with a particular group of "bad" people. These heavy abusers require our immediate attention. The rest of us are minor abusers of drugs from time to time; but because our acts are less serious, they can be conveniently ignored. Instead, public outrage is directed towards that special group of extreme individuals who are serious abusers. We direct programs and laws against the minority of serious trouble-makers rather than towards the majority of minor offenders.

The Curve with Two Humps

If one looks at the dotted line in Figure 12.1, instead of the solid line, the shape of this curve might describe reality if the heavy drug abusers were more numerous than moderate users and could be clearly distinguished from the rest. The dotted line describes a **curve with two humps**: abusers on the right side of the chart, leisure users on the left. Belief in this bi-modal curve leads to a distorted worldview. Most of us have no trouble with the peak on the left; paragons of virtue are rare, but most of us commit indiscretions that are not serious. The real problem, for those with a distorted view of reality, is with those who represent the smaller hump, the abusers. They need special handling. We can tolerate the large group of leisure users on the left but must take action against the abusers on the right. The basic flaw in this argument is with the shape of the curve; the solid line represents reality, not the broken line with two humps, and it is difficult to change drug use by concentrating on the few. One must move the entire curve to the left.

Most drug policies are ineffective because they are based on the mythical two-humped curve. Programs designed to change abusers are common, but an effective policy must alter the entire curve. Thus, programs that reduce the consumption of commonly used substances, such as tobacco and alcohol, would move the entire drug-using curve to the left. Thus, I oppose free drinks on airlines. We do not give out free marijuana, why free alcohol? Should Air Canada be a drug pusher? When people pay for their drugs, they consume less. Free alcohol (and cigarettes, etc.) increases consumption and moves the skewed curve to the right. Similarly, we allow drugs as business expenses, as part of entertainment. Heroin, cocaine, and marijuana are not included, but alcohol, tobacco, and the services of prostitutes (disguised in various ways) are allowed. I am not so naive as to believe that corporations will stop providing the last three items, but at least the taxpayer should not subsidize them. Small reductions in drug use among large numbers of people makes more sense than efforts to change smaller, select groups. By contrast, the focus on the latest "demon" drug discovered by the media in their search for something spectacular has little impact.

Admittedly, this argument is an oversimplification. Recent knowledge suggests that modest alcohol consumption has some health benefits. A harm-reduction strategy would emphasize low-alcohol beverages and the reduction of heavy-drinking occasions in settings where violence is more likely (Stockwell, 1997). For alcohol, encouraging light drinkers to abstain appears to have little effect. The main damage occurs when people get drunk and drive and become violent.

Reductions in drug use have taken place in North America in the cases of alcohol and tobacco. Canada has used taxes more effectively than the United States. Our tobacco prices rose 158 percent between 1979 and 1991, and teenage smoking fell by two-thirds. Unfortunately, provincial and federal governments lowered taxes to counter the smuggling from the U.S., which maintains the lowest tax rates of all industrialized countries. The June 1993 issue of the University of California at Berkeley *Wellness Letter* notes that a 10 percent increase in the price of cigarettes reduces consumption by 4 percent, even more with teenagers. Despite increases in the U.S. federal tax, tax represents a far smaller proportion of the cost of cigarettes than it did in the the 1950s. Tobacco lobbies, particularly in the U.S., are powerful, and their goal is to increase tobacco use. Canada has done better than the U.S. at moving the drug-using curve to the left, but it is tough going when the biggest drug pushers in the world are on your border and are supported by their government.

DRUG STRATEGIES: DECRIMINALIZATION, LEGALIZATION, OR STATE CONTROLS?

It would be difficult to design a more destructive drug policy than the one currently practised in the U.S. Illegal drug distribution is very lucrative and legitimate business is obviously excluded; this profitable business is reserved for criminals. In addition, it is most profitable for the most ruthless criminals. One might shame tobacco companies who hold smoking contests among children in developing countries in order to gain future customers, but publicity and shame have little impact on criminal drug lords. We invite corruption of police forces and entire governments. We place legitimate police forces in hopeless situations. It would be difficult to devise a more disastrous strategy.

The outcomes of various drug policies are difficult to anticipate (O'Malley and Mugford, 1991). When there was a strong attempt to eliminate marijuana, prices increased, which raised profitability so that more determined and violent criminal gangs replaced a more casual "hippy" distribution network. Crops of more potent strains of marijuana, such as sinsemilla, provided crops with higher value for their volume and replaced the bulkier, lower-grade version.

In Western Australia, efforts to reduce the supply of opiates led to the creation of a cottage industry which produced "homebake," an inferior substitute. There were risks of virus transmission and a variety of unpleasant side effects (Reynolds et al., 1997). The recent decline in the high levels of homebake manufacture in Western Australia appears to be the result of the increased availability of high-quality heroin. The basic lesson seems to be that attempts to reduce supply usually fail; *reducing the demand seems to be a more viable option.*

The illegality of a drug is said to increase the likelihood that a user will commit theft to obtain money for that drug. However, a Toronto study showed that most cocaine users bought drugs with their own money, others were given drugs, and the third most frequent strategy involved selling drugs to obtain cocaine. Only 10 percent used other crime to obtain money to purchase cocaine (Erickson and Weber, 1992). Erickson and Weber, along with other researchers, found a typical drop-off of cocaine use after a period of higher use. In other words, if cocaine were available through legal channels, it might reduce some secondary crime, but it is possible that this problem has also been overstated.

The Netherlands is unique in that policy-makers and drug researchers work together. Amsterdam may shock some North Americans, with a highly visible retail market for hard drugs operating as part of a deliberate policy (Grapendaal, 1991). This compromise is less damaging than the U.S. pattern. Despite complaints about noisy and unhygienic drug users who sleep and urinate in doorways, there are promising signs in the Netherlands. Very few "new" young users become involved in a junkie lifestyle (Grapendaal, 1991). Dutch drug users commit less property crime than their counterparts in the U.S. and the UK, and most Amsterdam addicts lead a lifestyle that, although deviant, has fewer harmful consequences for themselves and for others. The accessible retail drug market provides a portion of hard drug users with a source of income without recourse to committing property crime. The importance of this gain is usually lost on policy-makers with a moralistic rather than harm-reduction orientation. An additional gain comes from the decreased danger for police who work in these areas of the city.

A Harm-Reduction Drug Policy

Many Canadian drug researchers favour policies that focus on the reduction of harm (Erickson et al., 1997; Erickson and Butter, 1997; Boyd, 1991). Ideas from Pat O'Malley and Stephen Mugford in Australia (1991) fit this pattern. They distinguish among the different types of harm. Any progressive policy should attempt to reduce certain types of harm more than others. We should protect people from passive tobacco smoke, and warn smokers of the risk of their behaviour. Similarly, we should prevent heroin users from stealing to support their habits, and warn them of the risk of continued use. On the other hand, in a society that vigorously markets pleasure-producing commodities indiscriminately, it makes little sense to outlaw smoking or heroin use when the harm is to the user. Forgoing prohibition strategies, however, does not imply approval of drug use.

Drugs need to be assessed in terms of their harm, to individual users and to others. Alcohol, tobacco, and cocaine are higher on that scale than opiates. If opiate use is relatively stable, the effects are typically constipation and a reduced sex drive. A lifelong dependence on opiates is consistent with social productivity comparable to a lifelong dependence on tea or coffee (Appleby, 1998; Boyd, 1991: 5–6). Thus, we should discourage (not prohibit) those drugs that are more harmful. Similarly, some modes of use, such as injection, which is involved in the spread of AIDS, should be discouraged compared with less harmful modes of use, such as oral ingestion.

While Mugford and O'Malley oppose prohibition, they also disapprove of complete legalization. True, the ban on heroin has generated a black market, soaring prices, corruption, needle-sharing, and accelerated property crime to support habits, but complete legalization, as in the cases of alcohol and tobacco, is also undesirable. The extensive availability of drugs has taken a tremendous toll in terms of death and damaged health. Commercial merchants of death would probably succeed in increasing sales if they were given a broader selection of harmful products. Thus, to give the distribution of cannabis, heroin, and cocaine to the tobacco companies would mean that it would be vigorously pushed, along with tobacco, to teenagers in the Third World. Prohibition is too severe, but legalization, as it currently applies to tobacco and alcohol, is too soft. It appears that high profits for sellers and high damage for society are related to both prohibition *and* open legalization.

This does not mean banning alcohol and tobacco, but we could remove advertising, raise prices through taxes close to, but not past, the point at which substantial black-market alternatives would appear, and rigorously enforce age limits on purchase. With illegal drugs, one needs to move away from prohibition without causing a flood of use. Mugford and O'Malley would advocate **normalizing the user**: The addict should not be cast out of the society. "Junkies" are only a minority of drug users, and should not be pushed further towards harmful patterns and social irresponsibility. The Dutch, as noted above, have tried to normalize their users, expecting them to have normal rights and to display normal responsibilities.

However, we should not normalize drug use. It is unwise to rely on the market, since commercial forces glamorize drug use and influence peer groups to be like the "Marlboro Man" or some other "hip" or "cool" image. While junkies on illegal drugs are viewed as bums, junkies on legal drugs are portrayed as beautiful, sophisticated, virile, and having dazzling smiles. Government-supported advertising showing heavy tobacco and alcohol users as having diseased gums, bad breath, imperfect complexions, and so forth, would be more appropriate. Attractive advertising for all drugs should be banned, while educational and dissuasive advertising should be encouraged.

Harm reduction would make safer options more available. Coca tea might be made available more readily than cocaine, which in turn would be more available than "crack." Safer routes of administration would be encouraged, such as opium for smoking rather than morphine for injection. The cultivation, possession, and private sale of small amounts of cannabis would be decriminalized. Heroin would be available through a variety of prescription or licensing arrangements, but without incentives for new users (O'Malley and Mugford, 1991).

Don Weatherburn's (1992a) criticism of Mugford's proposals led to a useful debate in the *Australian and New Zealand Journal of Criminology* (Mugford, 1992; Weatherburn, 1992b). A detailed discussion of different drug policies is not possible here, but one can ask a broader question: are governments sincere in their desire to develop drug policies for the social good? I would like to believe that Canadian officials are sincere, if at times misguided. However, I share Mugford's view that hypocrisy characterizes drug policy in the United States.

Hypocrisy as a Major Barrier to Reasonable Drug Policies

While promoting a prohibitionist policy at home and pressuring other countries to do the same, the U.S. remains the largest exporter of tobacco, the source of the largest single set of health-care problems. The tobacco industry has successfully kept taxes lower than in any other industrial country, guaranteeing a major smuggling operation into Canada and providing lucrative opportunities for crime. While the U.S. government claims these exports are made by private companies, American trade negotiators have systematically threatened Japan, South Korea, Taiwan, and Thailand with retaliatory tariffs on these countries' exports if markets were not opened to its tobacco firms (*The Economist*, 1992). Increasingly worried about the success of health advocates in North America, and recently in Europe, tobacco companies are looking for markets elsewhere, with strong government support. Pressured by the tobacco lobby, the government displays further hypocrisy in failing to stop harmful advertising directed at children. Since 1988, RJR Nabisco has promoted Camel cigarettes with a sunglass-clad, macho-clothed, bulbous-nosed cartoon camel named Joe, designed to appeal to younger male smokers. The campaign clearly has worked. Efforts to develop addiction among children, strategies long used in North America, have been successful in other countries. Some marketing strategies target urban blacks, others focus on young, poorly educated women. The press obtained a letter from an RJR distributor that urged concentration in convenience stores "in close proximity to colleges, high schools or areas where there are a large number of young adults" (*The Economist*, 1992).

In Canada, Imperial Tobacco launched a program to push the Tempo cigarette with advertising aimed at the 18- to 24-year-old market. Civil suits brought a number of documents to public notice, including some produced by Imperial's "creative research group." One goal was to offer products "which could delay the quitting process" (Boyd, 1991: 189). The tobacco industry in Canada also hires influential people. Bill Neville, chief of staff when Joe Clark was prime minister and a member of Brian Mulroney's election campaign committee for 1988, has been president of the Canadian Tobacco Manufacturers' Council since 1987.

The hypocrisy of the U.S. government is particularly evident in its treatment of hard drugs, although probably not as damaging in terms of world health as its support for tobacco sales. Space does not permit elaboration here, but the illegal activities of various U.S. agencies have been reviewed in both the popular press and scholarly publications. These activities include: laundering of drug money through a bank in Sydney, Australia, for the purpose of funding clandestine and illegal activities, the selective crackdown on drug cartels and dictators in exchange for political favours, the gap between rhetoric and action for helping those affected by drugs, and the deliberate sabotaging of one U.S. drug-enforcement agency by the committee chaired by then vice-president George Bush (Boyd, 1991; Herman, 1991; Johns, 1992). The flagrant inconsistency between the public claims and actual behaviour of U.S. officials makes it impossible to develop a credible drug policy. It also makes it difficult for Canada and other countries to develop enlightened strategies, because the U.S. plays such a prominent role in the international drug scene.

Treating the Drug Addict: A Psychological or Social Issue?

Drug counselling is a common response to the "drug problem." The assumption is that the problems connected with alcohol, cocaine, glue-sniffing, heroin, etc., are rooted in personal characteristics. An alternative view is to look at the structure of society. To illustrate this perspective let us examine three situations: (1) the recent history of Ireland, (2) African Americans, and (3) Native peoples in Canada.

Irish People, African Americans, and First Nations People

The abuse of the Irish people by England is well documented. Unlike many conquests of the past, this one contained a pretext of "bringing civilization" to Ireland and giving the Irish people the benefits of English culture. In fact, the conquerers gave vast areas of land to English nobles, who treated the peasants as serfs. The most famous incident was the potato famine in the middle of the nineteenth century, when English landlords shipped grain out of Ireland with the knowledge that Irish peasants would starve. Unable to pay their rent, the peasants were driven off the land, their cottages destroyed, and the land used profitably by the landlords.

The activities of the powerful were often illegal and involved considerable corruption. The consequences for the Irish were profound. Unemployment drove the younger men to emigrate. Women married late. Economic impoverishment, deprivation, and a form of colonial servitude made for a rather bleak future.

But what has this to do with drugs? Like the rats in the steel cages in the Rat Park experiment, temporary escape from a miserable existence could be found in drugs. In the case of the Irish, home brew or other alcohol provided the means of temporary oblivion.

My second illustration, African Americans, offers some parallels. Theoretically, opportunities are open to all. In practice, there have been, and still are, many barriers to full participation in the American Dream. While African Americans are constantly bombarded by images of wealth in the media, the gap between the good life and the reality is greater for African Americans than it is for others. Is it surprising then that the incidence of cocaine or other mind-altering drugs is higher among young blacks in the U.S. and Canada?

The example of Canada's First Nations people also represents estrangement from a meaningful participation in a viable culture. The dominant culture simply moved in and took their territory. This conquest differs from others in that today's governments feel a bit of guilt. But the conditions that force people to seek solace in drugs remain.

The three illustrations given above apply to many situations in our modern world. Visions of the good life abound, and in fact many once-subjugated people succeed in the new system, adjust to it, and some even abandon their previous identity. As a group, however, there will be a higher proportion of alienated people who will look for some form of escape. As we saw in the experiment of the rats in the steel cages described above, the surroundings exacerbate the condition. Treating these issues as psychological matters—such as alcohol counselling for the Irish, cocaine programs for pregnant black mothers, and glue-sniffing therapy for Native children—simply misses the point. Perhaps individuals can be helped, but the source of drug problems lies with the larger society.

Early in this chapter, I suggested that people with fulfilling lives are less inclined to use drugs. It is not always possible for policy-makers to provide people with fulfilling lives, but there are certain target populations that can be helped. Marlene Webber (1991) and Bill McCarthy (Hagan and McCarthy, 1997) have studied youths living on the streets of cities in Canada. Many of these young people have experienced neglect and abuse, including rape and incest. The troubles they face can be overwhelming, and it is not surprising that they turn to drugs to "kill the pain." The same pattern applies to poverty-stricken countries where children rummage through garbage heaps to survive, but also use their meagre resources to buy marijuana. The reduction of pain among children would clearly be among our most potent weapons in the "war on drugs."

SUMMARY

1. Some "explanations" of drug use focus on pharmacology and fail to look at the social environment. The "Rat Park" studies suggest that rats living alone in steel cages are more likely to become addicted than those living in more stimulating environments.

2. The media and the public tend to ignore the greater health damage from alcohol and cigarettes while exaggerating the damage from illegal drugs. Politicians pander to public ignorance, which results in high rates of imprisonment.

3. U.S. drug policy was influenced by the desire to protect certain commercial interests, by moral entrepreneurship, and by an emphasis on punitive measures. The United Kingdom, by contrast, adopted a medical model. Canada started its drug policy with the Opium Act of 1908, which targeted Asians and made opium use illegal.

4. The "curve with two humps" approach leads to inappropriate strategies for reducing drug use. Instead, attempts to reduce *all* drug use, particularly common ones such as tobacco and alcohol, would probably have an impact on other drug use as well.

5. While it is difficult to point to a best strategy for reducing drug use, certain principles make sense: reducing demand is more viable than reducing supply; and harm-reduction strategies attempt to normalize the user but not drug use.

6. Instead of treating certain issues as psychological problems, it is more appropriate to recognize that some people lead less fullfilling lives than others and seek solace in alcohol and other drugs.

KEY TERMS

cultural lag model   193

the curve with two humps   196

distinct society model   193

harm reduction   193

moral entrepreneurs   190

normalizing the user   199

pharmacology of drugs   185

WEBLINKS

www.rcmp-grc.gc.ca/
The Royal Canadian Mounted Police: information on crime in Canada.

www.statcan.ca/english/Pgdb/State/justic.htm
Statistics Canada, Justice and Crime: current statistics on crime in Canada.

13

SOURCES OF VIOLENT CRIME[1]

This chapter will:

- Argue that corporate crime hurts more people than conventional crime.
- Describe subcultures of violence in which adherence to, rather than alienation from, certain norms leads to violence.
- Use war as an illustration of how cultures can become more violent.
- Examine the role of victimization, legal responses, and police responses to assault in the family.
- Note some of the recent trends in femicide in Canada.
- Argue for attempts to reduce the many minor incidents of violence as a way of reducing the rarer but more serious violent acts.
- Summarize recent evidence on family violence, child abuse, and future criminality.
- Discuss different government policies that could make a difference.

WHICH VIOLENT CRIMES SHOULD WE STUDY?

When we think of crimes of violence, murder, robbery, rape, and assault come to mind. We are less likely to think of family violence, which involves child abuse, sibling attacks on one another, and spousal abuse. However, family violence is more frequent and more lethal than those crimes we traditionally associate with violence. Most of us also give little thought to corporate violence, or actions taken by large organizations that do damage to others. Again, the damage done by corporations and governments clearly outweighs the damage done by conventional criminals. This chapter focuses on violence that does the greatest damage. The most lethal instrument in North America is the automobile. This book neglects the serious offence of drunk driving, and concentrates instead on deliberate actions taken by individuals that knowingly injure someone. Usually, those who deliberately cause someone else to die are called murderers. Should that label be attached to executives of the Ford Motor Company?

---

[1]Holly Johnson has been particularly helpful with this chapter. Her book *Dangerous Domains* (1996) reviews much material pertinent to Canada.

CORPORATE VIOLENCE: THE CASE OF THE FORD PINTO

According to one author (Dowie, 1977), exploding gas tanks on the badly designed Ford Pinto caused over 500, possibly 900, deaths by burning. These deaths would not have occurred with a properly designed automobile. The Ford Motor Company knew about the danger for seven years and calculated that about 180 burn deaths, 180 serious burn injuries, and 2100 burned vehicles would result. They calculated their costs, in terms of court settlements, to be about $50 million. However, if the company spent eleven dollars per vehicle to correct the problem, it would cost $137 million. The decision to accept the deaths and injuries was an economic one. The unusual aspect of this case is that it led to a charge of reckless homicide and a court trial (Cullen, Maakestad, and Cavender, 1991). Ford was acquitted of the charges, but the case helps us view **corporate violence** in a new light.

The Ford Pinto case is not unique. It is difficult to assess guilt and intent among corporations, but General Motors was in a similar situation. Since 1973, more than 300 people have been killed as a result of burning gas tanks in GM pickup trucks. Safety engineer George Carvil warned GM in 1970, and recommended moving the tank inside the frame rails (*Time*, November 30, 1992). The company acknowledged the problem in 1983, and has paid $200 million in settlements. The gas tank was moved to a more protected position in 1988. Criminal charges have not been laid against GM, but there are clear parallels with the Ford situation. Some corporate decisions knowingly risk the lives and welfare of others in order to make a larger profit.

The Costs of Corporate Violence

Charles Reasons, Lois Ross, and Craig Paterson (1981) point out that workers in Canada are at greater risk from job-related injuries than they are from "conventional" criminals. We think of crime as involving an easily identifiable victim and offender. When a company exposes workers to toxic substances, leading to their deaths, the company is not criminally liable, although it might be charged with violating health and safety regulations. Reasons and his colleagues describe a case involving Quasar Petroleum, which was found guilty of violations of safety regulations resulting in the deaths of three men. The company did not provide respiratory protective equipment and an external gauge on an enclosed tank. The men had to go inside the tank without protective equipment, and were overcome by the fumes (1981: 6–7). Nor had the company trained the workers concerning the hazards and the need for such equipment. The company was fined $5000. While the company did not intend to kill these men, it created the conditions for their deaths by violating the law. Reasons and his colleagues argue that armed robbers do not intend to kill victims, but their actions create the conditions for such violence. We have a growing literature on the illegal behaviour of large corporations (Ross, 1980), but the public rarely sees these activities as "real" crimes.

Although illegal and dangerous behaviour by corporations is rarely successfully challenged in the courts, strategies using reintegrative shaming may already be working. In the past, illegal and hazardous activities have largely been sheltered from shaming. Decisions leading to death and danger were easier to hide in the past, and executives may have supported each other. Today, business publications such as *Fortune* magazine discuss company lawlessness (Ross, 1980), and friends and families are more aware of corporate decisions that hurt others. Even if the criminal justice system is ineffective in dealing with corporate criminals, stripping away the shelter of anonymity from individual business leaders may make them vulnerable to shaming. If criminology is concerned with illegal acts that do great damage, then focusing on those in positions of power makes considerable sense. Not only might such people be susceptible to reintegrative shaming, they are also relatively good candidates for rehabilitation. Although they may not forgo all of their illegal activities, the possibility of reducing their most harmful behaviour is more promising than attempts to change conventional criminals. Let us now turn to more conventional violence.

SUBCULTURES OF VIOLENCE

Explanations of violence typically focus on individuals, while others look at cultures or subcultures in which prevailing norms favour, or at least permit, violence. Wolfgang and Ferracuti (1967) pioneered such ideas, and concluded that homicide should be viewed within a cultural context. They found that homicide was most prevalent among relatively homogeneous subcultural groups in most large urban communities. Some rural areas also shared similar characteristics. Ideas such as anomie are not appropriate here. Neither the killers nor their victims are alienated or marginal members of their subcultural groups. Rather, they are well integrated into a group of people who accept violence as the norm.

By distinguishing groups with high murder rates, Wolfgang and Ferracuti identified **subcultures of violence**. In some settings, a man jostling another may provoke a challenge. Derogatory remarks can be interpreted differently in some gatherings. Men are expected to defend their names and honour from any slurs or aspersions on their manhood, and quickly resort to physical combat. Carrying knives or other weapons is considered normal under these circumstances. In such settings, violence is not the result of deviant behaviour. Rather, conformity to these cultural norms and to this set of values leads to violence. In these settings, it is not always easy to distinguish offenders and victims. In data from Philadelphia, Wolfgang and Ferracuti note that 65 percent of the offenders and 47 percent of the victims had arrest records. While we sometimes think of murders being committed against innocent and uninvolved victims, in fact both offenders and victims are often committed to the norms of a violent subculture. The specific outcome as to who gets killed may be due to circumstances rather than intent.

The potency of these subcultural values regarding violence may be overrated. Sampson and Wilson (1995) suggest that the evidence for an indigenous subculture of violence in black ghettos is weak. While Wolfgang and Ferracuti emphasize subcultural norms, the dynamics of collective behaviour, how one event leads to another, as reviewed earlier in Chapter 6, on group dynamics, may be more important than static cultural norms. Coramae Mann (1996) suggests that the subcultural argument has little explanatory power concerning why women kill, most frequently in domestic situations. She finds no evidence of a black subculture of violence among the women. Similarly, she finds no subculture of violence among women from the southern United States, which have been viewed by others as having a subculture that supports violence.

Despite these reservations, the idea of a subculture of violence may be relevant to Native populations in Canada. Repressed aggression may characterize some Native people who do not attack outsiders but may respond violently to peers in bars or other settings in which alcohol leads to a reduction in inhibitions. In some working conditions groups of young males work and live together without the restraining influence of wives and children. In some settings, such as lumber camps, mining communities in the north, oil-rig crews, and so forth, where males make up the vast majority of the population, chauvinistic, individualistic norms characteristic of a subculture of violence could easily arise. Such subcultures have been identified in Canadian prisons (Mann 1967), and they appear in prison subcultures in other parts of the world.

If a violent subculture exists, then violence is not viewed as illicit or inappropriate conduct; hence there is little guilt about aggression. Psychiatrists who diagnose such offenders as psychopathic, assuming that a lack of remorse indicates abnormality, miss the essence of the subcultural norms. These men must respond in certain ways. It is simply considered bad luck if someone gets killed.

School girls who beat up on other girls may fit this pattern. Sibylle Artz (1997b) argues that adolescent school girls justify female-to-female violence because the victim "acted like a slut." That is, she showed signs of flirting or interacting sexually with males who were already spoken for. Such young women were fair game for a beating. Those called sluts must seek out those who have labelled them and make them take back the label. Either way, the path has been cleared for violence, which, in the minds of the participants, is entirely justified. These girls have a low assessment of women. Females are important only when they command the attention of men. Competition for the approval of men, who have more power and hence are "worth" more, is based on feelings of low personal worth.

Edgefield County, South Carolina, provides an illustration of a subculture of violence, and may offer a partial explanation of the high rates of violence in the United States (Butterfield, 1995). Even before the American Revolution, immigrants to South Carolina included white men quick to fight to the death for the slightest trespass on their honour. For the southern upper class, just as for the lower class, honour became a compelling passion, an overwhelming concern with one's reputation. Those who killed others in matters of honour were rarely punished by law, but were often elected to high office. In fact, Edgefield has produced many political leaders and has been the home of one of South Carolina's two U.S. senators for most of the period from 1842 to the present. Strom Thurmond, a native of Edgefield, has been in the Senate since 1954, making him its most senior member. His racist views have contributed to his reelection.

Violence and racism were not just characteristics of "rednecks" in South Carolina, but core attributes of the elite. In 1856, Edgefield politician Preston Brooks listened to Senator Charles Sumner of Massachusetts, a leading abolitionist, excoriate, in an insulting manner, a Southern senator because of his pro-slavery views. Under the code of honour, Brooks felt obligated to flog Sumner and did so with a gold-headed walking stick. It took Sumner three years to recover from the beating. Northerners were outraged, but in the South, Brooks became an instant hero.

The House of Representatives moved to expel Brooks but fell short of the two-thirds vote required. Every Southern congressman except one supported Brooks. Honour, along with violence, was part of the Southern heritage. In his account of the American tradition of violence, Fox Butterfield (1995) describes how this heritage contributed to the Civil War. After the war, leaders from Edgefield intimidated, murdered, and defrauded African-American voters. These activities, as epitomized by the Ku Klux Klan, spread from South Carolina. The racism, backed by violence which included murder, fed a subculture of violence. It infected both whites and blacks and still persists in the South today. How much progress has been made in overcoming these cultural elements is another topic, but Butterfield argues that violent blacks in the U.S. are to a large extent a product of the violence that was nurtured in the South.

Although I have used South Carolina as an illustration of the evolution of a subculture of violence, many places in the U. S. and the rest of the world fit the pattern. Texas, for example, was characterized in the nineteenth century by violence against Mexicans and Native peoples, and in the twentieth century, against African Americans. While in much of North America some sort of uneasy truce has been reached with the First Nations people, in Texas they were exterminated. True, the Comanche and Apache may have lived in a subculture of violence as well. Today, many Texans believe in carrying guns, and honour demands their use from time to time. Responses to crime are also violent and punitive. The death penalty is used frequently and a high percentage of young black males fill the prisons.

While the notion of a subculture of violence may apply to parts of the United States, it is relevant in other parts of the world as well—for example, Canada's North, Kosovo, the Middle East, and parts of Africa.

Rape and Subcultural Factors

Recent work on rape has produced a wealth of insights, but an older study by Menachim Amir (1971) fits with the subcultural argument. Amir is considered sexist by many critics for viewing rape as a sexual act, whereas most scholars view rape as violence and as a display of power. He also suggests that women sometimes contribute to the possibility of rape. Despite these criticisms, the study is informative.

The image of rapes being committed primarily by strangers who drag women into alleys is not supported. In fact, the most brutal rapes were between neighbours and acquaintances. The setting is likely to be the woman's apartment. Another common belief is that alcohol use is common, but only about one-third of the cases in Amir's study involved drinking. Although brutal acts were involved in about one-third of the cases, how does one interpret the statistic that half of the victims did not resist? Assessing the impact of verbal coercion is difficult.

Were the victims innocents? This is another place where Amir gets on shaky ground. One-fifth of the victims had prior arrest records, but half of the rapists had records. Another fifth of the victims had "bad reputations." Should the victims be seen as responsible for their victimization? Amir says no, except for about 19 percent of the cases. This issue is central to a subculture-of-violence argument. To what extent do attitudes and values about what women mean when they say "no" influence the incidence of rape? Are factors operating at the individual level, as distinct from the cultural level? There have been cases of women who decided to enter rape charges after changing their minds after the act, but using official records does not allow researchers to determine the frequency of such incidents, nor can we determine if this is an individual act of revenge or behaviour influenced by cultural factors.

Although analyses of individual characteristics are revealing, both subcultural factors and routine-activity theory provide insights into the conditions and settings that increase the likelihood of rape, thereby providing useful suggestions for policy changes. For example, Ruth Peterson and William Bailey (1988) found that relative inequality and other aspects of social disorganization were also related to rape. Concentrations of deprived people within a wealthy society breed violence, including rape.

Amir argues that a lower-class subculture of violence is the primary source of rape. It takes place disproportionately among lower-class, minority, chauvinistic, urban youth, a group in which similar subcultural elements encourage other violent crimes. Attitudes and values conducive to the use of violence are extended to sexist attitudes, which view females as sexual objects. While feminists are not fond of Amir's study, it calls attention to a larger subculture of violence. Responding to those subcultural elements may be more effective than treating rape as something distinct.

Conditions Fostering a Subculture of Violence

Policy-makers might well look at the broader conditions which create settings where violence is frequent. Although focusing on African Americans, Julie Phillips (1997) summarizes three theories that may also explain homicide in Canada:

1. When forms of social control such as family, churches, firms, and communities are weak, they are less able to restrain violence.

2. Discrimination and inequality have increased absolute and relative deprivation for blacks (or Natives), which produces frustration.

3. Violent activity may be a rational act for blacks (or Natives) faced with the reality of limited economic opportunities.

Phillips finds that all three explanations contribute, but the social control explanation gets the greatest support.

In reality these factors interact. The crack cocaine trade may have caused young blacks delivering expensive materials to carry guns for protection. The lethal competition may explain the increase in homicides (Blumstein and Wallman, 2000). In a sense, this may have created a temporary subculture. As the "rules of behaviour" developed different, and safer, ways to handle the drug trade, the murders decreased. These factors also interact when the absence of good jobs for young black (or Native) men eliminates an important social connection to conventional society. This results in lower absolute and relative economic status and power, which may tempt some men to choose more lucrative criminal activity (Krivo and Peterson, 1996). In a reciprocal manner, these conditions further disrupt the family mechanisms which normally constrain violence. One should not automatically assume that the same arguments would apply to Canada, but there are some clear parallels with First Nations people in this country.

Guns and a Subculture of Violence

One of the debates that profits from a comparison between the U.S. and Canada is gun ownership. Canadians have fewer guns in the home, and find it more difficult to purchase handguns. Canadian cities, such as Vancouver, have fewer handgun deaths than similar U.S. cities, such as Seattle (Sloan, Kellerman, and Reay, 1988). Some hypotheses suggest a less violent culture in Canada, independent of the use of handguns. Others see handgun ownership as an indicator of, and contributing factor to, the subculture of violence. A private firearm is six times more likely to be involved in a firearms accident than to be used in deterring a crime. On the other hand, some scholars question the methodology and conclusions of many of the studies (Wright, 1991: 453).

Gary Mauser's report for the Fraser Institute (2001) argues that there is no solid evidence linking Canadian gun laws to a decline in either crime rates or suicide rates. As in the U.S., urban areas have lower rates of legal gun ownership but higher rates of criminal violence. In 1995, the Canadian government passed the Firearms Act, which requires licensing all firearm owners and registering all firearms. Opponents argue that firearm registration is unworkable and just creates another costly bureaucracy. Canada already had in place a strict firearm regime: handguns have been registered since 1934; police scrutiny has been required for all firearm purchasers since 1977; a wide range of weapons were prohibited in 1977; and in 1991, large-capacity magazines and many semi-automatic rifles were prohibited or restricted. When firearm registration was introduced, it was claimed that it would cost taxpayers $85 million. By early 2001, Mauser argued that the known costs had already surpassed ten times that figure.

Gary Kleck (2001) argues that 1500 to 2800 felons were killed in the act of committing a crime annually by gun-using civilians in the U.S., far more than are killed by the police. A number of studies look at the self-defence aspect of gun ownership (Cook and Ludwig, 1998). Others view the frequency with which civilians use guns against criminals (300 000 times a year) as evidence of a violent culture. Clearly, guns are more lethal than knives, and guns of larger calibres are more lethal than guns of smaller calibres (Barlow and Schmidt, 1988).

The debate over gun legislation will go on, but requiring gun owners to take training courses, diligent licensing, and recording certain types of weapons may have some advantages. As with the debate over the amount of violence in the media, compromises with individual rights may not yield great gains, but, as in the case of seatbelts and safety glass for automobiles, some restrictions could lead to modest reductions in deaths. For example, there is some evidence that gun ownership is related to the risk of suicide (Miller and Hemenway, 1999). World Health Organization data from 21 countries suggest that guns in the home present a risk factor for suicide, as well as a threat to women (Killias, van Kesteren, and Rindlisbacher, 2001). However, the study does not show a correlation between guns in the home and the murder of males. One point, however, is clear. *Firearm regulation is overrated as a means of reducing crime. Changes in the way we raise children would have a much greater payoff.*

War and the Creation of Violent Cultures

The borderline between subcultures and the total culture of a society is debated by many criminologists. If the subculture differs considerably from the dominant society, conflict with the majority of the population and with the agents of social control is likely. On the other hand, if the larger culture is permeated by violent norms, different strategies might be appropriate to reduce violence. Dane Archer and Rosemary Gartner (1976) address the larger issue of elements that pervade an entire society. They, along with others, argue that wars contribute to violence, not just during the wars themselves, but afterwards.

The idea that war might increase domestic violence is not new, but Archer and Gartner test a number of different hypotheses, using 110 nations with data on wars and homicide rates. Such data are complicated, problematic, and difficult to interpret. During major wars, crime rates are lower because young males leave the civilian population for the military, convicts are released prematurely to enter the armed forces, those arrested are convicted and imprisoned less, and so forth. On the other hand, crimes might increase because families are disrupted, blackouts create criminal opportunities, and so on.

After a war, there are factors that might lead to a reduction of violence. Young men killed in action remove from the population those most likely to commit violent crimes in postwar years. Law-enforcement agencies return to normal staffing levels. But the return of young males might increase violent crime. In an attempt to sort out these arguments, Archer and Gartner identify seven theoretical models that attempt to explain the impact of war on homicide. I discuss only two:

1. The **catharsis model**. Wars substitute public violence for private violence. The catharsis model predicts that homicide would decrease during and after a war. The impact depends on how long the cathartic effects are thought to last. The model also suggests that societies that experienced the greatest violence would have the greatest catharsis and thus experience postwar decreases in violent crimes.

2. The **legitimation of violence model**. Wars influence homicide through the reduction of inhibitions and the legitimation of violence. Social approval of violence as a way of solving problems reduces inhibitions against taking human life. Wars legitimate killing people. The model predicts increases in homicide in postwar societies among both veterans and non-veterans.

The 110-nation Comparative Crime Data File, with rates of various offences for 1900 to 1970, enabled Archer and Gartner to examine many "nation-wars." My summary oversimplifies their sophisticated analysis and presentation. However, one way to test the catharsis model was to compare countries that suffered many battle deaths with those that had few. Those nations that saw "more" war—that is, suffered more battle deaths—showed the greatest postwar increase in homicide. This is clearly incompatible with the catharsis model.

Table 13.1 shows the postwar homicide rate changes in combatant nations and in nearby nations not involved in the fighting. For the combatant nations, six nation-wars were followed by decreases in homicide rates. This included Canada after World War I and the U.S. after World War II. Four nation-wars resulted in changes of less than 10 percent, including Canada after WW II. Seventeen nations were in the third category, which showed a distinct increase

TABLE 13.1   Homicide Rate Changes in Combatant and Non-Combatant Nations after WW I and WW II

Combatant Nations					
Decrease %		**No Change < 10%**		**Increase %**	
Canada (I)	−25%	Canada (II)	6%	Germany (I)	98%
U.S. (II)	−12%	England (I)	−5%	Italy(I)	52%
+4 others		+ 2 others		U.S. (I)	13%
				England (II)	13%
				France (II)	51%
				Italy (II)	133%
				Japan (II)	20%
				New Zealand (II)	313%
				Norway (II)	65%
				+ 8 Others	

Control Nations (Non-Combatant)					
Decrease %		**No Change**		**Increase %**	
Norway (I)	−37%	Ceylon (I)	8%	Finland (I)	124%
Ceylon (II)	−19%	Chile (I)	−3%	Thailand (I)	112%
Chile (II)	−67%	Netherlands (I)	−2%	Sweden (II)	14%
Switzerland (II)	−42%			+ 2 others	

Source: Based on material in Archer, Dane and Rosemary Gartner (1976). "Violent Acts and Violent Times: A Comparative Approach to Postwar Homicide Rates." *American Sociological Review* 41: 937–63.

in homicide rates after the two world wars. Clearly, increases were more common than decreases. By contrast, the non-combatant nations showed more decreases in homicide than increases. However, if we were to limit our arguments to Canada, England, and the U.S., decreases were just as common as increases. We would be misled. The social science research done on English-speaking societies might not be universal, despite what many anglophones would like to think.

Archer and Gartner examine other combinations to test seven different models. Only the legitimation-of-violence model is consistent with the frequent and pervasive postwar homicide increases in combatant nations. The other models are rejected. Sanctioned killing during war has a residual effect in peacetime. It is tempting to generalize this argument to other authorized violence, such as capital punishment. Do nations that use violence as a way to solve problems contribute to further violence?

Many criminologists, including those who are somewhat conventional in their orientation, share a growing consensus that coercive social control cannot reduce violent crime or solve social problems. War is one of those unsuccessful attempts to solve problems with violence.

PATTERNS OF FEMICIDE, FEMALE HOMICIDE, AND FAMILY VIOLENCE IN CANADA

Femicide (the killing of women) is similar in many respects to the killing of men. In general, women are less likely to be killed than men, who spend more time in dangerous situations. We tend to overlook, however, some of the differences between male and female victimization. (See also Chapter 11, on women's issues.)

Only recently has much attention been given to the family as a major source of violence. An analysis of 670 cases of femicide in Toronto and Vancouver from 1921 to 1988 confirms a general finding that women are more likely than men to be killed in intimate, family situations (Gartner and McCarthy, 1991). The role of employment may have changed the likelihood of victimization. Prior to 1970, Gartner and McCarthy found that employed women were over-represented as victims. After 1970 they were under-represented. In addition, single women were never at a disproportionately high risk of femicide. Married women were at a higher risk, and even more so prior to 1970. Is it possible that women are somewhat safer now because they are working more and getting married less?

A study of 246 women who were victims of femicide in Ontario between 1991 and 1994 can probably be generalized to most of Canada (Crawford, Gartner, and Dawson, 1997). Of the 224 cases in which the offender was identified, 159 (71 percent) were intimate femicides—that is, women killed by current or former legal spouses, common-law spouses, or boyfriends. During this period the rate at which women were killed by their spouses was over six times the rate at which men were killed by their spouses. Men may be at more risk of being murdered outside of the home, but the family setting appears to be more dangerous for women. In addition, the rate at which men are killed by their spouses has been declining over time, whereas the rate at which women are killed by their spouses has not.

A similar pattern exists in the U.S., with studies showing a dramatic decrease in the number of men killed by spouses from 1974 to 1994, with only a modest decline for women. According to Angela Browne and Kirk Williams (1989, 1993), the availability of resources that allow threatened women to escape violent domestic settings has benefited men more than women. Homicides involving unmarried women, however, followed a different pattern. From 1976 to 1987, the rate of unmarried women killed by their partners increased significantly (Browne and Williams, 1993).

Ontario's largest cities do not have intimate femicide rates substantially higher than average. In fact, Toronto, Ottawa, and Hamilton have lower rates than the provincial average (Crawford, Gartner, and Dawson, 1997). The majority of these femicide victims were over 30, living with a legal or common-law spouse, had at least one child, were working outside the home, were born in Canada, had no criminal record, and were not using alcohol or drugs when they were killed. The majority of the men who killed their partners did have a criminal record.

Forty percent of the victims were estranged from their partners at the time of the killing, and in at least one-third (probably more) of the cases, there had been police intervention in the past because of violence in the relationship. Women separated from their partners faced risks five to six times greater than other women. Three-fourths were killed in their own homes. Between 1991 and 1999 separated women were killed by estranged partners at a rate of 39 per million couples compared with 26 by current common-law partners and 5 by current husbands. By contrast, men were more likely to be killed by a current common-law partner than by an ex-partner (Hotton, 2001).

Comparing the 1993 Violence Against Women Survey with 1999 data suggests a moderate decrease in violence against women, but women separated from common-law partners still face a greater risk.

Crawford and her colleagues also found that, compared with an earlier period (1974–1990), the rate at which women were killed by strangers declined substantially, but the rate of intimate femicide did not. Murders by strangers, which generate the most fear and lead to the greatest demand for increased punitiveness, have not shown any systematic increase in the past 30 years. Focusing on family violence, instead of strangers lurking in the shadows, makes good sense if we are serious about reducing violence. (See the section "Police Response to Domestic Violence," on page 218.)

Silverman and Kennedy (1987) found that Canadian females kill males more often than they kill other females. Part of this finding is accounted for by the fact that they kill their husbands, but an examination of victims who are neither spouses nor children shows that 68 percent of the other victims are also male. Holly Johnson (1986) reports that most of the victims of women who committed non-lethal violent acts were females. At the same time, U.S. data show that females are almost twice as likely to be homicide victims as offenders (Wilbanks, 1982). Non-white women have the highest homicide victimization rate. Murders involving women of all races, whether the women are victims or offenders, are likely to be intraracial events. Wilbanks also found that U.S. women are unlikely to kill other women. They tend to kill men rather than members of their own sex, and are more likely to be killed by men.

Silverman and Kennedy also look at women who kill children. This is complicated by the distinction in the law made between infanticide, killing an infant under one year of age, and killing a child age one and over. In one case, a 16-year-old hid her pregnancy, gave birth to the child alone, was afraid of the consequences, and suffocated the infant. She was too psychologically confused to remember what she did. Her charge was reduced from first-degree murder, which carried a mandatory life sentence with no parole for 25 years, to infanticide, for which she received two years' probation. Infanticide may involve the assumption of post-partum depression, which may explain the maximum sentence of five years. In other words, the small number of infanticides (45) in Canada from 1961 to 1983, compared with the number of older children killed by their mothers (230), probably involved mitigating circumstances, which led to the lesser charge of infanticide being used.

When they kill their children, Canadian women are treated more leniently than men in the courts (Greenland, 1988). Comparing 37 women with 32 men prosecuted for child-abuse deaths, the women faced less serious charges, were more likely to receive a non-penal disposition, and received shorter prison terms when convicted.

In general, homicides by women take place largely within the family. Husbands and common-law husbands are the most likely victims, but 24 percent of the homicides were directed against children.

It is interesting to note that Native Canadian mothers are rarely charged with killing their children, even though they are involved in spousal homicide. Killing children is more likely among Caucasian mothers in Canada. Caucasian women appear to transfer their anger from the actual source of frustration, and use the child as an available target. Why is it, then, that Native women respond to domestic turmoil with violence against husbands, but rarely against their children? Since Native women are frequently incarcerated for violent crime (Johnson, 1986), it would be helpful to understand if there are factors that inhibit the murder of children. If Native women rarely kill their children, do they also abuse them less than non-Native women?

When mothers kill their children, they are declared mentally ill 67 percent of the time. However, this diagnosis is made by the police. William Wilbanks (1982) points out that killing children is inconsistent with the gender stereotype of motherhood. Thus, the reasoning goes, "if they killed their kids they must be crazy." However, infanticide may be unique. Women who commit infanticide are usually very young, unmarried, and very distressed about their pregnancy. This fits into a general pattern: female crime is often related to the perpetrators' marginality in the society and their limited means to influence their own destiny.

Women as Victims

It is not possible to understand female involvement in crime, or females' interaction with the criminal justice system, without examining the ways in which they are victimized.

So far, I have concentrated on the way agents of social control respond to females who are viewed as deviant. Another side of the same coin is the response to females who have been victims of sexual assault. Since many violent crimes take place between people who know each other, and since such crimes are viewed as less serious in comparison with crimes between strangers, victimized women are not always taken seriously (Stanko, 1985, 1995). In a ground-breaking Canadian study which called attention to this ignored area, Loreen Clark and Debra Lewis (1977) found that police procedures led to the "unfounding" of the majority of rapes that were reported—that is, the allegations were believed to be false and a crime was not considered to have taken place. When Clark and Lewis looked into these cases further, they found that only 10 percent were seen as false allegations—they were eliminated because of difficulties of predicting outcomes in court. Evidence of the victim's drinking, drug use, or sexual activity outside of marriage led jurors to doubt the defendant's guilt. LaFree, Reskin, and Visher (1985) also found that jurors were less likely to judge a male defendant guilty when the complainant was a black woman.

Changes to Canadian rape legislation in 1983 limited the questions that lawyers defending men accused of sexual assault could ask about the sexual history of the victim. This "rape-shield" provision (Section 246.6 of the Criminal Code) was struck down by the Supreme Court of Canada in a seven-to-two ruling in August 1991 (Comack, 1992). This issue continues to be debated in legal and criminological circles (Boyle, 1991; Currie, 1990; Hinch, 1985; Hinch, 1988).

Comack (1992) claims that male biases regarding sexual assault persist. During a 1984 case, a Manitoba judge told a Crown attorney he "would have to have grown up in a vacuum not to know women often at first resist sexual advances only to give in to their instincts eventually" (138). In 1989, a Quebec judge commented, "Rules are like women, they are made to be violated." A lawyer involved in the case responded: "Exactly." Comack also described a 1988 Vancouver case in which a man who admitted a sexual incident with a 3-year-old girl was given a suspended sentence, because the judge found the victim was "sexually aggressive."

When a gunman entered the École Polytechnique at the Université de Montréal on December 6, 1989, he yelled "You're all a bunch of feminists" before killing fourteen women and injuring thirteen others. Explaining the "Montreal massacre" is not easy, but the response by some men reflects continuing biases. In call-in radio shows, some men felt that the problem lay with women who make men feel insecure. Women are still to be blamed, to be seen as "legitimate," or at least "understandable," targets by a portion of the population.

The Battered Woman Syndrome: The Lavallée Case

The **battered woman syndrome** became an important legal consideration in a 1987 Winnipeg court case. Angélique Lavallée was charged with second-degree murder in the shooting death of her common-law partner. During the trial it was argued that she had been terrorized by her partner to the point of feeling trapped, vulnerable, worthless, and unable to escape this violent relationship. The shooting of her partner was described as a desperate act of self-defence by a woman who sincerely believed she would be killed.

Lavallée was acquitted and the decision was upheld by the Supreme Court of Canada in 1990. Did this decision give women in abusive situations a "licence to kill"? Not according to the Manitoba Association for Women and the Law, which argued that the decision recognized gender-biased presumptions inherent in the previous law on self-defence, which failed to consider self-defence from a female perspective (Comack, 1993).

Dating Violence

The Violence Against Women Survey estimates that about 24 percent of Canadian women aged 18–24 and 29 percent of women aged 25–34 have been involved in at least one incident of sexual or physical assault by a date or a boyfriend (Johnson, 1996). About 40 percent of these women reported acts of violence by more than one date or boyfriend. In their study of over 3000 Canadian college students, DeKeseredy and Kelly (1993) state that 45 percent of female students reported sexual abuse since leaving high school. By contrast, only 20 percent of male students said they had committed such acts. The percentage of women who reported forced sexual intercourse in dating situations was four times higher than the percentage of men who said they had committed a similar act (6.6 percent compared with 1.5 percent). Most researchers assume that the female reporting is more accurate for a variety of reasons. Many men do not admit to hurting their dating partners, some may have been drunk, and other men may not perceive or conceptualize sexual experiences in the same way, claiming for example that what they did was not rape.

Large discrepancies in the reports of wife battering given by wives and husbands may fit a general perception by men who view their behaviour as justified under the circumstances and therefore respond differently to survey questions than the women who were assaulted (Dobash and Dobash, 1992). During the 1998 Winter Olympics in Japan, the ice-skating world heard the story of a young Russian female skater who had been hit frequently by her former skating partner. This man did not view his own behaviour as criminal.

Wife Assault and the Impact on Children

When women experience domestic violence, they use one of three reporting strategies: turning to friends and family, seeking help from a social service agency, or calling the police. When a child is witness to the abuse the women are more likely to call the police (Kaukinen, 1997). If there is little access to family or when there is little money, they may seek help from a social service agency. Recent debate over the consequences of the choices made by women has generated some appropriate research. By the mid-1990s there were about 400 shelters for battered women in Canada (Johnson, 1996). The Violence Against Women Survey showed that 29 percent of all women who had ever been married or lived with a man had experienced spousal abuse.

In the past women tended to under-report domestic violence. The higher rates that are coming to light may be the product of a greater willingness to report combined with better data-gathering procedures. Increased awareness may have produced efforts that have in fact reduced violence against women, but if so, this should not imply that further efforts are not important. In fact, few endeavours have such a great potential for serious crime reduction than a focus on the reduction of domestic violence.

There is growing evidence that men who have peers with chauvinistic attitudes and who expect women to be obedient and dependent are more likely to be abusers. Battered women face increased danger when they attempt to leave violent husbands. At such times women are at serious risk of being killed. In an Ontario study, 40 percent of the victims were estranged from their partners at the time of the killing, and in at least one-third (probably more) of the cases, police had intervened in the past because of violence in the relationship (Crawford, Gartner, and Dawson, 1997). Women separated from their partners faced risks five to six times greater than other women. Three-fourths were killed in their own homes.

Witnessing violence against one's mother in childhood leads to an increased likelihood that children will use violence or be victims of violence as adults. Children experience considerable emotional trauma, see that violence is the basis of power and control, and learn that women have fewer rights and less value than men. Girls tend to become passive and withdrawn, boys identify with their fathers and have confused feelings about what their fathers have done. They become more aggressive, disobedient, and destructive. Both girls and boys feel partly responsible for the abuse.

Family Violence, Child Abuse, and Future Criminality

The gunman who killed fourteen women in the Montreal massacre had been abused as a child. Perhaps it is an oversimplification to claim that he transferred his family experience to his hatred of women, but such a conclusion is compatible with the evidence that violence in the family becomes a model for violence outside the home.

Cathy Spatz Widom, in a talk presented at a National Institute of Justice panel in 1997, summarized much of what we know about domestic violence. First, childhood victimization clearly increases a person's risk of arrest later in life. The odds are almost two times higher that an abused or neglected child will be arrested as a juvenile for a violent crime. Second, abused and neglected children are arrested at an earlier age, have more arrests, and are more likely to be repeat violent offenders. Third, being physically abused or neglected as a child leads to an increased risk of an arrest for violence. Fourth, victimization has differential impacts for females, males, and different ethnic groups. Many of these patterns are still poorly understood. Fifth, childhood victimization can also result in intellectual and mental health problems, higher rates of suicide attempts, alcohol abuse for women, unemployment, and lower rates of marital stability. Canada does not have as many studies with comparison groups as the U.S. but Catherine Trainor and Karen Mihorean (2001) make similar arguments.

However, certain interventions have been known to reduce the risk of domestic abuse. Home visitors working with mothers have been shown to improve parenting skills. Some home visitation programs rely on public health nurses, who establish contact with mothers during their pregnancy and provide frequent visits after birth. Home visitation reaches families who might not otherwise have access to services, such as rural families living in isolated areas, poor, isolated families in urban areas, or families who might be unwilling to travel to service providers, such as abusive or neglectful families.

The Kempe Center at the University of Colorado uses prenatal and infancy home visitation by nurses to prevent a wide range of health and development problems, including child abuse (Olds et al., 1998). Compared with families without these services, a fifteen-year follow-up in Elmira, New York, showed that those who received home visits had a 79 percent reduction in child abuse and neglect, a 44 percent reduction in maternal misbehaviour due to alcohol and drug use, and 69 percent fewer arrests among mothers. Among the 15-year-old adolescents there were 69 percent fewer convictions, 58 percent fewer sexual partners, 28 percent fewer cigarettes smoked, and 51 percent fewer days consuming alcohol.

Richard Tremblay: Developmental Crime Prevention

Richard Tremblay and a cluster of scholars with links to the Université de Montréal have been doing longitudinal studies that offer clear policy guidelines for crime prevention. Stated simply: start early! Efforts that help very young children and their parents to behave in a prosocial way prevent problems at a later time. These ideas are not new, but the empirical evidence is providing more concrete suggestions for prevention. Figure 13.1 illustrates the logic. Small children were observed from age 2 until age 6 to observe how often they hit, bit, or kicked another child. The pattern was clear: boys were more violent than girls in both the "often" and "sometimes" categories; most striking was the conclusion that both boys and girls were most violent at about 27 months of age.

Antisocial behaviour at an early age is a precursor of delinquent behaviour. Experiments to prevent crime have focused on socially disruptive behaviour and parenting skills. The Montreal Longitudinal Experimental Study worked on boys' social development from kindergarten to high school (Tremblay et al., 1992). The experimental treatment lasted two years, beginning about age 7. Parents were trained to: monitor their sons' behaviour, reinforce positive behaviour, punish effectively without being abusive, and manage family crises. Social skills training was done by professionals in the schools. Disruptive boys were included in small groups of prosocial peers in which coaching and peer modelling were among the techniques used to change behaviour.

Six years after the end of the treatment, when the boys were 15, they were assessed (Tremblay et al., 1994). Teacher-rated disruptive behaviour was less for the treated boys than for the untreated boys from ages 10 to 13, but the trend disappeared at age 14. For self-reported delinquency, the treated boys reported less delinquency from age 10 to 15. While having a significant effect on social development, the program had less impact on extreme cases.

The High/Scope Perry Preschool Project began in the 1960s with the Head Start programs for disadvantaged children in a poor African-American neighbourhood of Ypsilanti, Michigan

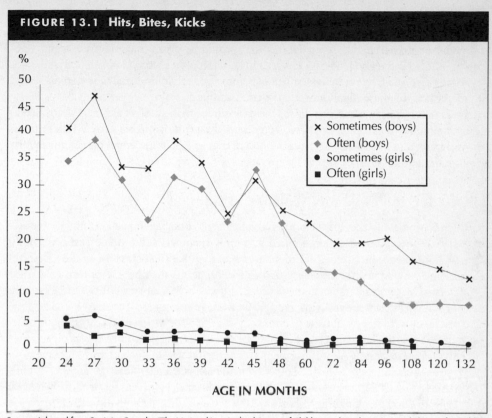

FIGURE 13.1 Hits, Bites, Kicks

Legend:
- × Sometimes (boys)
- ◆ Often (boys)
- ● Sometimes (girls)
- ■ Often (girls)

AGE IN MONTHS

Source: Adapted from Statistics Canada, "The National Longitudinal Survey of Children and Youth: An Essential Element for Building a Learning Society in Canada." Catalogue 89-550, November 20, 1996.

(Schweinhart, Barnes, and Weikart 1993). The program was aimed at stimulating cognitive development through active learning. Thirteen children attended the program from age 4 to 5; 33 participated from age 3 to 5. Compared with the control group, those in the program were doing better at age 14 on reading, arithmetic, and language achievement. By age 27, more had finished high school (71 percent compared with 54 percent for the controls). They earned more money per year, were more likely to own homes, received fewer social services, and had fewer arrests than the controls (mean = 2.3 versus 4.6).

The general thrust of this type of research is obviously simplified here. Developing effective programs is difficult. For example, individual characteristics of children and the nature of their peer associations can complicate matters, as illustrated by one study assessing the impact of deviant peers. Those who were already highly disruptive became delinquent *without* the need of deviant peers. By contrast, conforming boys were less vulnerable to the influence of peers (with respect to delinquency up to age 13, at least). However, deviant peers did influence moderately disruptive boys into becoming more delinquent (Vitaro, Tremblay, and Kerr, 1997).

Despite the complexity of assessing the impact of specific combinations of factors, and creating programs built on somewhat confusing knowledge, the ripple effect of much intervention is very likely. The Université de Montréal researchers focus primarily on psychological variables, but most of us would agree that combining this effort with structural changes would enhance effectiveness. If young fathers and mothers also had reasonable employment, had opportunities to further their education and to interact more effectively with their children, one might predict that they would be less attracted to drugs and alcohol, might read more about helpful topics, and so on. In other words, most integrated theories would agree that the cumulative effect of helping young children and their parents would be greater than the individual impact on single variables.

Since policy-makers must decide on where resources will go, Tremblay and Craig (1995) argue that money invested in early (e.g., preschool) prevention efforts with at-risk families will yield greater payoffs than money invested in later (e.g., adolescence) prevention efforts with the same families.

The Reduction of Family Violence in Canada

It is difficult to identify specific factors in Canada that have had an impact on family violence, but in 1999 the number of children killed by family members fell to its lowest level in 26 years. As noted earlier, families are the major source of serious violence. Of almost 2000 children and youth murdered between 1974 and 1999, family members were responsible for 63 percent of the deaths (Trainer and Mihorean, 2001: Ch. 2). Between 1993 and 1999 there was a decline in rates of spousal violence against women in most provinces. At the same time there was an upward trend in the use of criminal justice and social services by victims. Spousal homicide was particularly high among First Nations couples. For women it was eight times higher than it was for non-Aboriginal women. For men it was eighteen times higher.

Have shelters for abused women helped? There has been a decline in the number of children admitted to shelters, but the proportion of children in shelters for reasons of abuse increased from 1998 to 2000 (Trainor and Mihorean, 2001). Could this mean that more children are being rescued? There may have been a shift in attitudes and in practice in the past two decades.

Police Response to Domestic Violence

While it is easy to criticize past practices, it is not clear how the police should respond. A move toward laying criminal charges against men accused of assaulting their spouses began in the 1980s. The Minneapolis Domestic Violence Experiment appeared to find evidence that arrests reduced the likelihood of further violence (Sherman and Berk, 1984).

Peter Jaffe and his colleagues at the London Family Court Clinic in Ontario monitored the charging policy of the police and the level of repeat violence of men against their female partners prior to and following the implementation of the policy (Jaffe et al., 1993). They found reductions in violence when charges were laid. They also found increased satisfaction among victims with the help received from the police.

The Spouse Assault Replication Program

Assessing over 4000 cases of spousal assault in five different sites, Maxwell, Garner, and Fagan (2001) found that arrests resulted in fewer future assaults. The size of the reduction was modest compared with the effect of factors such as the batterer's age and prior criminal record. Regardless of whether the batterer was arrested, more than half of the suspects committed no subsequent criminal offence against their original victim during the follow-up period.

A minority of suspects continued to commit intimate partner violence whether they were arrested, counselled, or temporarily separated from their partner.

One should not confuse *arrests* with *mandatory charging*. In British Columbia such a policy in the late 1990s removed discretion from the prosecutors. They were required to proceed with all spousal assault cases. Suspected offenders found it advantageous to delay their court appearances. This left women vulnerable. Attempts to address family conflict situations were essentially stymied. Thus, arrest could interrupt dangerous dynamics and set the stage for positive action. Mandatory charging may have interfered with constructive steps as well as reducing the willingness of women to call the police.

Paternoster and his colleagues wanted to know what would happen when police adhered to fair procedures even when the suspect was arrested. They found that when the police listened to both sides of the story in a domestic dispute, appeared to be impartial, and treated the suspect with respect, the number of subsequent domestic assaults by the suspect was lower (Paternoster et al., 1997). *How* things are done may be as important as *what* is done.

Studies in six American cities produced mixed results. Arrests deterred some offenders and increased the rates of violence in others (Schmidt and Sherman, 1993). One fairly consistent finding, however, was that arrest seemed to deter employed men and white men, but it had the opposite effect for unemployed and African-American men. Does arrest matter if one has less to lose?

There have been a number of other innovative responses to wife battering. The Winnipeg Family Violence Court has tried to expedite court processing, increase victim cooperation, and provide sentencing that would protect victims, such as treatment for abusers and monitoring of offenders (Ursel, 1994). This project may have elevated the status of family cases from low-priority cases to complex matters requiring highly skilled personnel (MacLeod, 1995).

Another innovation is a community conferencing strategy borrowed from the Maori people of New Zealand (Braithwaite and Daly, 1994). This approach emphasizes shaming, apology, and the reaffirmation of community values rather than punishment, and is followed by reintegration into the community. By contrast, the typical court scene stigmatizes both the victim and offender and reinforces denial by the offender.

McMahon and Pence (1995) agree with the need for community involvement in domestic violence cases. However, they point out that community interventions need to appreciate how power works in families. For example, community interventions to protect children must recognize how a violent man's relationship with the mother of his children spills over into disputes about custody and access.

THE DISTRIBUTION OF VIOLENCE

Serious offences are less common than minor ones. Such a distribution is shown by the curve indicated by the solid line in Figure 13.2, in which I have attempted to diagram the frequency of violent acts committed by the total population, charted against the seriousness of each violent act. The horizontal axis goes from "not serious" to "very serious"; the vertical axis shows the frequency of the acts in each category. For the solid line, the single hump of the curve towards the left suggests that many people often commit minor acts of violence. Most people occasionally spank their children; many children get into minor fights. Towards the right of the curve are people who are truly violent. The main point is that the curve tapers off to the right; extreme behaviour is much less frequent.

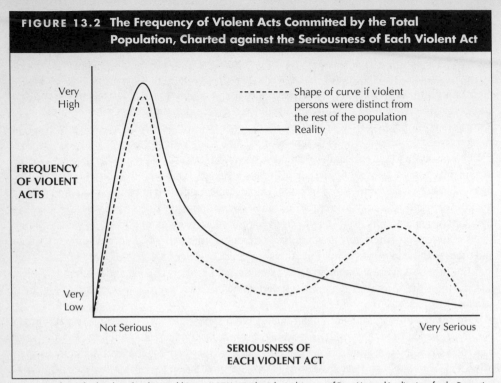

FIGURE 13.2 **The Frequency of Violent Acts Committed by the Total Population, Charted against the Seriousness of Each Violent Act**

Source: Based on Whitehead, Paul and Reginald Smart (1972). "Epidemiological Aspects of Drug Use and Implications for the Prevention of Drug Abuse." In Craig Boydell, Carl Grindstaff, and Paul Whitehead (eds.), *Deviant Behaviour and Societal Reaction*. Toronto: Holt, Rinehart, and Winston.

The *broken line* in Figure 13.2 has two humps. If extremely violent persons were clearly distinct and numerous, they might fall under the hump to the right. Most of us have no trouble with the peak on the left; the paragons of virtue are rare and most of us commit indiscretions that are not truly serious. The *real* problem is with those under the peak to the right, who are more dangerous, and therefore require special handling. The basic flaw in this argument is that the *solid* line represents the correct shape, and it is difficult to have much impact on the total violence curve by concentrating on the few. By now, the reader has certainly recognized that the logic demonstrated here is the same as that used in the chapter on drugs (Chapter 12).

Typically, we assume that the problem lies with a particular group of violent individuals who require our immediate attention. Others commit minor acts of violence from time to time, but because their acts are less serious and, taken individually, of little consequence, they can be conveniently ignored. Public outrage is directed at extreme individuals who commit serious crimes. Moral outrage must be distinguished from effective public policy. Programs and laws directed against the minority of serious trouble-makers, rather than towards the majority of minor offenders, have little impact. However, modest changes for many minor forms of violence would eventually influence the extreme and dangerous behaviour of the few, if we could change the *conditions* that influence violent behaviour in general. There is no distinct target population; serious offenders are simply at one end of a *smooth* continuum. Present policies make a few people the target of some anti-violence strategy. However, the *shape* of the curve remains constant; efforts directed towards that small population on the right of the curve will have little impact on the *entire* curve. The only way to reduce violence is to move the entire curve to the left.

A similar kind of logic can be applied to family violence. Instead of concentrating on extreme cases, policies should emphasize conditions that influence all cases. Women trapped in certain types of family situations are more likely to experience violence (Tong, 1984; Atkins and Hoggett, 1984; Brophy and Smart, 1985). Economic factors that make it difficult for women to leave dangerous family situations contribute to the potential for violence. Thus, social policies giving women more economic independence would reduce the frequency of conditions that lead to violence (Hackler, 1991a).

When Margaret Mitchell, Member of Parliament in Canada, told the House of Commons a couple of decades ago that one out of ten men regularly beats his wife, there were guffaws from some of the male MPs. Obviously, an initial task was to convince male-dominated policy-making bodies that a problem existed. There was also a tendency to make the battered wife the focus of attention. The battered woman is given "therapy" and shown how to "identify tensions in the marriage relationship" (Tierney, 1982), as if she, rather than the male-oriented values that influence social inequality, were the problem. The wife-beating problem has been medicalized, professionalized, individualized, and de-politicized while conditions that increase the likelihood of family stress have been ignored. One strategy was to "cool out" militant feminist groups by providing specific social services. The practice of "funding and defanging" them through manipulating funding, influencing hiring, and guiding referrals keeps some of these feminist groups more "manageable" (Burstyn, 1987). It is possible that by the 1990s such manipulation gave way to sensible programs spearheaded by feminists and their allies.

Laureen Snider (1998) points to remaining problems. The dependence on the criminal justice system to deal with wife assault and battery has benefited privileged white women at the expense of women of colour, Aboriginal, and immigrant women. Snider argues that the control of violence lies outside criminal justice institutions; the focus should be on how to create less-violent people (particularly men), families, communities, and societies—in other words, to move the violence curve to the left.

Using Child-Support Payments to Move the Violence Curve to the Left

Many mothers resort to using family court because a former husband has failed to make child-support payments. The father may also be facing financial difficulties. He tries to visit his children; the mother resists because he has not made payments; a fight ensues. If the state took on the task of paying child support and collecting from the husband, the situation could be quite different. Once child support is awarded, the state could guarantee those payments, providing better protection for children. Collecting payments from the father becomes a separate issue, which does not have to affect the family. An unemployed father might have difficulties, but this is between the court and the father, not between the mother and the father. Divorces already involve stress. By making the mother as independent as possible, we minimize the negative impact on the children. Chasing a former husband through the courts to recover overdue child-support payments is a poor way for a divorced mother to use her time or finances, and can lead to retaliation when the mother attempts to deny visitation rights to the father.

Our present situation penalizes the weakest and most vulnerable people. Economic factors frequently make it difficult for a woman to leave a violent situation. Society has a vested interest in enabling women to act independently when faced with stressful conditions. At present, we focus on families who are currently displaying serious violence. In reality, there is a continuum of family violence, from serious to minor, similar to the skewed curve in Figure 13.2. The target group is always unclear, so a truly effective strategy would include many who are marginal. Universal plans have an impact on many families, including those with severe problems.

Family Violence and Native Families in Canada

Although empirical data on violence in Native families in Canada are scarce, the murder rate for Native offenders doubled from 1961 to 1990. Murder is probably the best indicator of general violence over time. Changes in reporting practices have probably influenced crime statistics on sexual assault, child abuse, and wife-battering. Murder represents the most visible tip of the iceberg, but it is a mere tip. Thus, I suggest that the murder rate indicates that violence has increased among Native families from 1961 until the late 1970s. If violence is of concern in the population in general, it is much more serious among our Native population. Since violence among marginal families today leads to their children being violent in the future, improving family conditions for Native children should be of the highest priority. All of the points made above with regard to economic equality, and other factors that make women vulnerable, apply even more to Native women. Few areas of public policy have greater potential for reducing crime in the future.

The recent increases in homicide in Canada may be primarily due to the increases in Native homicides. Although the Native population is small in Canada, if we were to discount Native homicides, the increases in homicide rates for the rest of the population would be minimal. Similarly in the U.S. (where African Americans make up a larger portion of the total population than Native people in Canada), if one were to discount black homicides, increases in homicide rates for the rest of the population would be less apparent. This finding fits with a major theme in this book: *violence in recent years has increased most dramatically among members of those groups who have been marginalized by society rather than among members of the dominant society.* Policies that would improve the lot of marginalized people would probably contribute more to the reduction of violent crime than the repressive tactics that have been favoured in North America during the past two decades.

Can Government Policy Make a Difference in Reducing Violent Crime?

Government intervention reduces wife abuse. For example, the family allowance contributes toward the financial independence of women. Thus, stresses that lead to other forms of violent crime are reduced. Women raising small children either without a husband or with a non-supportive husband are vulnerable. Children raised in marginal families are more likely to become violent adults. Policy-makers overlook the criminogenic potential of such family conditions. If a woman is provided with the means to move away, circumstances conducive to violence might be avoided. Some of these changes may already be occurring in North America. When Straus and Gelles (1986) reported a decrease in child and wife abuse between 1975 and 1985, there was a mixed response from official agencies, since they had witnessed an increase in such cases. Broad-based social concern leading to a variety of programs could encourage women to seek help instead of enduring beatings. This would mean more contact with agencies, but also a decrease in actual beatings. When a society mobilizes, there is the potential for positive change. Unfortunately, broad-based programs that make modest contributions to the quality of family life for many families are often overlooked in favour of those programs that focus on the violent few.

Effective reduction in violent crime requires broad changes in the structure of society. The law-and-order mentality, which has emphasized increased punishment for the past dozen years, will not only fail but will contribute to greater violence. A couple of decades ago, the violence chapter of a criminology text would have focused on murderers, rapists, robbers, and other such individuals. Instead, this chapter has taken a broader approach and focused on corporate activities, cultural elements, and family violence. This approach will not satisfy those who think criminology should focus on conventional, "real" criminals. However, policies that take into account the points reviewed in this chapter would, in the long run, be more likely to reduce murder, rape, robbery, and the like, which are the by-products of subcultural conditions, child development, and government policies on the family.

SUMMARY

1. Corporate crime hurts more people and does more damage than conventional crime.

2. In violent subcultures adherence to, not alienation from, certain norms leads to violence.

3. War increases homicide by reducing inhibitions and legitimating violence. The use of capital punishment may characterize and reinforce violent societies.

4. Families can be dangerous places. Women estranged from their partners face a higher risk of being killed than if they are living together as a couple. Men are more likely to murdered by a current common-law partner.

5. Female crime is often linked to victimization. The Lavallée case is an illustration of the "battered woman syndrome."

6. Reducing the many minor incidents of violence is probably a good strategy for reducing the rarer but more serious violent acts.

7. Family violence and child abuse lead to future criminality and a variety of other problems.

8. Government policies could reduce violent crime in the long run by providing support for families with children.

KEY TERMS

battered woman syndrome	214	femicide	211
catharsis model	210	legitimation of violence model	210
corporate violence	204	subcultures of violence	205

WEBLINKS

www.canada.justice.gc.ca/en/ps/voc/index.html

The Policy Centre for Victims' Issues: a Department of Justice site providing information on federal government initiatives concerning crime victims.

www.crime-prevention.org/english/main.html

National Crime Prevention Council of Canada: provides information on federal government crime-prevention projects.

PROPERTY AND CORPORATE CRIMES: GREED, THRILLS, OR THE LUST FOR POWER?

This chapter will:

- Point out the difficulty of categorizing crimes in a way that would let us apply specific theories.

- Review some of the non-rational factors that seem to influence crime.

- Remind us that white-collar crime is our major property crime even though society responds less vigorously to it.

- Try to distinguish between occupational and corporate crime and examine some of its causes.

- Argue that a subculture of power abuse among corporate leaders creates a criminogenic mindset.

- Point out that conflict theories have been effective in calling attention to crimes of the powerful, as have traditional theories such as differential association.

- Note that technology and changing organizational activities constantly create new opportunities for crime and complicate attempts to explain them.

THE THIN LINES BETWEEN RATIONAL THEFT, VIOLENCE, AND GETTING ONE'S KICKS

Trying to categorize crimes as property crimes or violent attacks on people is convenient but is actually misleading. Many crimes are hard to classify. Take poaching, for example. First, there are major differences among poachers. One type hunts a few animals over the legal limit and shares with friends. Another exceeds limits simply for of the thrill of doing so. Still another sells animal parts or wild meat to other criminals and commercial trading rings. The latter are sophisticated, using modern technology such as airplanes and radio scanners to keep track of law enforcement officials (Gregorich, 1997). In some respects they are like other thieves. There is a market for their goods. South Korea, China, and Japan utilize bear paws. Gall bladders can bring $150 to $400. Is poaching a major or minor problem? British Columbia has 100 000 to 160 000 black bears. About 1000 to 2000 are killed illegally each year. In 1996 there were 194 investigations, twelve prosecutions, and four convictions. The professional poachers are often involved in other crime, such as drug trafficking, and are willing to use violence against law-enforcement officers.

The reason for discussing the crime of poaching is that it illustrates certain concerns we have about a lot of other crimes: (1) it does not fit neatly into a category; (2) effective enforcement is extremely difficult; and (3) it reflects a general disrespect and lack of concern for society in general. In other words, it tears at the social fabric.

Greed has been viewed as the major motivating factor for many crimes. This is a vast oversimplification, but it forms the basis of much criminological research. Crime represents a rational quest for a supposedly universal goal, which people seek in a variety of ways. In a modern society, that means money and all of the goods, services, privileges, and prestige that money can buy. Explanations such as the routine activities theory take these motivations for granted, as does opportunity theory. Both theories look at situations.

Another strategy, or formula, for explaining property crime is to look at characteristics of the criminal, such as age, gender, race, ethnicity, socioeconomic status, and education. These characteristics could be subdivided into traits that are more individual or more social. Researchers can focus on individual characteristics or on the way individuals interact with aspects of the society. Still another formula is to see crime as irrational, the manifestation of mental, or at least emotional, illness, to the extent that rational thought has been suspended.

Stealing: Rational Behaviour or Getting One's Kicks?

In his book, *Great Pretenders: Pursuits and Careers of Persistent Thieves*, Neal Shover (1996) studies the choices made by ordinary property offenders. These choices are limited and distorted by a common central fact: almost all of these offenders were born into a life of pervasive poverty. This point is crucial because many theories pay scant attention to how offenders arrive at the point where they actually contemplate committing an offence. Most of us have many opportunities to steal, but we also have many other options which are much more attractive.

Shover contends that poverty can stunt the dreams and imaginations of childhood, causing many youngsters to tune out of the school scene. This limits legitimate options at an early age. Poorly supervised at home, some of these children are attracted to the street corner, where a different set of values is shared. Seeing failure as normal in school, the street-corner culture offers "life as party." The emphasis is on "good times," with minimal concern for obligations and commitments to the larger community. Shared values include spontaneity, resourcefulness, and independence from the routine imposed by the world of school and work. Thus, gambling, drinking, and using drugs take priority. But because they are poor to begin with, their resources are soon exhausted—as is the patience and goodwill of employers, spouses, and law-abiding friends. With increased isolation from conventional others, and in need of money, they see crime as an option to keeping the party going. Inevitably this leads to prison, which further limits legitimate options upon release.

Those theorists who emphasize rational choice overlook the fact that these persistent criminals find themselves with few realistic alternatives. Similarly, the justice system is prepared to write off these offenders and consign them to a life behind bars. Shover notes, however, that even these people grow wiser with age, and many search for ways to change. However, just as they are contemplating going straight, they often receive the most severe penalties. This may be the time when increasing legitimate options and opportunities would have the greatest effect.

The Seductions of Crime: Shoplifting, Joyriding, Burglary, and Other Sneaky Thrills

In a book with the provocative title *The Seductions of Crime: Moral and Sensual Attractions of Doing Evil*, Jack Katz (1988) argues that the rational choice perspective is inadequate, because it does not capture the essence of the experience from the standpoint of the criminal. Crime cannot be explained without knowing what it means to the actor. Conventional criminology assumes that criminals want to acquire money or goods, get revenge, satisfy sexual urges, get high on drugs, and the like. Katz feels that criminologists, whether they are using quantitative or qualitative techniques, impose their own interpretation on what is going on in the mind of the criminal.

Material needs are often insufficient to account for the fleeting fascination with theft. Albert Cohen (1955) and many others suggest that for many criminals crime is fun. They steal for the "hell of it." When a youth steals a hat and then goes into store after store exchanging one hat for another, it would be hard to say that he had a great desire to have a hat. But it certainly makes him seem daring in the eyes of his peers. Katz used self-reports of students in his criminology courses to construct his ideas about the sneaky thrill of shoplifting, experiences that were not utilitarian and practical, but "eminently magical" (1988: 54). He emphasizes the reports of his female students. One student was fascinated with non-acquisitive burglary:

> When she was 13, she would enter neighbours' homes and roam around. Somehow being in a neighbour's house without express permission made the otherwise mundane environment charged.… She found that a familiar kitchen or living room was magically transformed into a provocative environment. The excitement was distinctly sensual. (69–70)

Katz notes that girls "seem seduced by items of makeup, jewellery, and clothes: things used to cover up the naked female self … to make the self dazzlingly attractive to a world blinded to the blemishes underneath" (71). In general, Katz downplays rational and practical elements. Much research shows that girls steal cosmetics, and while Katz sees this as sensual and seductive, others view such theft as rational.

Robbery: Rational Behaviour or Pleasurable Pursuit?

Katz argues that **distinctive sensual dynamics** emerge during the committing of a crime and must be understood. For most criminals doing wrong has authenticity, an attractiveness that uplifts, excites, and purifies. He argues that each crime has its own distinctive appeals.

Robbery is often classified with violent crimes, but some argue that banks are robbed because, as famous bank robber Willie Sutton pointed out, "that is where the money is." However, Nettler (1982) and others, in addition to Katz, have done cost-benefit analyses to show that monetary gain as the principal reward cannot account for robbery, or for most other property crime. Nettler captures the pleasure of theft by quoting from Willie Sutton, an intelligent and persistent bank robber:

> Why did I rob banks? Because I enjoyed it. I loved it. I was more alive when I was inside a bank, robbing it, than at any other time in my life. I enjoyed everything about it so much that one or two weeks later I'd be out looking for the next job. But to me the money was the chips, that's all. The winnings. I kept robbing banks, when, by all logic, it was foolish. When it could cost me far more than I could possibly gain. (Nettler, 1982: 96)

Katz would also agree that robbery is risky and, from a rational standpoint, a dangerous, difficult, and not particularly lucrative way to make a living. Those who persist spend time in jail and face considerable risk, but Katz argues that the sensual attraction comes from the excitement, the thrill, the pursuit, and the satisfaction of forcing others to bow to their will. In a section entitled "Constructing Subjective Moral Dominance," Katz describes how the robber creates *"an angle of moral superiority* over the intended victim" (169). Different types of robberies provide different rewards, including the pleasure of ridiculing and humiliating, as well as stealing from, the victim.

Although Katz offers some stimulating ideas, Erich Goode (1990), in reviewing the book, asks a number of questions: "How does the author know this? Where is his evidence? Is a different interpretation possible?" (10) Researchers who have worked more directly with offenders create different images of bank robbers. Fred Desroches (1995), for example, interviewed bank robbers in Ontario, and found that the modern bandit is typically a man who works alone, stands in line with customers, does not carry a weapon, uses minimal disguises, discreetly passes a note to a single teller, and walks out with $1500 to $2500. Some bandits walk around for hours, trying to decide whether or not to commit a robbery. Sometimes they walk away or, just as compulsively, do the robbery with a minimal amount of careful planning. Thus we have two different pictures of the typical bank robber: inept individuals who vacillate over decisions or daring men, open to anything, prepared for anything, and deliberately looking for excitement.

Montreal has a tradition of robbery that is unique in Canada (Gabor et al., 1987): "In Canada, the French Canadian minority is overrepresented in armed robbery in a significant way.... Québec accounts for 60 percent of all armed robberies in Canada while having only a quarter of Canada's population" (Gabor and Normandeau, 1989: 274). Is there something in French-Canadian culture that would encourage young males to seek thrills through robbery?

In the U.S., the African-American minority is over-represented in most crime categories, but even more so in robbery. Although Katz tells us that looking at age or ethnicity is not adequate for explaining crime, conventional thinking would reasonably ask why French Canadians and blacks are more likely to commit certain crimes. Gabor and Normandeau (1989) note many of the young male subjects they studied in Quebec took pleasure in humiliating their victims. Even if we are sympathetic to the "seduction-of-crime" argument, why is it that French Canadians find it more satisfying to humiliate victims than English Canadians?

Why do blacks search for thrills and danger in the excitement of pursuit, and in the domination of others? Conventional criminology has been criticized for its mundane habit of looking at "background" variables and correlating them with crime; but if we are to abandon this traditional line of inquiry, are we left to conclude that French Canadians and African Americans are more immoral than others, that their happiness comes in hurting and humiliating others? Clearly, Katz would not make such an argument, but a more conventional argument for French Canadians and blacks is made by Gabor and Normandeau:

> Both groups were going through considerable upheaval during the 1960s; a fact that may explain the intensification of their participation in robbery at that time. Both groups faced political oppression and exclusion from the economic elite. Both have faced the humiliations accorded those considered inferior in status. (1989: 274–75)

On the other hand, Gabor and his colleagues (1987) describe elements that are compatible with the argument made by Katz. Most of the robbers they studied did little planning, while others made elaborate preparations. Some decided spontaneously to commit a robbery. Younger robbers liked the thrills, status, and feelings of power. One boy said: "It's funny to see the expression of people when they have a .38 in their face. Sometimes I went home at night I thought of it and laughed.… Maybe I was just fascinated" (Gabor and Normandeau, 1989: 277).

Still other robbers told Gabor that they had a code of ethics. They excluded certain targets, such as small businesses in which the owners themselves were struggling to make a living. Such reasoning seems strange for evil, daring thrill-seekers. Most explanations do not fit all people or all situations. Perhaps some people do find magic, beauty, excitement, and gratification in doing evil, as Katz would argue, but many other criminals do not.

Roger Caron may be one of those people who found magic and satisfaction in crime. In his book *Go-Boy* (1978), Caron describes some of the brutalizing aspects of imprisonment. With its publication he became a well-known personality. One might assume that Caron's new-found fame as a writer and sought-after speaker would alter his pattern of criminal behaviour. Two more popular books appeared: *Bingo!* (1985) and *Jojo* (1988). His latest book, *Dreamcaper* (1992), features an old con who finally gets parole and decides to pull off his last big job. The book includes daring and ingenious escapes, a brilliantly executed heist, nasty and vindictive police, and the idyllic tropical setting where the successful criminal retires. Caron himself, of course, hoped for such criminal success, but in fact was a dismal failure. Ironically, the hero of *Dreamcaper* says, "all convicts suffer from defective reasoning; they never seem to learn from experience." About the time the book was published, Roger Caron was arrested for armed robbery. Few criminals had better chances for rehabilitation. Caron was clearly a failure as a crook; and even though he was a success as an author, the seduction of crime seemed to be too great.

Choosing among Explanatory Models of Street Crime

A number of questions come to mind. Are these scholars looking at the same type of people? Do they begin their research with preconceived ideas? If, as Katz would argue, crime is explained primarily by the pleasure it yields, then clearly some countries are enjoying it much more than others. Why are Americans getting so many kicks out of crime, compared with the Japanese? Why do Canadians find evil so much more pleasurable than northern Europeans, who have lower crime rates? Conventional criminologists have gathered facts about different amounts of crime by gender, race, social class, country, and so forth, but if pleasure explains crime, why do males, blacks, lower-class people, and so on, find crime more seductive than others?

Do peer pressure, collective behaviour, group dynamics, and other factors explain compulsive theft and robbery better than the arguments offered by Katz? Do the ecological models, including routine activity theories and other approaches emphasizing opportunities, offer more adequate explanations of burglary than the motivation of thrills? Is it also possible that the pleasure described in doing crime is partially a reconstruction of realities after the fact? In earlier chapters, we noted that people can use cognitive dissonance reduction to convince themselves that they had reasons for doing what they did. Qualitative research has clearly enriched our thinking, but it would be a mistake to believe that this work automatically provides clear and adequate explanations that can now replace the emphasis on evidence.

How Specialized Are Property Offenders?

Despite the wealth of research that concentrates on a particular type of offender, most property offenders are not particularly specialized. Shover (1996) has summarized the literature for burglary and concludes that those who think of themselves as burglars not only engage in a variety of other crimes, but increase their versatility with success. The issue of specialization is important for policy decisions. If unique explanations are required for each type of crime, it would be difficult to develop effective societal responses. If we acknowledge different causal factors for violent crime and property crime, how different are white-collar offenders from other greedy people? Do our theories cover a broad spectrum of those who lie, cheat, and steal, including white-collar criminals?

WHITE-COLLAR CRIME

In 1939, Edwin H. Sutherland introduced the term **white-collar crime** in his presidential address to the American Sociological Society, and criticized criminologists for the narrowness of their thinking about crime. Poverty, broken homes, and the traditional variables did not explain some of the most common and costly crimes. As criminologists looked beyond the lower classes and street crime, they discovered that crimes such as income tax evasion were very frequent and costly, but rarely studied as crime.

The borderlines of white-collar crime are sometimes difficult to discern. When an officer of a large corporation has insider information that would enable him to profit over others, it is a criminal offence to use that knowledge for personal gain. However, if a cab driver overhears a conversation, borrows money, and makes a killing on the stock market, it would not be a crime. White-collar crime refers to the abuse of power and privilege, and there is considerable agreement that modern, democratic, free-enterprise societies must strive for a reasonably level playing field if our pursuit of material wealth is to be conducted in an orderly fashion.

Recording and enforcement are also more problematic with white-collar crime. A former premier of British Columbia was considered an "insider" because of his holdings and his involvement in a certain company. When a phone call came to his office with devastating financial news about the company, was it just a coincidence that he sold his stock in the company a few moments later? At any rate, this former premier was acquitted in the BC courts.

In monetary terms, white-collar crime is of greater consequence than conventional crime. John Irwin and James Austin (1987) summarize these costs in the U.S. The total for all street crimes in a year is about $11 billion. The U.S. spends more than four times that amount ($45.6 billion) on the criminal justice system to fight property crimes. The medical costs related to tobacco smoking are around $50 billion a year, and the cost of white-collar crime is about $200 billion per year. Although many white-collar criminals argue that they do not "hurt" people, because they steal from the government or a large company, the same argument can be made for some safe-crackers. Harry King (1972) claimed that he kept insurance companies and safe companies in business. He specialized in large corporations, which could easily absorb the expenses he created for them. By contrast, the fraud committed by the Principal group of mutual funds in Alberta led to the loss of life savings for thousands of people and caused more pain and damage than most burglaries.

The ability to exploit an organization, such as a corporation, provides greater rewards for the criminally inclined. Hagan and Parker (1985) report that securities violators who use organizational resources commit crimes that involve more victims. When a president of a corporation presents a bank with false information as a way of defrauding shareholders, for example, he is more likely to be believed than a person acting alone. Organizations, and those who speak for them, are seen as more trustworthy than individuals. Thus, Hagan (1992) argues that people in organizations such as corporations have tremendous advantages that individual criminals do not have, and this leads to greater criminal gains. Hagan concludes that the social organization of work itself is criminogenic in the world of the modern corporation. Later I will return to crimes of the powerful, but for now it is appropriate to emphasize that white-collar crime is a major part of our crime problem and deserves more attention from policy-makers than it currently receives. Explanations of white-collar crime are compatible with conventional theories. Why powerful people steal is no mystery. What requires more attention is how structures arose that made it possible for those with power and wealth to abuse that power. In addition, we need to understand why societies respond less vigorously to this type of crime and fail to recognize the cost of such crime to society.

The Abuse of Power: Corporate and Occupational Crime

Conflict theorists have been particularly effective in calling attention to crimes committed by the powerful. In all societies, individuals differ in their influence. In some societies, those who have influence are given high status but are also expected to be more honourable than average and to provide help and assistance to those less privileged. But in practice those with power often forget the principle of *noblesse oblige*. Some scholars believe that capitalism has created a situation that increases crime, including crime by corporations. "Corporate crime ... actually does more harm, costs more money, and ruins more lives" than assaults, thefts, and rape (Snider, 1993: 1). It "causes more deaths in a month than all the mass murderers combined do in a decade. Canadians are killed on the job by unsafe (and illegal) working conditions; injured by dangerous products ... and robbed by illegal conspiracies that raise prices and eliminate consumer choice" (1).

Apologists for large corporations often argue that some damage is inevitable in the pursuit of larger goals that are socially worthwhile. Critics, however, question the social value of these major goals. In the chemical industry, for example, criminogenic conditions are built into the business. Crimes are produced routinely through the supposedly normal operations of the corporations (Pearce and Tombs, 1998).

Other Canadian scholars have documented the harm done by commercial crime in the workplace (Reasons, Ross, and Patterson, 1981). Ray Corrado (1991) has summarized the impact of political crime, and Gordon and Coneybeer (1991) and Hagan (1992) have reviewed white-collar offences committed by those in respected positions.

The brief illustrations in this chapter merely set the stage for a discussion of appropriate societal responses. First, we should distinguish between occupational and corporate crime. **Occupational crimes** are commercial (white-collar) crimes committed by people exclusively for personal gain (Coleman, 1985: 8). The victims include organizations, businesses, or government. These crimes include embezzlement of corporate funds, expense-account fraud, tax evasion, and most computer crime. Perhaps political corruption could be seen as an "occupational" crime.

The occupational crime connected with the business world takes many forms (Francis, 1988). One involves "boiler-room boys," who misrepresent stock over the telephone. Many of these Canadian-run fraudulent operations are international, since avoiding local enforcement authorities often requires moving to other countries. The behaviour of these criminals does not fit comfortably into our criminological theories. Amsterdam was seen as a "good gig" by one boiler-room boy. "All day you sell stocks, and every night most of the guys would go to the red-light district to get laid or just get a blow job" (1988: 240). The greed for money is obvious, but are the seductions and excitement described by Katz even more significant?

Diane Francis also describes illegal activities involving the Vancouver and Alberta stock exchanges, and highlights Canada's role in laundering money from drug transactions. "Canada is a gigantic loophole through which billions of dollars worth of drugs and dirty money pass annually. Canada is a smuggler's and money launderer's mecca. The narcotics business generates an incredible $150 billion a year in cash transactions" (1988: 240). Although these types of crimes have not attracted as much attention as violent crime, appropriate explanations are probably similar to other types of crimes of deceit.

In contrast to occupational crime, **corporate crimes** are committed by legitimate formal organizations, through the individuals inside them, with the aim of furthering the interests of the corporation as well as those of the individuals involved. Conspiracies among companies to restrict supplies of goods, and thereby raise prices, to dispose of hazardous wastes illegally, or to deliberately fail to maintain safe working conditions are criminal acts that benefit individuals within the corporation. Corporate crime serves both the organization and the individual criminal, while occupational crime benefits only the individual but victimizes a variety of others, including different corporations and organizations (Snider, 1992).

Explanations of corporate crime can be viewed from three overlapping perspectives: (1) the behaviour of individuals, (2) the nature and requirements of the organizations, and (3) the structure and demands of the economic system (Gordon and Coneybeer, 1991: 440–44). At the individual level, one asks why executives, owners, and supervisors implement, and sometimes plan, corporate crimes. Why do successful people commit such crimes? Questions of "need" are not very convincing. Even "greed" fails to provide a satisfactory explanation. "Opportunity" to satisfy wants may be relevant, but many non-criminals have opportunities as well. In the chapter on social interaction I discussed Sutherland's differential association as an explanation of crime in general. It appears to fit white-collar crime as well. Corporate leaders commit crimes as a result of learning from others both techniques and rationalizations that let them override or "neutralize" the moral restraints to violating the law. But what are the specific characteristics of modern companies that create criminogenic conditions?

Corporations create pressures on executives and managers to "cut corners," to achieve organizational goals for which they will be rewarded. Wrong-doing is often complex, making it hard for different supervisors and managers within the system to fully appreciate the implications of some of the illegal actions. Often, middle managers feel they have few options. One can appreciate pressures on the individual managers within the corporation, but why are there demands on the corporation itself?

Capitalism and free enterprise create certain demands. One of these is the continual pressure to make profits. If one corporation finds a cheap way to dump poisonous wastes into rivers, it has an advantage over a similar company that pays for the safe storage of wastes. There are similar pressures on oil companies to extract oil rapidly. Speed was a factor in the Hibernia oil fields off Newfoundland. Oil-rig owners took shortcuts in safety measures, which led to deaths in the Ocean Ranger disaster (House, 1986). Why are deliberate actions on the part of corporations that lead to death and injury not treated as crimes? One corporate strategy is to describe accidents as regrettable but unavoidable by-products of a system that yields other benefits. Snider (1993) argues that the relationship between the state and corporate interests leads to cooperation in creating misleading public images.

Governments are sensitive to projects that might lead to short-term "job creation," even though such commercial enterprises may, in the long run, decrease jobs. (For example, lumbering activities that pollute streams and destroy salmon spawning grounds may decrease jobs in fishing.) The state also creates agencies, such as workers' compensation boards, that supposedly help the worker but also encourage the continuance of dangerous and criminal practices. Corporations have been able to divert the responsibility and avoid the stigma resulting from deliberate decisions that damage others.

Regulating Corporate Crime versus Publicizing Unethical Practices

It is difficult for the state to regulate corporations, because the revenues of the state, its educational, welfare, military, and other programs, are dependent on the profitability of the private sector. On the other hand, some regulations compel industries to take actions in their own interests that they could not take unilaterally. The enforcement of regulations on all companies should influence profits equitably, and a healthier and happier labour force would be able to buy the products being produced. However, when competition also comes from branch plants in other countries, similar regulations are required worldwide (Snider, 1993: 178–98).

Ideological issues vary by country. The United States seems to have a widespread criminogenic business subculture which resists enforcement action. Lawsuits constantly challenge the legitimacy of the government to enforce rules. This is less common in Japan, Australia, the United Kingdom (Hawkins, 1984; Vogel, 1986), or Sweden (Kelman, 1981). Canadian corporations also have a tendency to resist regulation. The general characteristic of North Americans to resist regulation and to engage in questionable commercial practices may be part of a general set of values regarding the abuse of power. Therefore, I focus on the broad abuse of power, not just criminal activities. Can we publicize behaviour that is unethical as an indirect way of eventually reducing corporate criminality? For example, corporate executives control their own salaries. This is not criminal, but it is part of a **subculture of power abuse** which favours a few at the expense of many, and fosters an antisocial climate.

Although publicly traded companies are supposedly owned and controlled by the shareholders, most people realize that a select group of entrenched executives, who control the selection of directors who serve on boards, holds the real power. These directors are often executives in other companies. They vote high salaries for the top executives and generous fees for themselves, knowing that this will also be done in the companies they lead. Shareholders, as well as other employees, certainly would not award these inflated salaries if they had the power to resist. When an armed robber takes money from someone against her will, that is a crime. When executives take undeserved money that the owners (shareholders) of the company oppose, the shareholders are powerless. These self-serving actions on the part of executives are morally similar to other forms of corporate crime, despite rationalizations and justifications.

The argument that these executives display unusual skills and earn their high salaries is not consistent with the evidence. Corporate leaders have built-in guarantees that protect them even when the companies do badly, sometimes due to the incompetence of the executives. When the chief executive officer of Moore Corporation was given a $12-million bonus after having led the company badly for years, shareholders complained, but the money was not returned. When John Roth, the CEO of Nortel, received immense rewards, he was acclaimed CEO of the year. When Nortel dropped to 8 percent of its former value, Mr. Roth did not provide a refund. The structure of corporate enterprise creates criminogenic subcultures, and the environment created in the corporate boardroom is antisocial and criminogenic.

In Chapter 18, on criminogenic conditions, I will try to argue that publicizing this abuse of power, something which conflict theorists do rather well, offers a strategy for reducing not only corporate crime, but other crime as well. For now, however, let us simply acknowledge that corporations, as demonstrated so adequately by Sutherland over half a century ago, are major contributors to crime.

THE LIMITATIONS OF EXPLANATIONS FOR PROPERTY CRIMES

A number of perspectives provide plausible explanations for property crime, but none is complete. Despite the variety of "new" theories that arise from time to time, such as the work by Katz on the seductions of crime, we still find that background factors—information about types of people, neighbourhoods, situations, and even nations—are needed. Even explaining ordinary property crime seems to require consideration of many factors. For example, a Dutch study, based on interviews with 106 burglars, suggests that elements found in a variety of theories all seemed to be relevant (Netherlands Ministry of Justice, 1991). The burglars wanted to be accepted by peers, but they also needed money to buy drugs. Once involved in burglary, it was hard to quit: they became dependent on the money, the drugs, and on being part of the criminal subculture. At the same time, they expressed dislike for what they were doing. Many were addicted to drugs (43 percent), gambling (23 percent), or alcohol (18 percent). Clearly, differential association, subcultural, and other theories were relevant. In addition, there are potential problems of methodology. In the interviews, were the burglars making excuses or rationalizing? Environmental factors were also apparent: the burglars preferred to steal from detached, single-family houses, preferably those on street corners, usually in the burglars' home towns but not in their neighbourhoods.

When Louise Biron and Carol Ladouceur (1991) interviewed 25 teen-age burglars in Montreal, they also found that a combination of factors seemed to be operating. Perhaps we cannot develop a distinct explanation for property crimes. The facts surrounding property crime vary considerably, depending on circumstances, and therefore the number of variables that interact make prediction especially difficult. Opportunities for property crime can also change through technology. Credit cards and electronic banking create possibilities for different types of theft. Theft from the luggage of air travellers is of growing concern. Thus, finding theories for property crime that lead to intelligent policies may be particularly challenging.

Changing Technology, Changing Crimes, and Changing Explanations

Obviously, changing technology and changing organizational activities will lead to new crimes and problems that have not been anticipated. A small sample of these situations may illustrate why criminologists will have a difficult time developing satisfactory theories to explain them.

Finland is becoming a target for criminals from Russia (*Maclean's*, August 3, 1992: 20). Finnish police have arrested dozens of underworld members who entered Finland posing as refugees. They typically steal electronic goods, designer clothes, and luxury cars and smuggle them back to Russia, where confederates sell the contraband on the black market. One Finnish civic leader said it was better under the Kremlin dictatorship. "The Iron Curtain kept the criminals on the other side of the border."

David Slatter was settling into his seat on an Air Canada plane in the Miami airport, when he glanced out the window and saw an airport ramp worker unzip his bag on the conveyor belt (*The Globe and Mail*, February 29, 1992). He complained to a stewardess, but Air Canada would not delay the flight. When Mr. Slatter arrived in Toronto his $1300 camera was missing from his bag.

Airport baggage theft illustrates the changing opportunities for property crime in a modern society. In some situations a variety of protective techniques arise, and there is a competition in innovation as thieves and victims develop new strategies. In addition to the technological changes and opportunities for theft, the way human groups are organized will influence crime. In Canada, baggage handlers are members of the International Association of Machinists and Aerospace Workers, and theft from baggage in Canada appears to be low. By contrast, in Miami, where Air Canada contracts with Dynair Services to handle baggage, there have been many complaints. An investigation showed that 70 of Dynair's 350 workers had arrest records. Obviously, the subcultural norms among a group of workers can influence theft rates. Although I do not have direct information, the baggage handlers in Canada may share group norms and attitudes that would condemn an individual worker who stole from clients. In other organizations, such as some longshoreman unions, theft from cargoes was seen as normal and acceptable. Anyone who ships a vehicle from Europe knows that the car keys will be given to supposedly responsible people, but anything left in the locked trunk will probably be stolen. At the same time, the thieves have their rules—the valuable spare tires are rarely taken. Understanding the way subcultural norms develop among groups of employees might help us to understand and deal with theft in a specific setting, but it is not clear how well such a strategy would transfer to other settings.

Employee theft accounts for a considerable proportion of the thievery in North America. Therefore, it is reasonable to ask what strategies would best reduce this type of crime. Taking action against employee theft is difficult, and the criminal justice system will have little impact on the problem. Mr. Slatter, who lost his camera, filed a complaint. Two detectives flew to Toronto with pictures of several airport workers, and Mr. Slatter identified the culprit. When Slatter returned to Miami to testify, he said he only saw the ramp worker unzip the bag. That didn't prove he had stolen the camera. The prosecutor dropped the case. Mr. Slatter never saw his camera again.

Various crimes were chosen to illustrate the difficulties with using descriptions of what crooks do to create explanatory arguments. Many perspectives offer plausible arguments, but none provide precise theories. Perhaps this is an unreasonable goal. When we look at the range, variety, and ingenuity of crimes, we might assume that there is no hope: we simply live in a corrupt world. But there are degrees. Some countries, some communities, some families are less involved with crime than others.

Many years ago, I carelessly left my wallet in a phone booth while going for change. It was gone when I returned; however, I later received an envelope, stamped with double postage, containing all my credit cards and other papers. Even thieves have principles, and this thief had clearly not abandoned all societal values. The point I wish to make is that significant reductions in property crime will only result if almost everyone has reasonable access to basic needs, feels tied in to the norms of society, and has strong internal inhibitions against stealing. There are countries, neighbourhoods, work groups, and so forth, where such conditions and values are widespread. Developing a non-deviant "climate" is not an impossible task for human groups. Policy-makers should also be aware that the increased processing of cases by the criminal justice system will have little impact on creating such a society.

SUMMARY

1. Crimes for profit encompass a variety of activities, making it difficult to categorize them or apply theories. Non-rational factors, such as "getting one's kicks," clearly play a role, but current explanations are controversial.

2. White-collar crime is our major property crime. It may be easier to explain, but society responds less vigorously to it than to less-harmful crimes.

3. While occupational crimes such as embezzlement, fraud, and income tax evasion are usually done by individuals, corporate crimes are committed by legitimate organizations to further the interests of the organization as well as the individuals involved.

4. When a subculture of power abuse arises among corporate leaders, a criminogenic mindset can result.

5. Conflict theorists call attention to crimes of the powerful, as do traditional theories, such as differential association. In addition, pressures created by capitalism and free enterprise increase the likelihood of shortcuts and illegal practices.

6. Technology and changing organizational activities constantly create new opportunities for crime and complicate attempts to explain them. Despite the many opportunities for crime, many groups and cultures develop a "non-deviant" climate, which results in very little crime.

KEY TERMS

corporate crimes	232	seductions of crime	227
distinctive sensual dynamics	227	subculture of power abuse	233
occupational crimes	231	white-collar crime	230

WEBLINKS

www.scc-csc.gc.ca/index_e.htm
The Supreme Court of Canada: overview of the Canadian judicial system.

www.statcan.ca/english/Pgdb/State/justic.htm
Statistics Canada, Justice and Crime: current statistics on crime in Canada.

15

THE CRIMINALIZATION OF SEX

This chapter will:

- Review some of the issues surrounding public sex.

- Argue that research in this area sheds light on other areas of deviance.

- Note the link between marginality and criminality.

- Summarize research on prostitution and official responses to it.

- Challenge some assumptions made about the sex trade.

SEX IN PUBLIC PLACES: AN "ORDER MAINTENANCE" PROBLEM

One might assume that in the twenty-first century homosexuality would no longer be a topic for criminologists, but sex between men in public places is still an offence and brings a response from the police. Criminologists find it useful to look at activities that might better be defined as requiring "order maintenance," rather than crime control. In a number of crimes, such as drug use, prostitution, or homosexual activities in public toilets, who exactly constitutes the "victim" is unclear, and one might question the response of the criminal justice system.

Fred Desroches (1991) notes that in the past several years, police in Canada have invoked a crime-control model of enforcement in response to complaints of sexual activity in public washrooms. Public toilets that are frequently used for homosexual encounters are often referred to as "tearooms" (Humphreys, 1970a). The crime-control model results in the arrest and charging of numerous "tearoom" participants. Desroches studied the police response to the situation in five Canadian urban areas. Although successful in apprehending offenders and getting convictions, the police have been criticized for their use of intrusive surveillance techniques. The publication of accused persons' names by local newspapers and the resulting loss of jobs, break-up of families, and the suicide of one offender, have raised questions about the appropriateness of police investigative practices. Desroches suggests alternatives that are equally effective, less intrusive, more humane, and less costly than an aggressive arrest-and-charge crime-control strategy.

Of the five settings studied, there had been complaints in four, and in the fifth, the store security requested police involvement. The places included a public park, the basement of a theatre, three shopping centres, a department store, and the basement of a shopping mall. Between 27 and 62 men were arrested in each setting. Videotape was used in three places, and direct surveillance through air ducts in the other two.

The police in all five communities estimated that only 10 to 15 percent of the men used the washrooms for legitimate purposes. One officer said, "Given the percentage of legitimate usage, we may as well have taped everything." Although police attempted to use a separate tape for each offence, sexual activity sometimes occurred so quickly that as many as six offenders appear on a single tape. In each setting, the police terminated operations when they had a high proportion of repeat offenders.

Police in one community postponed their arrests until after Christmas so that family holidays would not be affected. In general, most of the men who were contacted asked to talk about their situation. They were quiet on the first visit to pick up their summonses, but on the second visit they wanted to talk. Some had not told their wives; some had.

Did the operation achieve deterrence? Routine observations in the same settings covered by the police operations indicated that the activity had increased to its former level. Desroches argues that instead of a **crime control model** this situation should be viewed as an **order maintenance problem**. Tearoom behaviour constitutes a low level of threat to society. Alternative strategies for security forces at universities, department stores, and shopping malls could include issuing trespassing notices to men observed lingering about public lavatories. Men could be identified and charged with trespassing if they return. There is reason to believe that cautions would work, at least for some of the men. In addition, the environmental design of areas should be considered. Tearoom participants prefer places rarely used by legitimate users. The location of restrooms can make a difference.

Considering the devastating impact of certain types of police action in the case described above, it is important to scrutinize the actions of agents of social control. Just as we are concerned about the damage done by crime, we should be concerned about the damage done by enforcement procedures. It appeared to be a promising sign when the Toronto police appointed a lesbian police officer to handle police–gay community relations.

Laud Humphreys: The Tearoom Trade—Why Do They Do It?

Since the consequences of these arrests have been so disastrous, the reader might well be puzzled that these men used public restrooms instead of developing homosexual relations in private. A unique study by Laud Humphreys (1970a, 1970b) provides some insights into the frequency and magnitude of this type of crime. I deliberately use the word *crime* because, in the eyes of the law, and from the perspective of shopping-mall managers, this is unacceptable behaviour and punishable under the Criminal Code.

Rarely can criminologists observe criminal behaviour directly, but the fear and suspicion of tearoom participants produces a mechanism that makes observation possible. A third man (usually one who obtains voyeuristic pleasure from the job) serves as a lookout, moving back and forth from door to windows. This "watchqueen" coughs when a police car stops nearby or when a stranger approaches. He nods affirmatively when he recognizes a man entering as a "regular." Laud Humphreys played the watchqueen role while observing hundreds of acts of fellatio.

Some of the tearooms were the scenes of a great deal of activity. These tearooms were usually located in parks on an island of grass, with roads and parking close by. The getaway car was just a few steps away; children were not apt to wander over from a playground; straight people rarely stopped there; the women's side was rarely used. Participants assured Humphreys that it was not uncommon for one man to fellate as many as ten others in a day. Some waited their turn for service. After leaving a place, Humphreys remarked to one man, "Kind of crowded in there, isn't it?" "Hell, yes," he answered. "It's getting so you have to take a number and wait in line in these places!" (Humphreys, 1970b).

Since Humphreys wanted to know more about men who take such risks, he engaged some in conversation outside the restrooms and eventually gained a dozen respondents whom he interviewed. In addition, Humphreys noted licence numbers of cars. To learn more about these men, the researcher faced an ethical concern. How could these covert deviants be interviewed? During this period, Humphreys was also working on a health survey. With permission from the survey's directors, he traced the addresses of the men he had observed, by means of the licence plates, and added them to the larger group to be interviewed as part of the health survey. After a year, he changed his hairstyle, attire, automobile, and glasses, and interviewed these men in their homes. They did not realize that he had observed them engaging in fellatio in a restroom over a year earlier. The ethics and risks involved have been the focus of other debates, but I will avoid that topic here.

Most of the men in Humphreys's study were married and living with their wives. Most of those marriages appeared to be stable, and the wives were unaware of their husbands' secret sexual activity. Indeed, the husbands chose tearooms to avoid such exposure.

Interviews from the health survey suggest that the tearoom participants were not particularly different from others. Some felt that their frequency of intercourse with their wives was somewhat restricted, because the wife objected to birth control devices. But how does one make the transition from normal to deviant sex? What is the nature of the tearoom experience that makes it so common, compared with other homosexual experiences? And finally, what makes a man progress from getting a blow job to giving one?

As Desroches (1991) found two decades later, participants tend to be strangers. Humphreys noted that they rarely spoke. Barring unusual events, an occasionally whispered "thanks" at the conclusion of the act constituted the bulk of the communication. But silence was not just the means to protect privacy; it guaranteed anonymity and assured the impersonality of the sexual liaison.

> Tearoom sex is distinctly less personal than any other form of sexual activity.... There is less emotional and physical involvement in restroom fellatio—less, even, than in the furtive action that takes place in autos and behind bushes.... In tearoom stalls, the only portions of the players' bodies that touch are the mouth of the insertee and the penis of insertor; and the mouths of these partners seldom open for speech. (Humphreys, 1970b: 13)

One might ask how such activities take place without attracting the attention of the public more often. While visiting a scenic Canadian city, my wife stopped to use a public restroom before we wandered through a forested area. A few days later, I was walking through the same area with a plainclothes policeman and a probation officer. One of their tasks was to warn homosexuals that a gang of youths were attacking "queers" in this same wooded area. It did not dawn on me, as I was walking with my wife, that the strollers in the woods were predominantly male. Later, when the policeman and I introduced ourselves to some of the men strolling in the woods, most of the men claimed to be "out-of-town visitors," and the warning about the youth gang was passed on. Those who were willing to talk told me that the restroom my wife used earlier was a tearoom, which was news to my policeman colleague.

Most of us are concerned with the question, "why do they do it?" A current debate about genetic make-up suggests that there is a biological basis for homosexuality. However, there are some obvious sociological components that suggest both learning and situational factors. One component concerns the "aging crisis"—as these men age, they are considered less attractive by prospective partners. Some participants are seen as "trade"—those men who make themselves available for acts of fellatio but who regard themselves as "straight." They do not reciprocate. In most cases, fellatio is performed by an older man upon a younger man, but references to the aging crisis were common.

> Well, I started off as the straight young thing. Everyone wanted to suck my cock. I wouldn't have been caught dead with one of the things in my mouth!… So, here I am … with grown kids … and the biggest cocksucker in [the city]! (Humphreys, 1970b: 16)

It is important to dispel the idea that men who engage in homosexual acts may be typed by any consistency of performance in one or another sexual role.

> Undoubtedly, there are preferences: few persons are so adaptable, their conditions so undifferentiated, that they fail to exercise choice between various sexual roles … Such preferences, however, are learned, and sexual repertories [sic] tend to expand with time and experience. (16)

Many of the men in this study considered themselves "normal" men who were simply looking for orgasms when they first discovered the tearoom activity. As people engage in heterosexual relationships, their repertoires also expand. Activities and positions that may not have been enjoyable initially often become defined as pleasurable.

Extending the Argument to Theft and Other Crime

This "socialization" argument could be expanded to crime in general. Sutherland's differential association theory suggests that crime is learned in group interaction with significant others. Humphreys suggests that individuals can also learn deviant behaviour from interacting with strangers. Men find themselves in learning environments that provide new definitions of sex. Peers acting as coaches help and encourage us, but, in addition, we work out our own adaptations to situations. Humphreys's argument can be applied to gradual involvement in a wide range of deviance. Circumstances matter. At an early age, one might discover the tearoom as an adventure. Later, the aging crisis makes the "straight" participant in the tearoom trade reconsider roles. According to the same logic, the trusted employee would not think of stealing at first, but times get tough, opportunities become available, and "borrowing" from the company becomes an alternative.

In most of the theories discussed in this book, I emphasize individuals operating in small groups within larger social settings; however, as individuals, humans are imaginative and can operate covertly in response to surrounding circumstances. To paraphrase Humphreys:

criminal preferences are also learned, and criminal repertoires tend to expand with time and experience. This process can be covert rather than open to the scrutiny of peers or others. Sociologists naturally think in terms of social networks and may overlook the creativity that individuals express in creating their own social reality.

The qualitative research referred to in previous chapters (e.g., Katz, 1988) may also make more sense in these types of situations. If armed robbers get a thrill out of their dangerous games, one can see how the men in the tearooms described above would take risks that do not make much sense from a rational point of view. My dissatisfaction with using excitement as the motivating factor in crime, or in tearoom activity, is that there should be *precursors* that indicate why some pursue the thrills and others decide that the risk is too great. I am inclined to see these precursors arising out of social interaction. What other factors influenced these tearoom participants that would sway them to move towards a pattern of deviant behaviour?

The Making of Marginal Men

George was considered "trade" in the tearoom business, and, like most of those who played the "straight" role, was married. His appearance and mannerisms were masculine. At 20, he had married a Roman Catholic girl. They had seven children, and his wife objected to any type of birth control other than the rhythm method. "How often do you have intercourse?" Humphreys asked, as part of the social health survey. "Not very much the last few years. It's up to when she feels like giving it to me—which ain't very often." Cooking hamburgers on an outdoor grill, George appeared relaxed. He mentioned how much he enjoyed his children, but there were strains with his wife, who did not like to go places with the kids. "She's an A-1 mother ... but don't cross her! She gets aggravated with me ... We fight all the time ... Mostly we argue about the kids. She's afraid of having more.... I won't suggest having sex anyway—and she doesn't want it anymore" (1970b: 18). Whatever caused George to turn from the marriage bed, the alternative must be quick, inexpensive, and impersonal. Any personal, ongoing, or expensive affair would threaten a marriage that was already shaky and jeopardize his standing as a father. There is little indication that men such as George seek homosexual contact as such; rather, they want orgasm-producing action.

George was affable and at ease during the interview. A year earlier, he had been nervous and cautious in the tearoom, engaging in furtive sex. For him, the aging crisis would also be an identity crisis. Only with reluctance would he turn to the insertee role. His socialization into homosexual activity may have taken place in a world in which it was permissible for young males to accept money from a "queer" for getting blown. Nor did George have a network of friends in the tearooms to help him adapt to change. Marginal to both heterosexual and homosexual worlds, men such as George shun involvement in the gay subculture. When asked how many close friends he had, George answered: "None. I haven't got time for that." At the end of the interview, he urged Humphreys to stay for supper. "I really wish you'd stay awhile. I haven't talked to anyone about myself in a hell of a long time!" (1970b: 19).

Humphreys describes four types of tearoom participants. In addition to "trade," he discusses "ambisexuals," who seem to enjoy sex in a variety of forms, and "gay guys," who correspond more closely to society's homosexual stereotype. The last type, the "closet queens," differ from trade in that they are more likely to be unmarried and are even more isolated. Some may have entered the tearoom trade as straights, while others were attracted to other men:

I can't remember a time when I didn't find men attractive.... I used to have terrible crushes on my gym teachers, but nothing sexual ever came of it. I just worshipped them, and wanted to be around them all the time. I had coitus with a woman when I was 16—she was 22. After it was over, she asked me what I thought of it. I told her I would rather masturbate. Boy, was she pissed off! I've always liked older men. If they are under 30, I just couldn't be less interested.... The trouble is that they always want sex—and sex isn't really what I want.... I just want to be loved by an older man. (1970b: 24)

Other closet queens prefer young boys, and this involvement obviously raises community concerns. Reports of molestations usually suggest these types of offenders. Although tearoom participants as well, many closet queens also want a personal relationship. One man, an alcoholic, spoke of his loneliness and endless search for love:

I don't find it in the tearooms—although I go there because it's handy to my work. But I suppose the [hustler's hangout] is really my meat. I just want to love every one of those kids! (1970b: 25)

Later, this man was murdered by a teenager he had picked up. It is tempting to look for psychological explanations for the preference of some closet queens for young boys, but there are also clear situational factors, such as marginality, which will be discussed below. Closet queens fear exposure and the stigmatization that might result from overt participation in the gay subculture. Their involvement with youths is obviously dangerous for themselves as well as for others.

Marginality and Criminality

Marginal men (or women) are more prone to other forms of deviance and crime. Control theory suggests that bonds with conventional others inhibit crime and ties to deviant peers increase the likelihood of crime (Linden and Hackler, 1973). Some of the men studied above had social bonds with their children that would inhibit deviance. They were not connected with deviant peer groups, but neither were they strongly bound to conventional society. While **marginality** may not lead people into deviance automatically, there may be a parallel between some types of crime and the lonely and isolated men who slip off the freeway for a few moments of impersonal sex in a toilet stall. Before a gunman killed fourteen women at the Université de Montréal, was he a marginal person? Do child molesters have satisfying lives? Are children who abuse their siblings isolated from rich human relationships? Some ethnic groups have been marginalized, such as blacks in the U.S. and Native peoples in Canada, and they experience more crime. A meaningful crime-reduction strategy would advocate social policies that improve family life (including gay family life), provide social networks among lonely individuals, or afford some measure of success to those who experience little of it. In other words, reducing marginality reduces deviance, and marginality may be one of the precursors, not only of tearoom activity, but of crime in general.

It is unfortunate that we cannot borrow practices from other societies that might, in fact, improve social relationships. For example, adolescent males receive extensive sexual instruction from older women and widows in some Polynesian communities (Marshall, 1972). The experience of mature lovers is passed on to youths, and helps them to become skilled and considerate lovers. Such a practice would hardly get the endorsement of Home and School organizations in Canada. On the other hand, sex education in the schools might contribute to better-quality relationships in the future, and hopefully, less need for the tearooms, not to mention less rape and sexual assault by heterosexual males against women.

Other government policies would have a more direct impact on marginality. When teenage girls give birth, the likelihood that they will have marginal lives and that their children will be criminal increases considerably. Crime reduction would be greatly enhanced by minimizing the number of teenage mothers. In some countries, the drug RU486, sometimes referred to as the abortion pill, is available. Its use, along with other practices, makes it possible to avoid teenage pregnancies almost completely today. Sweden reduced such pregnancies approximately sixteen-fold between 1959 and 1979. These ideas may seem to stray from the ideas presented in *Tearoom Trade*, but what makes people choose either tearooms or crime can often be traced to societal conditions that create marginality.

PROSTITUTION: THE MYTH OF LEGALITY[1]

Prostitution is technically legal in Canada, but it is almost impossible for a prostitute to work without violating laws. If she were to service customers regularly in the same room, in her home or in a hotel, the premises could be defined as a **bawdy house,** thereby violating the Criminal Code. Even a parking lot can be defined as a bawdy house. Cooperation with someone else, not necessarily a pimp, could lead to a charge of "procuring" or "living on the avails." Vagrancy statutes were used to control prostitutes during an earlier period (Backhouse, 1985; Lowman, 1991; McLaren, 1986; McLaren and Lowman, 1990), and in the 1980s municipal by-laws in some cities curtailed street prostitution. In 1983, the Supreme Court of Canada ruled that by-laws of this nature were not within the jurisdiction of cities, because this was criminal law, an area that is within federal jurisdiction. In 1985, new legislation was enacted, creating the offence of "communicating for the purpose of prostitution," usually referred to as soliciting. However, to see prostitution as not being against the law "is a legal fiction, since every avenue of its expression (save the transaction) contravenes other laws" (Brannigan and Fleischman, 1989: 91).

Public interest in prostitution has varied over time. For long periods, the activity was localized, the situation was accepted, and the public did not express great concern (Lowman, 1991). Since the 1970s, there has been more interest, and a variety of lobby groups have been advocating action, usually to eliminate prostitution; but other groups have formed to represent the prostitutes themselves, such as POWER (Prostitutes and Other Women for Equal Rights), CORP (Canadian Organization for the Rights of Prostitutes), and DANS LA RUE. The American organization COYOTE (Call Off Your Old Tired Ethics) has received much media attention.

Nick Larsen notes that police in four large Canadian cities responded to prostitution in different ways and were ambivalent regarding specific approaches that could be applied (Larsen, 1999). Police are in a no-win situation when it comes to enforcing or ignoring legislation. They realize that prostitution will not disappear, but various lobby groups pressure them to do something. Those pressures are not consistent. A Crown attorney told John Lowman (1989: 211) that he had been able to turn a blind eye to some of the realities of prostitution. Wearing blinders is practical, since no politician will speak publicly on behalf

---

[1]This brief survey borrows heavily from the work of John Lowman and Frances Shaver. Their review articles, noted in the Bibliography, provide a more extensive introduction to the topic.

of red-light districts—church groups and others would be up in arms—so there is a balancing act between a variety of conflicting interests. The lawmakers would have to come down firmly: either outlaw prostitution altogether or identify locations and settings where it can take place. The former makes little sense, and the latter would require courage and long-range vision. On the other hand, policies can influence where the sex trade takes place. When sex-trade cabarets in Vancouver were closed in 1975, it led to an expansion of street prostitution (Lowman, 1989).

Causes and Background

Erin Van Brunschot (1991) uses a pathology/rational choice dichotomy suggested by Gus Brannigan as a means of organizing "causes" of prostitution. The "pathology" category includes prostitutes who are dysfunctional in some way, possibly as a result of abuse or neglect. Unfortunate family backgrounds may contribute to psychological problems and personality disorders. "Rational choice" focuses more on present needs, such as money, and the belief that the prostitute is acting rationally, given the circumstances. The pathology view places more emphasis on background factors, while the rational choice perspective places more emphasis on current, situational (foreground) factors.

Different explanations of prostitution parallel explanations of crime. Lowman (1988) reviews these perspectives in six different categories. I will deliberately neglect the "prostitution-as-atavism," "psychopathology," and "sex-as-genetic-imperative" orientations. These three categories reflect certain negative individual biases that contribute little to a genuine explanation of prostitution. The "undersocialization/social-disorganization" approach also focuses on the individual, but one who was moulded in an undesirable environment.

Davis (1937) suggests that prostitution performs a *function* for the society. It solves contradictory expectations arising out of the double standard for men and women: females should follow a code of premarital chastity and postmarital fidelity, while premarital and extramarital sex are tolerated for men, supposedly because of their stronger innate sex drive. Thus, the prostitute becomes the protector of family stability. This view exposes the double standard, but it also tends to reinforce the status quo. In addition, when Davis assumes that prostitution serves the "latent function" of guarding marriages, he accepts the now-questionable belief about differing sex drives. We might ask, "functional for whom?" Prostitution may be functional for the male customer, who is viewed as a victim of his uncontrollable sex drive (unless channelled by prostitutes). At the same time, he is immune from sanctions because of the important social functions he performs. By contrast, the prostitute is powerless, less useful than the man, of marginal status, and an appropriate target for control mechanisms. Thus, if the needs of society are equated with the needs of men, then, indeed, prostitution might be seen as functional.

Lowman (1988) and many researchers favour aspects of the "feminist" perspective, which focuses on the patriarchal power structure of society. There is no single feminist perspective (Brock, 1984), but there are some common themes: Women are conditioned to be subservient to men, to be owned by men and transformed into commodities to be bought and sold.

Brock (1984) distinguishes three main types of feminism. **Liberal feminists** assert the right of a woman to retain sovereignty over her own body; decriminalization secures that right in the short term. The long-term goal is to change gender roles so that women are no longer subordinate. **Radical feminists** condemn prostitution as the ultimate example of male power, but pledge support to prostitutes as a necessary part of "sisterhood." **Socialist feminists** focus on the way the political and economic realities of capitalism shape patriarchy. The policy initiatives covered in this chapter draw on elements of various feminist perspectives.

Focus on the Individual: The Badgley Report

The **Badgley Committee** (Committee on Sexual Offenses Against Children and Youth, 1984) initiated considerable research on prostitution in Canada, with particular attention focused on youth (Lowman, 1988, 1991). Young prostitutes share characteristics of many young delinquents. Many had run away from home or had been thrown out. The Badgley Committee reported 52 percent of the females recall home life as characterized by continual fighting or arguments. In Vancouver, 65 percent of the prostitutes interviewed in one study reported family violence (Lowman, 1984). The majority of prostitutes were from the lower social strata. For the Badgley Committee, the logical way to deal with young prostitutes was to criminalize their behaviour, so they could be given "help." Like other young deviants, they were to be arrested and held so that they could be rehabilitated. Lowman (1987) is one of those who questions this logic.

Some obvious factors influence the choice of prostitution, if, in fact, there is a choice. Youth are part of the age group with the highest unemployment. They are not eligible for welfare. Prostitution provides a feeling of autonomy and financial independence. But the factors which lead a person into prostitution are not that obvious. Diana Gray (1973) presents a picture that is not in keeping with other studies but offers different insights.

Entering the Trade and Seeking a Pimp

In keeping with other studies, Gray (1973) found that parental ties and attachments were weak for teenage prostitutes. They did poorly in school and expressed little expectation of a happy marriage. Their families provided little that they wished to imitate. None of this necessarily leads directly to prostitution, although it makes girls vulnerable. These girls had sex rather early, but Gray did not discover incest or any particular promiscuity or activity that distinguished them from others of their social-class background.

What was different for these girls was knowing someone who was in the sex trade, a point also made by Van Brunschot (1991: 111) for Calgary. Sometimes it was a relative, at other times a friend. They were curious and sought out persons who "were in the life." There were attractions that were social as well as material. It was a way to be important, to be admired. Social rewards were recognized as readily as material rewards, even prior to their entry into prostitution. They were also aware of the negative side, such as having sex with the customer, arrest, and venereal disease. From a middle-class vantage point, it is difficult to see the attractions of prostitution; but if life is boring and living conditions are unstable, the fast life may have its appeal.

Gray's study differs from others in its argument that these girls *sought out pimps* so they could make it big on the stroll. Most of them turned their money over to the pimp and were satisfied with the way it was handled. They received social reinforcement from their "man" when they were able to provide him with large sums of money. Relationships with the pimps ranged from impersonal and businesslike to shockingly brutal. Gray acknowledges the difficulty in interpreting the meaning of these relationships. Many girls saw the verbal and physical abuses as justified: "We had fights, like we were married—married people have fights. He beat me a couple of times, but not very bad.… But after our fights he'd just be so lovey-dovey" (Gray, 1973: 416). Clearly, these girls did not think very highly of marriage.

Gray argues that the girls seek out their male partners, and consider them essential for success on the stroll. "If you want to make something of yourself out there in the fast life, you got to get a for-real man" (417). They believe they need a man to "take care of business" and give them social status. "I always managed to get with a different guy … who was more important, who had more strength … They have to have respect for another man's woman … When I got with James, that was the top. Nobody messed with me at all" (417).

Feminists, understandably, would be annoyed with these girls' acceptance of male domination, and all of us should be dismayed at their acceptance of violence as part of "family" life, but Gray calls attention to the prostitutes' need for acceptance, status, and relationships with others in some kind of world, even though that world is loaded with negatives.

Van Brunschot's study in Calgary (1991) does not support Gray's argument completely. According to this study, juveniles had no choice; they *had* to have a pimp to work, and were pressured by both other women and the pimps (119). However, smart pimps avoided the juveniles because they were "heat scores"—they attracted the attention of the police (121). The Badgley Committee felt that pimps kept girls in a sort of slavery and encouraged drug use to keep the girls dependent. Lowman (1987) feels the evidence is less clear. However, the Committee found that drug use was not as endemic as they had anticipated (Committee on Sexual Offenses, 1984: 1021). It is also not clear what pimping means. Melanie Lautt (1984) describes the *modus operandi* of pimps on the Prairies. She also asks if a prostitute can have friends or a lover. In Vancouver (Lowman, 1991), organizers of local prostitutes' rights groups estimate that about half of the city's prostitutes do not have pimps. Pimps may be more in evidence elsewhere, in Montreal, for example (Shaver, 1992).

Focus on the Structure of Society: The Feminist Debate and the Fraser Report

Many studies of a historical nature fit into the feminist argument about the consequences of a patriarchal society. Poverty-stricken women in the past century had few alternatives to working in menial, low-paying positions in agriculture, factories, or domestic service (Backhouse, 1985; McLaren, 1986). In frontier societies, in which men outnumbered women, the incentive for prostitution was even greater. Feminists generally call for the long-term elimination of prostitution because it represents the exploitation of women; but if women have the right to control their own bodies, do they not also have the right to sell sex (Bell, 1987)?

The **Fraser Committee** (Special Committee on Pornography and Prostitution, 1985) developed a political economy of prostitution, taking into account patriarchal social relationships. The committee stressed earning power, inequalities in job opportunities, and sexual socialization as factors in prostitution. Obviously, the main concern is for the reduction of prostitution, but a consideration of these factors also leads to some more realistic questions. For example, prostitution is a vital means of subsistence for many Native people in Canadian cities. Should we not be asking how the sex trade can continue in a way that minimizes damage to women and society?

Other issues and assumptions are traditionally ignored. In urban areas, there is a contest between the rights of residents and landowners and the rights of prostitutes to work. This is a one-sided dispute, because the public clearly favours residents and landowners, but is this the case for all disputes? When businesses, light-rail lines, large buildings, and other developments come into areas where people live, there are disputes. When airports, highways, and oil wells encroach upon farm lands, there are disputes. Governments mediate claims of various parties. Should this be done for those in the sex trade as well, instead of dealing one-sidedly with public nuisances (Lowman, 1989, 1991: 129)? What claims do prostitutes have against the rights of others?

Questions to Ask about the Sex Trade

Frances Shaver (1988, 1992) has asked some fundamental questions that need to be addressed and before one can develop intelligent policies towards prostitution. Many policies simply denounce prostitution as degrading, dangerous, and exploitative. Shaver challenges the assumptions behind these positions.

Commercial Sex as Degrading

It is often presumed that commercial sex is cold, impersonal, and impoverished. It dehumanizes sexual relations. Is the quality of purchased sex inferior to other forms of impersonal or recreational sex that do not involve payment? Non-commercial sex also is often characterized by brevity and lack of affection. Blatant sexual bargaining goes on in singles clubs, in the back seats of cars, in the office, and in marriage (Shaver, 1988). While sex can be degrading, so can other aspects of human relationships. Many prostitutes have unpleasant encounters with men, but so do waitresses, nurses' aides, flight attendants, secretaries, and factory workers. There is simply a great deal of variety in human and sexual relations, and the potential for inferior human interaction or inferior sex exists within both commercial and non-commercial settings.

Commercial Sex as Dangerous

Shaver notes that the vulnerability of prostitutes is due to gender bias and the application of the law, rather than to the commercialization of sexual services. Male hustlers are less likely to be attacked and are much less likely to be victims of "bad tricks" than are females (Perkins and Bennett, 1985: 238–41; Visano, 1987). Battered prostitutes need protection just as do battered wives; and if they bring charges against their abusers, they need to feel safe from reprisals.

Occupational dangers should be viewed in comparison with other potentially dangerous or "dirty" work. Infection is a risk, but this element is also inherent in the work of doctors, nurses, hospital attendants, morticians, domestic workers, and hotel cleaners. Prostitutes have also developed procedures for minimizing other dangers. They have regular medical check-ups, examine their customers for STD (sexually transmitted disease) symptoms, and require them to use condoms. Their organizations distribute "bad trick sheets," describing and identifying dangerous customers (Shaver, 1988: 85; Shaver, 1992: 19). They also learn techniques for avoiding unwanted men. When harassed, one can say, "I'm not working tonight," a ploy Shaver often used during her field work. If this does not work, she can shout down the street: "Hey Jan, this here jerk thinks he can get a blow-job for twenty-five bucks." The would-be harasser invariably moves away.

Prostitutes develop protective routines. They work in pairs, note when and with whom the other leaves; licence plates are remembered; desk clerks are tipped, and are expected to keep an eye on the time and to listen for the sound of violence.

Police practices and public policy could alter the conditions that influence danger. The removal of bawdy-house legislation might permit the creation of safer locales for the sex trade, since street prostitution exposes women to greater risks.

Commercial Sex as Exploitative

Studies of prostitutes that view them within the context of their profession do not describe them as powerless victims or passive partners (Shaver, 1988). Like other workers, their exploitation is related to a variety of structural features. For example, the role of pimps needs to be carefully examined. Male prostitutes are rarely pimped and report fewer rapes and beatings than women (Lowman, 1985: 35–36; Forbes, 1977; Special Committee, 1985: 379; Visano, 1987). Exploitation and danger are gender-based, rather than work-based. On the other hand, Van Brunschot (1991) notes that far fewer police patrol the male stroll area in Calgary than the female strolls. Thus, *reported* victimization may be less for the males.

Shaver and others also note that it is difficult to determine if a prostitute is being exploited, in contrast to being served, by a pimp. Legislation fails to distinguish between lover, business manager, or co-habitant. The Criminal Code defines a pimp as anyone who lives wholly or in part on the avails of prostitution. Appropriate legislation must differentiate between friend and parasite, and create conditions under which the woman is willing to bring charges.

Strategies for Intervention and Public Policy

Traditional methods of dealing with prostitution, such as harassing the prostitutes themselves, contribute little to improving the situation. By contrast, making life more fulfilling for girls and protecting them from abuse make a good deal of sense. The long-term reduction of prostitution, and other crime, requires the strengthening of family life and the protection of vulnerable youngsters when families break down. This requires an investment in helping services, rather than controlling functions; but Canada and the U.S., in contrast to northern European countries, seem to prefer the latter over the former.

Those who believe that it is necessary to criminalize juvenile prostitution, so that prostitutes can be saved, may perceive "control" to be the same as "help." Unfortunately, "street kids" in North America rarely see the agencies of social control as a source of genuine help. In contrast, French juveniles with problems normally talk about their juvenile court judge and compare notes with others as to how the judge helped them. To illustrate, one young prostitute went to her judge in Paris because she was hoping to escape from her pimp, who wished to take her away from the Paris area to another part of France. Putting a girl in custody for prostitution, or for any deviance for that matter, is simply outside the thinking of almost all French juvenile court judges. Providing help in a variety of ways is within their power and part of what is expected. In this case, the judge provided a plane ticket for the girl to stay with relatives in North Africa for a couple of months, until her pimp left Paris. She then returned to her family in Paris and gave up prostitution. French juvenile court judges are given flexible powers to deal with situations in ways that they feel are sensible.

In Canada, we spend vast amounts on charging, prosecuting, and defending juveniles. Once juveniles are found guilty, we invest heavily in custodial facilities, but are less generous in terms of support services. In other areas, such as France and northern Europe, resources are concentrated on helping juveniles.

Most research notes that those who work in the sex trade are almost all economically deprived women and juveniles, many of whom have suffered a history of physical and sexual abuse (Larsen, 1992). Similarly, early pregnancies increase the vulnerability of women. Universal programs, such as a guaranteed annual wage, widespread medical coverage, and low tuition for school and training programs, are seen as expensive, but, in fact, they may be less expensive than specialized programs that target some individuals while neglecting others. These universal programs are more crucial to women than men in terms of avoiding the deprived conditions that are often precursors to prostitution.

Some women need physical protection from men at times; thus, shelters for battered women indirectly make women less vulnerable, more able to gain control over their lives, and, to a degree, less likely to be involved in crime or prostitution. If any principle is clear in terms of the reduction of prostitution, it is that tougher laws yield minimal returns. Arresting prostitutes or their johns is an exercise in futility. Stricter criminal sanctions would probably force prostitutes to adopt riskier working styles. As prostitutes move off main thoroughfares onto poorly lighted lanes and side streets, or use hitchhiking, it reduces their ability to screen potential clients who appear to be dangerous. Similarly, if the law is successful in deterring "respectable" customers from frequenting the strolls, the dearth of customers may force prostitutes to accept customers they would otherwise reject.

There is little debate that prostitution will continue. Some societies manage it better than others. The brothels in Bremerhaven, Germany, appear to be safer places for the women and their customers. The bawdy-house provisions of the Criminal Code need to be repealed so that prostitutes can operate legally in fixed locations (Larsen, 1992). Street life is dangerous, and most prostitutes would prefer to be off the street if they could have enough customers.

The creation of "red-light areas" is naturally controversial, but advantages and disadvantages need to be assessed. In some European countries, local prostitutes are normal components of the neighbourhood and are not seen as disruptive. Tax concessions and compensation to residents and business owners could mitigate some concerns. Local committees of residents, business owners, police officials, politicians, and prostitutes could monitor the prostitution trade and liaise with others to resolve disputes. This has been done in Vancouver, Edmonton, and Ottawa with some success (Larsen, 1992). Committees that did not include prostitutes were less successful.

Pimps could be prosecuted under extortion laws (Lowman, 1991: 128), and patronizing juvenile prostitutes should still be illegal; but unless juveniles see agencies as a genuine source of help, enforcement practices need to be carefully assessed. Adult prostitutes might become allies of the authorities in trying to discourage juveniles in this area.

The government could provide some of the services usually offered by pimps. A knowledgeable government agent, possibly a social worker or nurse, or a former prostitute, would have some advantages over other pimps, because of reinforcement from police and other agencies, awareness of medical care, contacts with drug counsellors, and so on. While most pimps are attempting to keep women in the business, the goal of a government operation would be just the opposite—to encourage women to move into other roles. Failing that, the goal might be to make prostitution more of a "genuine" choice, hopefully safer and less exploitative (Lowman, 1993). In keeping with this line of thinking, prostitutes would pay into pension plans, employment insurance, and the like. Admittedly, this approach is somewhat naive, considering the status that may come from having a pimp. It is unclear whether a government "pimp" could provide the same status and sense of belonging, but she or he could provide more options, not only to make the business safer, but to prepare the prostitute for an alternate lifestyle.

SUMMARY

1. Many activities treated as crimes might better be seen as "order maintenance problems." These might include homosexual activities in public restrooms, prostitution, drug use (including alcohol and tobacco), driving over the speed limit, and a variety of other behaviours that cause legitimate concern. The criminal law is ill-equipped to respond effectively to these activities.

2. The research by Laud Humphreys suggests that learning theories could be applied as individuals expand their experiences with different sexual activities. In addition, marginality may influence tearoom activities. These factors may influence other crimes as well.

3. As mentioned earlier with regard to drug policies, strategies that minimize harm make more sense than those that try to legislate morality.

4. The root causes of prostitution are similar to those that lead to crime: the exposure of children to vulnerable situations; the inability of marginal people to partake fully in the riches of society; and clumsy and inadequate attempts by government agencies and institutions to aid those who have been marginalized.

5. The Badgley Committee argued for the criminalization of juvenile prostitution so that youth can be given "help." The Fraser Committee did not favour criminalizing juvenile prostitution.

6. Frances Shaver questions common assumptions about commercial sex as being degrading, dangerous, and exploitative, compared with other roles women play.

KEY TERMS

Badgley Committee 245	marginality 242
bawdy house 243	order maintenance vs. crime control 238
Fraser Committee 246	radical feminists 244
liberal feminists 244	socialist feminists 245

WEBLINKS

www.cprn.com/cprn.html
The Canadian Policy Research Networks: information on social and economic issues.

www.rcmp-grc.gc.ca/
The Royal Canadian Mounted Police: information on crime in Canada.

ORGANIZED CRIME
AND GANGS

This chapter will:

- Note some of the characteristics of organized crime and the impact of globalization on such crime.
- Describe some historical work on Chinese organized crime that suggests the problem is an old one in many societies.
- Offer a functionalist explanation as to how these patterns of organized crime have emerged.
- Provide one perspective on why gangs develop and why they persist.
- Trace the similarities in dynamics in various criminal groups, suggesting that some of our theories about traditional crime could also be applied to organized crime.

ASSOCIATIONS OF CRIMINALS OR CRIMINAL ASSOCIATIONS?

Defining organized crime, as distinct from other crime, has not been easy (Koenig, 1999). Tom Naylor (1996) identifies some assumed characteristics of organized crime: a durable hierarchy, the use of violence and corruption, very high rates of return, and the penetration of legitimate business. However, he does not see this operating in reality. Rather he and Jean-Paul Brodeur (1996) suggest that it is more accurate to conceptualize the situation as *associations of criminals rather than criminal associations.*

Margaret Baere (1996: 47) offers a model based on other assumptions, categorizing groups according to their varying degrees of dependence on organized crime activity:

1. On the more legitimate end of the continuum are groups that are independent of, and therefore separate from, organized crime. Criminal activity is secondary, but circumstances may encourage it. An example might be Aboriginal groups involved in smuggling cigarettes.

2. Toward the other end of the continuum might be a terrorist group with an ideological goal. Organized crime activity is accepted as a necessary part of the operation, but the group would exist without it. Some motorcycle gangs might fit here.

3. Asian triads and the Mafia are closer to the illegitimate end of the continuum. Ethnic cohesion is provided within a historical structure that began with a political ideology. Triads originated in the mid-seventeenth century in China to overthrow the ruling Manchu or Ch'ing Dynasty; the Mafia arose during the nineteenth century in Sicily when local leaders took control of selected economic activities because government was distant, ineffective, and unfair (Cavan and Cavan, 1968). With time the focus of these groups shifted more toward crime.

4. On the clearly illegitimate end of the continuum, some Russian, Jamaican, and Nigerian organized crime groups were created strictly for the purpose of efficiently carrying out crimes. Some of these newer groups are still in a state of flux.

Technical changes also create new opportunities for organized crime. Video lottery terminals created problems in Ontario, British Columbia, and Quebec (Coordinated Law Enforcement Unit [CLEU], 1995). Historical factors influenced the growth of organized crime in some communities. The Italian Mafia spread from the United States to Montreal rather than Toronto because of geographical proximity, but also because of the preexisting political corruption during the Duplessis regime in Quebec (Baere, 1996). Organized crime also evolves, changes, and takes advantage of new opportunities. The Criminal Intelligence Service of Canada (1996) states that one of the Quebec chapters of the Hells Angels, the Nomads, was founded specifically to expedite expansion and control of the Hells Angels' drug trafficking networks across Canada.

Legislation against the many different forms of organized crime is still being developed in Canada (Koenig, 1999). However, certain factors make enforcement difficult: (1) original entrepreneurs have typically thrived by providing goods or services demanded by the public when they are limited and illegal; (2) organized crime usually has mutually rewarding associations with legitimate companies and institutions; and (3) organized crime may be a smokescreen used to conceal a hidden agenda.

There is extensive material on the first two issues, but the question of hidden agendas is a topic of more recent exploration. The case of the Bank of Commerce and Credit International (BCCI) was a good example of the cosy relationship that may arise among drug traffickers, white-collar criminals, intelligence-gathering agencies, and leading politicians (Kappeler, Blumberg, and Potter, 1993). The BCCI laundered millions for the Colombia cocaine cartels, helped former president and dictator of the Philippines Ferdinand Marcos transfer money out of that country, and was a conduit for CIA funds for the Contras to support illegal arms deals and cocaine trafficking (Koenig, 1999). With its powerful political allies, such as Edwin Meese (Ronald Reagan's attorney general), it is hardly surprising that the U.S. Justice Department was slow to investigate the BCCI. The basic question which Koenig poses is: has the United States been genuinely serious about its wars on drugs and on organized crime? Are so many powerful interests using organized crime that there is little incentive to rock the boat?

The Organized Crime Agency of British Columbia has recently been formed to disrupt and suppress organized crime in BC. It has charged 170 people for possession of weapons, counterfeit credit cards, and drug trafficking. As I argue later, however, attacks on the supply side of drug trafficking have never been successful. Whether government enforcement agencies can actually suppress organized crime through traditional strategies is questionable.

Recently, criminologists have shown a greater interest in this area. In Canada, the Nathanson Centre for the Study of Organized Crime and Corruption has been established at the Osgoode Hall Law School of York University. For Canada, however, efforts to control organized crime may be compromised if there are hidden agendas, particularly in the United States, that maintain the links between criminal organizations and powerful elements that hold themselves up as legitimate.

The Impact of Globalization on Organized Crime

In a collection of articles, Pearce and Snider (1995) have raised a number of questions regarding the impact of globalization on organized crime. As trade and manufacturing become globalized, corporations become less vulnerable to controls from national governments. Transnational markets have weakened the bargaining power of workers, increasing worker vulnerability at home and abroad to unsafe employment. At the same time, "market" ideologies about the causes of worker "accidents" are reinforced. Illegal practices become "normal risks." The border becomes blurred between (1) supporting obvious illegal labour practices, (2) operating in countries that have labour laws but violate them, and (3) actively seeking countries that will permit practices which are illegal elsewhere.

Transnational corporations not only target lesser-developed countries for expansion purposes, but also locate within underdeveloped areas of developed countries—with deleterious results for the environment and the general public. The long arm of the law is shortened or eliminated when corporations are out of range or are courted and encouraged to bring jobs and economic development to disadvantaged areas.

As operating activities get scattered, companies are more internally competitive and less centralized, making it easier for top executives to look the other way. Corporate illegalities could be reduced if top managers wished to exercise a moral voice, but it is easy to view these issues as irrelevant to business concerns. The sort of "community" pressures that keep most people behaving ethically may be missing in the global marketplace. Clearly, the criminal law is ineffective in addressing most corporate wrongs (Snider, 1997). Fines are minimal for both individuals and companies, and guilty managers rarely receive harsh sanctions such as imprisonment.

At times governments do respond vigorously. The savings and loan frauds in the U.S. received aggressive treatment by the government, even though other elite offences are treated gently. The signficant financial threat posed by the frauds and the need for the state to buttress confidence in the financial system suggest that when corporate interests are threatened by crime, powerful forces spur the criminal justice system to action.

Passas (1998) suggests that the distinctions between international business and crime are blurred. Corporate offences and illegal enterprises can be traced to **criminogenic asymmetries**—that is, structural disjunctions, mismatches, and inequalities in politics, culture, the economy, and the law. Asymmetries, whereby corporations rival nations in terms of power, may increase the demand for illegal goods and services and generate incentives for illegal behaviour. In the global age, national governments will be less able to control corporations which have influence in many countries.

As national autonomy is eroded, so is the ability of national authorities to protect their citizens from serious crime. Efforts to develop international regulations are hampered since national authorities do not always agree. Offenders can slip through the gaps of municipal laws and enforcement. As new crime opportunities arise, cosmopolitan offenders can escape local regulators with ease.

Creating Opportunities for Crime: The Privatization of Medicine and Other Services

In the February 2, 1998, issue of U.S. *News & World Report*, a conservative publication, Stephen Hedges wrote, "Drug dealers and organized crime groups have invaded the Medicare system and are taking the government and citizens for a billion-dollar ride." As Canada considers changes in health care, we should be aware that certain bureaucratic structures increase the likelihood of crime. In the U.S. over one thousand insurance companies are involved in delivering health care. This has a number of consequences. The cost of financing the insurance business drains about one-third of the medical costs from actual medical care. Do some of these funds attract criminals? Privatization attracts those looking for new ways to make money. While legitimate businesses watch for these new opportunities, organized crime is even more alert. With large amounts of money and companies purchased for laundering illegal money, organized crime is well equipped to respond quickly and offer legitimate medical services. Gradually these services can be manipulated to skim off a little, and then a little more.

While the Scandinavian countries have a "culture of honesty" which probably includes medical doctors, a culture of cheating the government seems to pervade North America. This general point could be expanded to a wide range of attempts to privatize a variety of government services whether it is medical care or building prisons. State-run enterprises attract more snoopers from the press and the public. Selling public institutions to private investors sets the stage for opportunistic criminals.

After the reunification of Germany in 1990, the government decided to sell inefficient factories in former East Germany for a trivial amount of money. The idea was that efficient West German and other firms would invest in these outdated facilities, make them efficient, and create new jobs. In fact, some of the purchasers, including those well connected with organized crime, sold off the equipment and closed the plants.

Admittedly, government-run enterprises can have problems of their own, but they are also open to more public scrutiny. If one lives in a society that places an undue emphasis on wealth, the scrutiny which goes with public ownership is one way to inhibit crime.

Providing Illegal Services to Big Business

Chapter 14 looked specifically at corporate crime, but it is easy to see possible links with organized crime. One concern is that criminals may be taking over and subverting legal businesses. Naylor (1996) asks if the reverse may be true: legal businesses may be using criminal methods and contracting with career criminals to achieve profits. If so, the problem is the degradation of business ethics, something which requires a more profound explanation than the plotting of aging Italian godfathers. The toxic waste industry is a good illustration. Firms generating toxic waste successfully lobbied the U.S. government for legislation which permitted them to avoid responsibility for long-term consequences of hazardous waste if they signed over the material to licensed waste-disposal companies. Criminals already engaged in the solid waste business were ready to oblige. These "licensed" companies would then dump the wastes down sewers, into lakes, or add it to heating oil to be burned by hospitals and schools, thereby distributing the toxic material in smoke all over a city (Block and Scarpitti, 1985).

The toxic waste business is minor compared with the smuggling of cigarettes, the most widely smuggled commodity in the world (Naylor, 1996). Arms and drug smugglers usually learned their tricks from the tobacco trade with the implicit, and sometimes explicit, assistance of the big tobacco companies. The heroin and cocaine traffic used the infrastructure created with the help of the tobacco companies. The power of the tobacco lobby may explain why the Canadian government does not tax cigarettes at the plant. If Imperial Tobacco can ship cigarettes to the U.S. and have them smuggled back into Canada, it lowers the true tax on cigarettes. And lower taxes tend to increase cigarette sales.

The big tobacco companies offer some of the best illustrations of unethical and illegal corporate practices (Naylor, 1996). They stand accused of undermining public health, hooking children on cigarettes, promoting slave labour conditions on tobacco farms, pushing cigarettes in impoverished countries, and so forth. Their worst sin, however, may be the creation of the conditions in which criminal entrepreneurs and their organizations can flourish.

Are these criminal activities growing, or has the link between corruption, organized crime, and stable patterns of criminality always been part of complex societies? There is a similar debate over gangs. Are these the natural products of complex societies that produce groups of individuals who are not doing well in the mainstream of society? How well structured are these groupings? Are most youth gangs casual clusters or are they organized to systematically recruit new members? Some scholars suggest that we are dealing with an old rather than a new phenomenon. Current concerns, such as the Asian gangs that are becoming better known to the public in Canada, are the product of old forces, according to Jeffrey McIllwain.

From Tong War to Organized Crime

Chinese organized crime in North America is, contrary to conventional wisdom, neither "emerging" nor "non-traditional." Rather, it predates, in structure and sophistication, organizations that have previously been recognized as organized crime (McIllwain, 1997). Academics, the media, and the government recently "discovered" Chinese organized crime. McIllwain documents a **tong war** from 1899 to 1907 between two organizations heavily involved in organized crime that extended across the United States and to China itself. These tongs were involved with police and political corruption, labour racketeering, price fixing, prostitution, gambling, immigrant smuggling, slavery, drug trafficking, and violent crimes. They are still associated with these activities.

This view is in contrast to others that see contemporary Asian organized crime in North America as a new phenomenon (Kleinknecht, 1996). Scholars such as Chin, Kelly, and Fagan (1994) assert that Chinese organized crime has neither infiltrated the larger American society nor victimized people who are not Chinese. In Canada, many police departments are concerned about Asian gangs, but see them as victimizing their own ethnic groups primarily. McIllwain argues that these organizations date back to the earliest Chinese settlements on the West Coast, and that instead of supplanting La Cosa Nostra, and better-known mafias, they are simply expanding criminal enterprises which they have controlled for more than 100 years.

Essentially, this argument could be generalized. The mafia-type organizations, often dominated by one particular ethnic group, have always been with us. Therefore, one might look to general explanations as to how they came to be.

A TRADITIONAL FUNCTIONALIST ARGUMENT FOR CORRUPTION AND ORGANIZED CRIME

Conflict theorists have made a major contribution to revealing the extent of corporate crime in Western society, which was discussed in the chapter on property crime (Chapter 14). Unfortunately, there has been a tendency for criminologists to favour one perspective over another rather than see the links between them. One might call the "conflict" approach a "top-down" explanation: it focuses on those with power. A traditional **functionalist approach** might be called a "bottom-up" explanation: it seeks to know how ordinary persons or groups would respond if society were structured in a certain way. This perspective assumes that society is somewhat static and certain things are "given." Instead of asking about the nature of things, it focuses on what things *do*—that is, what *function* something has. Although the functionalist perspective is no longer popular, it still offers a credible explanation of the continued existence of organized crime.

Barriers to Legitimate Goals in Democratic Societies

Robert Merton (1968) distinguished between **manifest** (intended) **functions** and **latent** (unintended) **functions**. The manifest function of parole is to reduce time spent in prison. However, if judges assume defendants get parole and do not serve full sentences, the latent, or unintended, function of parole might be to create longer sentences. Judges could decide to "compensate" for the fact that they were sure offenders were going to be released early.

Merton looked at the functions (some of them latent) of the **political machine**. The borders between political crime, organized crime, and powerful members of the economic elite are admittedly blurred in this discussion, and I do not attempt to disentangle them.

Merton poses two questions: (1) Is society organized so that it is difficult, if not impossible, for legitimate tasks to be completed? If so, is a political machine necessary to fulfill legitimate needs, thereby giving rise to illegitimate tasks? (2) Are there certain distinctive subgroups within a society whose needs are unsatisfied, thus leading to political machines that meet those needs?

These two issues appear to be related to the structure of American and Canadian democracy. In democracies, there is a lack of highly centralized power. Governments have a check-and-balance system. Power is decentralized even on the local scene. There is rarely a single "boss" who can really act when something needs to be done. The mayor of Edmonton may wish to devote more resources to public transportation, but power in many city governments is distributed among many people. Thus, political action requires compromise.

Sometimes there may be tremendous barriers to accomplishing a sensible and legitimate task. Imagine that you want to dam a river in the north. This might raise the water level, produce electricity, and provide irrigation in one province, but it might flood farmers in another province. Let us also assume that the dam would lower water downstream, reducing the muskrat population and annoying Native people who trap the muskrat for their fur. Even if the overall project were very desirable and the gains outweighed the losses, many governments would be involved. Public figures and civil servants come and go. Political power is dispersed among federal, provincial, and local authorities. Tenure in office is limited in democracies. Usually there is no overall, powerful leader. If you were a legitimate person who wished to build this dam, which would be a boon to society, you might find yourself frustrated. Enter the political "boss."

The political "boss" has "influence." He has ways of convincing members of legislative bodies, ministers, local governments, and so forth. Even if there are elections with new people in power, the "boss" can deliver enough votes, persuade enough people, and manipulate enough situations to enable you to build your dam. Naturally, there will be a price. As an upstanding Canadian you would not think of paying a bribe, and you only want to do something that is perfectly legal. Merton suggests that the difficulty of getting legitimate jobs done in democratic societies gives rise to an illegitimate system that can overcome these barriers. North America is not unique. Bribes, payoffs, and the like are endemic to many societies. In Eastern Europe one of the major weaknesses in the communist system was its inefficiency and corruption. Merton would probably agree that the inability to do the jobs well through legal channels was a major factor in creating corruption.

The second point made by Merton is that certain subgroups are not well served in democratic societies. If you are an immigrant, and someone who speaks your language greets you after you clear customs and offers to help you get established, would you not be inclined to cast your vote for the person recommended by your benefactor? If the official bureaucracy works poorly, a more humane system could easily arise. Imagine that you are a member of a minority group that faces prejudice. The political machine may be more sensitive to people in the local community and neighbourhood. The precinct captain humanizes and personalizes all manner of assistance—food baskets, jobs, legal advice, scholarships for a bright kid. There is no need to fill out application forms. No middle-class social worker will snoop about your home. When your kid gets into trouble with the police, you want help, not justice, and the representative of the political boss has the power to help. There is no loss of self-respect. The precinct captain only wants your vote.

Thus, the political machine performs a function for diverse subgroups. Deprived classes may be among the subgroups that are helped. Similarly, business, primarily big business, is served by the boss. Business does not want open competition. It prefers a predictable economic czar rather than unpredictable legislative control, which would permit public scrutiny. Just as the Oil King or Lumber King performs integrating services for legitimate business, so does the Vice King provide similar services for prostitution and gambling. Just as business eliminates competition, so does the racketeer.

When we look at the formation of the Canadian Pacific Railway or the history of the Hudson's Bay Company in Canada, it is not difficult to find illustrations of dishonest activity. Compared with the U.S., Canada's power elite is more concentrated. The need for an outside political boss may not have been as compelling. Canadian leaders probably had little difficulty convincing themselves that their activities benefited the country as well as themselves. If someone could say that what was good for General Motors was good for the U.S., I suspect Sir William Van Horne (general manager of the Canadian Pacific Railway in the 1880s) probably thought that what was good for the Canadian Pacific Railway was good for Canada. At any rate, the captains of industry in both Canada and the U.S. might find engaging in corrupt activities an inevitable part of their business.

Merton asks if it makes sense to talk of the "evil" political machine. Does it provide social mobility for certain underprivileged people who have little access to conventional and legitimate means? In economic terms, it is difficult to distinguish between legitimate, illegitimate, and undesirable goods and services. Prostitution is big business. Prostitutes outnumber doctors. One might argue that if it were organized legally as a sex industry, like other businesses, prostitution would be less damaging to society. It is difficult to assess the consequences of gambling when it is organized illegally, rather than by the Canadian Legion and the churches. During the Duplessis period in Quebec the government broke laws, but did it also provide services? Do corrupt systems provide services better than honest ones at times? Seen from a functional perspective, one might understand why reform campaigns are typically short-lived. Merton summarizes his argument as follows:

> Any attempt to eliminate an existing social structure without providing alternatives for filling needs previously filled by the abolished organization is doomed to failure.... To seek social change, without due recognition of the manifest and latent functions performed by the social organization undergoing change, is to indulge in social ritual rather than social engineering. (Merton, 1968: 135)

This functional argument has generated many criticisms. It assumes that everything that exists performs some function. This becomes a tautology. If something were dysfunctional, one might argue that it would soon cease to exist. Despite weaknesses, however, the above argument leads to some thought-provoking issues. It suggests that democracies, or dictatorships for that matter, must be fairly well run if they are to operate without the type of corruption and crime that characterizes much of the world.

Can the Functionalist Argument Be Generalized?

A Case of Ineffective Government: The Rise of the Mafia

Explanations of the Mafia, organized crime, and political crime differ. One approach would emphasize the characteristics of criminals and their organizations, viewing them as cancers that invade and destroy healthy societies. By contrast, a functionalist approach would see deficiencies in the society, which would lead to new organizational structures arising to deal with these deficiencies. The description offered here fits the latter explanation.

In the 1860s and earlier, local organizations in Sicily served as an intermediary force between powerless peasants and the wealthy, local feudal lords who owned estates (Cavan and Cavan, 1968: Ch. 6). Government was remote and ineffective. Tax collectors and police were viewed by the peasants as predators. Informal structures, called Mafias, at the local level arose to fill the gap in authority. Originally, the term Mafia referred to a sign of bravado. Men settled disputes without reference to the authorities. A theft was a personal insult. The thief held his victim in contempt. These values were supported by *omerta*, a conspiracy of silence towards law-enforcement officers. It also required absolute obedience of younger persons.

Different Mafias might function independently in the same area. One might control the water from the local spring, another the marketing of a specific product. Frequently, alliances developed. Leaders were men of natural ability. Often, they were humble, courteous, reliable, but also firm and ruthless as disciplinarians. Once a part of a Mafia it was very difficult to withdraw or become a member of an opposing group. A young cousin of a Mafioso joined the police, and was later killed by family leaders to remove the stain on their honour. Some of the functions of Mafias would normally have been performed by an effective government.

Would the evolution of Mafias fit a functionalist argument? One could argue that these structures arose to fill societal needs. It is also possible that, once having come into being, organizations take on a life of their own. In the past, the Italian government has had little luck in eliminating Mafias. At times, the government has even cooperated with them and turned to them for political support. Today the Italian government appears to be making strenuous efforts to destroy them; but the functionalist approach provides a warning—if legitimate governments do not serve the needs of society effectively, illegitimate structures will arise.

Similarly, in parts of South America, wealthy drug lords are providing housing and other services to the poor. It would be a mistake to see this as a natural response to societal needs, but drug lords all over the world may be filling gaps left unfilled by governments. The Mertonian argument suggests that, as illegitimate organizations perform useful societal tasks, they will be particularly hard to eliminate.

The Criminal Tribes of India

When the British arrived in India, they found themselves dealing with "criminal tribes" (Bose, 1956). Crime was a central part of these groups' livelihood. These crimes were directed against outsiders, were carefully planned and organized by the local council, and were for financial gain only. If the elders were given a contract to murder someone, it was not because of anger or insult. It was business. Some writers believe the origin of these criminal tribes was in organized bands of "thugs," a word that is now part of English (Biswas, 1960; Curry, 1932). The British government recognized these activities as evolving out of tribal cultures, rather than as the work of gangs of marauders who did not have any particular social or cultural background. The result was that part of child training included stealing and other types of crime.

Sex inside the tribe was regulated, but prostitution outside was acceptable to get money and information on sources of wealth. Thus a prostitute would follow different rules within her own group. This principle applied to other crimes as well. One did not steal from "your own people." The British found it difficult to change the situation. When jobs were provided, men said that it was more rewarding, monetarily as well as psychologically, to pick pockets than to work in a factory.

Let us again pose the question: do these tribes perform a function? We might ask, a function for whom? From the standpoint of the total Indian society, the rest of the population would have functioned quite well without the criminal tribes. From the standpoint of the criminal tribe itself, perhaps crimes could be viewed as functional; but if the authorities decided to eliminate this source of trouble, crime would become dysfunctional. It is also difficult to explain this pattern of crime as the product of an ineffective government or society.

Gangs in a Low-Crime Society: The Boryokudan *in Japan*

Although Japan is a developed country with relatively little crime, it does have traditional organized criminal gangs. Frank Huang and Michael Vaughn (1992) point out that the word *yakuza*, used by Western scholars to describe Japanese organized crime gangs, is not suitable because it means something like "hooligan." They use the term *boryokudan* (violent groups). In the seventeenth and eighteenth centuries, peace and stability in Japan reduced the need for *samurai*, traditional Japanese warriors. Many turned to new roles in education and bureaucracy, but others did not abandon their principal calling, warfare. They became the founders of the earlier *boryokudan,* individuals who failed to adapt to the peaceful society and were alienated from the dominant culture (Hoshino, 1988). Along with others displaced by the changing society, they lost social status. A variety of gangs developed. Some used violence to gain control over small cafés, theatres, brothels, and the ricksha industry. Others controlled gambling. Although evidence is largely anecdotal, some of these groups may have united to form the modern *boryokudan*. They resolved territorial disputes with violence, their violent problem-solving techniques being in contrast to dominant values. This further alienated them from mainstream Japanese society.

Lower-class gangs are also reinforced by the 700 000 Japanese-born Koreans who are excluded from much of meaningful Japanese society (Huang and Vaughn, 1992; Weiner, 1989). They are required to carry alien registration cards and face a variety of discriminatory practices. Along with other modern outcasts, they cannot pursue a range of legitimate activities. A disproportionate number of women who work in the sex trade and entertainment districts are from such backgrounds. The *boryokudan* are one of the few groups in Japanese society in which being of Korean ancestry does not matter.

Because of the Korean War, the U.S. pumped billions of dollars into Japan, and prostitution and gambling flourished. In the late 1960s the police responded to rising threats and public concern with a variety of efforts to reduce the power of these groups, including attempts to stigmatize the *boryokudan* as embodying anti-Japanese values. Over time, however, symbiotic relationships evolved between the police and the gangs. The police tolerated gang activities in prostitution, protection rackets, and a variety of illicit businesses; however, when the gangs trafficked in narcotics, smuggled guns, and injured innocent law-abiding citizens, the police cracked down.

A number of ideas raised earlier seem to fit here. Gangsters are depicted romantically in the Japanese media, just as they are in some American films, even though average citizens are outraged at their violence. The functional argument comes into play in that there is a tremendous appetite for gambling, pornography, prostitution, and drugs. Gangs and criminal organizations in many societies fulfill these functions. In Japan, the gangs also keep lower-class areas relatively free of common crimes of which they and the residents do not approve. The functional perspective is further reinforced when one notes the many links between *boryokudan* gangs and the police, business, and government. In 1991, intimate relationships between the gangs and four of Japan's largest brokerage firms were revealed (Powell, Takayama, and Itoi, 1991). Despite weaknesses in the functionalist perspective, it seems to apply to societies with a collective mentality like Japan, as well as individualistic ones such as the U.S. Much organized crime is demand-driven. People want certain goods or services that may be illegal or in short supply.

GANGS: THEIR ATTRACTIONS, THE ROLES THEY PLAY, WHY THEY EXIST

Delinquent gangs have been studied in many countries for many years. Each generation of criminologists rediscovers street gangs and tries to explain them using the favourite theories of the period. In the U.S. during the 1920s, gangs were seen as the product of cultural dislocations and community disorganization resulting from large numbers of immigrants. By the 1930s the Great Depression provided obvious explanations: economic pressures, lack of work, enforced idleness. During the 1940s, World War II created unique conditions, and by the 1950s the period of affluence gave rise to emotional disturbances caused by the stress of modern life. Psychology had grown dramatically as a discipline, and gangs were seen as being composed of psychopathic personalities who came together in groups. In the 1960s and 1970s, sociology experienced exceptional growth. Many explanations focused on young males who had failed in conventional society and who turned to gangs for alternative experiences. As labelling theorists and the conflict theories became more popular, they influenced gang studies.

Is the Number of Gangs Increasing in Canada?

The public perception is that gangs, and particularly Asian gangs, are increasing in numbers in Canada. Certainly the police would make such an argument. Others, such as McIllwain (1997), would argue that the structures have been there a long time but are simply expanding. In British Columbia, the now-defunct Coordinated Law Enforcement Unit (CLEU) (1995) responded to a growing concern about gang activity in the Lower Mainland. A cooperative study with the police found that of 976 gang subjects listed, 45 percent were from Asian gangs and 39 percent were from non-Asian gangs, and only 5 percent were females. Only 8 percent were youths, with 92 percent being adults, mostly young adults. The average age of Asian gang subjects was 26 years, while the average age of non-Asian gang subjects was 20 years.

Immigration profiles show that 33 percent of gang subjects were born in Canada and 46 percent were foreign-born. The country of birth could not be determined for 21 percent. Thus, the criminal gang problem cannot be perceived solely as an "imported problem," although immigration remains a key aspect. Of the foreign-born gang subjects, 73 percent originated in Asia. Of these, 55 percent were born in Vietnam, the People's Republic of China, and Hong Kong (CLEU, 1995).

Before readers get the impression that Canada is being overwhelmed by dangerous immigrants, one must remember that immigrants have traditionally been less criminal than native-born individuals. That has been true in North America and in Europe despite the frequent claim that the "foreigners" are the problem. Of course, recent immigrants from countries going through crises may not have experienced the traditional socialization that their cultures normally provided. However, the success of Asian children in Canadian schools and businesses bodes well for the assimilation of these people in the larger society. In addition, the importance of the family to most Asian immigrants is a positive factor that will continue to reduce the number of Asians coming in conflict with the law. Rather than looking for something unique, let us first try to understand the attractions of gang membership for many young men.

The Anatomy of a Motorcycle Gang

In his book, *The Rebels: A Brotherhood of Outlaw Bikers* (1991), Daniel Wolf provides unusual insights into an outlaw motorcycle club in Edmonton, Alberta. He spent three years riding with the Rebels (their real name), and then gained permission to study them systematically for his doctoral dissertation in anthropology. Some anthropologists are criticized for "going native" and losing objectivity. Wolf, however, began as a "native," including sharing the lower-working-class background of other bikers.

Why does the lower working class produce candidates for a biker subculture? The worker is a cog in an impersonal machine, an anomic world with little psychological payoff in terms of life-expanding experiences (31). Work does not excite him, but on his motorcycle he creates the highly romanticized image of the hero, or rather, anti-hero. Speed spiced with danger satisfies his quest for thrills, and the machismo image provides a new basis for self-esteem. The biker uses his possessions to create an identity or social position. The motorcycle represents a departure from the rational, secure, and sensible (32). He adopts attitudes and behaviours centred on independence, toughness, impulsiveness, and masculinity. Becoming an outlaw biker, however, requires a lengthy socialization.

For the outlaw biker, there is only one motorcycle: the Harley-Davidson "Hog." Japanese two-wheelers are not considered motorcycles, but "rice-burners." Anyone can handle a

Japanese bike; he is a "ricer" and lacks the mechanical skill and commitment characteristic of a "true" biker. Riding "Jap Crap" is not considered respectable; it does not make a statement about personal freedom, macho self-reliance, and daring. For a true biker, the Hog is the basis of his lifestyle. The ricer regards his motorcycle as he does his Maytag washer. The true biker personalizes his Hog by rebuilding, customizing, and virtually redesigning it. The dress of leather vest, jeans, and cowboy boots is part of the aura. "The pretty yellow and orange rain suits are strictly for candy asses who ride riceburners" (52). Bikers face accidents with a cavalier attitude. "At one hundred miles an hour … if you hit a half-brick on the road you won't stop rolling for two days.… It's only a fatal twitch away, and your fate is finally in your own hands!… That's better than sex, drugs, anything you name" (54).

Of course, social rebellion does not go unpunished. After refusals by insurance companies, restaurants, and campgrounds, and hassles by police, the gang member grows contemptuous of a world that pays tribute to personal freedom but punishes those who are different. Some find the hassles too great and abandon the biker role, but others move further into psychological allegiance to the outlaw-biker subculture. Harassment from outsiders can result in greater solidarity for those in the group (Cohen, 1955). The biker wants to socialize, discuss, exchange information, and share the mystique. This eventually leads to the doorsteps of an outlaw club.

Socialization and social interactions are more complex than we had thought, as illustrated by the bikers' relationships with women. Chauvinism is the norm, but women relate to the club in different ways. "Broads" are casual and usually temporary, "Mamas" maintain an affiliation with the club as a whole, while "Ol' Ladies" have established relationships with individual members (132). Interestingly, members' personal ties with women are the major threat to the internal cohesion of an outlaw motorcycle club. The club demands almost complete allegiance, but many women do not share this allegiance. Marriage frequently means leaving the club. As one biker said, "There are no biker weddings, only ex-biker weddings."

Sharing similar attitudes brings bikers from different areas together under certain conditions, but the common bonds of biking are completely overridden when inter-club rivalry dictates warfare. From the outlaw-biker viewpoint a club did not exist unless it openly wore "colours," and its existence was automatically terminated when it lost those colours, often at the hands of a victorious club. One detects the Rebels' pride in their successful rivalry with other clubs. The colours of other clubs were draped upside down on a wall in the clubhouse, all seized from clubs that they had "taken off the road." Wolf argues that territoriality was both necessary and inescapable. Ironically, there is more violence when territorial dominance breaks down. The Rebels' dominance in Edmonton, allied with other clubs at times, and unofficially sanctioned by the police, kept Edmonton more peaceful than Calgary, where gang rivalries led to bloodshed and deaths.

Why do motorcycle gangs persist? Wolf portrays the Rebels as a product of urban industrial society, a collective social response to the conditions of alienation as experienced by young, working-class men. Bikers form a subculture in opposition to, and sometimes in criminal conflict with, the social norms of mainstream North America. They create an opportunity for meaningful participation at personal and social levels. The man who "earns his colours" becomes a member of an elite, which struts with a high profile. (One can imagine the same type of psychological strutting from a politician, athlete, successful businessman, academic, or student who has received an award.) At the personal level, the biker is part of a tightly knit social network, a brotherhood. He is not antisocial or fleeing from commitment. He is an organization man.

Does the study by Wolf help us to understand Quebec's Hells Angels, who appear to be heavily into the drug and sex trades? Perhaps the incentive to become part of a bike gang is part of the explanation, but the functionalist argument may also apply here. In addition, the "subculture of violence" perspective and differential association discussed earlier make sense. Strategies to counter some of these forces will have to include more than just law enforcement. However, while heavy use of the justice system may not be a useful strategy for juvenile thieves, one could argue that vigorous law enforcement, while not a long-term cure, is a very necessary component in responding to organized crime, especially when it is linked to corporate activities.

The Search for Respect

Philippe Bourgois (1995) also calls attention to the social dynamics involved in being respected as part of a group when he describes cocaine dealers in New York City's Spanish Harlem and the inevitable involvement in violence which is part of this lifestyle. These Latino men have had unpleasant encounters with schools, police, courts, and so on. It is difficult to identify where the circular chain of "causes" begins, but forming gangs and engaging in criminal activities, which admittedly are self-destructive, offer an opportunity to acquire a kind of self-respect:

> "Hell, yeah, I felt good when I owned the Game Room (the local crack house). In those days everybody be looking for me; everybody needed me. When I drove up, people be opening the door for me, and offering to wash my car. Even kids too little to understand anything about drugs looked up to me." Felix. (Bourgois, 1995: 77)

One can see parallels between the lower-class Japanese man who wishes to see himself in the image of the samurai warrior, the biker described by Daniel Wolf, and the Puerto Rican drug dealer in New York who is looking for respect. Policies to reduce organized gang crime will be less effective if they ignore the *meaning* of these activities to those involved.

Nor can we overlook the link between the agencies of control and organized crime. Just as the police in Edmonton looked the other way when the Rebels took competing gangs "off the road," and thereby reduced the likelihood of gang wars, the police and other authorities in other countries have selective relationships with organized gangs. These links may be at the highest levels of government, with agencies such as the CIA in the U.S., or at the street level, where honest police are simply doing the best they can.

Societal Conditions That Mitigate against Gang Formation

One could probably consider much organized crime and gangs as deviant subcultures. They are scarce in simpler, homogeneous societies. Modern democratic societies with heterogeneous populations may create conditions for some groups to fail. Other modern societies may create parallel opportunity structures that increase the likelihood of success for those less advantaged. Having lived in Vienna for different periods, I suggest that city has some characteristics that mitigate against the creation of gangs. Societies with **pluralistic social bases** may be less likely to create criminal subcultures. Unlike the U.S. and Canada, where we seem to have created an "underclass," Vienna has a viable working-class culture that parallels a middle-class culture. There are two power pyramids in the society instead of one. The schools reinforce this. At the age of 10, young people take examinations for admittance into the college preparatory *Mittelschule*. Those who fail spend four more years in the *Hauptschule*. Middle-class parents hire tutors and are very concerned that their children pass these exams.

Although one might argue that it is unfair to stream children at this early age, this system has compensations for working-class families. Those in skilled trades may do much better financially than those with university degrees who work in bookstores. Technical colleges are also open to promising working-class students who have not had the eight years of Latin required for the university. Talented writers can work for the socialist newspaper; those with political skills can run for office with a high likelihood of success in Vienna. At the national level, sharing power with the conservatives (*Volkspartei*) has long been part of a coalition mentality. The double social pyramid is even reflected during the famous Viennese ball season. Most workers would not wish to attend the snobbish and expensive Opera Ball or Hunters Ball, but the Socialist Party has its own ball, as do the streetcar conductors, butchers, and so forth.

Other aspects of life reflect the two power pyramids. Day-care centres, scouting groups, hiking groups, and a myriad of other activities are organized on party—and, in a sense, social-class, or at least philosophical—lines. One can succeed within either the "conservative" middle-class power pyramid or the "socialist" working-class power pyramid. Comfortable coalitions between the two power pyramids are evident everywhere.

Traditionally, Vienna offers working-class people realistically achievable ways of gaining status and sharing in a meaningful life. This works against the formation of deviant subgroups such as outlaw motorcycle gangs. Since gang membership increases delinquent behaviour (Battin et al., 1998), the creation of legitimate, fulfilling groups should be a societal concern. Does Vienna have less organized crime? Or is it simply less visible? North American culture and its school systems offer tremendous opportunities, but they label those who perform badly as failures. Those who fail in our middle-class-dominated institutions have no haven—no socially accepted way of rationalizing their failure. In Austria, as in much of Europe, a large working-class culture (subculture?) shares political power with a middle-class culture. This may counter the alienation that characterizes some working-class groups in North America and makes them susceptible to deviant subcultures.

In a nutshell, the gang-breaking activities used by social control agencies in North America will fail as long as lower-class males see few opportunities to participate in a rich and exciting life within the mainstream of society. The trick is to create genuine communities that fill interpersonal needs. The groups and organizations which evolved in Austria illustrate organizational forms which provide settings for meaningful participation. Can working-class males create their own "clubs" that fill personal needs without generating fear from the public and hostility from the agents of social control?

Modern societies contain a variety of subgroups that fulfill a myriad of needs. The formation of some of these subgroups, such as organized criminal groups or motorcycle gangs, appears to result from the demand for illegal goods and services, often coupled with the feeling that life in the dominant society is unrewarding. Societies that create broad access to the things that make life worthwhile may inhibit the formation of deviant subgroups. Such an argument is obviously an oversimplification. The desire for gambling, drugs, and prostitution will probably never be met by legitimate organizations. Thus, illegitimate organizations seem to be an ongoing part of complex societies. Modern societies contain subgroups whose primary allegiance is not to the society as a whole. Bringing marginal groups into the mainstream is a major task for democracies.

SUMMARY

1. Organized crime might be viewed as associations of criminals rather than criminal associations.

2. Globalization and various corporate activities provide increasing opportunities for links between organized and corporate crime.

3. The example of the tong wars suggests that organized crime has been well entrenched for some time.

4. While a conflict perspective calls attention to crimes by people at the top, a functionalist perspective calls attention to the needs and demands of ordinary people. Thus, eliminating a social structure that provides a service demanded by society—be it legal or illegal—without providing an alternative, will fail. The argument seems to apply to a low-crime society with a collective mentality, such as Japan, as well as to individualistic societies, such as Canada and the U.S.

5. Explanations of gangs change over time. One study suggests that young men with dull jobs may find gratification in biker gangs. Instead of being deviants, these people are "organization men" who conform to a different set of rules.

6. Some societies—Austria, for example—may create opportunities for meaningful participation within working-class subcultures. Such conditions mitigate against gang formation.

KEY TERMS

boryokudan 259

criminogenic asymmetries 253

functionalist approach 256

latent functions 256

manifest functions 256

pluralistic social bases 263

political machine 256

tong war 255

yakuza 259

WEBLINKS

www.yorku.ca/nathanson/default.htm
The Nathanson Centre for the Study of Organized Crime and Corruption through York University: extensive information on Canadian organized crime.

www.cisc.gc.ca
Criminal Intelligence Service of Canada (CISC): annual reports on organized crime in Canada.

www.canada.justice.gc.ca/en/index.html
The Federal Department of Justice: links to information on the Youth Criminal Justice Act.

IV

RESPONDING TO
CRIME

Chapter 17 outlines different ways society can respond to crime. Utilizing the community is a strategy that has resulted in some modest successes in the U.S. By contrast, the way we use courts seems to have little positive impact. By the time offenders appear in court, it is difficult to do anything constructive. The factors that lead to crime cannot be influenced to a great extent by the criminal justice system in terms of prevention. The chapter also reviews situations in which the adversarial system actually increases the probability of crime.

The final chapter (Chapter 18) may be viewed as pessimistic or optimistic depending on the degree of faith one has that authorities will act on certain issues. Clearly, many characteristics of Canadian society are criminogenic. The abuse of power by the elite of society moves the "morality curve" in a direction that influences everyone. It becomes easier to accept cheating and other behaviour that tears at the social fabric. Government policies could make a difference. Unless the economic elite are controlling the government, and some would argue that this is the case, democratically elected governments could check the abuses of those in power. However, when a dishonest Canadian Cabinet minister is "punished" by being made ambassador to Denmark, it sends a clear message to everyone that ethical behaviour is not highly valued.

On the other hand, government policies that care for the weak, such as systematic attempts to reduce child poverty, could move the "morality curve" in a prosocial direction. The social fabric is a closely knit web. Seemingly unconnected issues are, in fact, linked together. The morality of an entire society can be changed, and crime is part of that morality.

While crime will not disappear, some of our most damaging crime can be reduced, as demonstrated by research and findings from many countries. It remains to be seen whether policy-makers in Canada will utilize the knowledge that is currently available.

17

COMMUNITY AND JUSTICE SYSTEM RESPONSES TO CRIME

This chapter will:

- Note that creating changes in communities may be one of the more effective ways of responding to crime.

- Describe a project in Chicago that emphasized collective efficacy, defined as cohesion among neighbourhood residents combined with shared expectations for informal social control of public space.

- Warn against the dangers of focusing on legal procedure and missing the essence of underlying issues.

- Question the merits of a highly adversarial justice system.

- Suggest that our Youth Courts may be contributing to crime and describe how other countries do a better job.

FOCUSING ON THE COMMUNITY

In a "temptation" survey, *Reader's Digest* magazine deliberately "lost" more than 1100 wallets throughout several countries. Each wallet contained 50 dollars in local currency and the name and phone number of the owner. About 44 percent of the wallets disappeared. However, in Norway and Denmark every single wallet was returned. Other studies have also suggested that Scandinavians are more honest than people in many other parts of the world. Their prosocial behaviour cannot be explained by criminal laws or by the behaviour of the police and the criminal courts. The question we should ask ourselves is how can countries or neighbourhoods create conditions that would lead to lower crime rates?

Much of our knowledge about crime suggests that coordinated projects involving a number of agencies can have an impact on crime in the community. These projects are very expensive and difficult to evaluate. While Canada would have difficulty launching and evaluating the types of projects described here, the findings from some U.S. studies offer suggestions for Canadian crime-prevention efforts.

Creating Collective Efficacy in Neighbourhoods

In the March 1982 issue of *Atlantic Monthly* an article about "broken windows" by James Wilson and George Kelling had a major impact on crime-prevention thinking. They argued that if a community appears to be neglected—if there are many broken windows, if minor incivilities like drinking in the street and spray-painting graffiti are common—more serious crime will result. These ideas had a powerful influence on crime-control policies. Some governments interpreted this as a call to "get tough." Many cities adopted **zero-tolerance strategies**, cracking down hard on very minor offences. Some politicians took a simple-minded approach to the problem, assuming that punitive policies would automatically reduce disorder and hence crime.

Advocates of zero-tolerance policies point to the drop of homicides in New York City as proof of their success. However, many large cities witnessed major decreases in crime during the middle 1990s. Some cities actually moved toward softer rather than harsher strategies, such as community-oriented policing. Others did not change police strategies at all. Confusion arises when people simply assume that tougher policing tactics, more convictions in court, and longer sentences can be effective in addressing the underlying problems of disorder and crime. While the causes of the recent drop in crime in many parts of the U.S. are not obvious, it would be a mistake to assume that tough policing has been the major factor. Of course, policing strategies are easier to change than modifying childrearing practices, for example. We might agree that creating a less materialistic society would reduce crime in the long run, but in the short term that is not feasible. Thus, even minor gains in policing activities might yield modest gains in crime reduction.

The challenge is to use police, and other agencies, to maintain orderly neighbourhoods. This involves broader measures than just crime control. Decay in a neighbourhood suggests that residents are unwilling to intervene, to confront children doing damage, or to see the police as helpful allies. But is disorder the cause of crime? Is it an indicator of other ills? Or, more important, is it, like crime, the product of other underlying factors?

Choosing the correct causal sequence of factors is important. The left-hand portion of Figure 17.1 suggests that changes in disorder, as described above, would have a *direct* impact on crime. The right-hand part suggests that the relationship between disorder and crime is spurious. The relationship exists because *both* disorder and crime are caused by other factors. Public policy should be alert to these differences. The right-hand figure, for example, would

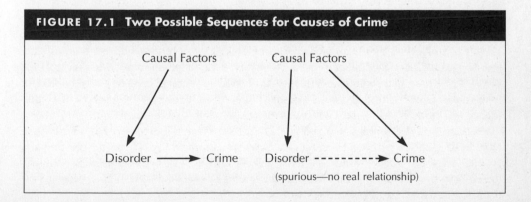

FIGURE 17.1 Two Possible Sequences for Causes of Crime

Causal Factors   Causal Factors

Disorder ⟶ Crime   Disorder ⇢ Crime

(spurious—no real relationship)

recommend *greater emphasis on the underlying causal factors*. The left-hand figure suggests that zero-tolerance strategies might work. (Actually, the interrelationships are much more complicated than the simple models above indicate.)

The Project on Human Development in Chicago Neighborhoods tried to sort out the impact of some of these factors. It looked at **collective efficacy**, defined as *cohesion among neighbourhood residents combined with shared expectations for informal social control of public space* (Sampson and Raudenbush, 2001). When there is mutual trust among neighbours and feelings of shared obligations, they are more likely to intervene for the common good. Residents might yell at teenagers who are doing damage or knock on the door of a neighbour if they hear sounds of spousal abuse.

The study also argued that both crime and disorder stem from structural characteristics, such as concentrated poverty and the absence of social resources. Structural constraints are not just economic. Residential stability, for example, helps residents build a stake in the community.

The study's findings offer some meaningful policy recommendations. Not surprisingly, disorder tends to be high when there is much poverty. In addition, concentrations of immigrant populations were related to disorder. (Past studies suggest that individual immigrants tend to have low rates of crime, but they tend to live in poorer neighbourhoods where the native-born have high crime rates and the younger generation frequently gets into trouble.)

In addition to these structural characteristics, factors involving human intervention influenced disorder. When collective efficacy was strong and neighbours were more willing to intervene, the levels of physical and social disorder tended to be lower. These findings are as predicted, but to which of the two models described above do the data apply better? The study found that there was little *direct* relationship between disorder and crime. Rather, disorder and crime appear to have similar roots. The right-hand part of Figure 17.1 fits the data better than the left-hand part. This strongly suggests that policies that try to reduce crime by eradicating disorder simply by using tough law enforcement are misdirected. *Underlying factors of both disorder and crime must be addressed*. For example, in Hamburg, Germany, the city used favourable tax policies to make it advantageous for people to stay in certain neighbourhoods, thereby creating more residential stability. People developed a stake in their community.

Other structural changes, such as the reduction of poverty, are more difficult to achieve. Scandinavian countries have less concentration of poverty in their neighbourhoods, but Canada and the U.S. have experienced an increasing gap between the wealthy and the poor. The reunification of Germany has resulted in rising crime rates in the 1990s in the former East Germany. The closing of factories, the loss of jobs, and the increasing gap between rich and poor are structural changes that have also reduced the collective efficacy that seemed to play a role in East Germany prior to unification.

But shouldn't one also try to fix the broken windows directly? Attempts to reduce physical disorder through community action could obviously produce some benefits. If residents rallied to engage in a neighbourhood cleanup, it might strengthen social ties and increase the residents' commitment to their neighbourhood. A community policing strategy might support such a mobilization. By contrast, Sampson and Raudenbush (2001) warn that a zero-tolerance crackdown could easily alienate residents who might have inclinations toward community cooperation.

Sometimes we forget that there are important links between communities and the criminal justice agencies. When courts operate as if in a cocoon, following legal rituals, and insulated from the public, they may be less effective. The next section looks at the criminal justice system.

FOCUSING ON PROCEDURES AND MISSING THE ESSENCE OF PROBLEMS

In an article entitled "Good People, Dirty System," I argue that the vast majority of those in the criminal justice system are able, upright, and compassionate people, but that the system itself makes it very difficult for them to achieve the intended, long-range goals of that system (Hackler, 1991b). When the criminal justice system focuses on procedures rather than on justice, the potential for deterrence is lost as well as the type of healing that characterizes the response to crime in many societies, including the Native peoples of Canada.

One problem with criminal justice can be illustrated by the following account of a trial for impaired driving. The only witness was the police officer who had followed the erratic driver to a parking lot. She testified that she "chartered" the defendant (local shorthand for reading the driver his rights) and then took him to the station for testing. The blood alcohol test was well over the legal limit. During the cross-examination, the defence lawyer did not ask the officer what she had meant by "chartering" the defendant, but in his closing arguments, he argued that the police officer had not said she had read the accused his rights, but simply that she had "chartered" him. He asked the judge to acquit. The judge, who was clearly uncomfortable with this argument, acquitted the defendant.

From a legal standpoint, I would certainly not question the decision, but magistrates in Asia, most of Europe, and ordinary Canadians might wonder about our legal system. The man was guilty, in the real, if not legal, sense of the word; the police officer acted properly; and everyone in the room, including the defendant and his lawyer, knew exactly what "chartered" meant. Why didn't (or, rather, couldn't) the judge simply ask the officer what she meant by "chartering" after the prosecution raised the issue?

But there is more. Legally trained people seemed to think the defence lawyer had done a "good" job. Even the police officer, who was chatting with the defendant during the break, was sympathetic when he mentioned that he had paid $7000 to his skilled defence lawyer. Nor did the prosecutor suggest that the system had failed. Instead, he apologized to the police officer for having goofed. It was clearly his fault; the system was OK. Non-legally trained people were more critical, seeing this case as another illustration of how our legal system serves society poorly.

Are these types of cases rare, or does our court system frequently create procedures that produce injustice? An Ontario lawyer who specializes in impaired driving had never lost a case at the time of a study done by Ericson (1981). Like the lawyer who defended the above case, this lawyer was also considered "good." He was highly respected and very well paid for his services, a person who obviously is making a worthwhile contribution to society. Again the non-legal mind might be excused for being critical of a system which rewards a professional whose specialty is helping people lie.

By contrast, the Norwegian or Dutch system might respond with a different logic. The prosecutor might be convinced that an offender is guilty, but decide that it is not in the best interests of the society to proceed to a trial. In the above case, the man was a first offender, embarrassed by his mistake, and unlikely to do it again. Thus, a Norwegian prosecutor might feel the goal of the system had been achieved without a trial.

Criminal courts are constantly faced with *social* issues, even though we deal with them by having judges make *legal* decisions. Family and Youth Court judges often try to decide what is best for a child. The setting is a contest in which both sides are striving to win. One response to this adversarial mentality is for the court to appoint an additional lawyer to represent the child. This process can be carried to extremes. In Australia, I observed a relatively straightforward case that had to determine whether an infant should be returned to a couple. The father had just been released from prison. Supposedly, the main concern was for the child and the competence of the parents. In fact, the self-interest of several different agencies was also involved. There were five lawyers presenting different arguments and representing different agencies, but at no time did the parents testify, nor were they asked for their opinions. The needs of the family were lost in this contest among lawyers. There is a parallel between changes in the juvenile and family courts and the rest of the justice system: the voices of the people affected are often lost, as agencies and other interests vie for influence.

Criminal matters are often connected to social issues involving a web of human relations. These issues have been "legalized." Lawyers argue among themselves and take these debates out of the hands of those most concerned (Christie, 1977). As a result, the clients of the system feel left out, and are more inclined to deny legitimacy to the system.

The main causes of crime lie in the structure of society itself. The response of the various components of the criminal justice system, at least as it operates now, cannot make a significant impact on criminal behaviour. However, the way the criminal justice system responds can have a long-range impact on the way people view the rules of society. When the system loses credibility and is seen as neither just nor effective, it can undermine the willingness of individuals to obey the rules or to have any confidence in the appropriateness of those rules.

Sally Merry (1991) describes the contest between clients of the system and the professionals who run it. She studies "the process of cultural domination exercised by the law over people who bring their personal problems to the lower courts" (9). The problems are important to the people involved, but they are not always amenable to legal solutions. Thus, the clients define their problems one way and the legal professionals another way. My contention is that the continuous expansion of a system ill-suited to resolving problems related to crime is, in the long run, criminogenic.

A Japanese Response to a Potential Crime

A North American husband and wife were working and studying in Japan. They had an argument. The man went out, got drunk, kicked in a garbage can, and damaged a door of an old woman's house. She called the police. Two officers arrived by bicycle and walked the offender to the police station. His Japanese was very poor, and he was belligerent at times. The police called the man's wife, who spoke Japanese. She came to the station, explained that there had been a domestic dispute and that the husband went out and got drunk. The police were sympathetic; but since the man was in a high-status position, they scolded him for acting so shamefully. In Japan, people of high status are expected to behave more responsibly than others. They sent the man home in the custody of his wife, and required that he go to the victim's house the next day and apologize, as well as pay for the damages. The apology was particularly important, and since his Japanese was poor and he might say the wrong thing, his wife was to translate. At the old woman's house the next day, the wife translated the apology, and the old woman also apologized for having her garbage can in an awkward place. Clearly there was an attempt to restore the peace, so even the victim made an effort. This is an illustration of restorative justice. Later I will discuss its recent discovery in North America.

Notice that no charge was laid, no judge was involved, there was no court process. Everything was done at the police and community level. In Canada, we might have laid charges, a defence lawyer could have asked for adjournments, and many months later the case might be resolved in an expensive and not particularly satisfactory manner. True, civil rights may not be as secure in Japan, but even serious crimes are often screened out at the prosecutorial level. Getting a conviction is not the goal of the system. Preventing further crime is. As long as the Canadian system is primarily concerned with punishing people, we must pretend that we are very careful about convicting people. In fact, our system convicts a very high percentage of lower-status defendants (Ericson and Baranek, 1982); it simply takes us a long time to do it. In such a system, the need for civil-rights protection is naturally greater. Unfortunately, we may have burdened ourselves with a system that is out of touch with the concerns of society.

The Consequences of an Adversarial System: The Pressure to Win

Many countries tend to believe that their legal systems are superior to the systems of others. North Americans are understandably proud of some legal achievements that speak to individual issues such as civil rights. Unfortunately, these accomplishments can lead to the naive assumption that a system has been created that responds constructively to the myriad of social issues that are so entwined with crime.

Investigating Crimes in Switzerland

A comparison with the Swiss canton of Vaud is revealing. An English scholar, who was familiar with the common-law system of England as well as with the Swiss system, said that if he were innocent, he would prefer to be tried under the Swiss system, but if he were guilty he would choose the common law in England or the United States (Godfrey, 1981: Ch. 16). In Switzerland, the innocent are more likely to be screened out early and never brought to trial, but the guilty are more likely to be convicted. The slower, drawn-out process in common-law countries, such as England and Canada, favour guilty persons with resources. In other words, the scholar believed the Swiss distinguished more accurately between guilt and innocence. Of course, this requires that the preliminary stage of the process, the police investigation, be rigorously fair. In North America, the adversarial system puts pressure on the police to produce charges that stick in court.

During a police investigation in Switzerland—the *instruction*, which is directed by a magistrate—the police gather information relevant to both sides of the case. The Swiss police have greater leeway than those in North America. Information such as hearsay evidence, which is considered privileged or inappropriate in Canada, is permitted in the Swiss canton of Vaud. Other protections available to suspects are not available in Switzerland. For example, the presumed suspect, the *prévenu*, can be held without charge. The investigation is secret until complete. (While the French system is similar, it differs on this point, and some French magistrates criticize this aspect of the system in Vaud.) When the file, or *dossier*, from the *instruction* is completed, it then becomes available to the defence, who can ask that the police gather more information. In other words, the ***juge d'instruction***, or investigating judge, instructs the investigating police to gather all relevant information. The failure to do this job fairly and thoroughly would bring criticism of the people involved.

By contrast, there is a tendency for the police in Canada, the U.S., and Australia to decide on the guilt of a suspect and then continue the investigation to make a strong case. Our system may have more safeguards during a trial, but police investigations are not neutral. There is pressure to build a strong case against the defendant. The police and prosecution are not rewarded for building a balanced case. The defence cannot insist that the police investigate in certain areas, whereas in France or Switzerland, the *juge d'instruction* is obligated to have the police search for evidence relevant to innocence as well.

The adversarial system, which is seen as sacred, places more emphasis on legal tricks and less on the search for truth and justice. When the defence has many resources, skilled lawyers not only protect innocent defendants, they also protect the guilty. A defendant with few resources will be convicted more easily. If the police are wrong, it is very difficult for an ordinary citizen to influence the system. Canada has joined the U.S. in creating a criminal justice system that is slow, out of touch with societal needs, biased against the underprivileged, and favourable towards upper-class defendants, experienced criminals, and those with resources.

Do Court Procedures Matter?

After criticizing our court system, we should, in fairness, look at some attempts to improve the system. Most criminologists would agree that the operations of the police, courts, and prisons have only a minor impact on actual crime. However, modest improvements in the criminal justice system are worth pursuing and may yield some unanticipated, long-term rewards. The Community Prosecution Project in Washington, DC, illustrates an attempt to make the courts and police more effective (Boland, 2001).

When the Community Prosecution pilot project began in 1996, the Metropolitan Police Department did not have a community-oriented focus. This changed with the appointment of prosecutors who got better acquainted with a specific community and worked more closely with the police. The project did not have a uniform set of strategies that were applied across neighbourhoods. Thus, the research did not lend itself to traditional evaluation methodologies designed to identify factors that could be assessed in terms of crime-prevention impact. Rather, prosecutors worked more closely with police and citizens to develop appropriate responses for that neighbourhood.

Recorded crime decreased over the next couple of years. To what extent this may have occurred because of decreased reporting or because of an actual decrease in criminal behaviour is hard to say. While no magic bullet or specific intervention technique comes out of this project, it suggests that *cooperation among the courts, the police, and the community can identify crime-producing settings and structures within a specific neighbourhood. Furthermore those settings can be altered.* The tendency to assume that the courts and police have no meaningful impact on crime overlooks the fact that when their activities are tuned to the community, they might bring about change or enable other agents in the neighbourhood to effect change.

Mobilizing and Coordinating Community Resources: Weed and Seed

The Weed and Seed project applied many of the principles discussed above (Dunworth and Mills, 1999). Beginning with three cities in the U.S., the project included 200 sites in 1999. Ten high-crime-rate sites were used for the evaluation. Neighbourhoods targeted for the program were compared with others. The project found success in some areas but less in others. The key components of this strategy were:

- Enhanced coordination—Coordinated analysis and planning of local problems and strategies to address them.
- **Weeding**—Concentrated law enforcement efforts to identify, arrest, and prosecute violent offenders, drug traffickers, and other criminals.
- Community policing—Proactive police/community engagement and problem solving with officers assigned to specified geographic locations.
- **Seeding**—Human services, including after-school, weekend, and summer youth activities, adult literacy classes, and neighbourhood revitalization efforts.

Not surprisingly, the evaluation found weak links in the chain of efforts. For example, a number of local prosecutors lacked the personnel to conduct enhanced prosecution when aggressive policing generated larger case loads. We should also not assume that more aggressive policing and charging are just another "get tough" strategy. In some communities citizens are terrorized by criminals and welcome police activities that curtail those who are preying on them. Charging a higher percentage of criminals who are known in the community as troublemakers increases the likelihood that a wrong-doer will be caught. Certainty of punishment is a more effective deterrent than severity of punishment. In Quebec, for example, the likelihood of biker gang members getting convicted has been rather low. Similarly, for income tax evaders, certainty rather than severity of punishment has more impact.

One caution about projects of this type is that politicians are more enthusiastic about the "weeding" and tend to neglect the "seeding." From what we know now, the investment in the "seeding" activities may pay the higher dividends in crime reduction in the long run.

The Weed and Seed efforts worked better in some areas than others, but it appears that the program was a stimulant to community coalition building. The evaluation and research committed to these projects are considerable and unlikely to be found in Canada. However, the knowledge from Weed and Seed and the Project on Human Development in Chicago Neighborhoods could provide guidelines for efforts in this country.

YOUTH COURTS AS A FACTOR IN INCREASED CRIME IN CANADA

Effective intervention with juveniles makes a difference in crime in general. The trend in North America is to "get tough on young criminals." This unimaginative approach probably contributes to an increase in crime in the future, because it avoids facing issues that might make a difference. The alienation of youth from the juvenile justice system becomes part of a general alienation from society. While it is unfair to expect the Youth Courts in Canada to prevent delinquency, they can make things worse by reinforcing feelings of injustice, lack of care, and lack of opportunity. By failing to expedite the reintegration of young people into the fabric of society, the juvenile justice system contributes to an increase in crime in Canada.

The critical position taken in this book should not obscure the fact that considerable progress has been made over the last century in developing more effective ways of dealing with youth and families in trouble. My point is that other parts of the world have done even better, and recent decades have not seen a continuation of the long-term progress in juvenile justice.

With the passage of the **Young Offenders Act (YOA)** in 1984, Juvenile Courts became Youth Courts. Prior to 1984, there had been a "welfare orientation" in Juvenile Courts. In her book, *From Punishment to Doing Good: Family Courts and Socialized Justice in Ontario 1880–1940*, Dorothy Chunn (1992) notes that the Family Courts developed a tradition that began recognizing problems and made efforts to help. Until recently, some of the Youth and Family Court judges were not trained as lawyers. A few came from a social-work background. The major contest, well into the early 1930s in Ontario, seemed to be between lawyer types and social-welfare types. But if there was a gradual shift towards helping people up until the 1940s, by the 1970s and 1980s there was clearly a move towards a more legalistic model.

By the 1980s, almost all Juvenile Court judges were trained as lawyers, marking a legalistic trend which continued with more legally trained prosecutors and the increasing appearance of defence attorneys. Duty counsels, defence lawyers who assist anyone who wants help, are found in most large Canadian Youth Courts today. Part of this trend was influenced by concerns that the welfare-oriented system was, in fact, punishing juveniles under the pretence of helping. While there is reason to believe that this happened, it also appears that these abuses were adjusted, over time, through changes in practices in juvenile courts. At any rate, Canadian Youth Courts today resemble adult courts more than they did in the past. To date there is no evidence that the presence of lawyers and the increased legalism is superior to the previous system (Corrado and Markwart, 1996). At present, many trivial cases appear in Youth Courts, delays and adjournments are common, and juveniles who are not dangerous spend time in custody. These points can be made more clearly with some specific cases.

Case 1

The 15-year-old girl was in court for theft. The parents were separated and lived in different cities. The daughter was with neither parent, but lived in a small town with a family who treated her like one of their own. She had been in no trouble in the community and had done well in school. However, she began to date a 20-year-old. The family did not approve. When the father, who had legal custody, heard of the situation, he drove to the small town, picked up his daughter, and moved her to his apartment in the larger city. The girl did not like the woman who lived with the father, stole 11 dollars from her father's wallet to buy a bus ticket back to the small town, and returned to the family with whom she had been living. The father swore out a warrant for her arrest for theft. The police picked up the girl, put her in the local detention centre, then brought her to the larger city and housed her in a larger detention centre, pending a hearing in juvenile court on a charge of theft. The social worker who looked into the case found it difficult to recommend any specific action.

In court, the girl expressed her desire to return to the small town. The father, who had legal custody, was concerned about the older boyfriend, even though the girl said she was no longer seeing him. The charge of petty theft remained. Duty counsel (the lawyer for the defence) recommended that the girl plead not guilty, which she did. Therefore, a trial had to be held. But what to do with the girl in the meantime? The judge did not wish to send her back to the detention centre, but the father refused to accept her in his apartment as long as she was pleading not guilty. The session adjourned with the girl being sent back to the detention centre. She turned to the social worker and asked, "Why did I plead not guilty?" After a couple of more days in detention, the girl came back, pleaded guilty to the theft before a different judge, and was sent home with her father.

I do not know the best way of dealing with family squabbles, but three different stays in detention centres and a criminal record may not be the best way of handling an argument between a father and daughter. We also saw good people doing dirty work: the police, a probation officer, a social worker, and two reluctant judges wishing there were a reasonable way of handling the situation. Unfortunately, the legalism of the system made it difficult to handle this family dispute intelligently. This is another illustration of **"stealing conflicts"** from those who are in a better position to make decisions (Christie, 1977). The Young Offenders Act has encouraged legally trained people to steal conflicts, whereas in the past, the social workers were perhaps guilty of being "professional usurpers" of other people's problems.

Case 2

The boy had been picked up on a Friday evening and held in detention until Monday morning. He was charged with missing appointments with his probation officer, not seeking work, and not living with the family to whom he had been assigned. The Crown prosecutor presented the case from the paperwork she had in front of her. However, no probation officer appeared and there was some confusion as to which probation officer was currently handling the case. The boy's employer had not arrived. (Would having an employer be relevant to the charge of not seeking work?) The boy was staying at home and his mother was in the courtroom, but evidently he was supposed to be staying in another home. There seemed to be some confusion about all three charges. Asked how he pleaded, the boy was confused but pleaded guilty. The duty counsel was also confused. At that point, the judge accepted the guilty plea and adjourned the case until Thursday, when he would decide on the sentence on the basis of a predisposition report. In the meantime, the boy would go back to the detention centre. No thought was given to the possibility that this dangerous criminal could go home with his mother. The mother tried to speak, but the judge cut her off, saying that she would be able to speak on Thursday, at the disposition hearing.

During the break, the distraught mother approached the prosecutor, saying, "I know my boy is a brat, but he shouldn't be shit on like that." After further discussion, the prosecutor agreed to raise the matter with the judge when he returned to the courtroom. When the judge returned and the prosecutor pointed out that the mother would like to say something about the case, the judge simply repeated that the boy had pleaded guilty and the mother would have adequate time to provide information at the time of sentencing. When the mother stomped out of the courtroom, the judge hurled threats of contempt of court at her as she disappeared through the doors.

In this case, a minor offender had two different stays in detention, at considerable cost to the taxpayer. It is most unlikely that he or his mother will have much faith in the justice, efficiency, or intelligence of the system. But even with skilled people handling such cases, there are some structural barriers to an intelligent response. First, in court we insist that juveniles plead guilty or not guilty. They cannot tell their story in their own way. They must conform to the rituals. Second, the prosecutor rarely has any personal background knowledge and usually has limited information, often having only some brief written reports. One prosecutor had to use photocopies that were almost unreadable. Third, the judge is inhibited from exploring confusing situations, or discussing topics not introduced in court. Findings of guilt are separate from sentencing decisions, when, in reality, the two are often entwined. These conditions frequently make a mockery of the Youth Court as a setting for the sensitive handling of complex problems. Fourth, once a situation has been botched, it is hard to correct. A judge cannot call up a detention centre and say he made a mistake, and that the mother should just drop by and pick up her son.

Better Alternatives for Handling Juveniles: France

Evidence for determining which juvenile justice systems are "better" is not readily available. We simply do not have measures of the impact of systems that can be compared from country to country. However, a majority of criminologists agree that locking up large numbers of juveniles, so they can share ideas with other delinquents, is counterproductive (Krisberg et al., 1986). Thus, countries that imprison many juveniles are probably doing more damage than good. Using rough estimates, it appears that the U.S. locks up about twenty times as many juveniles per capita as Paris, and the province of Alberta about ten times as many (Hackler, 1988).

At the adult level, the U.S. also locks up more people per capita than almost any other developed country, and Canada tends to be higher than almost all European countries (Pease and Hukkila, 1990). The trend is also frightening. Between 1980 and 1990, the incarceration rate in the U.S. increased 121 percent (Canadian Centre for Justice Statistics, 1992). By contrast, Canada has had a fairly stable prison rate until recently. The 1990s have seen some increase. Despite the rhetoric concerning the need to "get tough," those countries with high imprisonment rates are illustrations of societies that have failed in their response to crime.

Let us look at France, a country plagued by problems that are not so different from those in North America, and ask how it responds to juvenile delinquency. A British criminologist and a French juvenile court judge who know both the English and French systems (King and Petit, 1985/86) write that non-punitive responses to the vast majority of young offenders in France seem to avoid the stigmatization, the exclusion from the mainstream of society, and the consequent creation of delinquent subcultures that characterize the English scene. This is probably even more true in comparison with North America.

The attitudes of the French judges and the way they perform their tasks reflect differences from the North American mentality. Judges in North America often lock up children "for their own good," but the difference between being helped and punished is not always clear to the juveniles. The distinction in France is clear. The judge must either help or punish; the two functions are considered incompatible. Girls are rarely punished. A variety of help is offered, however, including accommodations in residential settings where there is no concern about custody.

If a juvenile spends a night (the legal maximum) in a police lock-up in France, the setting is usually unpleasant. However, the police in France usually try to contact an *éducateur* (correctional social worker) the same day a youth is picked up by the police. Prisons are used for detention, with either a wing or a separate section being used for young men under 25. Juveniles are held in a separate portion of this wing. Detention is not provided separately for those not yet proven guilty; thus a sentenced youth would go to the same place. These are not nice places, but when a judge finally uses this alternative, she usually considers the case a failure, after other alternatives have been tried.

There is a wide range of non-custodial group homes in France, but the essential difference from North America is that the juveniles have decided to be there. Such placements are negotiated with a judge, not the result of a decision after a trial. If a juvenile decides to leave a group home, she cannot be punished. The *éducateur* may be annoyed, the judge may be displeased, but putting a juvenile in jail for running away is not a choice that is even considered (Syndicat de la Magistrature, 1979). Failure to follow an administrative decision is not a crime, and children can only be imprisoned for committing crimes. If residential placement is to help a juvenile, judges and social workers in France agree that the child must want to stay there. Admittedly, the judge can exert pressure on a youth, but the threat of prison is not an alternative. To understand these different attitudes towards custody, it is necessary to review decision making at the early stages in the process.

Juvenile Justice Processing in France

The French police do not lay charges; they simply refer the case to the ***procureur***, a magistrate who performs a role comparable to our prosecutors. The *procureur* can screen out the case or send it to the juvenile court judge **(*juge des enfants*)**. Complicated cases or serious crimes go to the *juge d'instruction*, a magistrate who has the responsibility for more detailed investigations. Perhaps 90 percent of juvenile cases are handled informally in the judge's office. Juveniles who have been dealt with informally cannot be incarcerated. However, if the case is serious or if the child continues to offend, the judge refers the case to trial in the formal courtroom, where two lay judges sit with the *juge des enfants* (the same judge, incidentally) while the *procureur* and defence lawyer present their arguments. After a trial, a juvenile can be sentenced to the juvenile wing of prison, usually for a maximum of a few weeks. Rehabilitative efforts are not undertaken when youths are given punitive sentences, but despite this reasoning, I have seen teachers and social workers making modest helping efforts inside prisons.

Even without using the formal courtroom, the judge has considerable power. She can detain a juvenile temporarily prior to a trial, but this decision is limited to those who are considered dangerous. The numbers in detention are small compared with those in Canada. In practice, the judges, working from their offices, spend the vast majority of their time offering a wide range of welfare services (Girault, 1984).

The judge can assign a correctional social worker (an *éducateur*) to supervise the juvenile, but if the juvenile resists supervision, the judge cannot legally place her in a closed institution, i.e., prison. Of course, judges can harass or coerce juveniles in other ways. For example, they can have the police bring the youth to the office and can use the symbolic position of the judge in a very persuasive way; but unless the juvenile wishes to be "helped," little will be accomplished. Thus, when the judge forgoes a punitive sanction, the focus is on finding alternatives that are likely to gain the cooperation of the juvenile. When the judge decides not to use the formal court machinery, no distinction is made between delinquency and welfare cases; the emphasis turns to meeting the needs of the juvenile. Instead of handing down decisions, French judges concentrate on working out options and arranging services.

Judges discuss placements with juveniles rather extensively. If family ties are positive, arrangements can be flexible, making it easy for a juvenile to keep in touch with parents. Being placed in a residential facility becomes a matter of negotiation, rather than a "sentence." Nor are such placements designed to keep juveniles out of the community.

French judges are expected to be well informed about their cases, have background information, and use it constructively without being biased by it. By contrast, in our concern for the rights of juveniles in North America, we make it difficult for them to tell their story to someone who has the power to help. The Canadian Young Offenders Act mandates that a juvenile is not required to face a judge, police officer, or someone else in authority without having a parent, lawyer, or advocate at her side. A Canadian youth, afraid to talk in front of her parents, will have difficulty telling her story in private to the judge. In France, the judge frequently talks to the juvenile without the parents being present. Some French juveniles pointed out to me that the judge was the one person with whom they felt comfortable.

In contrast to French juvenile courts, Canadian courts are relatively unconcerned about adjusting their needs to those of the clients. When I was studying courts in southern France, the chief judge in Nice was meeting a family at 6:00 P.M. on a Friday. The parents would miss work at other times, the judge explained. Our system simply schedules cases; parents and others are expected to take time off work or make other sometimes difficult adjustments. Then they may spend only a few moments in court, often without having the opportunity to discuss matters that they felt were relevant.

One juvenile left a residential facility near Paris and went to the court to talk to "his" judge. The judge was away for a few days, but the juvenile did not wish to talk with anyone else or with another judge. The French respect the relationship between juveniles and "their" judges, so the juvenile was accommodated in a residence until "his" judge returned.

Solving Problems Rather Than Making Judicial Rulings

The difference in judicial practices between France and North America is illustrated by the case of a 14-year-old girl temporarily staying in a small group home near Paris. She was in conflict with her mother, who wanted her to continue in school; the girl wished to take a course in hairstyling. The girl ran away from home, stole food, and appeared before the judge in his office. The petty theft charge was immediately set aside, and arrangements were made for the girl to stay in the group home. The social workers were encouraging the girl to return home and go along with the mother to a greater degree. If the girl were older, for example 16, the judge might have considered helping the girl be on her own, but because she was only 14, both social worker and judge encouraged a family reconciliation. The judge was not acting against the juvenile so much as playing an intermediary role between parents and juvenile. Nor was the judge imposing a decision. Hopefully, the family would work it out, but in the meantime, shelter and food were provided. The petty theft charge that brought the girl to court was seen as unimportant.

In Canada, such flexibility would be unlikely. Social services would have to "apprehend" a child. The province would have to become the "guardian." Formal decisions must be made in court, with legal representation from all sides. The Canadian system does not simply provide temporary room and board while things get sorted out. The government bureaucracy cannot provide much support without "taking over."

A French judge was visiting an open-custody group home in Canada, where boys were serving sentences but were able to attend school in the community. One boy was doing very well but was finishing his six-month sentence. Therefore, he could no longer stay in this "correctional" facility, but would have to be placed somewhere by social services. The French judge asked, "If he is doing well, why can't he stay?" But in our system, juveniles "serve time" in one place under one bureaucracy, and are then transferred to another. The

French judge was amazed that a Canadian judge could not order a facility to keep housing a juvenile if the setting seemed to be working so well. Bureaucratic needs do not necessarily fit the needs of clients.

The French system has its weaknesses, but it seems better designed to deliver those services that make sense to an individual young person. In Canada, a juvenile is processed by many professionals who have varying degrees of power over her life. In France one person who knows a great deal about the juvenile—the judge—listens to the juvenile and then has the power to provide a wide range of help. If that fails, punishment is available.

Distributing Resources among Legal and Helping Services

The Canadian system spends scarce resources supporting legalistic rituals, most of which yield a poor return, and fiscal constraints lead to a decrease in helping services. Although the French system is too different from ours to be seriously considered, Melbourne, Australia, uses a legal system much like ours. However, four judges seem to be able to serve three million people, whereas in Edmonton eight judges serve 700 000. The way legal-aid lawyers are trained as public defenders and utilized in Melbourne seems to be a key factor in creating greater efficiency and more intelligent handling of juvenile cases (Hackler, 1992b). Within common-law systems in Canada, the U.S., England, and Australia, there are local systems that appear to be more effective. In Canada, for example, Quebec uses public defenders and prosecutors in a way that helps them gain experience in Youth Court. This may be one factor that reduces the flow of cases into institutions in Quebec. The study of local differences sometimes indicates that minor differences in practices can yield significant differences in outcomes (Hackler, 1991c). Alberta has introduced staff lawyers into the Youth Courts, which seems to have improved the system and also reduced costs (RPM Planning Associates, 1996).

The Youth Criminal Justice Act

In 2001 the federal government had been struggling for over two years with a proposed Youth Criminal Justice Act (YCJA) to replace the Young Offenders Act. I believe this was a political move to appease voters. To satisfy the right, the proposed act would allow an adult sentence for any youth 14 years old convicted of a serious offence. Although previous amendments of the YOA to make it harsher have rarely been used by judges, governments often feel they can win votes by "getting tough." In fact, those who think punishment is the cure to crime are never satisfied.

To appease others, the proposed act encourages greater use of alternative measures. In reality, the YOA offers the same opportunities. The police, judges, and others constantly look for alternatives. The actual use of these measures depends on the options available, not on the legislation. When the YOA was passed in 1984, it led to an increase in the formal use of the system. Legalistic practices may have interfered with informal strategies. For the past decade we have been seeing less use of the formal juvenile justice system, possibly because local agencies have finally learned to work together and use the YOA in a more innovative manner. I predict that the YCJA will create turmoil for several years and strain the local networks that have been established to respond with greater flexibility. Attention will again be directed to interpreting this clumsy proposed legislation, leaving less energy for constructive responses to troublesome juveniles.

Rediscovering Restorative Justice

Restorative justice focuses on correcting wrongs, on restitution of losses, including material damage and mental suffering (Bazemore and Walgrave, 1998). It involves face-to-face confrontation between offenders, victims, relatives, respected members of the community, and others. Victims are usually angry when they come face-to-face with offenders, but often offenders are ashamed and become involved in what can be a healing process. The shaming is designed to reintegrate the offender into the mainstream of society (Braithwaite, 1989). Sometimes complete restitution is not possible and even a repentant offender can only make partial repayment, but the gesture itself is important.

These ideas are not new. Many of the Native peoples in Canada have practised restorative justice for centuries, as have many parts of the world. About two decades ago, the Maori people of New Zealand convinced the government that the Native justice system was superior to the one imposed by the British Empire, not just for the Maoris, but for everyone (Morris and Maxwell, 1997). These ideas have taken root in places like Sparwood, BC, as well as in other parts of Canada.

Like other panaceas in the past, restorative justice is currently something of a fad. Barry Feld (1998) is cautious about jumping on this new bandwagon. Canadian systems have had a tendency to adopt ideas pioneered elsewhere without paying attention to pitfalls. Restorative justice looks promising, but assessing the views of critics like Feld should be part of any new programs.

A Cause for Optimism: The Adaptability of Local Systems

Despite the barriers to effective action created by some of our bureaucracies, resourceful individuals at the local level often overcome a variety of obstacles. In one small community, an experienced judge and an experienced prosecutor were faced with a man who had been charged with "leaving the scene of an accident." His car had turned over in the ditch, and the driver crawled out of the car and passed out in the tall grass nearby. When the RCMP discovered the car, they did not find the passed-out driver. In court, the defendant had no lawyer and repeatedly made it clear that he was drunk, even when the judge kept assuring him that he had not been charged with drunk driving. Neither the police nor the prosecutor was trying to be harsh, and the judge finally dismissed the case. The system did not try to crush the defendant. The point of this story is that, with experienced personnel who know how things operate, the system can be humanized, can become more efficient, and can possibly be made more just. A legal-aid lawyer defending this case would have earned more money by asking for adjournments and complicating the matter considerably. I am not arguing against legal aid, but if legal aid were to hire public defenders on a salary, instead of paying them according to the number of times they appear in court, the client and the public would be better served. Our present system is designed to reward inefficiency.

Despite my criticisms of the Canadian criminal justice system, and the juvenile system in particular, I have seen many illustrations of innovative and imaginative individuals making rigid bureaucracies perform more adequately.

The North American preoccupation with punishing people blinds policy-makers to the progress that has been made in other parts of the world. North Americans seem puzzled by the willingness of Europeans and others to use alternatives to punishment and legal rituals as a way of responding to criminal behaviour. Fortunately, the federal government in Canada is giving some thought to change. The Twelfth Report of the Standing Committee on Justice and the Solicitor General (1993) to the House of Commons actually stated, "If locking up those who violate the law contributed to safer societies, then the United States should be the safest country in the world" (2). The report went on to say that the U.S. affords a glaring example of the limited impact criminal justice responses have on crime. This argument has been made by criminologists for years, so it is gratifying that it is finally being heard by members of the House of Commons. Perhaps things will change if restitution and mediation become part of our response to crime. When victims receive restitution, their desire to punish the offender is greatly reduced. This frees the court to make punishment consistent with the rehabilitative needs of the offender, rather than the animosity of the victim.

At the same time Canadians need to overcome their smugness with regard to the U.S. and the research produced there. True, many things should not be imitated, but the U.S. has done many extensive evaluations of creative crime-prevention programs in many different settings. This offers a cafeteria of useful ideas that could counter our tendency to repeat ineffective strategies to reduce crime.

SUMMARY

1. The "broken windows" approach to crime prevention focuses on community disorder and encourages some "zero-tolerance" policing practices. This approach may have led to dealing with symptoms rather than causes.

2. The Project on Human Development in Chicago Neighborhoods looked at collective efficacy. When there is mutual trust among neighbours and feelings of shared obligations, they are more likely to intervene for the common good. The study also argued that both crime and disorder stem from structural characteristics. Residential stability, for example, helps residents build a stake in the community.

3. The North American tendency to concentrate on legal ritual and the adversarial nature of our proceedings can reduce the effectiveness of our criminal justice system.

4. Compared with systems in other countries, our Youth Courts may be contributing to crime by aggravating rather than helping family situations.

5. Professionals in local systems frequently show considerable creativity in making the formal system work better.

KEY TERMS

collective efficacy   270
éducateur   278
juge des enfants   279
juge d'instruction   273
procureur   279

restorative justice   282
"stealing conflicts"   277
"weeding and seeding"   275
Young Offenders Act (YOA)   276
zero-tolerance strategies   269

WEBLINKS

www.digeratiweb.com/sociorealm

National Crime Prevention Council: information on crime-prevention projects across Canada.

www.restorativejustice.org/

Restorative Justice Online: providing links to statutes, regulations, and articles on restorative justice.

CRIMINOGENIC CONDITIONS: IMPLICATIONS FOR CRIME REDUCTION

This chapter will:

- Argue that a subculture of power abuse among corporate leaders leads to a criminogenic mindset that influences the entire society.

- Explore ways of reducing crime by modifying the behaviour of elite members of society.

- Broaden our thinking about crime to include unethical behaviour and argue that using public policy to influence antisocial behaviour would eventually influence conventional crime.

- Suggest that "reintegrative shaming" can be used to counter the subculture of power abuse.

- Argue that societies that care for the weak and the poor more effectively also have less crime.

- Claim that increased use of prisons and other "get-tough" policies have not led to decreases in crime.

CHANGING THE CONDITIONS THAT LEAD TO CRIME

Is a high level of crime inevitable in modern society? Should we accept higher levels of crime as the price we must pay for the individualism, freedom, excitement, and material wealth generated by the free-enterprise system? Economists tell us that the human costs associated with increased efficiency are inevitable, but these costs will be balanced by the ultimate rewards that come from "progress" and economic growth.

Should we accept the notion that governments can do nothing meaningful about crime? Admittedly, most of the various "wars on crime" are cynical, politically motivated, and ill-founded; in fact, the U.S. has adopted crime-*producing* policies for decades, such as official responses to drug use. Admittedly, many creative projects have demonstrated modest success in local situations. While there are no grand cures, many countries have adopted strategies that are superior to those used in Canada. Unfortunately, Canada has been influenced by the punitive approach followed by most of the United States (Gordon, 1991), which has produced, and probably will continue to produce, ineffective responses to crime. Many people in the U.S. see crime as a reflection of the decline in individual morality rather than as evidence of flaws in the basic economic and social structure. Similarly, many who work in the Canadian justice system say they are serious about crime, but they are largely performing rituals that perpetuate the "justice juggernaut." Our responses to crime reflect the needs of politicians to win elections, of newspapers to make sales, and of the general population to blame someone else. Given the characteristics of modern society, are there any broad strategies that could decrease crime in general?

In Chapter 12, on drug crime, I argued that the distribution of drug use resembled a skewed curve and that a meaningful change in hard-drug use would require changes in all drug-use patterns. The point was that focusing on the worst offenders would make little difference because they were relatively rare. Violence is distributed the same way; a meaningful change in violence required changes in violent behaviour at all levels. Focusing on the few murderers would yield fewer returns than trying to change the frequent violent behaviour among children and in families. I would like to extend this logic to the moral behaviour of some of the most influential role models in society—the business elite.

Reducing Crime by Changing the Behaviour of the Elite

In the chapter on property crime (Chapter 14) I argued that a subculture of power abuse is part of corporate crime. Furthermore, this pattern not only is criminogenic for the business world but is generally antisocial. It is worth attempting to change this criminogenic climate for two reasons: (1) public policy can change corporate boardroom ethics more easily than actual corporate crime, and (2) prosocial changes in the corporate boardroom would probably lead to a decrease in corporate and other crime. Naturally, the reader will wonder how a decrease in corporate crime could influence other crime. This is far from obvious, but there is no clear line between behaviour that is immoral and unethical and that which is criminal. Thus, there is a link between crime and the subculture of power abuse. But how would changes in ethical behaviour actually reduce crime? Or specifically, how would prosocial changes in the corporate boardroom lead to a decrease in corporate and other crime? The reasoning is the same as the reasoning applied earlier regarding drugs and violence. If we were to lump together all "immoral acts" they could be distributed from ideal behaviour to very immoral behaviour on a continuum that one might call a **morality curve** (Figure 18.1).

The dotted line in Figure 18.1 suggests there are criminals in the corporate and public area who are distinct in their immorality: those who fall under the second hump on the right in the curve represented by the dotted line. A number of well-publicized cases indicate that some members of the business elite are clearly criminals. Many corporate executives would say that these corporate criminals are the exception, different from those who award wealth to themselves legally. The latter consider themselves "respectable" businesspeople. They do not see themselves as perfect, but neither do they believe they are cheaters.

This bifurcation of bad and good makes the same mistake I described earlier. It creates a mental set which claims that certain select people should be punished while the rest of us can continue as usual. In fact, the solid line, not the dotted line, represents reality. There is no clear border between those who engage in different degrees of immorality. The solid line indicates that people who are more immoral are fewer in numbers, but there is no clear distinction between the criminals and the unethical.

As with drug use and violent crime, one cannot change the *shape* of this curve, but it can be moved to the left or right. In the U.S., in contrast to Norway for example, the morality

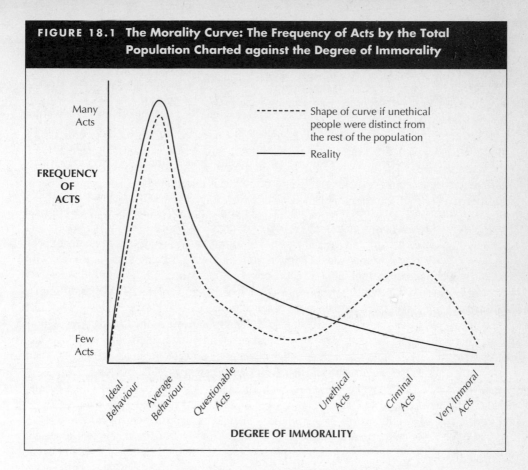

FIGURE 18.1 The Morality Curve: The Frequency of Acts by the Total Population Charted against the Degree of Immorality

curve has been pulled to the right in the business sector, as well as in the rest of the society. Corporate executives abuse power more, lawyers cheat more, and average citizens lie about their income tax more. The morality curve in North America spreads out to the right. Not surprisingly, lower-class people and those belonging to certain minorities, who feel neglected, recognize the lack of justice in their society and feel less guilt about cheating, stealing, or even burglarizing the homes of others.

Admittedly, I oversimplify the argument, but social life hangs together in an interconnected web of morality. A culture that values honesty and concern for others displays general concerns on moral issues. The situation represented by the dotted line in Figure 18.1 is the myth created by many. It suggests different responses for the bad and the good. Punish those *few* corporate criminals who get caught and ignore the rest. This has little impact on the morality curve. But if the *many* corporate executives currently abusing their power improved their behaviour, it could move the entire morality curve to the left. *These leaders have a greater-than-average impact on others; thus, the spread of higher moral principles among the powerful could eventually have an impact on all crime.*

Using Public Policy to Decrease Antisocial Behaviour among the Elite

Corporations sometimes need government to save them from ruthless competition that is potentially destructive. The competition to pay excessive salaries is influenced by these pressures. Prestige factors make it difficult for executives to accept more realistic salaries. What can governments do? Salaries, and other benefits, should be deductible as company expenses only up to a certain level. An executive salary of ten times that of the average worker might be the limit allowable as an expense to the corporation. Only $100 000 might be allotted to be divided among the board of directors. Benefits beyond these limits would come directly out of profits and require an explanation in the company's annual report and in a newsletter produced by the Toronto Stock Exchange.

American public companies must reveal the salaries of their CEOs to the stockholders. The Toronto Stock Exchange made a similar requirement in 1993, but the TSE could provide more information: who sits on how many boards of directors? What interest-free loans, stock options, and other privileges were they given? If you were the owner of a company or principal of a school, you would want to know if your employee is being paid for a second job and is neglecting her current job. CEOs are often getting paid for doing multiple jobs.

As long as the industrial elite has extensive power over government, it will be difficult to influence tax legislation, or to change the practice of the Toronto Stock Exchange; but such changes would be easier to achieve than would changes in some of the technical regulations and enforcement that currently exist in safety standards, pollution, and other areas in which corporate crime is common. Nor should such changes be unwelcome to all executives. There are many commercial leaders who find that the **intrinsic rewards** of doing a job well outweigh the **extrinsic rewards**, such as obscenely high salaries. Imagine an executive who is earning $250 000, is well respected, and performs her job well; she has created job security for her workers, reduced pollution and danger in the plant, and has a husband and children who are proud of her. A secure person in such a position might find that extrinsic compensations add little to her quality of life. Many such people take pleasure in their calling and are not overly concerned about material rewards. Some even have the respect of their business colleagues.

John Coleman was formerly chairman of the Federal Reserve Bank of Philadelphia, president of Haverford College, and president of the Edna McConnell Clark Foundation in New York City, which gives grants aimed at ameliorating social problems. But he also took time off from his more prestigious roles to work as a garbage man, ditch-digger, kitchen worker, roughneck on an oil rig, hired hand, and correctional officer in prison. He even assumed a different identity to spend time as an inmate in five prisons (Coleman, 1980). Mr. Coleman would be among those influential people who provide prosocial role models for leaders.

Baseball offers a similar analogy. In the April 11, 1998, *Globe and Mail*, Carl Hiebert describes the way Mennonites play baseball:

> There is not a lot of chatter and certainly no jeering. If someone drops a ball, there is no bemoaning the fact. If the runner says he is safe, he's safe. There is no dispute.... they often don't keep score. Everything is geared toward fun, not beating someone.

> [Some would argue that the qualities that make baseball are fire and grit—the killer instinct exemplified by Pete Rose running over the catcher at home plate.]

> It's baseball, but I don't think its a healthy interpretation compared to what the Mennonites play.... Is someone whose reflexes are 30-per-cent better than someone else's worth $7-million

a year? Is the world a better place?... I see the Mennonite way as a much more healthy way of being.

Mennonite attitudes are rare in corporate boardrooms, but it still may be possible to shame powerful people who engage in antisocial behaviour.

Using Reintegrative Shaming to Counter a "Subculture of Power Abuse"

Reintegrative shaming can be used to make conventional criminals feel ashamed and make them wish to redeem themselves in order to become acceptable members of society. By the same token, could it not also be used even more effectively on those members of the elite who have behaved in an antisocial manner? After all, many of them claim to be upright members of society.

A newsletter put out by the Toronto Stock Exchange should comment critically on corporate leaders who gouge their corporations and the public. If a tobacco company conducts smoking contests among children in developing countries to get them addicted to nicotine, it is impossible to convict the chief executive officer of the tobacco company. However, he could be identified in the press, along with photographs. If he goes to church, the preacher should refuse to shake his hand, and reject his contribution to the church. In other words, he should be shamed. The families of such individuals should be ashamed of them. Such shame could be a powerful force in changing unethical behaviour generated by the criminogenic subculture that pervades the highly concentrated business elite in Canada. At the same time, business leaders who make genuine contributions and strive to make their corporations more socially responsible should be recognized. Furthermore, executives who abandon their abusive practices and acknowledge the misuse of their positions should be "reintegrated" into the world of honourable persons. This lies at the heart of the concept of reintegrative shaming (Braithwaite, 1989).

Although powerful people can easily resist technical regulations designed to keep them from harming others, self-esteem is still important to them. Threats to that self-esteem can result in change. Medical doctors who exploit their positions, lawyers who misuse others, commercial leaders who swindle society, and professors who abuse students are part of a subculture of power abuse that characterizes a portion of the elite in North American society. I would generalize the findings of Hawkins (1984), Vogel (1986), and Kelman (1981) beyond the directly criminogenic business subculture that distinguishes North America from Japan, the UK, Australia, and Sweden. Not only do structural imperatives in North America lead to more corporate crime, they contribute to unethical corporate practices that support leaders who share in this subculture of power abuse. A circular pattern develops, which perpetuates itself.

If societal responses to commercial deviance are limited to the criminal justice system, few unethical people will be shamed. This will not move the morality curve to the left. On the other hand, if we focus on common offences, such as the income-tax evasion of many wealthy people, we include a much larger number of wrong-doers. The sanctions against income-tax evaders do not have to be severe, nor do they have to involve the criminal justice system, but they should threaten the self-images of these supposedly decent citizens. Professors who accept salaries when they are on sabbatical, or dentists who purchase expensive art works for their offices, depreciate them over five years, and then take them home, are illustrations of unethical behaviour. They are rarely convicted of crimes, but can they be shamed?

Other legal activities could certainly be questioned; accounting practices, for example. Accounting firms sometimes look the other way when crimes are discovered. "Senior executives are embarrassed by the revelation of fraud in their backyard," said Robert Chambers of Toronto-based KPMG Peat Marwick Thorne (*Maclean's*, July 27, 1992). It reflects on their competence. As the London *Times* editorialized, "Accountants are the private police force of capitalism.... If accountancy is rotten, then that rottenness spreads through the system and confidence is shaken" (*Times*, March 16, 1992). It is unlikely that accounting firms will be disciplined by regulations; but because of the pervasiveness of their role in the business world, exposing unethical accounting practices and naming the people involved could influence the behaviour of accountants and businesses.

The subculture of power abuse also applies to other professions. The economic structure of law, medicine, and many other disciplines encourages an emphasis on material wealth. The "worth" of some professionals is judged by their income. Rarely is this characteristic of our society viewed as criminogenic. Actions that improve the ethical behaviour of many people who commit a wide range of questionable acts can move the entire morality curve to the left. By contrast, actions that have a severe impact on the few people who are on the extreme right of the curve do not move the morality curve very much.

I am not suggesting abandoning the enforcement of rules against corporate crime. Rather, I suggest broadening the criticism and shaming of individuals involved in unethical behaviour. Treating powerful people in society as uniformly venal and selfish is unrealistic, but identifying *individuals* who abuse their power is realistic. Braithwaite and Grabosky (1985) feel that it is worthwhile beginning with the assumption that business leaders think of themselves as upright citizens making a contribution to the society. Perhaps this assumption is naive, but even if wrong, giving it lip-service may counter the growth of a subculture of power abuse.

To summarize, criminalizing *specific* corporate deviance may help to identify areas of concern, but it will have little impact on the reduction of crime. Enforcing criminal rules has been very difficult and largely ineffective. On the other hand, shaming those who are the models of society might erode the subculture of power abuse and move significant numbers of influential leaders in the direction of prosocial behaviour. *A little success with many has more impact than the rare success with the truly corrupt*, and would move the entire morality curve to the left.

CARING FOR THE WEAK AND THE LINK TO CRIME

The second theme of this chapter suggests that societies that take better care of the weak have less crime. Today we have a **"selfish majority,"** an economically comfortable population that accepts increasing destitution for a growing underclass and a deteriorating public sector (Hackler, 1993). This encourages short-sightedness and the mistaken belief that private riches and public squalor will adequately serve a modern society (Galbraith, 1992). It is difficult to win elections by appealing to altruism, even though the quality of life for all of us is related to how well we deal with environmental issues, mass transportation, education, and other areas of public concern.

One way to look at the impact of the contented majority on the way a society serves its total population is to look at infant mortality rates, that is, the number of infant (under the age of one) deaths per 1000 live births. This is acknowledged to be the best measure for comparing countries in terms of medical care. The infant mortality rate may also reflect our concern for mothers and children as well as our success in helping the vulnerable members of society.

How does infant mortality in Canada and the United States compare with the rate in the rest of the world? The United States spends more money on medical care per capita than any other country in the world. Canada is second. Over the past 30 years the U.S. has dropped from around sixth in the world to around thirtieth.

Most of us are aware that Northern Europe is ahead of Canada and the U.S. in terms of health care, but Table 18.1, showing mortality rates of selected countries from the 1996 World Population Data Sheet, may include some surprises.

TABLE 18.1 Infant Mortality Rates—1996			
Singapore	4.0	Canada	6.2
Japan	4.2	Netherlands Antilles	6.3
Sweden	4.4	Slovenia	6.5
Hong Kong	5.0	Israel	6.9
Taiwan	5.1	Spain	7.2
Ireland	5.9	Brunei	7.4
Martinique	6.0	San Marino	7.5
Macao	6.0	United States	7.5

The left-hand column shows rates better than Canada's 6.2. The right-hand column lists additional countries with rates equal to or better than the U.S. rate of 7.5. Admittedly, the difference between some of these rates is small, and the rankings change somewhat from year to year. However, the U.S. normally ranks with the Czech Republic, Greece, and Portugal, with Cuba and Malta not far behind. It is not a world leader. Canadians like to think of themselves as a bit superior. We may acknowledge that Northern Europe has better medical care, but can we say that Taiwan is more concerned about its children? Or Ireland? Or Macao?

Looking at the second column, should we conclude that Spain, Slovenia, and Brunei have created more caring societies? The U.S. government response to the inferior medical care given to many Americans has been to propose tax credits so people can purchase medical insurance. Tax credits, of course, mean little to the impoverished. Furthermore, the thousand-plus health insurance companies in the U.S. are in business to make a profit. Their goal is to insure healthy people and avoid insuring sick people. Health is one of the many social concerns that cannot be well served by the profit motive. When we hear about the various ways of improving medical care, or providing social services in general, looking to the U.S. for guidance is like asking the Taliban how to improve women's rights in Afghanistan.

In general, countries with low infant mortality rates have lower crime rates. Naturally, correlation is not the same as causality. However, *caring for the weak probably reduces crime.*

Child Poverty and Crime Reduction

This is not a book about social welfare, medical care, and child poverty. It should be obvious, however, that child poverty leads to crime. Furthermore, it is much more economical for a society to take action early, rather than pay for the consequences later. Every dollar spent helping pregnant women buy nutritious food and teaching them about diet saves nearly three dollars in health-care costs in one year alone (Canadian Centre on Substance Abuse, 1992). Proper nutrition reduces the rate of low-birth-weight babies by 25 percent. Low birth weight contributes to mental retardation, cerebral palsy, vision and hearing loss, and impaired school performance. Doing badly in school is clearly related to delinquency and future crime. Child poverty is criminogenic. The real question is: how well have we been protecting children?

The sources of income of families of poor children in the U.S. have changed. The contribution from fathers fell sharply from the 1960s to the 1980s, caused by the decline in the earning potential of young adults and the shift towards one-parent, mostly female-headed, households. An increased proportion of the income of poor families comes from public-assistance programs, especially the food-stamp program (Bane and Ellwood, 1989). This contributes to a "culture of poverty." The children of such households are less likely to escape poverty as they become adults. For the selfish majority, they are now "welfare bums."

This logic could be extended to issues such as homelessness. Hagan and McCarthy (1997a) found that homeless adolescents participated in more serious crimes after they left home. They also noted that changes in criminal activity did not appear to be due to the direct effects of background variables. In other words, regardless of race, education, and gender, being poor and homeless creates the potential for crime.

The Manitoba Basic Annual Income Experiment (Mincome) was an experimental test of guaranteed income (Hum and Simpson, 1991). Many fear that a guaranteed annual income would reduce the incentive to work. The study concludes that such fears are largely misplaced. Ideas about systematic income distribution in general should be taken seriously. Between 1974 and 1988 in the U.S., the income share of the nation's richest one-fifth increased from 41 to 44 percent, while the share received by the poorest one-fifth fell from 5.5 percent to 4.6 percent (Phillips, 1990). Despite a booming economy toward the turn of the century, the gap between rich and poor continues to widen. This should be criminogenic, but actually crime rates have gone down slightly. It is possible that efforts to reduce violence in the home are beginning to bear fruit even though other factors still tear at the societal fabric.

Blumstein and Wallman (2000) attribute the recent drop in violent crime to a decrease in the lethal violence connected with crack cocaine dealings, in which young black males carry guns to protect their valuable cargo. In the long run, however, legitimate opportunities to success would offer alternatives to drug dealing.

These ideas are not original. In his book, *Confronting Crime* (1985), Elliot Currie writes, "If we are serious about attacking the roots [of crime] ... we must build a society that is less unequal, less depriving, less insecure, less disruptive of community ties, less corrosive of cooperative values. In short, we must begin to take on the enormous task of creating the conditions of community life in which individuals can live together in compassionate and cooperative ways" (225–26). Policy-makers in the U.S. and Canada have encouraged, directly or by default, social and economic forces that undermine social cohesion. This increases crime, with the result that we "invoke a grossly outsized penal system to contain the predictable consequences, without notable success" (226).

The Bankruptcy of Prisons and of the "Get-Tough" Approach

Despite evidence that deviance is a product of marginality, the U.S. has been caught up in an unproductive "get-tough" approach to crime for several decades. California offers an excellent model of what should be avoided (Blomberg and Cohen, 1995). That state ignored scientific knowledge in favour of political expediency. From 1980 to 1995, the state's prison population grew by 600 percent. To pay for the fivefold increase in the corrections budget, California has sacrificed other services, such as education. The Department of Corrections estimated that it will need 20 more prisons in addition to the current 28 plus the 12 on the drawing board. By 2001, California anticipates 109 000 more prisoners behind bars serving life sentences. Admittedly, this pattern is beginning to change. The prison-building boom means that larger numbers of inmates will soon complete their sentences and return to the community as alienated and bitter men. Many will be African Americans and Hispanics, and they will move to the cities. Even California politicians recognize this as a potentially explosive situation.

Japan provides a contrast to California. In 1990, Japan's imprisonment rate was only 11 percent of that in the U.S. and was declining (Elmer Johnson, 1996). Criminals in Japan are expected to feel shame, confess, display repentance, ask forgiveness from the victim, and provide monetary payments to those hurt. When they act according to these cultural norms, they are diverted from prisons. Imprisonment does not work well in Japan either. It leads to recidivism.

Malta is also a highly integrated society with a strong sense of community and commitment to family life. Consistent with most criminological knowledge, this is correlated with low levels of crime and incarceration. However, those who are imprisoned become recidivists. It seems that prisons don't help much in Malta either (Baumer, 1997).

It is possible that well-integrated societies influence the *initiation* of criminal behaviour but have little impact on the *continuation* of such behaviour once it has begun. For those already involved in crime, participation in criminal subcultures, such as prison, may support continuance of criminal behaviour (Smith and Brame, 1994).

Malta may practise *disintegrative shaming* or stigmatization instead of integrative shaming. Some tightly knit communities are intolerant of individual deviants. This can make reintegration difficult. All modern societies have crime and prisons. However, more progressive countries recognize that prisons are part of the problem, not the cure. Criminologists seem to be better at offering things to *avoid* than providing clear guidelines as to what should be done. Past mistakes are easier to analyze. Imprisonment seems to fit this pattern. We can learn from the dramatic increase in prison sentences in the U.S. That country clearly has more violent crime than other stable democracies. Its homicide rate is seven times that of England and Wales. Its murder rate for young men is 52 times higher (Young, 1999). Both men and women systematically avoid parts of many American cities. Since the U.S. is a more dangerous place to live, many lawmakers believe (or think that voters believe) long sentences (and capital punishment) are necessary.

I would argue that societies that use punishment extensively use resources unproductively and fail to consider more fruitful alternatives. For example, investment in education has many payoffs, but *Mother Jones* magazine (July 2001) reports that, since 1980, spending on prisons in the U.S. has grown six times faster than spending on higher education. In addition, the extensive use of punishment sends the wrong message: those with power rely on coercion to solve problems. This can create social conditions that lead to more crime.

Has imprisonment helped? Those who advocate longer sentences say yes. Overall, crime has declined recently in the U.S. However, crime also declined in the majority of advanced industrial countries during this period. Others point to ways in which high rates of imprisonment have torn the social fabric. Supposedly, the U.S. is making progress in terms of racial prejudice, but one in nine of African-American males aged 20 to 29 is in prison.

Despite this high risk of imprisonment, violence continues to decimate the black community. In Canada, First Nations people are over-represented in prison. Has the high incarceration rate deterred crime among First Nations people?

The U.S. provides some excellent research that could help Canada develop more intelligent responses to crime, but U.S. social policies, which largely ignore the research, do not offer useful guidelines. The get-tough approaches, such as more imprisonment or punishing the parents of juveniles, may contain grains of truth, but such strategies obscure the larger lesson: *If an advanced society requires heavy-handed police tactics, punitive courts, and the extensive use of prisons to keep the underclass in line, then the society itself is functioning badly and should be changed.*

Canada has been resisting the U.S. pattern. During the 1990s conditional sentences in the community increased slightly, federal incarcerations (two years and longer) went down slightly, while provincial incarcerations (under two years) remained fairly stable (Lonmo, 2001). Custodial remand, however, increased.

The decreasing crime rate in Canada may be leading to fewer incarcerations, but it is also possible that Correctional Services Canada has been able to resist the political pressures to use imprisonment the way it has been used in parts of the U.S.

A Cautionary Note on Oversimplifying Cures

Even if we reduced the criminogenic pressures that arise from the neglect of weaker members in a society, there would still be crime. However, the conflict theorists, along with liberal humanists, who emphasize structural variables, come closest to identifying the major sources of crime. They may not agree on specific policy strategies, but as we look around the world for societies that have done better than North America, a number of northern European countries come to mind. Sweden provides better opportunities than does Canada for the adequate nurturance of children. Sweden still has delinquency and crime and, like the U.S. and Canada, a small group of serious offenders who contribute disproportionately (Sarnecki, 1986).

Social policies form a **hierarchy of effectiveness.** Those societies, such as Canada, that have considerable structural inequality, would probably reduce crime the most by policies that reduce such inequality. The more socially developed countries of northern Europe have already applied the principles argued by the conflict theorists and those criminologists who emphasize structural variables. Next would be policies that strengthen the family and the quality of community life. Again, more effective models exist in Europe than in North America, although programs in North America regarding family violence may be yielding modest gains. At a lower level of effectiveness, theoretical orientations emphasizing group processes, such as control theory, become more relevant.

Sarnecki (1989) notes that in Sweden the economic interdependence that links different generations has diminished. Children do not feel as obligated to, or have the need to, support parents. The opportunity for youth to interact with adults as part of meaningful jobs has been reduced. Children are less likely to follow the occupation of their parents. Youth are not socially integrated through work, as they were with farm work, apprenticeships, and the like. Paul Friday argues that adolescents in Sweden are more socially isolated and dependent on the peer group. "The more dependent one is on that group, the more the group's definitions prevail.... The earlier the emancipation, the greater the group dependency" (1992: 242) and the greater the likelihood of crime.

Having reduced the explanatory power of social class and dealt more effectively with major criminogenic conditions, more egalitarian societies may find that social psychological theories, routine activities theory, psychological orientations, and perhaps even biological factors become more relevant. However, it is unrealistic to think that we can take a young Native man in a Canadian prison, who has grown up in criminogenic conditions, counsel him, then release him in downtown Vancouver, and assume that he has been "cured" of criminal behaviour. The fact that we naively continue to "counsel" offenders to go straight is a reflection of the power of the counselling industry, rather than an intelligent approach to crime.

Let me close this book with a sociological bias. Specific tinkering could make modest contributions to crime reduction, and we should not ignore these possibilities. But there is also the possibility of creating a *culture* that is less criminogenic. Few people probably believe that changing corporate crime would have an impact on predatory street crime, but I feel that the morality of a society is part of a common social fabric. Powerful and wealthy people influence that morality more than others. While the courts and regulations may have little impact on corporate behaviour, publicity and exposure of their practices could help to control the subculture of power abuse.

While crime is inevitable in complex industrial societies, the level of predatory crime that exists in North America is not. The way our criminal justice system functions probably increases crime; and a range of other social policies work against social cohesiveness, destroy the institutional infrastructure of communities, and interfere with the capacity of families to socialize children into non-deviant adults. Despite the lip-service given by governments to crime prevention, the knowledge for reducing crime has been available and has been applied, at least moderately, in many parts of the world. Canada has a choice: it can continue to mimic the failed governmental practices of the U.S., or it can utilize the knowledge accumulated by criminologists, many of them Americans, and applied with a modest degree of success in other countries of the world.

SUMMARY

1. Focusing on the misbehaviour of the most powerful in society would be a more effective way of reducing crime than concentrating on the conviction of the worst offenders.

2. By responding to a broad range of unethical behaviour and not simply crime, public policy could influence antisocial behaviour that would eventually influence conventional crime.

3. Strategies such as reintegrative shaming could be used for powerful people who behave unethically. This could counter the subculture of power abuse and move the "morality curve" in the direction of higher morality and less crime.

4. Those societies that respond more effectively to the health, education, and general well-being of their children tend to have less crime. Thus, these factors are crucial for crime prevention.

5. The increased use of prisons and other "get-tough" policies have not led to decreases in crime.

6. Societies that have already dealt more effectively with factors like structural inequality may then find that theories emphasizing small-group processes become more relevant.

KEY TERMS

extrinsic rewards   288

hierarchy of effectiveness   294

intrinsic rewards   288

morality curve   286

reintegrative shaming   289

"selfish majority"   290

WEBLINK

www.crime-prevention.org/english/main.html
National Crime Prevention Council of Canada: provides information on federal government crime-prevention projects.

Bibliography

The most useful source of Canadian crime statistics is probably the Juristat series produced by Statistics Canada. The series is available on-line at http://dsp-psd.pwgsc.gc.ca/Collection-R/Statcan/85-002-XIE/85-002-XIE.html.

Adams, Samuel Hopkins. 1955. "The Juke Myth." Saturday Review 38: 13, 48–49.

Addiction Research Foundation. 1989. Annual Report, 1988–89. Toronto: Addiction Research Foundation.

Adelberg, Ellen and Claudia Currie. 1987. Too Few to Count: Canadian Women in Conflict with the Law. Vancouver: Press Gang.

Adler, Freda. 1975. Sisters in Crime: The Rise of the New Female Criminal. New York: McGraw-Hill.

Ageton, Suzanne S. 1983. "The Dynamics of Female Delinquency, 1976–1980." Criminology 21: 555–84.

Agnew, Robert. 1991. "A Longitudinal Test of Social Control Theory and Delinquency." Journal of Research in Crime and Delinquency 28: 126–56.

Agnew, Robert. 1992. "Foundation for a General Strain Theory of Crime and Delinquency." Criminology 30: 47–87.

Agnew, Robert. 1997a. "Stability and Crime over the Life Course: A Strain Theory Explanation." In Terrence P. Thornberry (ed.), Advances in Criminological Theory, Vol. 7: Developmental Theories of Crime and Delinquency. New Brunswick, NJ: Transaction.

Agnew, Robert. 1997b. "The Nature and Determinants of Strain." In Nikos Passas and Robert Agnew (eds.), The Future of Anomie Theory. Boston: Northeastern University Press.

Agnew, Robert and Helene Raskin White. 1992. "An Empirical Test of General Strain Theory." Criminology 30: 475–99.

Agnew, Robert, Francis T. Cullen, Velmer S. Burton Jr., T. David Evans, and R. Gregory Dunaway. 1996. "A New Test of Classic Strain Theory." Justice Quarterly 13: 681–704.

Akers, Ronald L. 1985. Deviant Behavior: A Social Learning Approach (3rd ed.). Belmont, CA: Wadsworth.

Akers, Ronald. L. 1991. "Addiction: The Troublesome Concept." Journal of Drug Issues 21: 777–92.

Alexander, Bruce K., Patricia Hadaway, and Robert Coambs. 1988. "Rat Park Chronicle." In Judith C. Blackwell and Patricia G. Erickson (eds.), Illicit Drugs in Canada: A Risky Business. Scarborough, ON: Nelson Canada.

Allen, H. 1987a. Justice Unbalanced: Gender, Psychiatry, and Judicial Decisions. Milton Keynes, UK: Open University Press.

Allen, H. 1987b. "Rendering Them Harmless: The Professional Portrayal of Women Charged with Serious Violent Crimes." In P. Carlen and A. Worrall (eds.), Gender, Crime and Justice. Milton Keynes, UK: Open University Press.

Amir, Menachim. 1971. Patterns of Forcible Rape. Chicago: University of Chicago Press.

Anderson, John. (forthcoming). "Transcending the Residual Self: Towards a Substantive Theory of Leaving Crime." PhD dissertation. University of Victoria.

Andrews, Don A., Ivan Zinger, Robert D. Hoge, James Bonta, Paul Gendreau, and Francis T. Cullen. 1990. "Does Correctional Treatment Work? A Clinically and Psychologically Informed Meta-analysis." Criminology 28: 369–404.

Appleby, Timothy. 1998. "Crime and Disease Cut by Project." The Globe and Mail, April 14.

Archer, Dane and Rosemary Gartner. 1976. "Violent Acts and Violent Times: A Comparative Approach to Postwar Homicide Rates." American Sociological Review 41: 937–63.

Artz, Sibylle. 1997a. Sex, Power, and the Violent School Girl. Toronto: Trifolium Books.

Artz, Sibylle. 1997b. "On Becoming an Object." Journal of Child and Youth Care 11: 17–37.

Atkins, S. and B. Hoggett. 1984. Women and the Law. Oxford: Basil Blackwell.

Bachman, Jerald G., Lloyd D. Johnston, and Patrick M. O'Malley. 1990. "Explaining the Recent Decline in Drug Use among Young Adults: Further Evidence That Perceived Risks and Disapproval Lead to Reduced Use." Journal of Health and Social Behaviour 31: 173–84.

Bachman, Jerald G., Lloyd D. Johnston, Patrick M. O'Malley, and Ronald H. Humphrey. 1988. "Explaining the Recent Decline in Marijuana Use: Differentiating the Effects of Perceived Risks, Disapproval, and General Lifestyle Factors." Journal of Health and Social Behaviour 29: 92–112.

Backhouse, Constance. 1985. "Nineteenth Century Canadian Prostitution Law: Reflection of a Discriminatory Society." Social History 53: 387–423.

Baere, Margaret. 1996. Criminal Conspiracies: Organized Crime in Canada. Scarborough, ON: Nelson Canada

Baldwin, John. 1979. "Ecological and Areal Studies in Great Britain and the United States." In Norval Morris and Michael Tonry (eds.), Crime and Justice: An Annual Review of Research, Vol. 1. Chicago: University of Chicago Press.

Ball-Rokeach, Sandra J. 1973. "Values and Violence: A Test of the Subculture of Violence Thesis." American Sociological Review 31: 736–49.

Bandura, A. 1973. Aggression: A Social Learning Analysis. Englewood Cliffs, NJ: Prentice-Hall.

Bane, Mary Jo and David Ellwood. 1989. "One Fifth of the Nation's Children: Why Are They Poor?" Science 245: 1047–53.

Barak, Gregg. 1991. Crimes by the Capitalist State: An Introduction to State Criminality. Albany: State University of New York Press.

Barlow, Hugh D. and Lynne Schmidt. 1988. "More on the Role of Weapons in Homicidal Violence." Medicine and Law 7: 347–58.

Barth, Tom, Walter Watson, and Wayne Blanchard. 1966. "Parent–Child Relations in Mass Society." In Jeanette R. Folta and Edith S. Deck (eds.), A Sociological Framework for Patient Care. New York: Wiley.

Bartol, Curt R. and Anne M. Bartol. 1986. Criminal Behavior: A Psychosocial Approach (2nd ed.). Englewood Cliffs, NJ: Prentice-Hall.

Bartusch, Dawn R. Jeglum, Donald R. Lynam, Terrie E. Moffitt, and Phil A. Silva. 1997. "Is Age Important? Testing a General versus a Developmental Theory of Antisocial Behaviour." Criminology 35: 13–48.

Bass, Ellen and Laura Davis. 1997. The Courage to Heal. London: Vermillion.

Battin, Sara R., Karl G. Hill, Robert D. Abbott, Richard F. Calano, and J. David Hawkins. 1998. "The Contribution of Gang Membership to Delinquency beyond Delinquent Friends." Criminology 36: 93–115.

Baumer, Eric. 1997. "Levels and Predictors of Recidivism: The Malta Experience." Criminology 35: 601–28.

Bazemore, Gordon and Lode Walgrave (eds). 1998. Restorative Juvenile Justice. Monsey, NY: Criminal Justice Press.

Beauchesne, Line. 1997. "Legalization of Drugs: Responsible Action towards Health Promotion and Effective Harm Reduction Strategies." In Patricia G. Erickson, Diane M. Riley, Yuet W. Cheung, and Patrick A. O'Hare (eds.), Harm Reduction: A New Direction for Drug Policies and Programs. Toronto: University of Toronto Press.

Beccaria, Cesare. 1963. On Crimes and Punishments. Trans. Henry Paolucci. Indianapolis: Bobbs-Merrill.

Becker, Howard. 1963. Outsiders. New York: Free Press of Glencoe.

Bell, Laurie (ed.). 1987. Good Girls/Bad Girls: Sex Trade Workers and Feminist Face to Face. Toronto: Women's Press.

Bensman, Joseph and Israel Gerver. 1963. "Crime and Punishment in the Factory: The Function of Deviancy in Maintaining the Social System." American Sociological Review 28: 588–98.

Bernard, Thomas. 1987a. "Testing Structural Strain Theories." Journal of Research in Crime and Delinquency 24: 262–80.

Bernard, Thomas. 1987b. "Reply to Agnew." Journal of Research in Crime and Delinquency 24: 287–90.

Bertrand, Marie-Andrée. 1969. "Self-Image and Delinquency: A Contribution to the Study of Female Criminality and Women's Image." Acta criminologica: Études sur la conduite antisociale 2: 71–144.

Bertrand, Marie-Andrée. 1979. La femme et le crime. Montréal: L'Aurore.

Bertrand, Marie-Andrée. 1983. "Femmes et justice: Problèmes d'intervention." Criminologie 16.

Bertrand, Marie-Andrée. 1984. "The Drug Laws: Their Continuing Perverse Effects and Resistance to Change." Unpublished paper. University of Montreal.

Besserer, Sandra. 1998. "Criminal Victimization: An International Perspective." Juristat Vol. 18, No. 6. Ottawa: Statistics Canada.

Besserer, Sandra and Catherine Trainor. 2000. "Criminal Victimization in Canada, 1999." Juristat Vol. 20, No. 10. Ottawa: Statistics Canada.

Biron, Louise L. and Carol Ladouceur. 1991. "The Boy Next Door: Local Teen-Age Burglars in Montréal." Security Journal 2: 200–4.

Biswas, P. C. 1960. The Ex-Criminal Tribes of Delhi State. Delhi: University of Delhi.

Blackwell, Brenda Sims. 2000. "Perceived Sanction Threats, Gender, and Crime: A Test and Elaboration of Power Control Theory." Criminology 38: 439–88.

Block, Alan and Frank Scarpitti. 1985. Poisoning for Profit: The Mafia and Toxic Waste in America. New York: William Morrow.

Blomberg, Thomas G. and Stanley Cohen. 1995. "Punishment and Social Control." In Thomas G. Blomberg and Stanley Cohen (eds.), Punishment and Social Control: Essays in Honor of Sheldon L. Messinger. New York: Aldine de Gruyter.

Blumer, Herbert. 1951. "Collective Behaviour." In A. M. Lee (ed.), Principles of Sociology. New York: Barnes and Noble.

Blumstein, Alfred and Joel Wallman. 2000. The Crime Drop in America. Cambridge: Cambridge University Press.

Boggs, Sarah. 1965. "Urban Crime Patterns." American Sociological Review 30: 899–908.

Boland, Barbara. 2001. Community Prosecution in Washington, DC: The U.S.

Attorney's Fifth District Pilot Project. Washington, DC: National Institute of Justice.

Bonta, James, Suzanne Marie Wallace-Capretta, and Jennifer Rooney. 2000. "Can Electronic Monitoring Make a Difference? An Evaluation of Three Canadian Programs." Crime and Delinquency 46: 61–75.

Bose, G. 1956. "Delinquency in India." In K. R. Eissler (ed.), Searchlights on Delinquency. New York: International Universities Press.

Bourgois, Philippe. 1995. In Search of Respect: Selling Crack in El Barrio. New York: Cambridge University Press.

Bourgois, Philippe, Mark Lettiere, and James Quesada. 1997. "Social Misery and the Sanctions of Substance Abuse: Confronting HIV Risk among Homeless Heroin Addicts in San Francisco." Social Problems 44: 155–73.

Bowker, Lee H. (ed.). 1997. Masculinities and Violence. Thousand Oaks, CA: Sage.

Box, Steven. 1971. Deviance, Reality, and Society. London: Holt, Rinehart, and Winston.

Boyd, Neil. 1991. High Society: Legal and Illegal Drugs in Canada. Toronto: Key Porter Books.

Boyle, Christine. 1991. "Sexual Assault: A Case Study of Legal Policy Decisions." In Margaret Jackson and Curt Griffiths (eds.), Canadian Criminology: Perspectives on Crime and Criminality. Toronto: Harcourt Brace Jovanovich Canada.

Braithwaite, John. 1989. Crime, Shame and Reintegration. Cambridge: Cambridge University Press.

Braithwaite, John and Kathleen Daly. 1994. "Masculinities, Violence, and Communitarian Control." In Tim Newburn and Elizabeth Stanko (eds.), Just Boys Doing Business? Men, Masculinities, and Crime. London: Routledge.

Braithwaite, John and Peter Grabosky. 1985. Occupational Health and Safety Enforcement in Australia. Canberra: Australian Institute of Criminology.

Brannigan, Augustine and John Fleischman. 1989. "Juvenile Prostitution and Mental Health: Policing Delinquency or Treating Pathology." Canadian Journal of Law and Society 4: 77–98.

Brantingham, Patricia L. and Paul J. Brantingham. 1981. "Notes on the Geometry of Crime." In Paul Brantingham and Patricia Brantingham (eds.), Environmental Criminology. Beverly Hills, CA: Sage.

Brantingham, Patricia L. and Paul J. Brantingham.1995. "Criminality of Place: Crime Generators and Crime Attractors." European Journal of Criminal Policy and Research 3: 5–26.

Brickey, Stephen and Elizabeth Comack (eds). 1986. The Social Basis of Law. Toronto: Garamond Press.

Brock, Debi R. 1984. Feminist Perspectives on Prostitution: Addressing the Canadian Dilemma. MA thesis, Department of Sociology and Anthropology, Carleton University, Ottawa.

Brodeur, Jean-Paul. 1996. Organized Crime: Trends in the Literature. Presented at the Forum on Organized Crime, September 27–28, in Ottawa.

Brophy, Jane and Carol Smart (eds.). 1985. Women-in-Law. London: Routledge and Kegan Paul.

Brown, David and Russell Hogg. 1992. "Essentialism, Radical Criminology, and Left Realism." Australian and New Zealand Journal of Criminology 25: 195–230.

Brown, Lorne and Caroline Brown. 1973. An Unauthorized History of the RCMP. Toronto: James Lewis and Samuel.

Brown, Stephen E., Finn-Age Esbensen, and Gilbert Geis. 1991. Criminology:

Explaining Crime and Its Context. Cincinnati: Anderson.

Browne, Angela and Kirk Williams. 1989. "Exploring the Effect of Resource Availability and the Likelihood of Female-Perpetrated Homicides." Law and Society Review 23: 75–92.

Browne, Angela and Kirk Williams. 1993. "Gender, Intimacy, and Lethal Violence: Trends from 1976 through 1987." Gender & Society 7: 78–98.

Bryan, J. H. and M. A. Test. 1967. "Models and Helping: Naturalistic Studies in Aiding Behaviour." Journal of Personality and Social Psychology 6: 400–7.

Burns, M. O. and M. E. P. Seligman. 1989. "Exploratory Style across the Life Span: Evidence for Stability over 52 Years." Journal of Personality and Social Psychology 56: 471–7.

Burstyn, Varda. 1987. "The Left and the Porn Wars: A Case Study in Sexual Politics." In Howard Buchbinder et al. (eds.), Who's on Top? The Politics of Heterosexuality. Toronto: Garamond Press.

Burton, R. V. 1963. "Generality of Honesty Reconsidered." Psychological Review 70: 481–99.

Burton, R. V. 1976. "Honesty and Dishonesty." In T. Lickona (ed.), Moral Development and Behavior. New York: Holt, Rinehart & Winston.

Butterfield, Fox. 1995. All God's Children: The Bosket Family and the American Tradition of Violence. New York: Knopf.

Campbell, M. 1973. Halfbreed. Toronto: McClelland and Stewart.

Canada. 1981. Second Report of the Commission of Inquiry Concerning Certain Activities of the Royal Canadian Mounted Police: Freedom and Security under the Law (The MacDonald Report, 2 volumes). Ottawa: Minister of Supply and Services.

Canadian Centre for Justice Statistics. 1990. The Development of Data Quality Assessment Procedures for the Uniform Crime Reporting Survey: A Case Study of Calgary-Edmonton. Ottawa: Canadian Centre for Justice Statistics.

Canadian Centre for Justice Statistics. 1992. Just Info. Spring/Summer.

Canadian Centre on Substance Abuse. 1992. Action News 3(3): 5.

Canadian Pacific Limited. 1992. Notice of Annual Meeting of Stockholders.

Canter, Rachelle J. 1982. "Sex Differences in Self-Report Delinquency." Criminology 20: 373–93.

Carlen, Pat. 1983. Women's Imprisonment: A Study in Social Control. London: Routledge & Kegan Paul.

Carrington, Peter. 1999. "Trends in Youth Crime in Canada, 1977–1996." Canadian Journal of Criminology 41: 1–32.

Carter, Ronald L. and Kim Q. Hill. 1979. The Criminal's Image of the City. New York: Pergamon.

Cavan, Ruth Shonle and Jordan T. Cavan. 1968. Delinquency and Crime: Cross-Cultural Perspectives. Philadelphia: J. B. Lippincott.

Cernkovich, Stephen A. and Peggy C. Giordano. 1979a. "On Complicating the Relationship between Liberation and Delinquency." Social Problems 26: 467–81.

Cernkovich, Stephen A. and Peggy C. Giordano. 1979b. "A Comparative Analysis of Male and Female Delinquency." The Sociological Quarterly 20: 131–45.

Caron, Roger. 1978. Go-Boy. Toronto: McGraw-Hill Ryerson.

Caron, Roger. 1985. Bingo. Toronto: Stoddart.

Caron, Roger. 1988. Jojo. Toronto: Stoddart.

Caron, Roger. 1992. Dreamcaper. Toronto: Stoddart.

Chambliss, William. 1964. "A Sociological Analysis of the Law of Vagrancy." Social Problems 12: 67–77.

Chambliss, William. 1975. "Toward a Political Economy of Crime." Theory and Society 2: 149–70.

Chambliss, William. 1988. On the Take: From Petty Crooks to Presidents. Bloomington: Indiana University Press.

Chambliss, William J. and Robert Seidman. 1982. Law, Order and Power (2nd ed.). Reading, MA: Addison-Wesley.

Chambliss, William. 1989. "State Organized Crime." Criminology 27: 183–208.

Chamlin, Mitchell B. and John K. Cochran. 1997. "Social Altruism and Crime." Criminology 35: 203–27.

Chein, Isadore, D. L. Gerrard, R. S. Lee, and E. Rosenfeld. 1964. The Road to H. New York: Basic Books.

Chesney-Lind, Meda. 1973. "Judicial Enforcement and the Female Delinquent." Issues in Criminology 8: 51–59.

Chesney-Lind, Meda. 1986. "Women and Crime: The Female Offender." Signs: Journal of Women in Culture and Society 12: 78–96.

Chesney-Lind, Meda. 1988. "Girls and Status Offenses: Is Juvenile Justice Still Sexist?" Criminal Justice Abstracts 20: 144–65.

Chesney-Lind, Meda. 1989. "Girls' Crime and Women's Place: Toward a Feminist Model of Female Delinquency." Crime and Delinquency 35: 5–29.

Chesney-Lind, Meda. 1995. "Girls, Delinquency, and Juvenile Justice: Toward a Feminist Theory of Young Women's Crime." In Barbara Raffel Price and Natalie Sokoloff (eds.), The Criminal Justice System and Women. New York: McGraw-Hill.

Chesney-Lind, Meda. 1997. The Female Offender: Girls, Women, and Crime. Thousand Oaks, CA: Sage.

Chesney-Lind, Meda and Barbara Bloom. 1997. "Feminist Criminology: Thinking about Women and Crime." In Brian MacLean and Dragan Milovanic, (eds.), Thinking Critically about Crime. Vancouver: Collective Press.

Cheung, Y. W. and P. G. Erickson. 1997. "Crack Use in Canada: A Distant American Cousin." In C. Reinarman and H. Levine (eds.), Crack in Context: Demon Drugs and Social Justice. Berkeley, CA: University of California Press.

Chin, Ko-lin, Robert J. Kelly, and Jeffrey Fagan. 1994. "Chinese Organized Crime in America." In R. J. Kelley, K. Chin, and R. Schatzberg (eds.), Handbook of Organized Crime in the United States. Westport, CT: Greenwood.

Christie, Nils. 1977. "Conflicts as Property." British Journal of Criminology 17: 1–26.

Chunn, Dorothy. 1992. From Punishment to Doing Good: Family Courts and Socialized Justice in Ontario 1880–1940. Toronto: University of Toronto Press.

Chunn, Dorothy E. and Shelley A. M. Gavigan. 1991. "Women and Crime in Canada." In Margaret Jackson and Curt Griffiths (eds.), Canadian Criminology: Perspectives on Crime and Criminality. Toronto: Harcourt Brace Jovanovich Canada.

Chunn, Dorothy and Robert Menzies. 1996. "Canadian Criminology and the Woman Question." In Nicole Hahn Rafter and Frances Heidensohn (eds.), International Feminist Perspectives in Criminology: Engendering a Discipline. Buckingham: Open University Press.

Clark, Loreen and Debra Lewis. 1977. Rape: The Price of Coercive Sexuality. Toronto: The Women's Press.

Cloud, John. 1998. "A Way Out for Junkies?" Time. January 19.

Cloward, Richard. 1959. "Illegitimate Means, Anomie, and Deviant Behaviour." American Sociological Review 24: 164–76.

Cloward, Richard and Lloyd Ohlin. 1960. Delinquency and Opportunity. Glencoe, IL: Free Press.

Cohen, Albert K. 1955. Delinquent Boys: The Culture of the Gang. Glencoe, IL: Free Press.

Cohen, Albert K. 1966. Deviance and Control. Englewood Cliffs, NJ: Prentice Hall.

Cohen, Deborah. 1995. "Ethics and Crime in Business Firms: Organizational Culture and the Impact of Anomie." In Freda Adler and William S. Laufer (eds.), Advances in Criminological Theory, Vol. 6: The Legacy of Anomie. New Brunswick, NJ: Transaction.

Cohen, Lawrence. 1981. "Modeling Crime Trends: A Criminal Opportunity Perspective." Journal of Research in Crime and Delinquency 18: 138–62.

Cohen, Lawrence and Marcus Felson. 1979. "Social Change and Crime Rate Trends; A Routine Activities Approach." American Sociological Review 44: 588–608.

Cohen, Lawrence, James R. Kluegel, and Kenneth C. Land. 1981. "Social Inequality and Predatory Criminal Victimization: An Exposition and Test of a Formal Theory." American Sociological Review 46: 505–24.

Cohen, Stanley. 1985. Visions of Social Control. Cambridge: Polity Press.

Coleman, James W. 1985. The Criminal Elite: The Sociology of White Collar Crime. New York: St. Martin's Press.

Coleman, John R. 1980. "What I Learned Last Summer." Psychology Today 14(11): 17–20.

Colvin, Mark and John Pauly. 1983. "A Critique of Criminology: Toward an Integrated Structural-Marxist Theory of Delinquency Production." American Journal of Sociology 89: 513–51.

Comack, Elizabeth. 1992. "Women and Crime." In Rick Linden (ed.), Criminology: A Canadian Perspective (2nd ed.). Toronto: Harcourt Brace Jovanovich Canada.

Comack, Elizabeth. 1993. "Women Offenders' Experiences with Physical and Sexual Abuse." Presentation at the Canadian Law and Society Meetings at Carleton University in Ottawa.

Comack, Elizabeth. 1996. Feminist Engagement with the Law: The Legal Recognition of the Battered Woman Syndrome. Ottawa: Canadian Research Institute for the Advancement of Women.

Comack, Elizabeth and Stephen Brickey (eds.). 1991. The Social Basis of Law (2nd. ed.). Halifax: Garamond Press.

Commission of Inquiry into the Non-Medical Use of Drugs. 1973. Final Report. Ottawa: Information Canada.

Committee on Sexual Offenses Against Children and Youth. 1984. Sexual Offenses against Children. Ottawa: Department of Supply & Services.

Cook, Philip J. and Jens Ludwig. 1998. "Defensive Gun Uses: New Evidence from a National Survey." Journal of Quantitative Criminology 14: 111–31

Coordinated Law Enforcement Unit, Policy Analysis Division (British Columbia Ministry of Attorney General). 1995. VLTs: Video Lottery Terminal Gaming. Victoria, BC: The Queen's Printer.

Corrado, Ray. 1991. "Contemporary Political Crime: National and International Terrorism." In Margaret Jackson and Curt Griffiths (eds.), Canadian Criminology. Toronto: Harcourt Brace Jovanovich Canada.

Corrado, Ray and Alan Markwart. 1996. "Canada." In Donald Shoemaker (ed.), International Handbook on Juvenile Justice. Westport, CT: Greenwood Press.

Cossins, Diane. 1991. Canadian Juvenile Justice before and after the Young Offenders Act. MA thesis, Department of Sociology, University of Alberta, Edmonton, Alberta.

Crawford, Maria, Rosemary Gartner, and Myrna Dawson. 1997. Intimate Femicide in Ontario. Toronto: Ontario Women's Directorate.

Criminal Intelligence Service Canada. 1996. Annual Report on Organized Crime in Canada, 1996. Ottawa: CISC.

Crutchfield, Robert D. 1995. "Ethnicity, Labor Markets, and Crime." In Darnell F. Hawkins (ed.), Ethnicity, Race and Crime: Perspectives across Time and Place. Albany: State University of New York Press.

Cullen, Francis. 1984. Rethinking Crime and Deviance Theory: The Emergence of a Structuring Tradition. Totowa, NJ: Rowman and Allanheld.

Cullen, Francis. 1988. "Were Cloward and Ohlin Strain Theorists? Delinquency and Opportunity Revisited." Journal of Research in Crime and Delinquency 25: 214–41.

Cullen, Frances T. 1994. "Social Support as an Organizing Concept for Criminology." Justice Quarterly 11: 527–59.

Cullen, Frances T. and John Paul Wright. 1997. "Liberating the Anomie-Strain Paradigm: Implications from Social Support Theory." In Nikos Passas and Robert Agnew (eds.), The Future of Anomie Theory. Boston: Northeastern University Press.

Cullen, Francis T., William J. Maakestad, and Gray Cavender. 1991. "The Ford Pinto Case and Beyond: Assessing Blame." In Michael C. Braswell, Belinda R. McCarthy, and Bernard J. McCarthy (eds.), Justice, Crime and Ethics. Cincinnati: Anderson.

Currie, Dawn. 1990. "Battered Women and the State: From the Failure of Theory to a Theory of Failure." Journal of Human Justice 1: 77–96.

Currie, Elliott. 1985. Confronting Crime. New York: Pantheon Books.

Currie, Elliott. 1987. What Kind of Future? Violence and Public Safety in the Year 2000. San Francisco: National Council on Crime and Delinquency

Curry, J. C. 1932. The Indian Police. London: Faber and Faber.

Dahrendorf, Ralf. 1959. Class and Class Conflict in Industrial Society. Stanford, CA: Stanford University Press.

Daly, Kathleen. 1989. "Criminal Justice Ideologies and Practices in Different Voices: Some Feminist Questions about Justice." International Journal of the Sociology of Law 17: 1–18.

Daly, Kathleen. 1990. "New Feminist Definitions of Justice." Proceedings of the First Annual Women's Policy Research Conference. Washington, DC: Institute for Women's Policy Research.

Daly, Kathleen and Meda Chesney-Lind. 1988. "Feminism and Criminology." Justice Quarterly 5: 497–538.

Darley, J. M. and B. Latané. 1968. "Bystander Intervention in Emergencies: Diffusion of Responsibility." Journal of Personality and Social Psychology 8: 377–83.

Davies, Robertson. 1972. The Manticore. Toronto: Macmillan.

Davis, Kingsley. 1937. "The Sociology of Prostitution." American Sociological Review 2: 744–55.

DeKeseredy, Walter and Katherine Kelly. 1993. "Woman Abuse in University and College Dating Relationships: The Contribution of Ideology of Familial Patriarchy." Journal of Human Justice 4: 25–52.

DeKeseredy, Walter and Ron Hinch. 1992. Woman Abuse: Sociological Perspectives. Toronto: Thomson Educational Publishers.

Denno, Deborah. 1984. "Neuropsychological and Early Environmental Correlates of Sex Differences in Crime." International Journal of Neuroscience 23: 199–214.

Denno, Deborah. 1985. "Sociological and Human Developmental Explanations of Crime." Criminology 23: 711–41.

Denno, Deborah. 1990. Biology and Violence: From Birth to Adulthood. New York: Cambridge University Press.

Denno, Deborah. 1993. "Considering Lead Poisoning as a Criminal Defense." Fordham Urban Law Journal 20: 377.

Denno, Deborah. 1994. "Gender, Crime, and the Criminal Law Defenses." Journal of Criminal Law and Criminology 85: 80.

de Rahm, Edith. 1969. How Could She Do That? New York: Clarkson N. Potter.

Desroches, Fred. 1991. "Tearoom Trade: A Law Enforcement Problem." Canadian Journal of Criminology 33: 1–21.

Desroches, Frederick J. 1995. Force and Fear: Robbery in Canada. Scarborough, ON: Nelson Canada.

Dobash, Rebecca E. and Russell Dobash. 1992. Women, Violence, and Social Change. London, UK: Routledge.

Dolan, L. J., S. G. Kellam, C. H. Brown, L. Werthamer-Larsson, G. W. Rebok, L. S. Mayer, J. Laudoff, J. Turkkan, C. Ford, and L. Wheeller. 1993. "The Short-Term Impact of Two Classroom-Based Preventive Interventions on Aggressive and Shy Behaviors and Poor Achievement." Journal of Applied Developmental Psychology 14: 317–45.

Doob, Anthony N. and Jane B. Sprott. 1996. "Interprovincial Variation in the Use of Youth Court." Canadian Journal of Criminology 38: 401–12.

Doob, Anthony N., Voula Marinos, and Kimberly N. Varna. 1995. Youth Crime and the Youth Justice System in Canada: A Research Perspective. Toronto: Centre of Criminology.

Dowie, Mark. 1977. "Pinto Madness." Mother Jones (Sept.-Oct.): 18–32.

Dunworth, Terence and Gregory Mills. 1999. National Evaluation of Weed and Seed. Research Brief. Washington, DC: National Institute of Justice.

Durkheim, Émile. 1933. The Division of Labor in Society. New York: Free Press.

Durkheim, Émile. 1951. Suicide. New York: Free Press.

Du Wors, Richard. 1997. "The Justice Data Factfinder." Juristat Vol. 17, No. 13. Ottawa: Statistics Canada.

Dyer, Gwynn. 1997. "Lion's Share of Genetic Diversity Belongs to Africa." Times-Colonist, 17 August.

Economist, The. 1992. "The Tobacco Trade: The Search for Eldorado." 323 (May 16): 21–24.

Elliot, Delbert S. and Scott Menard. 1996. "Delinquent Friends and Delinquent Behavior: Temporal and Developmental Patterns." In J. David Hawkins (ed.), Delinquency and Crime: Current Theories. Cambridge, UK: Cambridge University Press.

Engels, Frederick. 1958. The Condition of the Working Class in England. Trans. and ed. W. O. Henderson and W. H. Chaloner. Oxford: Basil Blackwell.

Erickson, Patricia G. 1992. "Recent Trends in Canadian Drug Policy: The Decline and Resurgence of Prohibitionism." Daedalus 121: 239–67.

Erickson, Patricia G. and Reginald Smart. 1988. "The LeDain Commission Recommendations." In Judith C. Blackwell and Patricia G. Erickson (eds.), Illicit Drugs in Canada: A Risky Business. Scarborough, ON: Nelson Canada.

Erickson, Patricia G. and Tim Weber. 1992. "Cocaine, Control and Crime." Paper presented at the annual meeting of the

American Society of Criminology, New Orleans.

Erickson, Patricia G., Edward Adlaf, Glenn Murray, and Reginald Smart. 1987. The Steel Drug: Cocaine in Perspective. Lexington, MA: Lexington Books, D. C. Heath.

Erickson, Patricia G., Diane M. Riley, Yuet W. Cheung, and Patrick A. O'Hare (eds.). 1997. Harm Reduction: A New Direction for Drug Policies and Programs. Toronto: University of Toronto Press.

Ericson, Richard V. 1981. Making Crime. Toronto: University of Toronto Press.

Ericson, Richard V. 1982. Reproducing Order. Toronto: University of Toronto Press.

Ericson, Richard V. and Patricia M. Baranek. 1982. The Ordering of Justice: A Study of Accused Persons as Dependents in the Criminal Process. Toronto: University of Toronto Press.

Ericson, Richard V., Patricia Baranek, and Janet B. L. Chan. 1987. Visualizing Deviance: A Study of News Organization. Toronto: University of Toronto Press.

Ericson, Richard V., Patricia Baranek, and Janet B. L. Chan. 1989. Negotiating Control: A Study of News Sources. Toronto: University of Toronto Press.

Farnworth, Margaret and Michael Leiber. 1989. "Strain Theory Revisited." American Sociological Review 54: 263–74.

Fattah, Ezzat. 1971. La victime est-elle coupable? Montréal: Les Presses de l'Université de Montréal.

Fattah, Ezzat A. 1987. "Ideological Biases in the Evaluation of Criminal Justice Reform." In R. S. Ratner and John L. McMullan (eds.), State Control: Criminal Justice Politics in Canada. Vancouver: University of British Columbia Press.

Fattah, Ezzat A. 1997. Criminology, Past, Present and Future: A Critical Overview. New York: St. Martin's.

Fedorowycz, Orest. 2000. "Homicide in Canada—1999." Juristat Vol. 20, No. 9. Ottawa: Statistics Canada.

Feinman, Clarice. 1980. Women in the Criminal Justice System. New York: Praeger.

Feld, Barry. 1998. "Rehabilitation, Retribution, and Restorative Justice: Alternative Conceptions of Juvenile Justice." In Gordon Bazemore and Lode Walgrave (eds.), Restorative Juvenile Justice. Monsey, NY: Criminal Justice Press.

Ferri, Enrico. 1901. Criminal Sociology. Boston: Little, Brown.

Festinger, Leon. 1957. A Theory of Cognitive Dissonance. New York: Harper and Row.

Figueira-McDonough, Josefina and Elaine Selo. 1980. "A Reformulation of the 'Equal Opportunity' Explanation of Female Delinquency." Crime and Delinquency 26: 333–43.

Finkelhor, David and Larry Baron. 1986. "Risk Factors for Child Sexual Abuse." Journal of Interpersonal Violence 1: 43–71.

Fischer, Stanley I. 1979. Moving Millions: An Inside Look at Mass Transit. New York: Harper and Row.

Fogelman, E. and V. L Wiener. 1985. "The Few, the Brave, the Noble." Psychology Today 19: 61–65.

Forbes, G. A. 1977. Street Prostitution in Vancouver's West End. Vancouver: Vancouver Police Report.

Forge, K. L. and S. Phemister. 1987. "The Effect of Prosocial Cartoons on Preschool Children." Child Study Journal 17: 83–88.

Fox, John and Timothy Hartnagel. 1979. "Changing Social Roles and Female Crime in Canada: A Time Series Analysis." Canadian Review of Sociology and Anthropology 16: 96–104.

Francis, Diane. 1988. Contrepreneurs. Toronto: Macmillan.

Freud, Sigmund. 1965. New Introductory Lectures on Psychoanalysis. New York: W. W. Norton.

Friday, Paul C. 1992. "Delinquency in Sweden: Current Trends and Theoretical Implications." International Journal of Comparative and Applied Criminal Justice 16: 231–46.

Gabor, Thomas and André Normandeau. 1989. "Armed Robbery: Highlights of a Canadian Study." Canadian Police College Journal 13: 273–82.

Gabor, Thomas, Micheline Baril, Maurice Cusson, Daniel Elie, Marc LeBlanc, and André Normandeau. 1987. Armed Robbery: Cops, Robbers, and Victims. Springfield, IL: Charles C. Thomas.

Galbraith, John Kenneth. 1992. The Culture of Contentment. Boston: Houghton Mifflin Co.

Gannon, Maive. 2001. "Crime Comparisons between Canada and the United States." Juristat Vol. 21, No. 11. Ottawa: Statistics Canada.

Gartner, Rosemary and Bill McCarthy. 1991. "The Social Distribution of Femicide in Urban Canada, 1921–1988." Law and Society Review 25: 287–311.

Gavigan, Shelley A. M. 1983. "Women's Crime and Feminist Critiques." Canadian Criminology Forum 6: 75–90.

Gavigan, Shelley A. M. 1986. "Women, Law, and Patriarchal Relations. Perspectives within the Sociology of Law." In Neil Boyd (ed.), Social Dimensions of Law. Scarborough, ON: Prentice-Hall Canada.

Gavigan, Shelley A. M. 1987. "Women's Crime: New Perspectives and Old Theories." In Ellen Adelberg and Claudia Currie (eds.), Too Few to Count: Canadian Women in Conflict with the Law. Vancouver: Press Gang.

Gaylord, Mark S. 1990. "The Chinese Laundry: International Drug Trafficking and Hong Kong's Banking Industry." Contemporary Crises 14: 23–37.

Gaylord, Mark S. and John F. Galliher. 1991. "Riding the Underground Dragon: Crime Control and Public Order on Hong Kong's Mass Transit Railway." British Journal of Criminology 31: 15–26.

Geis, Gil. 1965. Juvenile Gangs. Washington, DC: President's Committee on Juvenile Delinquency and Youth Crime.

Geis, Gilbert. 1972. "Jeremy Bentham." In Herman Mannheim (ed.), Pioneers in Criminology. Montclair, NJ: Patterson Smith.

Gelsthorpe, Lorraine. 1986. "Towards a Skeptical Look at Sexism." International Journal of the Sociology of Law 14: 125–52.

Gelsthorpe, Lorraine and Allison Morris. 1988. "Feminism and Criminology in Britain." British Journal of Criminology 28: 223–40.

Gibbons, Don C. 1987. Society, Crime, and Criminal Careers (5th ed.) Englewood Cliffs, NJ: Prentice-Hall.

Giffen, P. J. 1965. "Official Rates of Crime and Delinquency." In W. T. McGrath (ed.), Crime and Its Treatment in Canada. Toronto: Macmillan.

Giffen, P. J. 1966. "The Revolving Door: A Functional Interpretation." Canadian Review of Sociology and Anthropology 3: 154–66.

Giffen, P. J. 1976. "Official Rates of Crime and Delinquency." In W.T. McGrath (ed.), Crime and Its Treatment in Canada (2nd ed.) Toronto: University of Toronto Press.

Giffen, P. J. and Sylvia Lambert. 1988. "What Happened on the Way to Law Reform?" In Judith C. Blackwell and Patricia G. Erickson (eds.), Illicit Drugs in Canada: A Risky Business. Scarborough, ON: Nelson Canada.

Giffen, P. J., Shirley Endicott, and Sylvia Lambert. 1991. Panic and Indifference: The Politics of Canada's Drug Laws. Ottawa: Canadian Centre on Substance Abuse.

Gilligan, Carol. 1982. In a Different Voice. Cambridge, MA: Harvard University Press.

Gilligan, Carol. 1987. "Moral Orientation and Moral Development." In E. Kittay and D. Meyers (eds.), Women and Moral Theory. Totowa, NJ: Rowman and Littlefield.

Gillis, A. R. 1973. "Types of Human Population Density and Social Pathology." Discussion Paper No. 7. Edmonton: The University of Alberta Population Research Laboratory.

Gillis, A. R. and John Hagan. 1982. "Density, Delinquency, and Design: Formal and Informal Control and the Built Environment." Criminology 19: 514–29.

Gillis, A. R. and John Hagan. 1990. "Delinquent Samaritans: Network Structure, Social Conflict, and the Willingness to Intervene." Journal of Research in Crime and Delinquency 27: 30–51.

Giordano, Peggy C., Sandra Kerbel, and Sandra Dudley. 1981. "The Economics of Female Criminality: An Analysis of Police Blotters, 1890–1975." In Lee H. Bowker (ed.), Women and Crime in America. New York: MacMillan.

Girault, Henriette. 1984. "La détention provisoire des mineurs." Unpublished paper, Centre de recherche interdisciplinaire, Vaucresson.

Glueck, Sheldon and Eleanor Glueck. 1950. Unravelling Juvenile Delinquency. New York: Commonwealth Fund.

Godfrey, Ellen. 1981. By Reason of Doubt: The Belshaw Case. Vancouver: Clarke, Irwin and Co.

Goff, Colin H. and Charles E. Reasons. 1978. Corporate Crime in Canada. Scarborough, ON: Prentice-Hall Canada.

Goode, Erich. 1990. "Crime Can Be Fun: The Deviant Experience." Contemporary Sociology 19: 5–12.

Gordon, Robert M. and Ian T. Coneybeer. 1991. "Corporate Crime." In Margaret Jackson and Curt Griffiths (eds.), Canadian Criminology. Toronto: Harcourt Brace Jovanovich Canada.

Goring, Charles. 1913. The English Convict. London: H. M. Stationery Office.

Gould, Leroy C. 1969. "The Changing Structure of Property Crime in an Affluent Society." Social Forces 48: 50–59.

Grapendaal, M. 1991. "Dutch Drug Policy and the Economics of Crime." Paper present at the American Society of Criminology Meetings, San Francisco.

Grapendaal, M., E. Leuw, and H. Nelen. 1995. A World of Opportunities: Lifestyle and Economic Behavior of Heroin Addicts in Amsterdam. Albany: State University of New York Press.

Gray, Diana. 1973. "Turning Out: A Study of Teenage Prostitution." Urban Life and Culture (January): 401–25.

Greenberg, David F. 1979. Mathematical Criminology. New Brunswick, NJ: Rutgers University Press.

Greenberg, David. 1981. Crime and Capitalism. Palo Alto, CA: Mayfield.

Greenland, Cyril. 1988. Preventing CAN Deaths: An International Study of Deaths Due to Child Abuse and Neglect. London: Tavistock.

Gregorich, L. J. 1997. Poaching and the Illegal Trade in Wildlife and Wildlife Parts in Canada. Ottawa: Canadian Wildlife Federation.

Gurr, Ted. 1981. "Historical Forces in Violent Crime." In Michael Tonry and Norval Morris (eds.), Crime and Justice. Vol. 3. Chicago: University of Chicago Press.

Hackler, James C. 1966. "Boys, Blisters, and Behaviour: The Impact of a Work Program in an Urban Central Area." Journal of Research in Crime and Delinquency 3: 155–64.

Hackler, James C. 1970. "Testing a Causal Model of Delinquency." Sociological Quarterly 11: 511–22.

Hackler, James C. 1978. The Great Stumble Forward: The Prevention of Youthful Crime. Toronto: Methuen.

Hackler, James C. 1988a. "A Developmental Theory of Delinquency." In Ronald A. Farrell and Victoria Lynn Swigert (eds.), Social Deviance (3rd ed.). Belmont, CA: Wadsworth.

Hackler, James C. 1988b. Practising in France What Americans Have Preached: The Response of French Judges to Juveniles. Crime and Delinquency 34: 467–85.

Hackler, James C. 1991a. "The Reduction of Violent Crime through Economic Equality for Women." Journal of Family Violence 6: 199–216.

Hackler, James C. 1991b. "Good People, Dirty System: The YOA and Organizational Failure." In Alan Leschied, Peter Jaffe, and Wayne Willis (eds.), The Young Offenders Act: A Revolution in Canadian Juvenile Justice. Toronto: University of Toronto Press.

Hackler, James C. 1991c. "Two Strategies for Defending Juveniles in Australia: Which Does the Least Damage?" In James C. Hackler (ed.), Official Responses to Problem Juveniles: Some International Reflections. Oñati, Spain: International Institute for the Sociology of Law.

Hackler, James C. 1992. "The Manifest Functions of Legal Aid." International Criminal Justice Review 2: 58–75.

Hackler, James C. 1993. "The Selfish Majority: Is Canada Also Heading for Private Riches and Public Squalor?" Policy Options 13(10): 44–45.

Hackler, James C. 1996. "Anglophone Juvenile Justice: Why Canada, England, the USA, and Australia Are behind Other Developed Countries." In John Winterdyk (ed.), Issues and Perspectives on Young Offenders in Canada. Toronto: HBJ-Holt Canada.

Hackler, James C. 2000. "Strain Theories." In Rick Linden (ed.), Criminology: A Canadian Perspective (4th ed.). Toronto: Harcourt Brace Canada.

Hackler, James C. and Kim Don. 1989. "Screening Juveniles and the Central City Phenomenon: Using Official Statistics to Understand the Dynamics of Police Systems." Canadian Police College Journal 13: 1–17.

Hackler, James C. and John Hagan. 1975. "Work and Teaching Machines as Delinquency Prevention Tools: A Four Year Follow-up." Social Service Review 49: 92–106.

Hackler, James C., Diane Cossins, and Kim Don. 1990. "Comparing Crime Rates: When Are They Meaningful?" Discussion Paper 24, Edmonton: Centre for Criminological Research.

Hackler, James C., Kwai-yiu Ho, and Carol Urquhart-Ross. 1974. "The Willingness to Intervene: Differing Community Characteristics." Social Problems 21: 328–44.

Hagan, Frank. 1986. Introduction to Criminology: Theories, Methods and Criminal Behaviour. Chicago: Nelson-Hall.

Hagan, John. 1973. "Labelling and Deviance: A Case Study in the 'Sociology of the Interesting.' " Social Problems 20: 447–58.

Hagan, John. 1985. Modern Criminology: Crime, Criminal Behaviour, and Its Control. New York: McGraw-Hill.

Hagan, John. 1987. "White Collar and Corporate Crime." In Rick Linden (ed.), Criminology: A Canadian Perspective. Toronto: Holt, Rinehart, and Winston Canada.

Hagan, John. 1991. The Disreputable Pleasures: Crime and Deviance in Canada (3rd ed.). Toronto: McGraw-Hill Ryerson.

Hagan, John. 1992. "White-Collar and Corporate Crime." In Rick Linden (ed.), Criminology: A Canadian Perspective (2nd ed.). Toronto: Harcourt Brace Jovanovich Canada.

Hagan, John and Jeffrey Leon.
1977. "Rediscovering Delinquency: Social History, Political Ideology, and the Sociology of Law." American Sociological Review 42: 587–98.

Hagan, John and Bill McCarthy. 1997a.
Mean Streets: Youth Homelessness and Crime. New York: Cambridge University Press.

Hagan, John and Bill McCarthy. 1997b.
"Anomie, Social Capital, and Street Criminology." In Nikos Passas and Robert Agnew (eds.), The Future of Anomie Theory. Boston: Northeastern University Press.

Hagan, John and Patricia Parker.
1985. "White Collar Crime and Punishment: The Class Structure and Legal Sanctioning of Securities Violations." American Sociological Review 50: 302–16.

Hagan, John and Ruth Peterson (eds.). 1995. Crime and Inequality. Stanford, CA: Stanford University Press.

Hagan, John, A. R. Gillis, and John Simpson. 1985. "The Class Structure of Gender and Delinquency: Toward a Power-Control Theory of Common Delinquent Behaviour." American Journal of Sociology 90: 1, 151, 178.

Hagan, John, A. R. Gillis, and John Simpson. 1987. "Class in the Household: A Power-Control Theory of Gender and Delinquency." American Journal of Sociology 92: 788–816.

Hancock, Linda. 1981. "The Myth That Females Are Treated More Leniently Than Males in the Juvenile Justice System." Australian and New Zealand Journal of Sociology 16: 4–14.

Hanmer, J. and M. Maynard (eds.).
1987. Women, Violence, and Social Control. Atlantic Highlands, NJ: Humanities Press International.

Hare, R. D. 1970. Psychopathy: Theory and Research. New York: Wiley.

Hare, R. D. 1980. "A Research Scale for the Assessment of Psychopathy in Criminal Populations." Personality and Individual Differences 1: 111–19.

Hare, R. D. 1985. "A Comparison of Procedures for the Assessment of Psychopathy." Journal of Consulting and Clinical Psychology 53: 7–16.

Hare, R. D. and L. McPherson.
1984. "Violent and Aggressive Behaviour by Criminal Psychopaths." International Journal of Law and Psychiatry 7: 35–50.

Hartnagel, Timothy F. 1982. "Modernization, Female Social Roles, and Female Crime: A Cross-National Investigation." Sociological Quarterly 23: 477–90.

Hartnagel, Timothy F. 1997. "Crime among the Provinces." Canadian Journal of Criminology 39: 387–402.

Hartshorne, H. and M. A. May.
1928–30. Studies in the Nature of Character (3 vols.). New York: Macmillan.

Hawkins, K. 1984. Environment and Enforcement: Regulation and the Social Definition of Pollution. Oxford: Clarendon Press.

Hayner, Norman. 1942. "Five Cities in the Pacific Northwest." In Clifford Shaw and Henry McKay (eds.), Juvenile Delinquency and Urban Areas. Chicago: University of Chicago Press.

Heidensohn, Frances. 1996. "Feminist Perspectives and Their Impact on Criminology and Criminal Justice in Great Britain." In Nicole Hahn Rafter and Frances Heidensohn (eds.), International Feminist Perspectives in Criminology: Engendering a Discipline. Buckingham: Open University Press.

Hempel, Carl G. 1952. Fundamentals of Concept Formation in Empirical Science. Chicago: University of Chicago Press.

Hendrick, Dianne. 1996. "Youth Statistics 1995–96 Highlights." Juristat Vol. 17, No. 10. Ottawa: Statistics Canada.

Henshel, Richard L. 1990. Thinking about Social Problems. San Diego: Harcourt Brace Jovanovich.

Herman, Edward S. 1991. "Drug 'Wars': Appearance and Reality." Social Justice 18: 76–84.

Herman, Edward S. and Noam Chomsky. 1988. Manufacturing Consent: The Political Economy of the Mass Media. New York: Pantheon.

Herrnstein, Richard and Charles Murray. 1994. The Bell Curve: Intelligence and Class Structure in American Life. New York: Free Press.

Hinch, Ronald. 1983. "Marxist Criminology in the 1970s: Clarifying the Clutter." Crime and Social Justice (Summer): 65–74.

Hinch, Ronald. 1985. "Canada's New Sexual Assault Laws: A Step Forward for Women?" Contemporary Crises 9: 33–44.

Hinch, Ronald. 1988. "Inconsistencies and Contradictions in Canada's Sexual Assault Law." Canadian Public Policy 14: 282–94.

Hinch, Ronald (ed.). 1994. Readings in Critical Criminology. Scarborough, ON: Prentice-Hall Canada.

Hinch, Ronald. 1999. "Conflict and Marxist Theories." In Rick Linden (ed.), Criminology: A Canadian Perspective. Toronto: Harcourt Brace Canada.

Hirschi, Travis. 1969. Causes of Delinquency. Berkeley: University of California Press.

Hirschi, Travis and Hanan Selvin. 1967. Delinquency Research: An Appraisal of Analytic Methods. New York: The Free Press.

Hooton, Ernest. 1939. The American Criminal. Cambridge, MA: Harvard University Press.

Hoshino, K. 1988. "Organized Crime and Its Origins in Japan." Paper presented at the American Society of Criminology Meetings, Chicago.

Hotton, Tina. 2001. "Spousal Violence after Marital Separation." Juristat Vol. 21, No. 7. Ottawa: Statistics Canada.

House, J. D. 1986. "Working Offshore: The Other Price of Newfoundland's Oil." In K. P. Lundy and B. Warme (eds.), Work in the Canadian Context. Toronto: Butterworths.

Huang, Frank F. Y. and Michael S. Vaughn. 1992. "A Descriptive Analysis of Japanese Organized Crime: The Boryokudan from 1945 to 1988." International Criminal Justice Review 2: 19–57.

Hubbard, Ruth. 1982. "Have Only Men Evolved?" In Ruth Hubbard, M. S. Henifin, and Barbara Fried (eds.), Biological Woman—The Convenient Myth. Cambridge, MA: Schenkman.

Hudson, Diane. 1987. "You Can't Commit Violence against an Object: Women, Psychiatry, and Psychosurgery." In J. Hanmer and M. Maynard (eds.), Women, Violence, and Social Control. Houndsmills, Basingstoke, Hampshire: Macmillan Press.

Hum, Derek and Wayne Simpson. 1991. Income Maintenance, Work Effort, and the Canadian Mincome Experiment. Ottawa: Economic Council of Canada.

Humphreys, Laud. 1970a. Tearoom Trade: Impersonal Sex in Public Places. Chicago: Aldine.

Humphreys, Laud. 1970b. "Tearoom Trade: Impersonal Sex in Public Places." Transaction 7(3): 10–25.

Irwin, John and James Austin. 1987. It's About Time: Solving America's Prison Crowding Crisis. San Francisco: National Council on Crime and Delinquency.

Jacobs, Jane. 1961. The Death and Life of Great American Cities. New York: Random House.

Jaffe, P. G., E. Hastings, D. Reitzel, and G. W. Austin. 1993. "The Impact of Police Laying Charges." In N. Zoe Hilton (ed.), Legal Responses to Wife Assault. Newbury Park, CA: Sage.

Janhevich, Derek. 1998. "Violence Committed by Strangers." Juristat Vol. 18, No. 9. Ottawa: Statistics Canada.

Jennings, W. S., R. Kilkenny, and L. Kohlberg. 1983. "Moral-Development Theory and Practices for Youthful and Adult Offenders." In W. S. Laufer and S. M. Day (eds.), Personality Theory, Moral Development, and Criminal Behavior. Lexington, MA: Lexington Books.

Jensen, Gary F. 1995. "Salvaging Structure through Strain: A Theoretical and Empirical Critique." In Freda Adler and William S. Laufer (eds.), Advances in Criminological Theory, Vol. 6: The Legacy of Anomie. New Brunswick, NJ: Transaction.

Jepsen, Jorgen. 1988. "Drugs, Crime and Social Control in Scandinavia: International Moral Entrepreneurism in Action and Research." Paper presented at the International Conference on Crime, Drugs, and Social Control, Research Committee for the Sociology of Deviance and Control, University of Hong Kong.

Johns, Christina. 1992. State Power, Ideology, and the War on Drugs: Nothing Succeeds Like Failure. New York: Praeger.

Johnson, Elmer. 1996. Japanese Corrections: Managing Convicted Offenders in an Orderly Society. Carbondale: Southern Illinois University Press.

Johnson, Holly. 1986. Women and Crime in Canada. Ottawa: Solicitor General of Canada.

Johnson, Holly. 1987. "Getting the Facts Straight: A Statistical Overview." In Ellen Adelberg and Claudia Currie (eds.), Too Few to Count: Canadian Women in Conflict with the Law. Vancouver: Press Gang.

Johnson, Holly. 1996. Dangerous Domains. Scarborough, ON: Nelson Canada.

Joy, L. A., M. M. Kimball, and M. L. Zabrack. 1986. "Television and Aggressive Behaviour." In T. M. Williams (ed.), The Impact of Television: A Natural Experiment Involving Three Towns. New York: Academic Press.

Kamin, Leon. 1986. "Is Crime in the Genes? The Answer May Depend on Who Chooses What Evidence." Scientific American (February): 22–27.

Kappeler, Victor E., Mark Blumberg, and Gary W. Potter. 1993. The Mythology of Crime and Criminal Justice. Prospect Heights, IL: Waveland Press.

Katz, Jack. 1988. The Seductions of Crime: Moral and Sensual Attractions in Doing Evil. New York: Basic Books.

Kaukinen, Catherine. 1997. "An Integrative Approach to Domestic Violence: An Examination of Factors Influencing Reporting." Annual Meeting of the American Society of Criminology, San Diego.

Keane, Carl, A. R. Gillis, and John Hagan. 1989. "Deterrence and Amplification of Juvenile Delinquency by Police Contact." British Journal of Criminology 29: 336–52.

Kellam, S. G., G. W. Rebok, N. Ialongo, and L. S. Mayer. 1994. "The Course and Malleability of Aggressive Behavior from Early First Grade into Middle School: Results of a Developmental Epidemiologically-Based Preventative Trial." Journal of Child Psychology and Psychiatry 35: 259–82.

Kelly, Liz and Jill Radford. 1996. "'Nothing Really Happened': The Invalidation of Women's Experiences of Sexual Violence." In Marianne Hester, Liz Kelly, and Jill Radford (eds.), Women, Violence, and Male Power. Buckingham: Open University Press.

Kelman, S. 1981. Regulating America, Regulating Sweden: A Comparative Study of Occupational Safety and Health Policy. Cambridge, MA: MIT Press.

Kennedy, Leslie W. and David Forde. 1990. "Risky Lifestyles and Dangerous Results: Routine Activities and Exposure to Crime." Sociology and Social Research 74: 208–11.

Kennedy, Leslie W. and David Veitch. 1997. "Why Are Crime Rates Going Down? A Case Study in Edmonton." Canadian Journal of Criminology 39: 51–69.

Killias, Martin, John van Kesteren, and Martin Rindlisbacher. 2001. "Guns, Violent Crime, and Suicide in 21 Countries." Canadian Journal of Criminology 43: 429–48.

King, Harry. 1972. Box Man: A Professional Thief's Journey. New York: Harper and Row.

King, Michael and Marie-Agnes Petit. 1985/86. "Thin Stick and Fat Carrot: The French Juvenile Justice System." Youth and Policy 15: 26–31.

Kingsley, R. 1996. "Assault." In L. W. Kennedy and V. Sacco, Crime Counts. Scarborough, ON: Nelson Canada.

Kleck, Gary. 2001. Armed: New Perspectives on Gun Control. Amherst, NY: Prometheus.

Klein, Dorie. 1973. "The Etiology of Female Crime: A Review of the Literature." Issues in Criminology 8: 3–30.

Kleinknecht, W. 1996. The New Ethnic Mobs: The Changing Face of Organized Crime in America. New York: Free Press.

Kobrin, Sol. 1951. "The Conflict of Values in Delinquency Areas." American Sociological Review 16: 653–61.

Koenig, Dan. 1996. "Do Police Cause Crime?" In R. Silverman, J. Teevan, and V. Sacco (eds.), Crime in Canadian Society. Toronto: Harcourt Brace, Canada.

Koenig, Daniel J. 1999 . "Take the Money: Enterprise Crime and Canada's Response." In Jay Albanese, Dilip Das, and Arvind Verma (eds.), Organized Crime: A Global Perspective. Ineline, NV: Copperhouse Publishing.

Kohlberg, Lawrence. 1976. "Moral Stages and Moralization: The Cognitive-Developmental Approach." In T. Lickona (ed.), Moral Development and Behaviour. New York: Holt, Rinehart & Winston.

Kornhauser, Ruth. 1978. Social Sources of Delinquency. Chicago: University of Chicago Press.

Kowalski, Melanie. 2000. " Break and Enter, 1999." Juristat Vol. 20, No. 13. Ottawa: Statistics Canada

Krisberg, Barry, Ira Schwartz, Paul Litsky, and James Austin. 1986. "The Watershed of Juvenile Justice Reform." Crime and Delinquency 32: 5–38

Krivo, Lauren J. and Ruth D. Peterson. 1996. "Extremely Disadvantaged Neighborhoods and Urban Crime." Social Forces 75: 619–50.

Kvale, Steiner. 1996. Interviews: An Introduction to Qualitative Research Interviewing. Thousand Oaks, CA: Sage.

LaFramboise, Donna. 1997. "Who's the Victim Now?" The Globe and Mail (November 8).

LaFree, Gary D., Barbara F. Reskin, and Christy A. Visher. 1985. "Jurors' Responses to Victims' Behaviour and Legal Issues in Sexual Assault Trials." Social Problems 32: 389–407.

LaPrairie, Carol. 1987. "Native Women and Crime: A Theoretical Model." In Ellen Adelberg and Claudia Currie (eds.), Too Few to Count: Canadian Women in Conflict with the Law. Vancouver: Press Gang.

LaPrairie, Carol. 1990. "The Role of Sentencing in the Over-Representation of Aboriginal People in Correctional Institutions." Canadian Journal of Corrections 32: 429–40.

Larsen, Nick. 1992. "Time to Legalize Prostitution." Policy Options 13(7): 21–22

Larsen, Nick. 1999. "The Politics of Law Reform: Prostitution Policy in Canada, 1985–1995." In N. Larsen and B. Burtch (eds.), Law in Society: Canadian Readings. Toronto: Harcourt Brace Canada.

Latané, Bibb and Judith Rodin. 1969. "A Lady in Distress: Inhibiting Effects of

Friends and Strangers on Bystander Intervention. Journal of Experimental Social Psychology 5: 189–202.

Latané, Bibb, John Darley, and J. M. Darley. 1968. "Group Inhibition of Bystander Intervention." Journal of Personality and Social Psychology 10: 215–21.

Laub, John H. and Robert J. Sampson. 1993. "Turning Points in the Life Course: Why Change Matters to the Study of Crime." Criminology 31: 301–25.

Lautt, Melanie. 1984. A Report on Prostitution in the Prairie Provinces. Working Papers on Pornography and Prostitution, Report No. 9. Ottawa: Department of Justice.

LaVigne, Nancy G. 1997. "Visibility and Vigilance: Metro's Situational Approach to Preventing Subway Crime." Research in Brief. Washington, DC: National Institute of Justice.

Leuw, Ed. 1991. "Drugs and Drug Policy in the Netherlands." In Michael Tonry (ed.), Crime and Justice: A Review of Research 14. Chicago: University of Chicago Press.

Linden, Rick. 1987. "Social Control Theory." In Rick Linden (ed.), Criminology: A Canadian Perspective. Toronto: Holt, Rinehart and Winston of Canada

Linden, Rick (ed.). 1992. Criminology: A Canadian Perspective (2nd ed.). Toronto: Harcourt Brace Jovanovich Canada.

Linden, Rick and Cathy Fillmore. 1981. "A Comparative Study of Delinquency Involvement." Canadian Review of Sociology and Anthropology 18: 343–61.

Linden, Rick and James C. Hackler. 1973. "Affective Ties and Delinquency." Pacific Sociological Review 16: 27–46.

Lindesmith, Alfred R. 1965. The Addict and the Law. Bloomington: Indiana University Press.

Link, Bruce G. 1987. "Understanding Labeling Effects in the Area of Mental Disorders: An Empirical Assessment of the Effects of Expectations of Rejection." American Sociological Review 52: 96–112.

Link, Bruce G., Francis T. Cullen, Elmer Struening, Patrick E. Shrout, and Bruce P. Dohrenwend. 1989. "A Modified Labeling Theory Approach to Mental Disorders." American Sociological Review 54: 400–23.

Linsky, Arnold S., Ronet Bachman, and Murray A. Strauss. 1995. Stress, Culture and Aggression. New Haven: Yale University Press.

Liska, Allen E. and Mark D. Reed. 1985. "Ties to Conventional Institutions and Delinquency: Estimating Reciprocal Effects." American Sociological Review 50: 547–60.

Lofland, John. 1969. Deviance and Identity. Englewood Cliffs, NJ: Prentice Hall.

Logan, Ron. 2001. "Crime Statistics in Canada." Juristat Vol. 21, No. 8. Ottawa: Statistics Canada

Lombroso, Cesare. 1911. Crime, Its Causes and Remedies. Boston: Little, Brown.

Lombroso, Cesare and William Ferrero. 1895. The Female Offender. London: Unwin Fisher.

Lonmo, Charlene. 2001. "Adult Correctional Services in Canada." Juristat Vol. 21, No. 5. Ottawa: Statistics Canada.

Lowman, John. 1984. Vancouver Field Study of Prostitution. Working Papers on Pornography and Prostitution, Report No. 8. Ottawa: Department of Justice.

Lowman, John. 1985. "Prostitution in Canada." Resources for Feminist Research 14(4): 35–37.

Lowman, John. 1987. "Taking Young Prostitutes Seriously." The Canadian Review of Sociology and Anthropology 24: 99–116.

Lowman, John. 1988. "Street Prostitution." In Vincent F. Sacco (ed.), Deviance:

Conformity and Control in Canadian Society. Scarborough, ON: Prentice-Hall Canada.

Lowman, John. 1989. Street Prostitution: Assessing the Impact of the Law: Vancouver. Ottawa: Department of Justice.

Lowman, John. 1991. "Prostitution in Canada." In Margaret Jackson and Curt Griffiths (eds.), Canadian Criminology. Toronto: Harcourt Brace Jovanovich Canada.

Lowman, John. 1992. Personal correspondence, November 19.

MacLeod, Linda. 1980. Wife Battering in Canada: The Vicious Circle. Ottawa: CAACSW.

MacLeod, Linda. 1995. "Expanding the Dialogue: Report of a Workshop to Explore the Criminal Justice System Response to Violence against Women." In Mariana Valverde, Linda MacLeod, and Kirsten Johnson (eds.), Wife Assault and the Canadian Justice System. Toronto: Centre for Criminology, University of Toronto.

Maestro, Marcello. 1973. Cesare Beccaria and the Origins of Penal Reform. Philadelphia: Temple University Press.

Mann, Coramae Richey. 1993. Unequal Justice: A Question of Color. Bloomington: Indiana University Press.

Mann, Coramae Richey. 1995. "Women of Color and the Criminal Justice System." In Barbara Raffel Price and Natalie Sokoloff (eds.), The Criminal Justice System and Women. New York: McGraw-Hill.

Mann, Coramae Richey. 1996. When Women Kill. Albany: State University of New York Press.

Mann, W.E. 1967. Society behind Bars. Toronto: Social Science Publishers.

Marshall, Donald S. 1972. "Too Much in Mangaia." Change: Readings in Society and Human Behaviour. Del Mar, CA: Communications Research Machines.

Martin, Randy, Robert J. Mutchnick, and W. Timothy Austin. 1990. Criminological Thought: Pioneers Past and Present. New York: Macmillan

Massey, James, Marvin Krohn, and Lisa Bonati. 1989. "Property Crime and the Routine Activities of Individuals." Journal of Research in Crime and Delinquency 26: 378–400.

Mauser, Gary A. 2001. Misfire: Firearm Registration in Canada. Vancouver: Fraser Institute.

Maxim, Paul S. and Carl Keane. 1992. "Gender, Age, and the Risk of Violent Death in Canada, 1950–1986." Canadian Review of Sociology and Anthropology 29: 329–45.

Maxwell, Christopher D., Joel H. Garner, and Jeffrey A. Fagan. 2001. The Effects of Arrest on Intimate Partner Violence: New Evidence from the Spousal Assault Replication Program. Washington, DC: National Institute of Justice.

McIllwain, Jeffrey Scott. 1997. "From Tong War to Organized Crime: Revising the Historical Perception of Violence in Chinatown." Justice Quarterly 14: 25–52.

McLaren, John. 1986. "Chasing the Social Evil: Moral Fervour and the Evolution of Canada's Laws, 1867–1917." Canadian Journal of Law and Society 1: 125–65.

McLaren, John and John Lowman. 1990. "Prostitution Law and Law Enforcement, 1892–1920: Unravelling Rhetoric and Practice." In Martin Friedland (ed.), Securing Compliance: Seven Case Studies. Toronto: University of Toronto Press.

McMahon, Maeve W. and Richard V. Ericson. 1987. "Reforming the Police and Policing Reform." In R. S. Ratner and John L. McMullan (eds.), State Control: Criminal Justice Politics in Canada. Vancouver: University of British Columbia Press.

McMahon, Martha and Ellen Pence. 1995. "Doing More Harm Than Good? Some

Cautions on Visitation Centers." In Einat Peled, Peter Jaffe, and Jeffrey Edleson (eds.), Ending the Cycle of Violence: Community Responses to Children of Battered Women. Thousand Oaks, CA: Sage.

McMullan, John L. 1992. Beyond the Limits of the Law: Corporate Crime and Law and Order. Halifax: Fernwood.

McPhie, Paul and Francis Remedios. 1992. "Legal Aid in Canada: 1990–91." Juristat Service Bulletin, Canadian Centre for Justice Statistics 12 (23).

Mednick, Sarnoff. 1985. "Crime in the Family Tree." Psychology Today 19 (3): 58–61.

Mednick, S. A. and K. Christiansen (eds.). 1977. Biosocial Bases of Criminal Behaviour. New York: Gardner.

Mednick, S. A. and J. Volavaka. 1980. "Biology and Crime." In N. Morris and M. Tonry (eds.), Crime and Justice: An Annual Review of Research. Vol 2. Chicago: University of Chicago Press.

Menard, Scott. 1995. "A Developmental Test of Mertonian Anomie Theory." Journal of Research in Crime and Delinquency 32: 136–74.

Menard, Scott. 1997. "A Developmental Test of Cloward's Differential Opportunity Theory." In Nikos Passas and Robert Agnew (eds.), The Future of Anomie Theory. Boston: Northeastern University Press.

Menard, Scott and David Huizinga. 1994. "Changes in Conventional Attitudes and Delinquent Behavior in Adolescence." Youth and Society 26: 23–53.

Menzies, Robert J., Dorothy E. Chunn, and Christopher D. Webster. 1992. "Female Follies: The Forensic Psychiatric Assessment of Women Defendants." International Journal of Law and Psychiatry 15: 179–93.

Merry, Sally Engle. 1991. Getting Justice and Getting Even: Legal Consciousness among Working-Class Americans. Chicago: University of Chicago Press.

Merton, Robert K. 1938. "Social Structure and Anomie." American Sociological Review 3: 672–82.

Merton, Robert K. 1968. Social Theory and Social Structure. New York: Free Press.

Messerschmidt, James. 1986. Capitalism, Patriarchy, and Crime: Toward a Socialist Feminist Criminology. Totowa, NJ: Rowman and Littlefield.

Messerschmidt, James W. 1993. Masculinities and Crime: Critique and Reconceptualization of Theory. Lanham, MD: Rowman and Littlefield.

Messner, Steven and Kenneth Tardiff. 1985. "The Social Ecology of Urban Homicide: An Application of the 'Routine Activities' Approach." Criminology 23: 241–67.

Messner, Steven F. and Richard Rosenfeld. 1997a. Crime and the American Dream (2nd ed.). Belmont, CA: Wadsworth.

Messner, Steven F. and Richard Rosenfeld. 1997b. "Political Restraint of the Market and Levels of Criminal Homicide: A Cross-National Application of Institutional-Anomie Theory." Social Forces 75: 1393–1416.

Mihorean, Steve. 1992. "Correctional Expenditures and Personnel in Canada, 1991–92." Juristat Vol. 12, No. 22. Canadian Centre for Justice Statistics. Ottawa: Publications Division, Statistics Canada.

Milgram, Stanley. 1963. "Behavioral Study of Obedience." Journal of Applied Social Psychology 67: 371–78.

Milgram, Stanley. 1974. Obedience to Authority. New York: Harper and Row.

Miller, Eleanor M. 1986. Street Woman. Philadelphia: Temple University Press.

Miller, Jody. 1998. "Up It Up: Gender and the Accomplishment of Street Robbery." Criminology 36: 37–66.

Miller, Matthew and David Hemenway.
1999. "The Relationship between Firearms
and Suicide: A Review of the Literature."
Aggression and Violent Behavior 4: 59–75.

Moldon, Mary Bess and Damir Kukec.
2000. "Youth Custody and Community
Services in Canada." Juristat Vol. 20, No.
8. Ottawa: Statistics Canada.

Morash, Merry and Meda Chesney-Lind.
1991. "A Reformulation and Partial Test of
the Power Control Theory of Delinquency."
Justice Quarterly 8: 347–77.

Morgan, John P. and Lynn Zimmer. 1997.
"Animal Self-Administration of Cocaine:
Misinterpretation, Misrepresentation, and
Invalid Extrapolation to Humans." In
Patricia G. Erickson, Diane M. Riley, Yuet
W. Cheung, and Patrick A. O'Hare (eds.),
Harm Reduction: A New Direction for
Drug Policies and Programs. Toronto:
University of Toronto Press.

Morris, Allison. 1987. Women, Crime, and
Criminal Justice. Oxford: Basil Blackwell.

Morris, Allison and Gabrielle Maxwell.
1997. "Reforming Juvenile Justice: The
New Zealand Experiment." The Prison
Journal 77: 125–34.

Mugford, Stephen. 1992. "Crime and the
Partial Legalization of Heroin: Comments
and Caveats." The Australian and New
Zealand Journal of Criminology 25: 27–40.

Murphy, Emily F. 1922. The Black Candle.
Toronto: T. Allen.

Naffine, Ngaire. 1987. Female Crime: The
Construction of Women in Criminology.
Sydney: Allen and Unwin.

Naylor, R. T. 1996. The Theory and Practice
of Enterprise Crime: Public Perceptions and
Legislative Responses. Presented at the
Forum on Organized Crime, September
27–28, in Ottawa.

Nease, Barbara. 1971. "Measuring Juvenile
Delinquency in Hamilton." In W. E. Mann
(ed.), Social Deviance in Canada.
Vancouver: Copp Clark.

Netherlands Ministry of Justice.
1991. "Woningbraak: Motieven en
Werkwijzen Vanuit Daderperspectief.
(Domestic Burglary: Motives and Modus
Operandi from the Offender's Perspective.)
Gravenhage, Netherlands.: Crime
Prevention Directorate. (From Criminal
Justice Abstracts 24, June 1992: #0406.)

Nettler, Gwynne. 1982. Lying, Cheating, and
Stealing. Cincinnati, OH: Anderson.

Nettler, Gwynne. 1984. Explaining Crime
(3rd ed.). New York: McGraw-Hill.

Newman, Oscar. 1973. Architectural Design
for Crime Prevention. Washington, DC:
U.S. Government Printing Office.

Nielsen, Marianne. 1979. RCMP Policing: A
Question of Style. Master's thesis,
University of Alberta, Edmonton.

Noble, Amanda. 1997. "Is Prenatal Drug
Use Child Abuse? Reporting Practices
and Coerced Treatment in California."
In Patricia G. Erickson, Diane M. Riley,
Yuet W. Cheung, and Patrick A.
O'Hare (eds.), Harm Reduction:
A New Direction for Drug Policies
and Programs. Toronto: University of
Toronto Press.

Nye, F. Ivan and James F. Short, Jr.
1957. "Scaling Delinquent Behaviour."
American Sociological Review 22: 326–31.

**Nye, F. Ivan, James F. Short, Jr., and Virgil
J. Olsen. 1958.** "Socioeconomic Status and
Delinquent Behaviour." American Journal
of Sociology 53: 381–89.

Nylund, Marianne. 1991. "Young Offenders
and the Mediation Program in Finland." In
James Hackler (ed.), Official Responses to
Problem Juveniles: Some International
Reflections. Oñati, Spain: Oñati Institute
for the Sociology of Law.

**O'Brien, C. P., E. P. Nace, J. Mintz, A. L.
Meyers, and N. Ream. 1980.** "Follow-up
of Vietnam Veterans: I. Relapse to Drug
Use after Vietnam Service." Drug and
Alcohol Dependence 5: 333–40.

O'Brien, Robert. 1989. "Relative Cohort Size and Age-Specific Crime Rates: An Age-Period-Relative-Cohort-Size Model." Criminology 27: 57–78.

Office of National Drug Control Policy. 2001. Pulse Check: Trends in Drug Abuse, Midyear 2000 (Special Topic: Ecstasy and Other Club Drugs). Washington, DC: U.S. Department of Justice.

Olds, D., C. R. Henderson, R. Cole, J. Eckenrode, H. Kitzman, D. Luckey, L. Pettit, K. Sidera, P. Morris, and J. Powers. 1998. "Long Term Effects of Nurse Home Visitation on Children's Criminal and Antisocial Behavior." Journal of the American Medical Association 280: 1238–44.

O'Malley, Pat and Stephen Mugford. 1991. "The Demand for Intoxicating Commodities: Implications for the 'War on Drugs.'" Social Justice 18: 49–74.

Panitch, L. 1977. The Canadian State: Political Economy and Political Power. Toronto: University of Toronto Press.

Passas, Nikos. 1997. "Anomie, Reference Groups, and Relative Deprivation." In Nikos Passas and Robert Agnew (eds.), The Future of Anomie Theory. Boston: Northeastern University Press.

Passas, Nikos. 1998. "Globalisation and Economic Crime." In Urlich Beck (ed.), Perspektiven der Weltgesellschaft (Edition Zweite Moderne). Frankfurt: Suhrkamp.

Paternoster, Raymond, Robert Brame, Ronet Bachman, and Lawrence Sherman. 1997. "Do Fair Procedures Matter? The Effect of Procedural Justice on Spouse Assault." Law and Society Review 31: 163–204.

Pearce, Frank and Laureen Snider (eds.). 1995. Corporate Crime: Contemporary Debates. Toronto: University of Toronto Press.

Pearce, Frank and Steve Tombs. 1998. Toxic Capitalism: Corporate Crime and the Chemical Industry. Brookfield, VT: Ashgate.

Pease, Ken and Kristiina Hukkila. 1990. Criminal Justice Systems in Europe and North America. Helsinki: Helsinki Institute for Crime Prevention and Control.

Perkins, Roberta and Garry Bennett. 1985. Being a Prostitute. Winchester, MA: Allen and Unwin.

Perrone, Paul A. and Meda Chesney-Lind. 1997. "Media Presentation of Gangs and Delinquency: Wild in the Streets?" Social Justice 24: 96–117.

Peterson, Ruth D. and William C. Bailey. 1988. "Forcible Rape, Poverty, and Economic Inequality in U.S. Metropolitan Communities." Journal of Quantitative Criminology 4: 99–119.

Phelan, G. F. 1977. "Testing Architecturally Defensible Design: How Burglars Perceive Clues of Residential Vulnerability." Paper presented at the American Society of Criminology, Atlanta, Georgia.

Phillips, Julie A. 1997. "Variation in African-American Homicide Rates: An Assessment of Potential Explanations." Criminology 35: 527–59.

Phillips, Kevin. 1990. The Politics of Rich and Poor: Wealth and the American Electorate in the Reagan Aftermath. New York: Random House.

Piaget, Jean. 1952. The Origins of Intelligence in Children. New York: International Universities Press.

Pierce, Gregory R., Barbara R. Sarason, and Irwin G. Sarason (eds.). 1996. Handbook of Social Support and the Family. New York: Plenum.

Platt, Anthony M. 1969. The Child Savers. Chicago: University of Chicago Press.

Platt, Anthony. 1974. "The Triumph of Benevolence: The Origins of the Juvenile Justice System in the United States." In Richard Quinney (ed.), Criminal Justice in America. Boston: Little, Brown.

Ploeger, Matthew. 1997. "Youth Employment

and Delinquency: Reconsidering a Problematic Relationship." Criminology 35: 659–75.

Pollak, Otto. 1961. The Criminality of Women. New York: Barnes.

Popham, Robert E., Wolfgang Schmidt, and Jan de Lint. 1976. "The Prevention of Hazardous Drinking: Implications for Research on the Effects of Government Control Measures." In J. A. Edwing and B. A. Rouse (eds.), Drinking. Chicago: Nelson-Hall.

Poulantzas, Nico. 1973. Political Power and Social Classes. London: New Left Books.

Powell, B., H. Takayama, and K. Itoi. 1991. "Tokyo's Power Club." Newsweek 118(2): 40–42.

Prus, Robert. 1996. Symbolic Interaction and Ethnographic Research. New York: State University.

Quinney, Richard. 1975. "Crime Control in a Capitalist Society." In Ian Taylor, Paul Walton, and Jock Young (eds.), Critical Criminology. London: Routledge and Kegan Paul.

Rafter, Nicole Hahn. 1986. "Left Out by the Left." Socialist Review 16: 7–23.

Rafter, Nicole Hann. 1990. Partial Justice: Women in State Prisons, 1800–1935 (2nd ed.). Boston: Northeastern University Press.

Rafter, Nicole Hahn. 1997. Creating Born Criminals. Champaign: University of Illinois Press.

Ratner, Robert. 1984. "Inside the Liberal Boot: The Criminological Enterprise in Canada." Studies in Political Economy 13: 145–64.

Ratner, R. S. 1998. "Tracking Crime: A Professional Odyssey." In James E. Hodgson (ed.), Criminal Justice System: Alternative Measures. Toronto: Canadian Scholars Press.

Ratner, Robert S. and John L. McMullan (eds.). 1987. State Control: Criminal Justice Politics in Canada. Vancouver: University of British Columbia Press.

Ratner, Robert and John McMullan. 1989. "State Intervention and the Control of Labour in British Columbia: A Capital-Logic Approach." In Tullio Caputo, Mark Kennedy, Charles Reasons, and Augustine Brannigan (eds.), Law and Society: A Critical Perspective. Toronto: Harcourt Brace Jovanovich Canada.

Reasons, Charles E. (ed.). 1984. Stampede City: Power and Politics in the West. Toronto: Between the Lines.

Reasons, Charles E., Lois L. Ross, and Craig Paterson. 1981. Assault on the Worker: Occupational Health and Safety in Canada. Toronto: Butterworths.

Reckless, Walter. 1967. The Crime Problem. New York: Appleton, Century, Crofts.

Reckless, Walter C., Simon Dinltz, and Ellen Murray. 1956. "Self Concept as an Insulator against Delinquency." American Sociological Review 21: 744–46.

Redl, F. and Hans Toch. 1979. "The Psychoanalytic Perspective." In Hans Toch (ed.), Psychology of Crime and Criminal Jusice. New York: Holt, Rinehart, and Winston.

Reeg, Axel R. 1988. "Recent Developments of Western-European Criminal Drug Law Policies." Paper presented at the International Conference on Crime, Drugs, and Social Control, Research Committee for the Sociology of Deviance and Control, University of Hong Kong.

Reiman, Jeffrey. 1990. The Rich Get Richer and the Poor Get Prison (3rd ed.). New York: Macmillan.

Reitsma-Street, Marge. 1999. "Justice for Canadian Girls: A 1990s Update." Canadian Journal of Criminology 41: 335–63.

Reynolds, Henry. 1981. The Other Side of the Frontier. Townsville, NE Queensland, Australia: James Cook University, History Department.

Reynolds, Julia, Simon Lenton, Mike Charlton, and Jane Caporn. 1997. "Shopping, Baking, and Using: The Manufacture, Use, and Problems Associated with Heroin Made in the Home from Codeine-Based Pharmaceuticals." In Patricia G. Erickson, Diane M. Riley, Yuet W. Cheung, and Patrick A. O'Hare (eds.), Harm Reduction: A New Direction for Drug Policies and Programs. Toronto: University of Toronto Press.

Robins, L. N. 1966. Deviant Children Grow Up. Baltimore: Williams and Wilkins.

Robins, Lee. 1992. "Antisocial Personality and Crime: Separable or Synonymous." Edwin H. Sutherland Award Presentation Address, American Society of Criminology, New Orleans.

Robinson, Jennifer B. 1998. "Transit Stations as Crime Generators: A Study of Vancouver." Paper presented at fiftieth annual meeting of the American Society of Criminology, Washington, DC, November 11–14.

Rosenbaum, Jill. 1989. "Family Dysfunction and Female Delinquency." Crime and Delinquency 35: 31–44.

Rosenfeld, Richard and Steven F. Messner. 1997. "Markets, Morality, and an Institutional-Anomie Theory of Crime." In Nikos Passas and Robert Agnew (eds.), The Future of Anomie Theory. Boston: Northeastern University Press.

Ross, I. 1980. "How Lawless Are Big Companies?" Fortune 102 (December 1): 56–64.

Rossmo, D. Kim. 1997. "Geographic Profiling." In Janet L. Jackson and Debra A. Berkerian (eds.), Offender Profiling. Chichester: John Wiley and Sons.

RPM Planning Associates Ltd. 1996. Evaluation of the Staff Lawyer Pilot Project. Edmonton: Legal Aid Society of Alberta.

Rushton, J. P. 1988. "Race Differences in Behaviour: A Review and Evolutionary Analysis." Personality and Individual Differences 9: 1009–24.

Rushton, J. P. and A. F. Bogaert. 1987. "Race Differences in Sexual Behaviour: Testing an Evolutionary Hypothesis." Journal of Research in Personality 21: 529–51.

Sacco, Vincent F. and Holly Johnson. 1990. Patterns of Criminal Victimization in Canada. Ottawa: Statistics Canada.

Sampson, Robert J. and John H. Laub. 1993. Crime in the Making: Pathways and Turning Points through Life. Cambridge, MA: Harvard University Press.

Sampson, Robert J. and Stephen W. Raudenbush. 2001. "Disorder in Urban Neighborhoods—Does It Lead to Crime?" Washington, DC: National Institute of Justice

Sampson, Robert J. and William Julius Wilson. 1995. "Toward a Theory of Race, Crime, and Urban Inequality." In John Hagan and Ruth Peterson (eds.), Crime and Inequality. Stanford, CA: Stanford University Press.

Sarnecki, Jerzy. 1986. Delinquent Networks. Stockholm: The National Council for Crime Prevention Sweden.

Sarnecki, Jerzy. 1989. Juvenile Delinquency in Sweden: An Overview. Stockholm: The National Council for Crime Prevention Sweden.

Schechter, S. 1982. Women and Male Violence. Boston: South End Press.

Schissel, Bernard. 1997. Blaming Children: Youth Crime, Moral Panics and the Politics of Hate. Halifax: Fernwood Publishing

Schmidt, Janell and Lawrence Sherman. 1993. "Does Arrest Deter Domestic Violence?" American Behavioral Scientist 36: 601–9.

Schmidt, Wolfgang and Robert E. Popham. 1978 "The Single Distribution Theory of Alcohol Consumption." Journal of Studies on Alcohol 39: 400–19

Schneider, Stephen R. 1997. Obstacles to Collective Action in Socially Disadvantaged Neighbourhoods: Toward a Radical Planning Theory of Community Crime Prevention. Doctoral dissertation, School of Community and Regional Planning, University of British Columbia.

Schrag, Clarence. 1971. Crime and Justice: American Style. Rockville, MD: National Institute of Mental Health.

Schwartz, Michael and Sandra Tangri. 1965. "A Note on Self-Concept as an Insulator against Delinquency." American Sociological Review 30: 922–26.

Schweinhart, L. L., H. V. Barnes, and D. P. Weikart. 1993. Significant Benefits: The High/Scope Perry Preschool Study through Age 27. Ypsilanti, MI: High/Scope Press.

Schwendinger, Herman and Julia Schwendinger. 1967. "Delinquent Stereotypes of Probable Victims." In Malcolm Klein (ed.), Juvenile Gangs in Context: Theory, Research, and Action. Englewood Cliffs, NJ: Prentice Hall.

Sellin, Thorsten. 1938. Culture Conflict and Crime. New York: Social Science Research Council.

Shaver, Frances M. 1988. "A Critique of the Feminist Charges Against Prostitution." Atlantis 4: 82–89.

Shaver, Frances M. 1992. "The Regulation of Prostitution: Avoiding the Morality Trap." Paper presented at Canadian Law and Society Meetings, Charlottetown, PEI.

Shaw, Margaret. 1991. The Federal Female Offender: Report on a Preliminary Study. User Report 1991–3. Ottawa: Solicitor General Canada.

Shaw, Margaret, with Karen Rodgers, Johanne Blanchette, Tina Hattem, Lee Seto Thomas, and Lada Tamarack. 1992. Paying the Price: Federally Sentenced Women in Context. User Report 1992–13. Ottawa: Corrections Branch, Solicitor General Canada.

Sheldon, William. 1940. The Varieties of Human Physique: An Introduction to Constitutional Psychology. New York: Harper and Row.

Shelley, Louise. 1981. Crime and Modernization. Carbondale: Southern Illinois Press.

Sherman, Lawrence and Richard Berk. 1984. "The Specific Deterrent Effects of Arrest for Domestic Assault." American Sociological Review 49: 261–72.

Short, James F., Jr. and Fred L. Strodtbeck. 1965. Group Process and Gang Delinquency. Chicago: University of Chicago Press.

Shover, Neal. 1996. Great Pretenders: Pursuits and Careers of Persistent Thieves. Boulder, CO: Westview Press.

Silverman, Robert A. and Leslie W. Kennedy. 1987. "The Female Perpetrator of Homicide in Canada." Discussion Paper No. 11. Edmonton, AB: Centre for Criminological Research.

Silverman, Robert A., James J. Teevan, Jr., and Vincent F. Sacco (eds.). 1991. Crime in Canadian Society (4th ed.). Toronto: Butterworths.

Simon, Rita and Jean Landis. 1991. The Crimes Women Commit, The Punishments They Receive. Lexington, MA: Lexington Books.

Simon, Rita. 1975a. The Contemporary Woman and Crime. Washington, DC: U.S. Government Printing Office.

Simon, Rita. 1975b. Women and Crime. Lexington, MA: Lexington Books.

Singer, Simon I. and Murray Levine. 1988. "Power-Control Theory, Gender, and Delinquency: A Partial Replication with Additional Evidence on the Effects of Peers." Criminology 26: 627–47.

Sloan, John Henry, Arthur L. Kellerman, and Donald T. Reay. 1988. "Handgun Regulations, Crime, Assaults, and

Homicide." New England Journal of Medicine 319: 1256–62.

Small, Shirley. 1978. "Canadian Narcotics Legislation, 1908–1923: A Conflict Model Interpretation." In William K. Greenaway and Stephen L. Brickey (eds.), Law and Social Control in Canada. Scarborough, ON: Prentice-Hall Canada.

Smandych, Russell. 1985. "Marxism and the Creation of Law: Re-examining the Origins of Canadian Anti-Combines Legislation 1890–1910." In Thomas Fleming (ed.), The New Criminologies in Canada: Crime, State, and Control. Toronto: Oxford University Press.

Smart, Carol. 1976. Women, Crime, and Criminology. London: Routledge and Kegan Paul.

Smart, Reginald G. 1986. "Cocaine Use and Problems in North America." Canadian Journal of Criminology 28: 109–29.

Smart, Reginald G. and Edward M. Adlaf. 1992. "Recent Studies of Cocaine Use and Abuse in Canada." Canadian Journal of Criminology 34: 1–13.

Smith, Douglas A. and Raymond Paternoster. 1987. "The Gender Gap in Theories of Deviance: Issues and Evidence." Journal of Research in Crime and Delinquency 24: 140–72.

Smith, Douglas and Robert Brame. 1994. "On the Initiation and Continuation of Delinquency." Criminology 32: 607–29.

Snider, Laureen. 1978. "Corporate Crime in Canada: A Preliminary Report." Canadian Journal of Criminology 20: 142–68.

Snider, Laureen. 1992. "Commercial Crime." In Vince Sacco (ed.), Deviance: Conformity and Control in Canadian Society (2nd ed.). Scarborough, ON: Prentice-Hall Canada.

Snider, Laureen. 1993. Bad Business: Corporate Crime in Canada. Scarborough, ON: Nelson Canada.

Snider, Laureen. 1997. "Nouvelle donne législative et causes de la criminalité 'corporative.'" Criminologie 30: 9–34.

Snider, Laureen. 1998. "Towards Safer Societies: Punishment, Masculinities, and Violence against Women." British Journal of Criminology 38: 1–39.

Special Committee on Pornography and Prostitution (Fraser Committee). 1985. Pornography and Prostitution in Canada. Ottawa: Department of Supply and Services.

Sprott, Jane B., Anthony N. Doob, and Jennifer M. Jenkins. 2001. "Problem Behaviour and Delinquency in Children and Youth." Juristat Vol. 21, No. 4. Ottawa: Statistics Canada.

Stack, Carol. 1974. All Our Kin: Strategies for Survival in a Black Community. New York: Harper Colophon Books.

Stack, Steven. 1982. "Social Structure and Swedish Crime Rates: A Time Series Analysis, 1950–1979." Criminology 20: 499–513.

Stanko, Elizabeth. 1985. Intimate Intrusions: Women's Experiences of Male Violence. Boston: Routledge and Kegan Paul.

Stanko, Elizabeth. 1995. "Women, Crime, and Fear." Annals of the American Academy of Political and Social Sciences 539: 46–58.

Stark, Rodney. 1987. "Deviant Places: A Theory of the Ecology of Crime." Criminology 25: 893–909.

Statistics Canada. 2001. Graphical Overview of Criminal Justice Indicators, 1999–2000. 85-227-XIE. Ottawa: Statistics Canada.

Steffensmeier, Darrell J. 1981. "Crime and the Contemporary Woman: An Analysis of Changing Levels of Female Property Crime, 1960–1975." In Lee Bowker (ed.), Women and Crime in America. New York: Macmillan.

Steinhoff, P. G. 1991. "Political Offenders in the Japanese Criminal Justice System."

Paper presented at the American Society of Criminology Meetings, San Francisco.

Stephens, Richard C. 1991. The Street Addict Role: A Theory of Heroin Addiction. Albany: SUNY Press.

Stockwell, Tim. 1997. "Harm Reduction and Licensed Drinking Settings." In Patricia G. Erickson, Diane M. Riley, Yuet W. Cheung, and Patrick A. O'Hare (eds.), Harm Reduction: A New Direction for Drug Policies and Programs. Toronto: University of Toronto.

Straus, Murray and Richard Gelles. 1986. "Societal Change and Change in Family Violence from 1975 to 1985 as Revealed by Two National Surveys." Journal of Marriage and the Family 48: 465–79.

Sudworth, Mark and Paul deSouza. 2001. "Youth Court Statistics, 1999/00." Juristat Vol. 21, No. 3. Ottawa: Statistics Canada.

Sumner, Colin. 1994. Sociology of Deviance: An Obituary. New York: Continuum.

Sutherland, Edwin H. 1949. White Collar Crime. New York: Dryden

Sutherland, Edwin H. and Donald R. Cressey. 1978. Criminology (10th ed.). Philadelphia: J. B. Lippincott.

Syndicat de la Magistrature. 1979. "Mineurs: L'art de la fugue." Justice 69: no pages on reprint.

Tannenbaum, Frank. 1938. Crime and Community. Boston: Ginn & Co.

Tappan, Paul. 1947. "Who Is the Criminal?" American Sociological Review 12: 96–102.

Thomas, Charles and John Hepburn. Crime, Criminal Law, and Criminology. Dubuque, IA: William C. Brown.

Thomas, William I. 1923. The Unadjusted Girl: With Cases and Standpoint for Behaviour Analysis. New York: Harper and Row.

Thornberry, Terence P. 1987. "Toward an Interactional Theory of Delinquency." Criminology 25: 863–91.

Thornberry, Terence P., Alan J. Lizotte, Marvin D. Krohn, Margaret Farnworth, and Sung Joon Jang. 1991. "Testing Interactional Theory: An Examination of Reciprocal Causal Relationships among Family, School, and Delinquency." Journal of Criminal Law and Criminology 82: 3–35.

Thrasher, A. 1976. Skid Row Eskimo. Toronto: Griffin House.

Tierney, Kathleen J. 1982. "The Battered Women Movement and the Wife Beating Problem." Social Problems 29: 207–20.

Tong, Rosemarie. 1984. Women, Sex, and the Law. Totowa, NJ: Rowman and Allanheld.

Trainor, Catherine and Karen Mihorean (eds.). 2001. Family Violence in Canada: A Statistical Profile 2001. Catalogue no. 85-224. Ottawa: Canadian Centre for Justice Statistics.

Trasler, Gordon. 1962. The Explanation of Criminality. London: Routledge & Kegan Paul.

Tremlay, R. E., B. Boulerice, P. W. Harden, P. McDuff, D. Pérusse, R. O. Pihl, and M. Zoccolillo. 1996. "Do Children in Canada Become More Aggressive as They Approach Adolescence?" In Human Resources Development Canada and Statistics Canada (eds.), Growing Up in Canada: National Longitudinal Survey of Children and Youth. Ottawa: Statistics Canada.

Tremblay, R. E. and Wendy M. Craig. 1995. "Developmental Crime Prevention." In M. Tonry and D. P. Farrington (eds.), Building a Safer Society: Strategic Approaches to Crime Prevention. Vol 19. Chicago: University of Chicago Press.

Tremblay, R. E., L. Kurtz, L. C. Masse, F. Vitaro, and R. O. Pihl. 1995. "A Bimodal Preventive Intervention for Disruptive Kindergarten Boys: Its Impact through Mid-Adolescence." Journal of Consulting and Clinical Psychology 63: 560–68.

Tremblay, R. E., F. Vitaro, L. Bertrand, M. LeBlanc, H. Beaucesne, H. Boileau, and H. David. 1992. "Parent and Child

Training to Prevent Early Onset of Delinquency: The Montreal Longitudinal-Experimental Study." In J. McCord and R. E. Tremblay (eds.), Preventing Antisocial Behavior: Interventions from Birth through Adolescence. New York: Guilford.

Ursel, Jane. 1994. "The Winnipeg Family Violence Court." Juristat Vol. 14, No 12. Ottawa: Statistics Canada.

Van Brunschot, Erin Elan Gibbs. 1991. "Working Girls: A Study of Youthful Involvement in Calgary Street Prostitution." MA thesis, Department of Sociology, University of Calgary.

Vaughan, Diane. 1997. "Anomie Theory and Organizations: Culture and the Normalization of Deviance." In Nikos Passas and Robert Agnew (eds.), The Future of Anomie Theory. Boston: Northeastern University Press.

Visano, Livy A. 1987. This Idle Trade: The Occupational Patterns of Male Prostitution. Concord, ON: VitaSana Books.

Visher, Cathy. 1983. "Gender, Police Arrest Decisions, and Notions of Chivalry." Criminology 21: 5–28.

Vitaro, Frank, Richard Tremblay, and Margaret Kerr. 1997. "Disruptiveness, Friends' Characteristics, and Delinquency in Early Adolescence: A Test of Two Competing Models of Development." Working Paper No. 19. Toronto: L'Institut canadien de recherches avancées.

Vogel, D. 1986. National Styles of Regulation: Environmental Policy in Great Britain and the United States. Ithaca, NY: Cornell University Press.

Vold, George. 1958. Theoretical Criminology. New York: Oxford University Press.

Wade, Andrew L. 1967. "Social Processes in the Act of Juvenile Vandalism." In Marshall B. Clinard and Richard Quinney, (eds.), Criminal Behaviour Systems: A Typology. New York: Holt, Rinehart, and Winston.

Wahlsten, D. 1990. "Insensitivity of the Analysis of Variance to Heredity–Environment Interaction." Behavioral and Brain Sciences 13: 109–61.

Wahlsten, D. 1992. "Betwixt Gene and Behaviour." Behavior Genetics 22: 11–14.

Waldo, Gordon and Simon Dinitz. 1967. "Personality Attributes of the Criminal: An Analysis of Research Studies 1950–1965." Journal of Research in Crime and Delinquency 4: 185–202.

Weatherburn, Don. 1992a. "Crime and Partial Legislation of Heroin." The Australian and New Zealand Journal of Criminology 25: 11–26.

Weatherburn, Don. 1992b. "Rejoinder to Mugford." The Australian and New Zealand Journal of Criminology 25: 41–43.

Webber, Marlene. 1991. Street Kids: The Tragedy of Canada's Runaways. Toronto: University of Toronto Press.

Weiner, M. 1989. The Origins of the Korean Community in Japan (1910–1923). Atlantic Heights, NJ: Humanities Press International.

Weizmann, F., N. I. Weiner, D. L. Wiesenthal, and M. Ziegler. 1990. "Differential K Theory and Racial Hierarchies." Canadian Psychology 31: 1–13.

West, Donald. 1969. Present Conduct and Future Delinquency. New York: International Universities Press.

Whitehead, Paul and Reginald Smart. 1972. "Epidemiological Aspects of Drug Use and Implications for the Prevention of Drug Abuse." In Craig Boydell, Carl Grindstaff, and Paul Whitehead (eds.), Deviant Behaviour and Societal Reaction. Toronto: Holt, Rinehart, and Winston.

Widom, Cathy Spatz. 1986. "Early Child Abuse, Neglect, and Later Violent Criminal Behaviour." Paper to the conference on Perinatal and Early Childhood Factors in Deviant Development, Palm Springs.

Wilbanks, William. 1982. "Murdered Women and Women Who Murder: A Critique of the Literature." In Elizabeth Stanko and Nicole Hann Rafter (eds.), Judge, Lawyer, Victim, Thief. Boston: Northeastern University Press.

Wilbanks, William. 1987. The Myth of a Racist Criminal Justice System. Monterey, CA: Brooks-Cole.

Williams, Franklin P., III. 1980. "Conflict Theory and Differential Processing: An Analysis of the Research Literature." In James Inciardi (ed.), Radical Criminology: The Coming Crisis. Beverly Hills: Sage.

Wilson, Barbara, Dale Kunkel, Dan Linz, James Potter, Ed Donnerstein, Stacy Smith, Eva Blumenthal, and Timothy Gray. 1997. National Television Violence Study. Vol 1. Thousand Oaks, CA: Sage.

Wilson, James Q. and Richard J. Herrnstein. 1985. Crime and Human Nature. New York: Simon & Schuster.

Wilson, William Julius. 1987. The Truly Disadvantaged: The Inner City, the Underclass, and Public Policy. Chicago: University of Chicago Press.

Wolf, Daniel R. 1991. The Rebels: A Brotherhood of Outlaw Bikers. Toronto: University of Toronto Press.

Wolfgang, Marvin. 1972. "Cesare Lombroso." In Herman Mannheim (ed.), Pioneers in Criminology. Montclair, NJ: Patterson Smith.

Wolfgang, Marvin E. and Franco Ferracuti. 1967. The Subculture of Violence. London: Social Science Pap

Wong, S. 1984. The Criminal and Institutional Behaviours of Psychopaths. Programs Branch User Report. Ottawa: Ministry of the Solicitor General.

Wright, James D. 1991. "Guns and Crime." In Joseph Sheley (ed.), Criminology: A Contemporary Handbook. Belmont, CA: Wadsworth.

Wright, John Paul and Francis T. Cullen. 1996. "Parental Support and Delinquent Behavior: The Limits of Control Theory?" Paper presented at the annual meeting of the American Society of Criminology, Chicago.

Young, Jock. 1986. "The Failure of Criminology: The Need for a Radical Realism." In Roger Matthews and Jock Young (eds.), Confronting Crime. London: Sage.

Young, Jock. 1999. The Exclusive Society. Sage: London.

Zimbardo, Philip G. 1970. "The Human Choice: Individuation, Reason, and Order versus Deindividuation, Impulse, and Chaos." In W. J. Arnold and D. Levine (eds.), Nebraska Symposium on Motivation, 1969. Lincoln, NE: University of Nebraska Press.

Zimbardo, Philip G. 1973. "The Psychological Power and Pathology of Imprisonment." In T. R. Sarbin (ed.), Social Psychology. New York: Van Nostrand.

Name Index

Subject Index